ReportLab: PDF Processing with Python

Michael Driscoll

© 2018 Michael Driscoll

Published by Michael Driscoll
Ankeny, IA

Copyright © 2018 by Michael Driscoll. All rights reserved.

No portion of this book may be reproduced, stored in a retrieval system or transmitted in any form or by any means – electronic, photocopy, recording, or any other – except for brief quotations in printed reviews, without the prior permission of the author / publisher.

Cover art by Therese Larsson

Contents

Introduction 1
    About the Author 2
    Conventions 2
    Setting up & Activating a Virtual Environment 2
    Dependencies 4
    Installation 4
    Configuration 5
    Reader Feedback 6
    Errata 6
    Code Examples 6

Part I - The ReportLab Toolkit 7

Chapter 1 - Getting Started with Reportlab 8
    The Canvas Object 9
    Canvas Methods 13
    Using Colors in ReportLab 23
    Adding a Photo 27
    The textobject 29
    Create a Page Break 35
    Canvas Orientation (Portrait vs. Landscape) 36
    Other methods 36
    A Simple Sample Application 37
    Wrapping Up 38

Chapter 2 - ReportLab and Fonts 39
    Unicode / UTF8 is the Default 39
    The Standard Fonts 39
    Other Type-1 Fonts 41
    TrueType Fonts 44
    Asian Fonts 46
    Switching Between Fonts 50
    Wrapping Up 52

CONTENTS

Chapter 3 - Intro to Page Layout 53
    The Basics of PLATYPUS 53
    Changing Fixed Elements Across Pages 61
    Flowable Methods 63
    Frame Basics 65
    Templates 67
    Flowable Orientation (Portrait vs. Landscape) 68
    Wrapping Up 71

Chapter 4 - Paragraphs 72
    Paragraph Styles 72
    Paragraph Markup Tags 76
    The Outermost Markup Tags 76
    Using Intra-Paragraph Markup 79
    Working with Fonts 82
    Superscripts & Subscripts 85
    Inserting Inline Images 87
    Numbering Paragraphs / Sections 89
    Bullets 90
    Wrapping Up 92

Chapter 5 - Tables 93
    The Table's Methods 95
    Applying Style to Your Table 95
    Cell Formatting 97
    Changing Fonts in Tables 99
    Line Commands 103
    Cell Alignment 106
    Alternating Background Colors 110
    Putting Paragraphs in Your Cells 112
    Adding Images to Cells 113
    Spanning 115
    Wrapping Up 116

Chapter 6 - Other Flowables 117
    Preformatted 117
    XPreformatted 119
    The Image Flowable 120
    The Spacer Flowable 125
    PageBreak 127
    CondPageBreak 128
    KeepTogether 128
    How to Add a Table of Contents 128

CONTENTS

 SimpleIndex 131
 ListFlowable / ListItem 134
 Wrapping Up 137

Chapter 7 - Creating Your Own Flowables 138
 Creating a Line Flowable 138
 Creating a Bordered Textbox + Line Flowable 140
 Modifying a Pre-Existing Flowable 143
 Wrapping Up 143

Chapter 8 - Intro to Graphics and Charts 144
 What is a Drawing? 144
 ReportLab's Renderers 144
 The Coordinate System 145
 A Simple Drawing 145
 Supported Outputs 146
 Verifying Attributes 147
 Naming Shapes 148
 Charts and Graphs 149
 Labels 149
 Axes 152
 Bar Charts 156
 Line Charts 167
 Line Plots 171
 Pie Charts 174
 Adding Titles and Legends 182
 Odds and Ends 186
 Wrapping Up 186

Chapter 9 - Other Graphics 188
 Shapes 188
 Widgets 198
 Bar Codes 202
 Wrapping Up 214

Chapter 10 - Creating Special Features in Your PDF 216
 File Annotations 216
 Bookmarks 217
 Page Transitions 220
 Encryption 221
 Interactive Forms 224
 Wrapping Up 240

CONTENTS

Part II - Tutorials and How-Tos 241

Chapter 11 - Turning Data into PDFs 242
    Getting Started 243
    Creating the Base Template Class 244
    Refactoring the EOB Class 251
    Creating a Multipage Document 257
    Using Real Data 259
    Consuming XML 260
    Wrapping Up 266

Chapter 12 - Custom Headers and Footers 267
    A Naive Header 268
    Putting the Header on Every Page 270
    Adding a Logo 273
    Configurable Logos 275
    Adding Page Numbers 284
    Adding a Page Number of Total 286
    Headers + Footers 289
    Wrapping Up 291

Chapter 13 - Creating a PDF Library 292
    Accepting Different Data Formats 292
    Multipage Data Files 297
    Custom Stylesheets 307
    Configuring Your Application 311
    Adding a Graphical User Interface 316
    Finishing the User Interface 324
    Wrapping Up 330

Chapter 14 - The PyPDF2 Package 332
    Installation 332
    Extracting Metadata from PDFs 333
    Extracting Text from PDFs 334
    Splitting PDFs 335
    Merging Multiple PDFs Together 336
    Rotating Pages 339
    Overlaying / Watermarking Pages 339
    PDF Encryption 341
    Wrapping Up 342

Chapter 15 - The pdfrw Package 343
    Installation 343

Extracting Information from PDF 343
Splitting 345
Merging / Concatenating 345
Rotating 346
Overlaying / Watermarking Pages 347
Scaling 348
Combining pdfrw and ReportLab 350
Wrapping Up 352

Chapter 16 - Extracting and Exporting Data from PDFs 353
Extracting Text with PDFMiner 353
Exporting Text via pdf2txt.py 356
Extracting Text with Slate 359
Exporting Your Data 361
Exporting to XML 361
Exporting to JSON 363
Exporting to CSV 364
Extracting Images 366
Wrapping Up 368

Chapter 17 - Filling in PDF Forms 369
Creating a Simple Form 369
Merging Overlays 371
Other Ways to Fill Forms 374
Using the pdfforms Package 375
Wrapping Up 376

Chapter 18 - Converting Markup to PDF 377
rst2pdf 377
WeasyPrint 379
Pandoc 381
LaTeX 382
Wrapping Up 382

Chapter 19 - The PyFPDF Package 383
Installation 383
Basic Usage 383
Working with Fonts 385
Drawing 388
Adding Images 391
Multipage Documents 392
Headers and Footers 393
Tables 397

CONTENTS

    Transform HTML to PDF 399
    Web2Py 400
    Templates 400
    Wrapping Up 400

Appendix A - Adding SVG Files in ReportLab 402
    Dependencies 402
    Installation 402
    Usage 403
    Drawing on the Canvas 403
    Adding an SVG to a Flowable 405
    Scaling SVGs in ReportLab 407
    Using SVG Plots from matplotlib in ReportLab 409
    Using svg2pdf 411
    Wrapping Up 412

Appendix B - Getting System Fonts 413
    The fontTools Package 413
    Getting the System's Fonts 413
    Wrapping Up 417

Appendix C - Creating a Color Demo 418
    Getting the Colors 418
    Wrapping Up 419

Afterword and Thanks 420

Introduction

The Reportlab PDF Toolkit started life in the year 2000 by a company called "Reportlab Inc.". Reportlab is now owned by "ReportLab Europe Ltd". They produce the open source version of Reportlab. The Reportlab toolkit is actually the foundation of their commercial product, **Report Markup Language** which is available in their **Reportlab PLUS** package. This book is focused on the open source version of Reportlab. The Reportlab PDF Toolkit allows you to create in Adobe's Portable Document Format (PDF) quickly and efficiently in the Python programming language. Reportlab is the defacto method of generating PDFs in Python. You can also use Reportlab to create charts and graphics in bimap and vector formats in addition to PDF. Reportlab is known for its ability to generate a PDF fast. In fact, Wikipedia chose Reportlab as their tool of choice for generating PDFs of their content. Anytime you click the "Download as PDF" link on the left side of a Wikipedia page, it uses Python and Reportlab to create the PDF!

In this book, you will learn how to use Reportlab to create PDFs too. This book will be split into three sections. We will be covering the following topics in the first section:

- The canvas
- Drawing
- Working with fonts
- PLATYPUS
- Paragraphs
- Tables
- Other Flowables
- Graphics
- and More!

In the second section, we will learn about data processing. The idea here is to take in several different data formats and turn them into PDFs. For example, it is quite common to receive data in XML or JSON. But learning how to take that information and turn it into a report is something that isn't covered very often. You will learn how to do that here. In the process we will discover how to make multipage documents with paragraphs and tables that flow across the pages correctly.

The last section of the book will cover some of the other libraries you might need when working with PDFs with Python. In this section we will learn about the following:

- PyPDF2
- pdfminer
- PyFPDF

About the Author

You may be wondering about who I am and why I might be knowledgeable enough about Python to write about it, so I thought I'd give you a little information about myself. I started programming in Python in the Spring of 2006 for a job. My first assignment was to port Windows login scripts from Kixtart to Python. My second project was to port VBA code (basically a GUI on top of Microsoft Office products) to Python, which is how I first got started in wxPython. I've been using Python ever since, doing a variation of backend programming and desktop front end user interfaces as well as automated tests.

I realized that one way for me to remember how to do certain things in Python was to write about them and that's how my Python blog came about: http://www.blog.pythonlibrary.org/. As I wrote, I would receive feedback from my readers and I ended up expanding the blog to include tips, tutorials, Python news, and Python book reviews. I work regularly with Packt Publishing as a technical reviewer, which means that I get to try to check for errors in the books before they're published. I also have written for the Developer Zone (DZone) and i-programmer websites as well as the Python Software Foundation. In November 2013, DZone published **The Essential Core Python Cheat Sheet** that I co-authored. I have also self-published the following books:

- **Python 101** - June 2014
- **Python 201: Intermediate Python** - Sept. 2016
- **wxPython Cookbook** - Dec. 2016

Conventions

As with most technical books, this one includes a few conventions that you need to be aware of. New topics and terminology will be in **bold**. You will also see some examples that look like the following:

```
>>> myString = "Welcome to Python!"
```

The >>> is a Python prompt symbol. You will see this in the Python **interpreter** and in **IDLE**. Other code examples will be shown in a similar manner, but without the >>>. Most of the book will be done creating examples in regular Python files, so you won't be seeing the Python prompt symbol all that often.

Setting up & Activating a Virtual Environment

If you don't want to add ReportLab into your system's Python installation, then you can use a virtual environment. In Python 2.x - 3.2, you would need to install a package called **virtualenv** to create a virtual environment for Python. The idea is that it will create a folder with a copy of Python and pip.

You activate the virtual environment, run the virtual pip and install whatever you need to. Python 3.3 added a module to Python called **venv** that does the same thing as the virtualenv package, for the most part.

Here are some links on how all that works:

- https://docs.python.org/3/library/venv.html (Python 3 only)
- https://pypi.python.org/pypi/virtualenv (Python 2 and 3)

When you are using a Python Virtual Environment, you will need to first activate it. Activation of a virtual environment is like starting a virtual machine up in VirtualBox or VMWare, except that in this case, it's just a Python Virtual Environment instead of an entire operating system.

Creating a virtual sandbox with the virtualenv package is quite easy. On Mac and Linux, all you need to do is the following in your terminal or command prompt:

```
virtualenv FOLDER_NAME
```

To activate a virtual environment on Linux or Mac, you just need to change directories to your newly created folder. Inside that folder should be another folder called **bin** along with a few other folders and a file or two. Now you can run the following command:

```
source bin/activate
```

On Windows, things are slightly different. To create a virtual environment, you will probably need to use the full path to virtualenv:

```
c:\Python27\Scripts\virtualenv.exe
```

You should still change directories into your new folder, but instead of **bin**, there will be a **Scripts** folder that can run **activate** out of:

```
Scripts\activate
```

Once activated, you can install any other 3rd party Python package.

Note: It is recommended that you install all 3rd party packages, such as ReportLab or Pillow, in a Python Virtual Environment or a user folder. This prevents you from installing a lot of cruft in your system Python installation.

I would also like to mention that **pip** supports a –**user** flag that tells it to install the package just for the current user if the platform supports it. There is also an –**update** flag (or just -**U**) that you an use to update a package. You can use this flag as follows:

Introduction

```
python -m pip install PACKAGE_NAME --upgrade
```

While you can also use pip install PACKAGE_NAME, it is now becoming a recommended practice to use the python -m approach. What this does differently is that it uses whatever Python is on your path and installs to that Python version. The **-m** flag tells Python to load or run a module which in this case is **pip**. This can be important when you have multiple versions of Python installed and you don't know which version of Python pip itself will install to. Thus, by using the python -m pip approach, you know that it will install to the Python that is mapped to your "python" command.

Now let's learn what we need to install to get ReportLab working!

Dependencies

You will need the Python language installed on your maching to use ReportLab. Python is pre-installed on Mac OS and most Linux distribututions. Reportlab 3 works with both Python 2.7 and Python 3.3+. You can get Python at https://www.python.org/. They have detailed instructions for installing and configuring Python as well as building Python should you need to do so.

ReportLab depends on the Python Imaging Library for adding images to PDFs. The Python Imaging Library itself hasn't been maintained in years, but you can use the **Pillow** (https://pillow.readthedocs.io/en/latest/) package instead. **Pillow** is a fork of the Python Imaging Library that supports Python 2 and Python 3 and has lots of new enhancements that the original package didn't have. You can install it with pip as well:

```
python -m pip install pillow
```

You may need to run **pip** as root or Administer depending on where your Python is installed or if you are installing to a virtualenv. You may find that you enjoy Pillow so much that you want to install it in your system Python in addition to your virtual environment.

We are ready to move on and learn how to install ReportLab!

Installation

Reportlab 3 works with both Python 2.7 and Python 3.3+. This book will be focusing on using Python 3 and ReportLab 3.x, but you can install ReportLab 3 the same way in both versions of Python using pip:

```
python -m pip install reportlab
```

If you are using an older version of Python such as Python 2.6 or less, then you will need to use ReportLab 2.x. These older versions of ReportLab have *.exe installers for Windows or a tarball for other operating systems. If you happen to run a ReportLab exe installer, it will install to Python's system environment and not your virtual environment.

If you run into issues installing ReportLab, please go to their website and read the documentation on the subject at https://www.reportlab.com/

Now you should be ready to use ReportLab!

Configuration

ReportLab supports a few options that you can configure globally on your machine or server. This configuration file can be found in the following file: **reportlab/rl_settings.py** (ex. C:\PythonXX\Lib\site-packages\reportlab). There are a few dozen options that are commented in the source. Here's a sampling:

- **verbose** - A range of integer values that can be used to control diagnostic output
- **shapeChecking** - Defaults to 1. Set to 0 to turn off most error checking in ReportLab's graphics modules
- **defaultEncoding** - WinAnsiEncoding (default) or MacRomanEncoding
- **defaultPageSize** - A4 is the default, but you can change it to something else, such as letter or legal
- **pageCompression** - What compression level to use. The documentation doesn't say what values can be used though
- **showBoundary** - Defaults to 0, but can be set to 1 to get boundary lines drawn
- **T1SearchPath** - A Python list of strings that are paths to T1Font fonts
- **TTFSearchPath** - A Python list of strings that are paths to TrueType fonts

As I said, there are a lot of other settings that you can modify in that Python script. I highly recommend opening it up and reading through the various options to see if there's anything that you will need to modify for your environment. In fact, you can do so in your Python interpreter by doing the following:

```
>>> from reportlab import rl_settings
>>> rl_settings.verbose
0
>>> rl_settings.shapeChecking
1
```

You can now easily check out each of the settings in an interactive manner.

Reader Feedback

I welcome your feedback. If you'd like to let me know what you thought of this book, you can send comments to the following email address:

comments@pythonlibrary.org

Errata

I try my best not to publish errors in my writings, but it happens from time to time. If you happen to see an error in this book, feel free to let me know by emailing me at the following:

errata@pythonlibrary.org

Code Examples

Code from the book can be downloaded from Github at the following address:

- https://github.com/driscollis/reportlabbookcode

Here's an alternate shortlink to the above as well:

- http://bit.ly/2nc7sbP

Now, let's get started!

Part I - The ReportLab Toolkit

Welcome to Part I! In this section you will learn all the major aspects of the ReportLab toolkit. Here is a listing of the chapters contained in this part of the book:

- Chapter 1 - The Canvas
- Chapter 2 - All about Fonts
- Chapter 3 - Page Layout and Typography Using Scripts (PLATYPUS)
- Chapter 4 - Paragraphs
- Chapter 5 - Tables
- Chapter 6 - Other Flowables
- Chapter 7 - Custom Flowables
- Chapter 8 - Charts / Graphics
- Chapter 9 - Other Graphics
- Chapter 10 - PDF Special Features

In this section of the book, you will learn how to create PDFs using ReportLab's low level **canvas** API. You will then move on to learn how to create PDFs using ReportLab's Flowable via their PLATYPUS sub-module. Then we will wrap up Part I by learning about ReportLab's graphics capabilities and the special features you can apply to a PDF such as page transitions and encryption.

Let's get started!

Chapter 1 - Getting Started with Reportlab

ReportLab is a very powerful library. With a little effort, you can make pretty much any layout that you can think of. I have used it to replicate many complex page layouts over the years. In this chapter we will be learning how to use ReportLab's **pdfgen** package. You will discover how to do the following:

- Draw text
- Learn about fonts and text colors
- Creating a text object
- Draw lines
- Draw various shapes

The pdfgen package is very low level. You will be drawing or "painting" on a canvas to create your PDF. The canvas gets imported from the pdfgen package. When you go to paint on your canvas, you will need to specify X/Y coordinates that tell ReportLab where to start painting. The default is (0,0) whose origin is at the lowest left corner of the page. Many desktop user interface kits, such as wxPython, Tkinter, etc, also have this concept. You can place buttons absolutely in many of these kits using X/Y coordinates as well. This allows for very precise placement of the elements that you are adding to the page.

The other item that I need to make mention of is that when you are positioning an item in a PDF, you are positioning by the number of **points** you are from the origin. It's points, not pixels or millimeters or inches. Points! Let's take a look at how many points are on a letter sized page:

```
>>> from reportlab.lib.pagesizes import letter
>>> letter
(612.0, 792.0)
```

Here we learn that a letter is 612 points wide and 792 points high. Let's find out how many points are in an inch and a millimeter, respectively:

```
>>> from reportlab.lib.units import inch
>>> inch
72.0
>>> from reportlab.lib.units import mm
>>> mm
2.834645669291339
```

This information will help us position our drawings on our painting. At this point, we're ready to create a PDF!

The Canvas Object

The canvas object lives in the pdfgen package. Let's import it and paint some text:

```
# hello_reportlab.py

from reportlab.pdfgen import canvas

c = canvas.Canvas("hello.pdf")
c.drawString(100, 100, "Welcome to Reportlab!")
c.showPage()
c.save()
```

In this example, we import the canvas object and then instantiate a Canvas object. You will note that the only requirement argument is a filename or path. Next we call **drawString()** on our canvas object and tell it to start drawing the string 100 points to the right of the origin and 100 points up. After that we call **showPage()** method. The **showPage()** method will save the current page of the canvas. It's actually not required, but it is recommended. The **showPage()** method also ends the current page. If you draw another string or some other element after calling showPage(), that object will be drawn to a new page. Finally we call the canvas object's **save()** method, which save the document to disk. Now we can open it up and see what our PDF looks like:

Fig. 1-1: **Welcome to ReportLab**

What you might notice is that our text is near the bottom of the document. The reason for this is that the origin, (0,0), is the bottom left corner of the document. So when we told ReportLab to paint our text, we were telling it to start painting 100 points from the left-hand side and 100 points from the bottom. This is in contrast to creating a user interface in Tkinter or wxPython where to origin is the top left.

Also note that since we didn't specify a page size, it defaults to whatever is in the ReportLab config, which is usually A4. There are some common page sizes that can be found in **reportlab.lib.pagesizes**.

Let's look at the Canvas's constructor to see what it takes for arguments:

```
def __init__(self,filename,
            pagesize=None,
            bottomup = 1,
            pageCompression=None,
            invariant = None,
            verbosity=0,
            encrypt=None,
            cropMarks=None,
            pdfVersion=None,
            enforceColorSpace=None,
            ):
```

Here we can see that we can pass in the **pagesize** as an argument. The **pagesize** is actually a tuple of width and height in points. If you want to change the origin from the default of bottom left, then you can set the **bottomup** argument to **0**, which will change the origin to the top left.

The **pageCompression** argument is defaulted to zero or off. Basically it will tell ReportLab whether or not to compress each page. When compression is enabled, the file generation process is slowed. If your work needs your PDFs to be generated as quickly as possible, then you'll want to keep the default of zero. However if speed isn't a concern and you'd like to use less disk space, then you can turn on page compression. Note that images in PDFs will always be compressed, so the primary use case for turning on page compression is when you have a huge amount of text or lots of vector graphics per page.

ReportLab's User Guide makes no mention of what the **invariant** argument is used for, so I took a look at the source code. According to the source, it *produces repeatable, identical PDFs with same timestamp info (for regression testing)*. I have never seen anyone use this argument in their code and since the source says it is for regression testing, I think we can safely ignore it.

The next argument is **verbosity**, which is used for logging levels. At zero (0), ReportLab will allow other applications to capture the PDF from standard output. If you set it to one (1), a confirmation message will be printed out every time a PDF is created. There may be additional levels added, but at the time of writing, these were the only two documented.

The **encrypt** argument is used to determine if the PDF should be encrypted as well as how it is encrypted. The default is obviously **None**, which means no encryption at all. If you pass a string to **encrypt**, that string will be the password for the PDF. If you want to encrypt the PDF, then you will need to create an instance of **reportlab.lib.pdfencrypt.StandardEncryption** and pass that to the **encrypt** argument.

The **cropMarks** argument can be set to True, False or to an object. Crop marks are used by printing houses to know where to crop a page. When you set cropMarks to True in ReportLab, the page will become 3 mm larger than what you set the page size to and add some crop marks to the corners. The object that you can pass to cropMarks contains the following parameters: borderWidth, markColor, markWidth and markLength. The object allows you to customize the crop marks.

The **pdfVersion** argument is used for ensuring that the PDF version is greater than or equal to what was passed in. Currently ReportLab supports versions 1-4.

Finally, the **enforceColorSpace** argument is used to enforce appropriate color settings within the PDF. You can set it to one of the following:

- cmyk
- rgb
- sep
- sep_black
- sep_cmyk

When one of these is set, a standard **_PDFColorSetter** callable will be used to do the color enforcement. You can also pass in a callable for color enforcement.

Let's go back to our original example and update it just a bit. Now as I mentioned earlier, in ReportLab you can position your elements (text, images, etc) using points. But thinking in points is kind of hard when we are used to using millimeters or inches. So I found a clever function we can use to help us on StackOverflow (http://stackoverflow.com/questions/4726011/wrap-text-in-a-table-reportlab):

```python
def coord(x, y, height, unit=1):
    x, y = x * unit, height - y * unit
    return x, y
```

This function requires your x and y coordinates as well as the height of the page. You can also pass in a unit size. This will allow you to do the following:

```python
# canvas_coords.py

from reportlab.pdfgen import canvas
from reportlab.lib.pagesizes import letter
from reportlab.lib.units import mm

def coord(x, y, height, unit=1):
    x, y = x * unit, height - y * unit
    return x, y

c = canvas.Canvas("hello.pdf", pagesize=letter)
width, height = letter

c.drawString(*coord(15, 20, height, mm), text="Welcome to Reportlab!")
c.showPage()
c.save()
```

In this example we pass the **coord** function the x and y coordinates, but we tell it to use millimeters as our unit. So instead of thinking in points, we are telling ReportLab that we want the text to start 15 mm from the left and 20 mm from the top of the page. Yes, you read that right. When we use the **coord** function, it uses the height to swap the origin's y from the bottom to the top. If you had set your Canvas's **bottomUp** parameter to zero, then this function wouldn't work as expected. In fact, we could simplify the coord function to just the following:

```python
def coord(x, y, unit=1):
    x, y = x * unit, y * unit
    return x, y
```

Now we can update the previous example like this:

```python
# canvas_coords2.py

from reportlab.pdfgen import canvas
from reportlab.lib.units import mm

def coord(x, y, unit=1):
    x, y = x * unit, y * unit
    return x, y

c = canvas.Canvas("hello.pdf", bottomup=0)

c.drawString(*coord(15, 20, mm), text="Welcome to Reportlab!")
c.showPage()
c.save()
```

That seems pretty straight-forward. You should take a minute or two and play around with both examples. Try changing the x and y coordinates that you pass in. Then try changing the text too and see what happens!

Canvas Methods

The **canvas** object has many methods. Let's learn how we can use some of them to make our PDF documents more interesting. One of the easiest methods to use **setFont**, which will let you use a PostScript font name to specify what font you want to use. Here is a simple example:

```python
# font_demo.py

from reportlab.lib.pagesizes import letter
from reportlab.pdfgen import canvas

def font_demo(my_canvas, fonts):
    pos_y = 750
    for font in fonts:
        my_canvas.setFont(font, 12)
        my_canvas.drawString(30, pos_y, font)
        pos_y -= 10

if __name__ == '__main__':
    my_canvas = canvas.Canvas("fonts.pdf",
                              pagesize=letter)
    fonts = my_canvas.getAvailableFonts()
    font_demo(my_canvas, fonts)
    my_canvas.save()
```

To make things a bit more interesting, we will use the **getAvailableFonts** canvas method to grab all the available fonts that we can use on the system that the code is ran on. Then we will pass the canvas object and the list of font names to our **font_demo** function. Here we loop over the font names, set the font and call the **drawString** method to draw each font's name to the page. You will also note that we have set a variable for the starting Y position that we then decrement by 10 each time we loop through. This is to make each text string draw on a separate line. If we didn't do this, the strings would write on top of each other and you would end up with a mess.

Here is the result when you run the font demo:

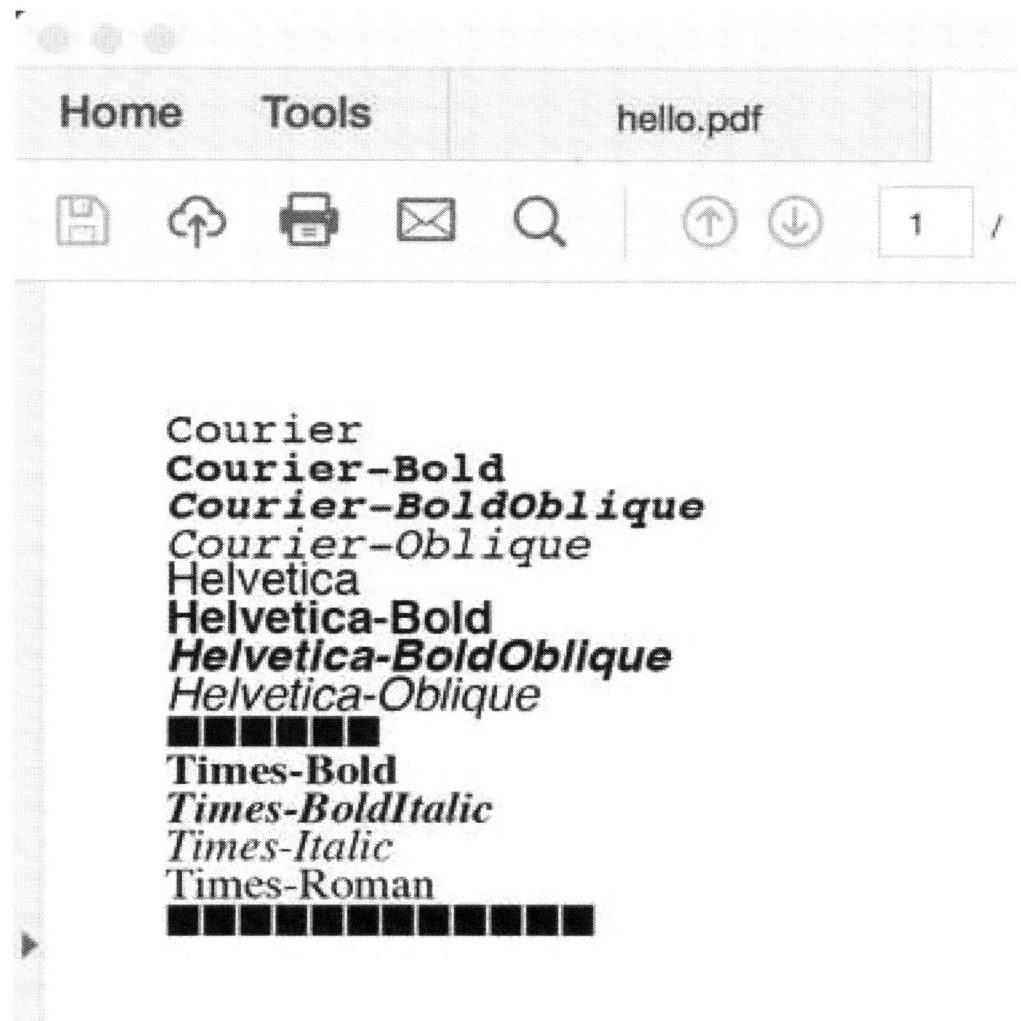

Fig. 1-2: Available fonts in ReportLab

If you want to change the font color using a canvas method, then you would want to look at **setFillColor** or one of its related methods. As long as you call that before you draw the string, the color of the text will change as well.

Another fun thing you can is use the canvas's **rotate** method to draw text at different angles. We will also learn how to use the **translate** method. Let's take a look at an example:

```
# rotating_demo.py

from reportlab.lib.pagesizes import letter
from reportlab.lib.units import inch
from reportlab.pdfgen import canvas

def rotate_demo():
    my_canvas = canvas.Canvas("rotated.pdf",
                              pagesize=letter)
    my_canvas.translate(inch, inch)
    my_canvas.setFont('Helvetica', 14)
    my_canvas.drawString(inch, inch, 'Normal')
    my_canvas.line(inch, inch, inch+100, inch)

    my_canvas.rotate(45)
    my_canvas.drawString(inch, -inch, '45 degrees')
    my_canvas.line(inch, inch, inch+100, inch)

    my_canvas.rotate(45)
    my_canvas.drawString(inch, -inch, '90 degrees')
    my_canvas.line(inch, inch, inch+100, inch)

    my_canvas.save()

if __name__ == '__main__':
    rotate_demo()
```

Here we use the **translate** method to set our origin from the bottom left to an inch from the bottom left and an inch up. Then we set out font face and font size. Next write out some text normally and then we rotate the coordinate system itself 45 degrees before we draw a string. According to the ReportLab user guide, you will want to specify the y coordinate in the negative since the coordinate system is now in a rotated state. If you don't do that, your string will be drawn outside the page's boundary and you won't see it. Finally we rotate the coordinate system another 45 degrees for a total of 90 degrees, write out one last string and draw the last line.

It is interesting to look at how the lines moved each time we rotated the coordinate system. You can see that the origin of the last line moved all the way to the very left-hand edge of the page.

Here is the result when I ran this code:

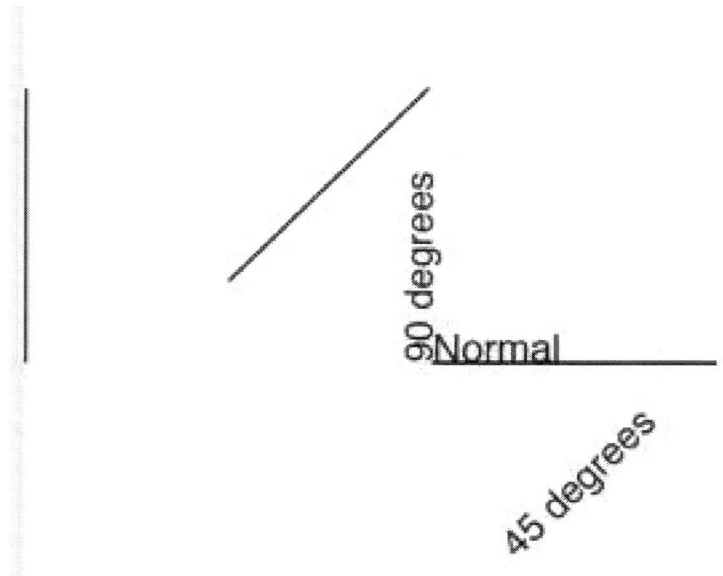

Fig. 1-3: Rotated text

Now let's take a moment learn about alignment.

String Alignment

The canvas supports more string methods than just the plain **drawString** method. You can also use **drawRightString**, which will draw your string right-aligned to the x-coordinate. You can also use **drawAlignedString**, which will draw a string aligned to the first pivot character, which defaults to the period. This is useful if you want to line up a series of floating point numbers on the page. Finally, there is the **drawCentredString** method, which will draw a string that is "centred" on the x-coordinate. Let's take a look:

```python
# string_alignment.py

from reportlab.pdfgen import canvas
from reportlab.lib.pagesizes import letter


def string_alignment(my_canvas):
    width, height = letter

    my_canvas.drawString(80, 700, 'Standard String')
    my_canvas.drawRightString(80, 680, 'Right String')

    numbers = [987.15, 42, -1,234.56, (456.78)]
```

```
    y = 650
    for number in numbers:
        my_canvas.drawAlignedString(80, y, str(number))
        y -= 20

    my_canvas.drawCentredString(width / 2, 550, 'Centered String')

    my_canvas.showPage()


if __name__ == '__main__':
    my_canvas = canvas.Canvas("string_alignment.pdf")
    string_alignment(my_canvas)
    my_canvas.save()
```

When you run this code, you will quickly see how each f these strings get aligned. Personally I thought the **drawAlignedString** method was the most interesting, but the others are certainly handy in their own right. Here is the result of running the code:

Standard String

Right String

987.15

42

-1

234.56

456.78

Centered String

Fig. 1-4: String Alignment

The next canvas methods we will learn about are how to draw lines, rectangles and grids!

Drawing lines on the canvas

Drawing a line in ReportLab is actually quite easy. Once you get used to it, you can actually create very complex drawings in your documents, especially when you combine it with some of

ReportLab's other features. The method to draw a straight line is simply **line**. Let's take a look at a simple example:

```
# drawing_lines.py

from reportlab.lib.pagesizes import letter
from reportlab.pdfgen import canvas

def draw_lines(my_canvas):
    my_canvas.setLineWidth(.3)

    start_y = 710
    my_canvas.line(30, start_y, 580, start_y)

    for x in range(10):
        start_y -= 10
        my_canvas.line(30, start_y, 580, start_y)


if __name__ == '__main__':
    my_canvas = canvas.Canvas("lines.pdf", pagesize=letter)
    draw_lines(my_canvas)
    my_canvas.save()
```

Here we create a simple **draw_lines** function that accepts a canvas object as its sole parameter. Then we set the line's width via the **setLineWidth** method. Finally we create a single line. You will notice that the **line** method accepts four arguments: x1, y1, x2, y2. These are the beginning x and y coordinates as well as the ending x and y coordinates. We add another 10 lines by using a **for** loop. If you run this code, your output will look something like this:

Chapter 1 - Getting Started with Reportlab

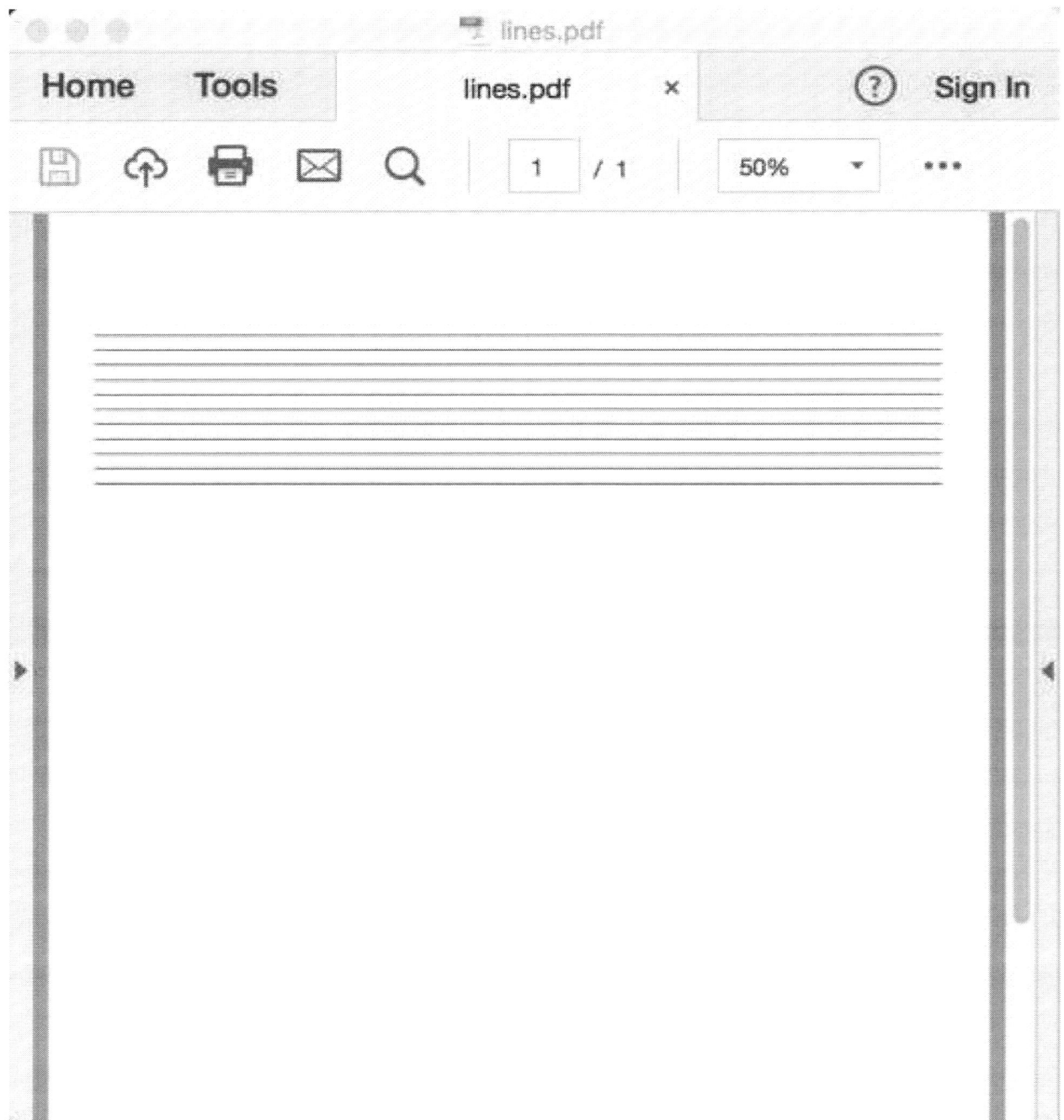

Fig. 1-5: Drawing lines on the canvas

The canvas supports several other drawing operations. For example, you can also draw rectangles, wedges and circles. Here's a simple demo:

```
# drawing_polygons.py

from reportlab.lib.pagesizes import letter
from reportlab.pdfgen import canvas

def draw_shapes():
    c = canvas.Canvas("draw_other.pdf")
    c.setStrokeColorRGB(0.2, 0.5, 0.3)
    c.rect(10, 740, 100, 80, stroke=1, fill=0)
    c.ellipse(10, 680, 100, 630, stroke=1, fill=1)
    c.wedge(10, 600, 100, 550, 45, 90, stroke=1, fill=0)
    c.circle(300, 600, 50)
    c.save()

if __name__ == '__main__':
    draw_shapes()
```

When you run this code, you should end up with a document that draws something like this:

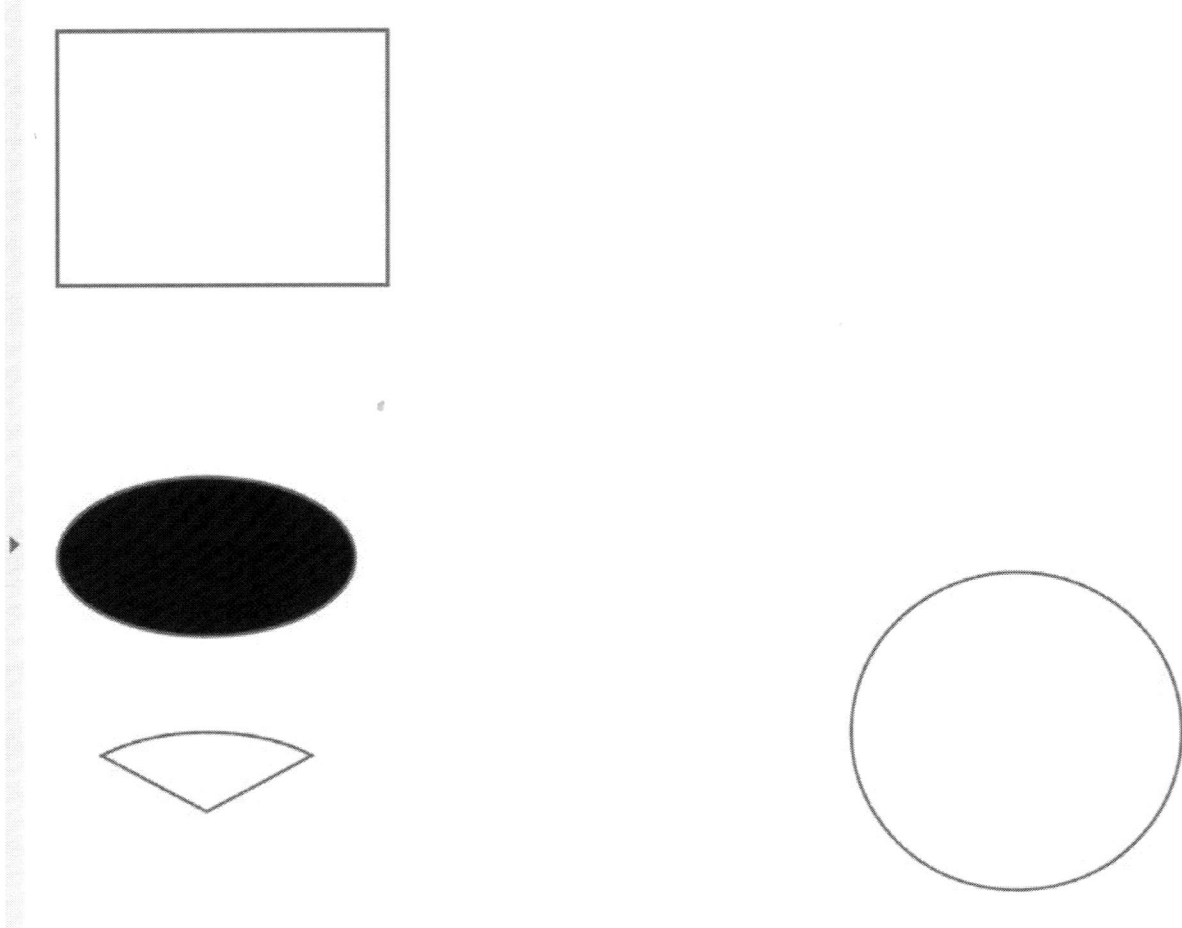

Fig. 1-6: Drawing polygons on the canvas

Let's take a few moments to go over the various arguments that each of these polygon methods accept. The **rect**'s code signature looks like this:

def rect(self, x, y, width, height, stroke=1, fill=0):

That means that you set the lower left-hand corner of the rectangle's position via its x/y parameters. Then you set its width and height. The stroke parameter tells ReportLab if it should draw the lines, so in the demo code I set **stroke=1**, or True. The fill parameter tells ReportLab to fill the interior of the polygon that I drew with a color.

Now let's look at the **ellipse**'s definition:

def ellipse(self, x1, y1, x2, y2, stroke=1, fill=0):

This one is very similar to the rect. According to method's docstring, the x1, y1, x2, y2 parameters are the corner points of the enclosing rectangle. The stroke and fill parameters operate the same way as the rect's. Just for fun, we went ahead and set the ellipse's fill to 1.

Next we have the wedge:

```
def wedge(self, x1,y1, x2,y2, startAng, extent, stroke=1, fill=0):
```

The x1,y1, x2,y2 parameters for the wedge actually correspond to the coordinates of an invisible enclosing rectangle that goes around a full 360 degree circle version of the wedge. So you will need to imagine that the full circle with a rectangle around it to help you position a wedge correctly. It also has a starting angle parameter (**startAng**) and the **extent** parameter, which basically tells the wedge how far out to arc to. The other parameters have already been explained.

Finally we reach the **circle** polygon. It's method looks like this:

```
def circle(self, x_cen, y_cen, r, stroke=1, fill=0):
```

The circle's arguments are probably the most self-explanatory of all of the polygons we have looked at. The **x_cen** and **y_cen** arguments are the x/y coordinates of the center of the circle. The **r** argument is the radius. The stroke and fill arguments are pretty obvious.

All the poloygons have the ability to set the stroke (or line) color via the **setStrokeColorRGB** method. It accepts Red, Green, Blue values for its parameters. You can also set the stroke color by using the **setStrokeColor** or the **setStrokeColorCMYK** method.

There are corresponding fill color setters too (i.e. setFillColor, setFillColorRGB, setFillColorCMYK), although I didn't show those in the demo code. The reason that wasn't covered above is that we are going to cover it in the very next section!

Using Colors in ReportLab

ReportLab has support for applying colors in several different ways. You can add a color to a drawing using one of two methods: RGB or CMYK. In the case of RGB, there are actually three different methods:

- By specifying red/green/blue values (i.e. values must be between zero and one)
- By name or
- By gray level

Frankly I think the gray level specification is a bit misleading in that you're really only specifying what level of gray you want, not any other color. Let's start with gray levels though and work our way up through the other methods!

```python
# gray_color_demo.py

from reportlab.lib.pagesizes import letter
from reportlab.pdfgen import canvas


def gray_color_demo():
    my_canvas = canvas.Canvas("grays.pdf",
                              pagesize=letter)
    my_canvas.setFont('Helvetica', 10)
    x = 30

    grays = [0.0, 0.25, 0.50, 0.75, 1.0]

    for gray in grays:
        my_canvas.setFillGray(gray)
        my_canvas.circle(x, 730, 20, fill=1)
        gray_str = "Gray={gray}".format(gray=gray)
        my_canvas.setFillGray(0.0)
        my_canvas.drawString(x-10, 700, gray_str)
        x += 75

    my_canvas.save()

if __name__ == '__main__':
    gray_color_demo()
```

This code should be pretty self-explanatory, but let's break it down anyway. First off, we create a list of different gray values. Then we set the fill color using **setFillGray**. After that we draw a circle and tell it to fill. Finally we create a string and draw it underneath each circle so we have the circles labeled with their gray value. When you run this code, you should see something like this:

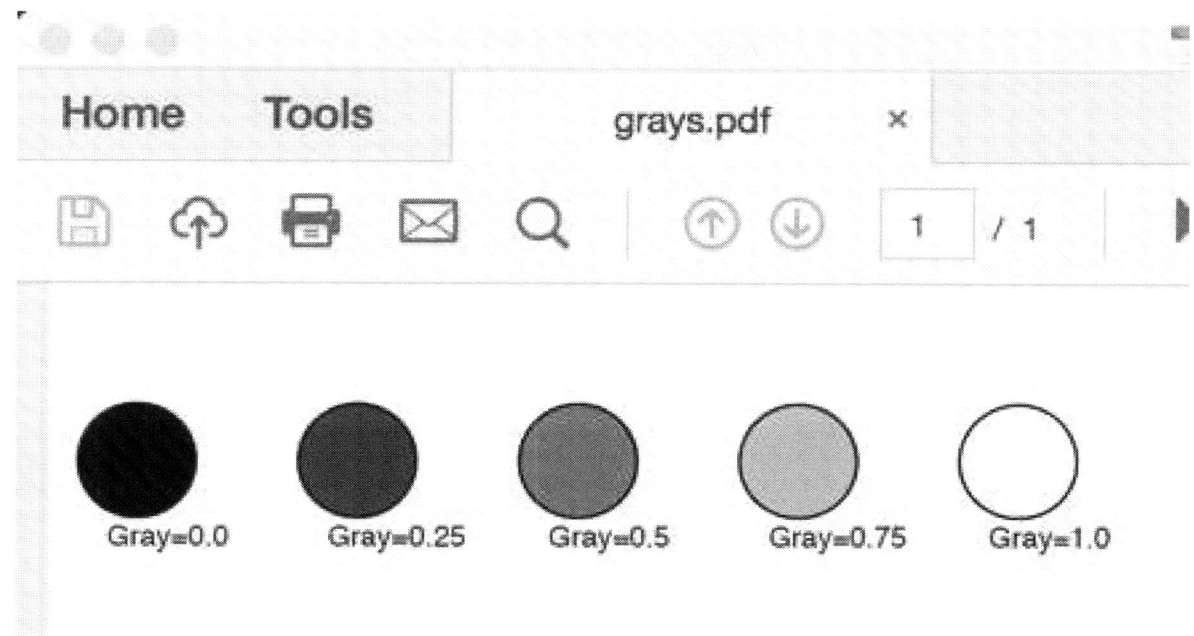

Fig. 1-7: ReportLab's shades of gray

Let's move on to learn how to add some color. The first method we will look at is setting the fill color by name:

```
# colors_demo.py

from reportlab.lib import colors
from reportlab.lib.pagesizes import letter
from reportlab.pdfgen import canvas


def color_demo():
    my_canvas = canvas.Canvas("colors.pdf",
                              pagesize=letter)
    my_canvas.setFont('Helvetica', 10)
    x = 30

    sample_colors = [colors.aliceblue,
                     colors.aquamarine,
                     colors.lavender,
                     colors.beige,
                     colors.chocolate]

    for color in sample_colors:
        my_canvas.setFillColor(color)
```

```
            my_canvas.circle(x, 730, 20, fill=1)
            color_str = "{color}".format(color=color._lookupName())
            my_canvas.setFillColor(colors.black)
            my_canvas.drawString(x-10, 700, color_str)
            x += 75

        my_canvas.save()

if __name__ == '__main__':
    color_demo()
```

Here we import the **colors** sub-module from ReportLab. Then we create a list of sample colors to iterate over like we did with the gray demo earlier. Then we do the loop and call **setFillColor** with the color's name. Now if you actually were to print the color to standard out, so you would see something like this:

```
>>> print(colors.aliceblue)
Color(.941176,.972549,1,1)
```

So these aren't exactly just names. In fact, they are ReportLab Color objects with RGB values and an intensity level between 0 (dark) and 1 (full intensity). Anyway, the next piece of code of note is where we grab the color's name via the **_lookupName()** method. The rest of the code is pretty easy to figure out.

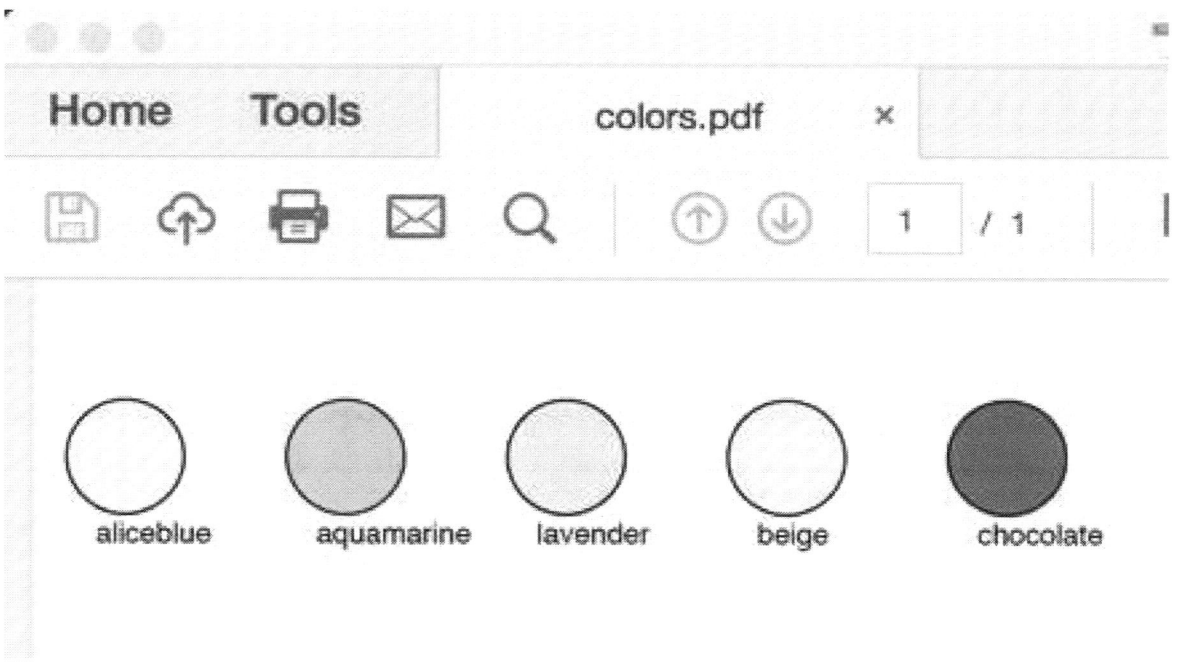

Fig. 1-8: **Example colors**

Chapter 1 - Getting Started with Reportlab

If you want to use straight-up RGB or CMYK values, then you can edit the example above to call **setFillColorRGB** or **setFillColorCMYK** respectively. They accept RGB or CMYK colors plus an alpha parameter respectively. The primary reason to use CMYK is for when you want more control over how the ink in your printer is applied to the printer. Of course you will need a printer that support CMYK for this to be really useful.

Adding a Photo

ReportLab supports adding images to your PDFs via the **Python Imaging Library (PIL)** package. Note that PIL is no longer supported and it is recommended that you download the **Pillow** project, a fork of PIL that works with both Python 2 and Python 3, something that the original PIL didn't do. To install Pillow, you just need to issue the pip command in your terminal, although you will only need to run this if it didn't automatically install when you installed ReportLab itself:

```
pip install pillow
```

Now that we have Pillow installed, let's talk about how to insert a photo into your PDF. The ReportLab canvas object supports two methods: **drawInlineImage** and **drawImage**. It is recommended that you use the newer **drawImage** method as it will cache the image and allow you to draw it many times while only being stored once in the PDF. If you use **drawInlineImage**, it will embed the image into the page stream itself, which makes it much less efficient as the image will be added multiple times to the document if you draw it more than once. While the documentation doesn't mention this, I would assume that this can also make the PDF larger in file size.

In this book, we will be using the **drawImage** method. Here's an example:

```python
# image_on_canvas.py

from reportlab.lib.pagesizes import letter
from reportlab.pdfgen import canvas


def add_image(image_path):
    my_canvas = canvas.Canvas("canvas_image.pdf",
                              pagesize=letter)
    my_canvas.drawImage(image_path, 30, 600,
                        width=100, height=100)
    my_canvas.save()

if __name__ == '__main__':
    image_path = 'snakehead.jpg'
    add_image(image_path)
```

As you can see, the **drawImage** method accepts the image's file path and its x / y position. These arguments are required. You can also specify the width and height of the image. Note that this will not automatically scale the image or keep its aspect ratio, so you may end up stretching the image if you don't know what you are doing. Finally you can also supply a **mask** parameter which will allow you to create a transparent image. This parameter is a list of 6 numbers which allows to define a range of RGB values which will be masked.

In ReportLab version 2 and newer, there is a **preserveAspectRatio** parameter that you can set as well as an **anchor** parameter. See the docstring for the **drawImage** method for more information on their proper usage.

If you are curious, here's what the PDF ended up looking:

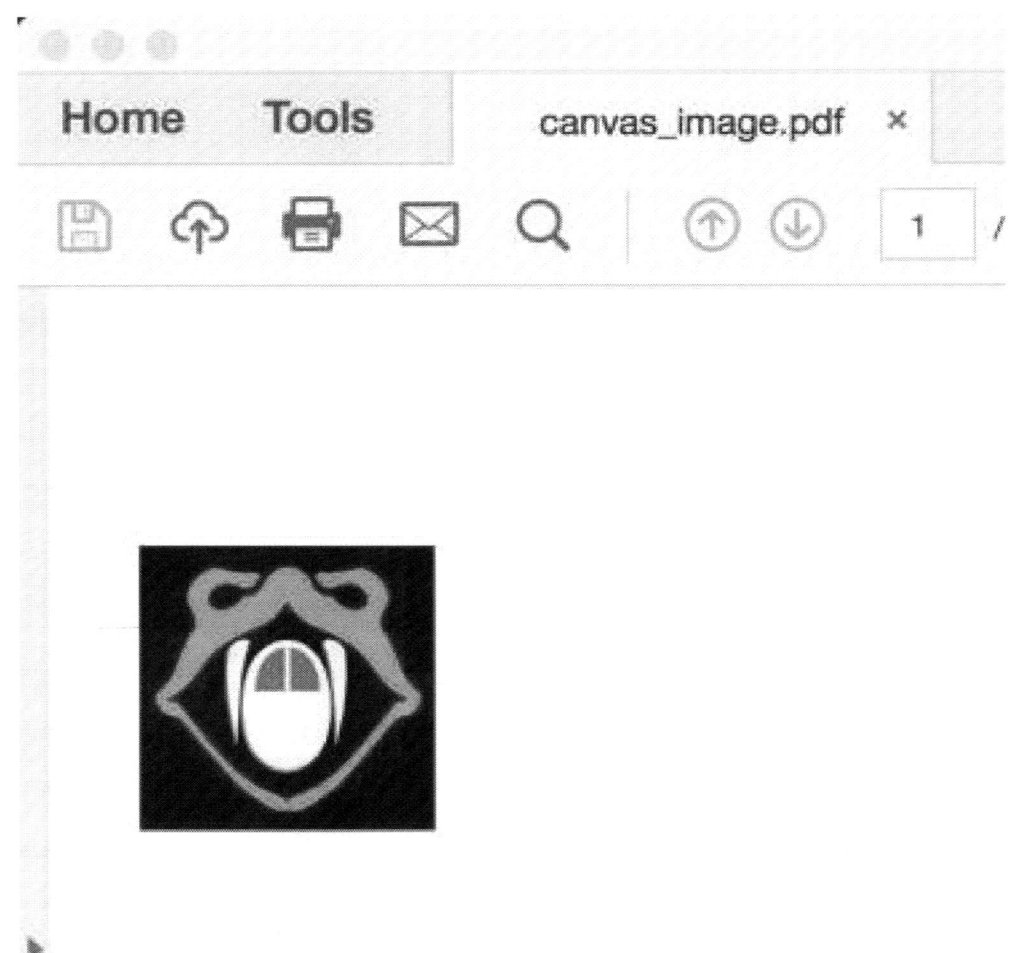

Fig. 1-9: Adding an image

The textobject

For additional control of your text's presentation, you can also use a **textobject**. Frankly I have never had the need for one of these as ReportLab's **Paragraph** class gives you more than enough control over the presentation of your text. But to be thorough, I will show you how to create and use a textobject. One benefit to use the textobject is that it will make the PDF generation faster if you use it instead of making separate calls to **drawString**.

Let's see a quick little demo:

```python
# textobject_demo.py

from reportlab.lib import colors
from reportlab.lib.pagesizes import letter
from reportlab.pdfgen import canvas


def textobject_demo():
    my_canvas = canvas.Canvas("txt_obj.pdf",
                              pagesize=letter)
    # Create textobject
    textobject = my_canvas.beginText()

    # Set text location (x, y)
    textobject.setTextOrigin(10, 730)

    # Set font face and size
    textobject.setFont('Times-Roman', 12)

    # Write a line of text + carriage return
    textobject.textLine(text='Python rocks!')

    # Change text color
    textobject.setFillColor(colors.red)

    # Write red text
    textobject.textLine(text='Python rocks in red!')

    # Write text to the canvas
    my_canvas.drawText(textobject)

    my_canvas.save()
```

```
if __name__ == '__main__':
    textobject_demo()
```

Here we learn that to create a **textobject**, we need to call the canvas's **beginText** method. If you happen to print out the textobject, you will find that it's technically an instance of **reportlab.pdfgen.textobject.PDFTextObject**. Anyway, now that we have a textobject, we can set its cursor position using a call to **setTextOrigin**. Then we set the font face and size as we saw before. The next new item is the call to **textLine**, which will allow you to write a string to the buffer plus what is basically a carriage return. The docstring for this method states that it makes the "text cursor moves down", but that amounts to a carriage return in my eyes. There is also a **textLines** method that allows you to write a multiline string out as well. If you want to control the location of the cursor, then you might want to use **textOut** as it won't add a carriage return to the end of the string.

The next thing we do is set the font color by calling **setFillColor**. In this example, we set the the next string of text to a red color. The last step is to call **drawText**, which will actually draw whatever you have in your textobject. If you skip calling **drawText**, then your text won't be written out and you may end up with an empty PDF document.

Here's the resulting PDF:

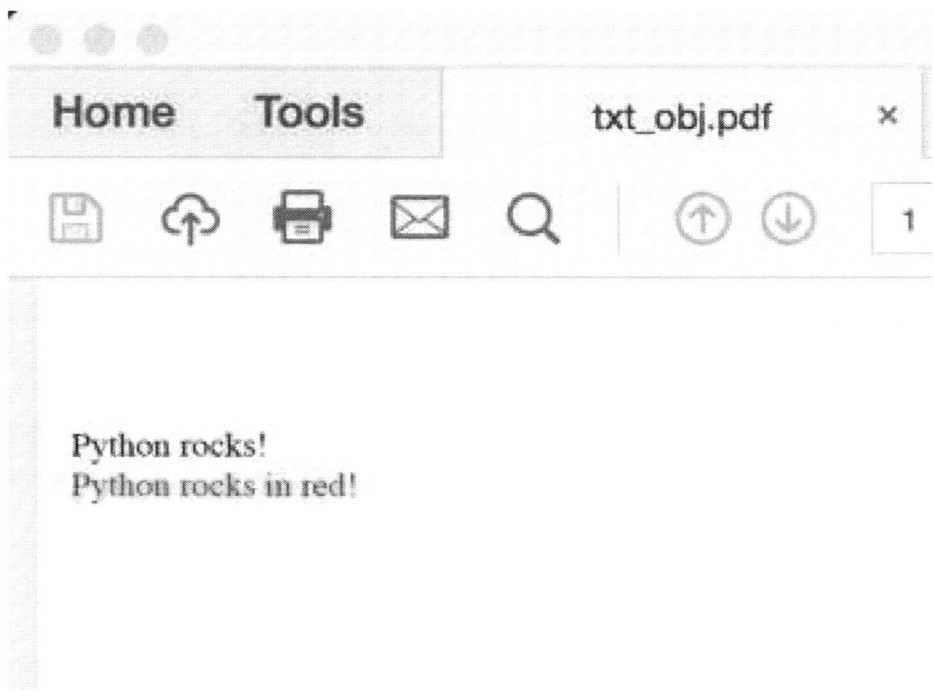

Fig. 1-10: Using a textobject

There are a lot of other methods you can call from your textobject. For example, if you want to move your cursor's position somewhere other than the very next line, you can call **moveCursor**. Let's take a look:

Chapter 1 - Getting Started with Reportlab

```python
# cursor_moving.py

from reportlab.lib.pagesizes import letter
from reportlab.pdfgen import canvas


def textobject_cursor():
    canvas_obj = canvas.Canvas("textobj_cursor.pdf", pagesize=letter)

    # Create textobject
    textobject = canvas_obj.beginText()

    # Set text location (x, y)
    textobject.setTextOrigin(10, 730)

    for indent in range(4):
        textobject.textLine('ReportLab cursor demo')
        textobject.moveCursor(15, 15)

    canvas_obj.drawText(textobject)
    canvas_obj.save()


if __name__ == '__main__':
    textobject_cursor()
```

Here we just set up a loop that will print out the same string four times, but at four different positions. You will note that we move the cursor 15 points to the right and 15 points down the page with each iteration of the loop. Yes, when using a textobject, a positive y number will move you down.

Now, let's say you would like to change the inter-character spacing; all you need to do is call **setCharSpace**. In fact, you can do a lot of interesting spacing tricks with textobject, such as changing the space between word using **setWordSpace** or the space between lines by calling **setLeading**. Let's take a look at how we might change the spacing of our text:

```python
# char_spacing_demo.py

from reportlab.lib.pagesizes import letter
from reportlab.pdfgen import canvas


def textobject_char_spacing():
    canvas_obj = canvas.Canvas("textobj_char_spacing.pdf",
                               pagesize=letter)
```

```python
    # Create textobject
    textobject = canvas_obj.beginText()

    # Set text location (x, y)
    textobject.setTextOrigin(10, 730)

    spacing = 0
    for indent in range(8):
        textobject.setCharSpace(spacing)
        line = '{} - ReportLab spacing demo'.format(spacing)
        textobject.textLine(line)
        spacing += 0.7

    canvas_obj.drawText(textobject)
    canvas_obj.save()


if __name__ == '__main__':
    textobject_char_spacing()
```

In this example, we increase the loop factor to 8 iterations and call **setCharSpace()** each time through the loop. We start with zero spacing and then add 0.7 in each iteration. You can see the result here:

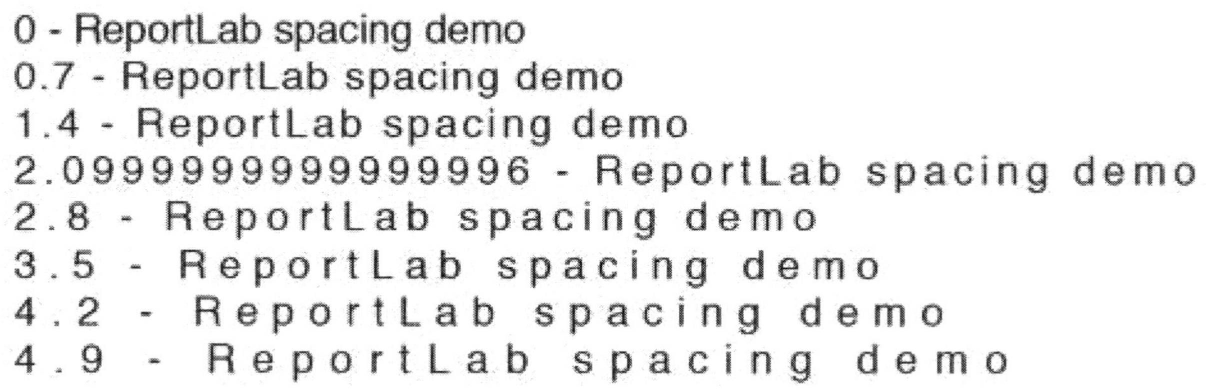

```
0 - ReportLab spacing demo
0.7 - ReportLab spacing demo
1.4 - ReportLab spacing demo
2.0999999999999996 - ReportLab spacing demo
2.8 - ReportLab spacing demo
3.5 - ReportLab spacing demo
4.2 - ReportLab spacing demo
4.9 - ReportLab spacing demo
```

Fig. 1-11: Character spacing with the textobject

Now let's see how applying word spacing effects our text:

```python
# wordspacing_demo.py

from reportlab.lib.pagesizes import letter
from reportlab.pdfgen import canvas


def wordspacer():
    canvas_obj = canvas.Canvas("textobj_word_spacing.pdf",
                               pagesize=letter)

    # Create textobject
    textobject = canvas_obj.beginText()

    # Set text location (x, y)
    textobject.setTextOrigin(10, 730)

    word_spacing = 0
    for indent in range(8):
        textobject.setWordSpace(word_spacing)
        line = '{} - ReportLab spacing demo'.format(word_spacing)
        textobject.textLine(line)
        word_spacing += 1.5

    canvas_obj.drawText(textobject)
    canvas_obj.save()

if __name__ == '__main__':
    wordspacer()
```

This example is pretty much the same as the previous one, but you will note that we are calling **setWordSpace()** instead of **setCharSpace()** and we are increasing the spacing by a factor of 1.5 in this example. The resulting text looks like this:

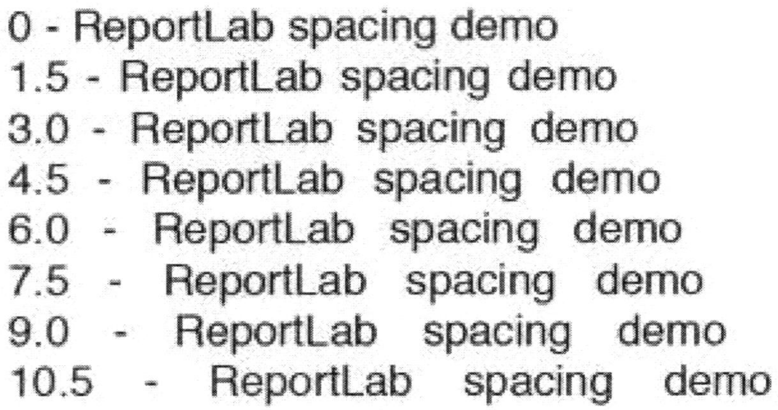

```
0 - ReportLab spacing demo
1.5 - ReportLab spacing demo
3.0 - ReportLab spacing demo
4.5 - ReportLab spacing demo
6.0 - ReportLab spacing demo
7.5 - ReportLab spacing demo
9.0 - ReportLab spacing demo
10.5 - ReportLab spacing demo
```

Fig. 1-12: Word spacing with the textobject

If you would like to create a superscript or subscript, then you would want to call **setRise** on your textobject. Let's create a demo that demonstrates how setting the rise works in ReportLab:

```python
# canvas_rising.py

from reportlab.lib.pagesizes import letter
from reportlab.pdfgen import canvas

def apply_scripting(textobject, text, rise):
    textobject.setFont("Helvetica-Oblique", 8)
    textobject.setRise(rise)
    textobject.textOut(text)
    textobject.setFont("Helvetica-Oblique", 12)
    textobject.setRise(0)


def main():
    canvas_obj = canvas.Canvas("textobj_rising.pdf",
                               pagesize=letter)

    # Create textobject
    textobject = canvas_obj.beginText()
    textobject.setFont("Helvetica-Oblique", 12)

    # Set text location (x, y)
    textobject.setTextOrigin(10, 730)

    textobject.textOut('ReportLab ')
```

```
    apply_scripting(textobject, 'superscript ', 7)

    textobject.textOut('and ')

    apply_scripting(textobject, 'subscript ', -7)

    canvas_obj.drawText(textobject)
    canvas_obj.save()

if __name__ == '__main__':
    main()
```

Here we create a couple of functions, **apply_scripting** and **main**. The main function will create our canvas and all the other bits and pieces we need. Then we write out some normal text. The next few lines are where we apply superscripting (positive) and subscripting (negative). Note that we need to set the rise back to zero between the superscript and subscript to make the word, "and", appear in the right location. As soon as you apply a rising value, it will continue to apply from that point on. So you will want to reset it to zero to make sure the text stays in a normal location. You will also note that we set the font size for the super and subscripts to be smaller than the regular text. Here is the result of running this example:

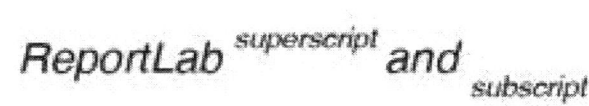

Fig. 1-13: Canvas rising with the textobject

Check out ReportLab's user guide for more interesting things you can do or check the source code itself.

Create a Page Break

One of the first things I wanted to know when I was creating PDFs with ReportLab was how to add a page break so I could have multipage PDF documents. The canvas object allows you to do this via the **showPage** method. Note however that for complex documents, you will almost certainly use ReportLab's **flowables**, which are special classes specifically for "flowing" your documents across multiple pages. Flowables are kind of mind bending in their own right, but they are also a lot nicer to use than trying to keep track of which page you are on and where your cursor position is at all times.

Canvas Orientation (Portrait vs. Landscape)

ReportLab defaults its page orientation to Portrait, which is what all word processors do as well. But sometimes you will want to use a page in **landscape** instead. There are at least two ways to tell Reportlab to use a landscape orientation. The first one is a convenience function called landscape that you can import from **reportlab.lib.pagesizes**. You would use it like this:

```
from reportlab.lib.pagesizes import landscape, letter
from reportlab.pdfgen import canvas

c = canvas.Canvas('test.pdf', pagesize=letter)
c.setPageSize( landscape(letter) )
```

The other way to set landscape is just set the page size explicitly:

```
from reportlab.lib.pagesizes import letter
from reportlab.pdfgen import canvas
from reportlab.lib.units import inch

c = canvas.Canvas('test.pdf', pagesize=letter)
c.setPageSize( (11*inch, 8.5*inch) )
```

You could make this more generic by doing something like this though:

```
from reportlab.lib.pagesizes import letter
from reportlab.pdfgen import canvas

width, height = letter

c = canvas.Canvas('test.pdf', pagesize=letter)
c.setPageSize( (height, width) )
```

This might make more sense, especially if you wanted to use other popular page sizes, like A4.

Other methods

There are a bunch of additional methods that I'm not even going to cover in this chapter. For example, there are methods to set some metadata for your PDF, such as the author (**setAuthor**), title (**setTitle**) and subject (**setSubject**). The **bookmarkPage** method is actually useful if you want to create bookmarks in your PDF though. There are also methods for creating a named form and then interacting with it (**beginForm**, **endForm**, etc). Just go look through the ReportLab's user guide for a complete list or check out the canvas's source.

A Simple Sample Application

Sometimes it's nice to see how you can take what you've learned and see if applied. So let's take some of the methods we've learned about here and create a simple application that create a form:

```python
# sample_form_letter.py

from reportlab.lib.pagesizes import letter
from reportlab.pdfgen import canvas

def create_form(filename, date, amount, receiver):
    """
    @param date: The date to use
    @param amount: The amount owed
    @param receiver: The person who received the amount owed
    """
    my_canvas = canvas.Canvas(filename, pagesize=letter)
    my_canvas.setLineWidth(.3)
    my_canvas.setFont('Helvetica', 12)

    my_canvas.drawString(30, 750, 'OFFICIAL COMMUNIQUE')
    my_canvas.drawString(30, 735, 'OF ACME INDUSTRIES')

    my_canvas.drawString(500, 750, date)
    my_canvas.line(480, 747, 580, 747)

    my_canvas.drawString(275, 725, 'AMOUNT OWED:')
    my_canvas.drawString(500, 725, amount)
    my_canvas.line(378, 723, 580, 723)

    my_canvas.drawString(30, 703, 'RECEIVED BY:')
    my_canvas.line(120, 700, 580, 700)
    my_canvas.drawString(120, 703, receiver)

    my_canvas.save()

if __name__ == '__main__':
    create_form('form.pdf', '01/23/2018',
                '$1,999', 'Mike')
```

Here we just create a simple function called **create_form** that accepts the filename, the date we want for our form, the amount owed and the person who receives the amount owed. Then we paint everything in the desired locations and save the file. When you run this, you will see the following:

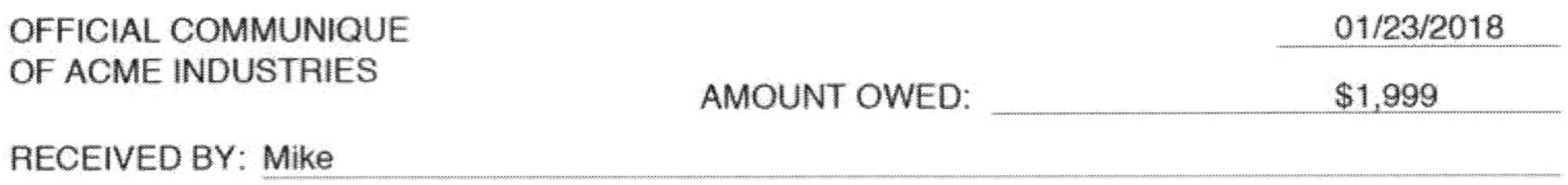

```
OFFICIAL COMMUNIQUE                                              01/23/2018
OF ACME INDUSTRIES
                              AMOUNT OWED:                        $1,999

RECEIVED BY: Mike
```

Fig. 1-14: A Sample Form letter

That looks pretty professional for a short piece of code.

Wrapping Up

We covered a lot of information in this chapter. You should now know how to create a pretty basic PDF. I highly recommend trying out the examples in this chapter and then going back and editing them a bit to see what all you can accomplish on your own. Once you are done playing around the canvas methods mentioned here, prepare yourselves as the next chapter will be about how ReportLab handles fonts.

Chapter 2 - ReportLab and Fonts

We covered a little information about fonts in chapter 1, but I thought it was important to talk a little about ReportLab's font support. A few years ago, ReportLab added support for Asian languages. They also support TrueType fonts and Type-1 fonts. It's also worth talking about encodings in this chapter, which is what we will discuss next.

Unicode / UTF8 is the Default

Way back in 2006, ReportLab made it so that all text you provide to their APIs should be in UTF8 or as Python Unicode objects. This should be done with the **canvas.DrawString** methods as well as in the flowables that accept text (i.e. strings) as their argument. Fortunately Python 3's "strings" are Unicode by default, so you won't even have to think all that much about this topic if you just use the latest Python. However if you are using an older version of Python AND your string is not encoded as UTF8, then you will get a **UnicodeDecodeError** if you give it any character that is not ASCII.

The fix is to just encode your text as UTF8 or use a Unicode object. Just keep that in mind if you run into these sorts of issues.

The Standard Fonts

ReportLab comes with a set of fonts by default. They don't need to be stored/embedded in your PDF as Adobe's Acrobat Reader guarantees that they will be there. You can get a list of the fonts available by calling the **getAvailableFonts()** canvas method. This is the list I received:

- Courier
- Courier-Bold
- Courier-BoldOblique
- Courier-Oblique
- Helvetica
- Helvetica-Bold
- Helvetica-BoldOblique
- Helvetica-Oblique
- Symbol
- Times-Bold
- Times-BoldItalic
- Times-Italic

- Times-Roman
- ZapfDingbats

ReportLab supports limited automatic font substitution. This will happen only if the ReportLab engine detects a character that is not in your font of choice. In these cases, ReportLab's engine will attempt to switch to Symbol or ZapfDingbats to display said character. Here's a quick demo:

```python
# basic_font_demo.py

from reportlab.lib.pagesizes import letter
from reportlab.pdfgen import canvas

def font_demo(my_canvas, fonts):
    pos_y = 750
    for font in fonts:
        my_canvas.setFont(font, 12)
        my_canvas.drawString(30, pos_y, font)
        pos_y -= 10

if __name__ == '__main__':
    my_canvas = canvas.Canvas("basic_font_demo.pdf",
                              pagesize=letter)
    fonts = my_canvas.getAvailableFonts()
    font_demo(my_canvas, fonts)
    my_canvas.save()
```

You will note that all we need to do to get a list of fonts is to call the **getAvailableFonts** method. When you run this code, you will get the following in your PDF:

```
Courier
Courier-Bold
Courier-BoldOblique
Courier-Oblique
Helvetica
Helvetica-Bold
Helvetica-BoldOblique
Helvetica-Oblique
■■■■■■
Times-Bold
Times-BoldItalic
Times-Italic
Times-Roman
■■■■■■■■■■■
```

Fig. 2-1: The standard fonts

Now let's learn about embedding fonts in your PDF document.

Other Type-1 Fonts

If you need to embed a non-standard font, then you will need a couple of font description files. One needs to be in the Adobe AFM (Adobe Font Metrics) format and the other needs to be in PFB (Printer Font Binary) format. The Adobe AFM file is actually ASCII and tells ReportLab about the glyph's of the font. A font's glyph describes the height, width, bounding box information and other font metrics. The PFB describes the shapes of the font and is in binary format, so you won't be able to read it without a hex editor or similar. I have had to use these files for embedding a check font into a PDF before.

Fortunately, ReportLab actually includes an open source font called *DarkGardenMK* that they distribute with ReportLab in their fonts folder. Let's write a little demo that shows how to embed this font in our PDF:

```python
# type1_font_demo.py

import os
import reportlab

from reportlab.lib.pagesizes import letter
from reportlab.pdfbase import pdfmetrics
from reportlab.pdfgen import canvas


def embedded_font_demo():
    my_canvas = canvas.Canvas("type1_font_demo.pdf",
                              pagesize=letter)
    reportlab_folder = os.path.dirname(reportlab.__file__)
    fonts_folder = os.path.join(reportlab_folder, 'fonts')
    print('ReportLab font folder is located at {}'.format(
        fonts_folder))

    afm = os.path.join(fonts_folder, 'DarkGardenMK.afm')
    pfb = os.path.join(fonts_folder, 'DarkGardenMK.pfb')

    # Register the font so we can use it
    font_face = pdfmetrics.EmbeddedType1Face(afm, pfb)
    pdfmetrics.registerTypeFace(font_face)

    face_name = 'DarkGardenMK'
    font = pdfmetrics.Font('DarkGardenMK',
                           face_name,
                           'WinAnsiEncoding')
    pdfmetrics.registerFont(font)

    # Use the font!
    my_canvas.setFont('DarkGardenMK', 40)
    my_canvas.drawString(10, 730, 'The DarkGardenMK font')
    my_canvas.save()

if __name__ == '__main__':
    embedded_font_demo()
```

This is a fairly complex process. First we have our imports. Note that we need **pdfmetrics** to register the font. Then we create our demo function and build the font folder by getting ReportLab's install location. I added a **print()** statement so that you could find out where this folder is located in case you would like to browse through it. Next we get the paths to the AFM and PFB files. Now we're finally ready to register the font with ReportLab. That process begins by instantiating the pdfmetrics's **EmbeddedType1Face** class and passing it the AFM and PFB file paths. Next we register the font's face via the call to **registerTypeFace**. Funnily enough, I accidentally discovered that if I don't call that function, the code works just fine, so I am actually not sure why this is needed other than possibly a sanity check.

Anyway, the next step is to instantiate the **Font** class by passing it the name of the font, the face name and the encoding. Then you can just register the font by calling **registerFont**. Now we can actually use the font in our PDF. This is the result I got when I ran this code:

Fig. 2-2: Embedding a Type-1 Font

I don't know when you would want to use this font other than possibly for when a dragon speaks, but it looks kind of neat!

You can also edit the T1 font search path in **rl_settings.py**, which is located in your ReportLab installation location. The variable you will need to set is called **T1SearchPath**. On my system, the default looks like this:

```
>>> from reportlab import rl_settings
>>> rl_settings.T1SearchPath
('c:/Program Files/Adobe/Acrobat 9.0/Resource/Font',
 'c:/Program Files/Adobe/Acrobat 8.0/Resource/Font',
 'c:/Program Files/Adobe/Acrobat 7.0/Resource/Font',
 'c:/Program Files/Adobe/Acrobat 6.0/Resource/Font',
 'c:/Program Files/Adobe/Acrobat 5.0/Resource/Font',
 'c:/Program Files/Adobe/Acrobat 4.0/Resource/Font',
 '%(disk)s/Applications/Python %(sys_version)s/reportlab/fonts',
 '/usr/lib/Acrobat9/Resource/Font',
 '/usr/lib/Acrobat8/Resource/Font',
 '/usr/lib/Acrobat7/Resource/Font',
 '/usr/lib/Acrobat6/Resource/Font',
 '/usr/lib/Acrobat5/Resource/Font',
 '/usr/lib/Acrobat4/Resource/Font',
 '/usr/local/Acrobat9/Resource/Font',
 '/usr/local/Acrobat8/Resource/Font',
 '/usr/local/Acrobat7/Resource/Font',
 '/usr/local/Acrobat6/Resource/Font',
 '/usr/local/Acrobat5/Resource/Font',
 '/usr/local/Acrobat4/Resource/Font',
 '/usr/share/fonts/default/Type1',
```

```
    '%(REPORTLAB_DIR)s/fonts',
    '%(REPORTLAB_DIR)s/../fonts',
    '%(REPORTLAB_DIR)s/../../fonts',
    '%(CWD)s/fonts',
    '~/fonts',
    '~/.fonts',
    '%(XDG_DATA_HOME)s/fonts',
    '~/.local/share/fonts',
    '/usr/share/fonts/type1/gsfonts')
```

TrueType Fonts

Adding TrueType fonts in your PDF using ReportLab is a bit less complicated than embedding Type-1 Fonts. Let's take a look and see how TrueType font embedding differs from Type-1:

```python
# truetype_font_demo.py

import os
import reportlab

from reportlab.lib.pagesizes import letter
from reportlab.pdfbase import pdfmetrics
from reportlab.pdfbase.ttfonts import TTFont
from reportlab.pdfgen import canvas


def embedded_font_demo():
    my_canvas = canvas.Canvas("truetype_font_demo.pdf",
                              pagesize=letter)
    reportlab_folder = os.path.dirname(reportlab.__file__)
    fonts_folder = os.path.join(reportlab_folder, 'fonts')
    print('ReportLab font folder is located at {}'.format(
        fonts_folder))

    # Register the font so we can use it
    vera_font_path = os.path.join(fonts_folder, 'Vera.ttf')

    # Usage: TTFont(name, filename)
    vera_font = TTFont('Vera', vera_font_path)
    pdfmetrics.registerFont(vera_font)
```

```python
    # Use a generic font
    my_canvas.setFont('Helvetica', 40)
    my_canvas.drawString(10, 730, 'The Helvetica font')

    # Use the font!
    my_canvas.setFont('Vera', 40)
    my_canvas.drawString(10, 690, 'The Vera font')
    my_canvas.save()

if __name__ == '__main__':
    embedded_font_demo()
```

One of the first changes is that we need to import **TTFont** from **reportlab.pdfbase.ttfonts**. Then we make an instance of that class by passing it the font's name and the font's file path. Then we call **registerFont** as we did with the Type-1 fonts in the previous section. The rest of the code is pretty much the same.

I would also like to point out that there is a **registerFontFamily** method that you should be aware of. This method will allow you to map the bold, italic and bolditalic versions of the font to the same name. Of course if you have all the different versions of the font, than you can use this function to register those name too. Here's the signature you would use for the **Vera** font:

```
registerFontFamily('Vera', normal='Vera',bold='VeraBd',italic='VeraIt',boldItali\
c='VeraBI')
```

As you can see, you just pass the name of the various flavors of the font to the appropriate parameter.

An alternative way to include TrueType fonts is to set the font search path in **rl_settings.py** in much the same way that you did the T1 search path. For TrueType fonts, you will want to set the **TTFSearchPath** variable. The defaults paths that ReportLab looks in are as follows:

```
>>> from reportlab import rl_settings
>>> rl_settings.TTFSearchPath
('c:/winnt/fonts',
 'c:/windows/fonts',
 '/usr/lib/X11/fonts/TrueType/',
 '/usr/share/fonts/truetype',
 '/usr/share/fonts',
 '/usr/share/fonts/dejavu',
 '%(REPORTLAB_DIR)s/fonts',
 '%(REPORTLAB_DIR)s/../fonts',
 '%(REPORTLAB_DIR)s/../../fonts',
 '%(CWD)s/fonts',
```

```
'~/fonts',
'~/.fonts',
'%(XDG_DATA_HOME)s/fonts',
'~/.local/share/fonts',
'~/Library/Fonts',
'/Library/Fonts',
'/Network/Library/Fonts',
'/System/Library/Fonts',
'/usr/share/fonts/truetype',
'/usr/share/fonts/truetype/kacst-one',
'/usr/share/fonts/truetype/freefont',
'/usr/share/fonts/truetype/nanum',
'/usr/share/fonts/truetype/ttf-khmeros-core',
'/usr/share/fonts/truetype/lohit-punjabi',
'/usr/share/fonts/truetype/takao-gothic',
'/usr/share/fonts/truetype/sinhala',
'/usr/share/fonts/truetype/ancient-scripts',
'/usr/share/fonts/truetype/tlwg',
'/usr/share/fonts/truetype/lyx',
'/usr/share/fonts/truetype/lao',
'/usr/share/fonts/truetype/fonts-guru-extra',
'/usr/share/fonts/truetype/abyssinica',
'/usr/share/fonts/truetype/dejavu',
'/usr/share/fonts/truetype/tibetan-machine',
'/usr/share/fonts/truetype/ubuntu-font-family',
'/usr/share/fonts/truetype/ttf-bitstream-vera',
'/usr/share/fonts/truetype/kacst',
'/usr/share/fonts/truetype/openoffice',
'/usr/share/fonts/truetype/liberation',
'/usr/share/fonts/truetype/noto',
'/usr/share/fonts/truetype/padauk')
```

If your font is in one of those paths, then you can simplify your code a bit because you won't need to include the entire path any longer:

```
vera_font = TTFont('Vera', 'Vera.ttf')
pdfmetrics.registerFont(vera_font)
```

Asian Fonts

A few years ago, ReportLab added support for Asian fonts. ReportLab currently supports, Japanese, Traditional Chinese (Taiwan / Hong Kong), Simplified Chinese (mainland China) and Korean. They

Chapter 2 - ReportLab and Fonts

do this by supporting the following fonts:

- chs = Chinese Simplified (mainland): 'STSong-Light'
- cht = Chinese Traditional (Taiwan): 'MSung-Light', 'MHei-Medium'
- kor = Korean: 'HYSMyeongJoStd-Medium','HYGothic-Medium'
- jpn = Japanese: 'HeiseiMin-W3', 'HeiseiKakuGo-W5'

If you use one of these fonts in your PDF, then you will likely discover that it isn't installed and Adobe's Reader may pop up a dialog like the following:

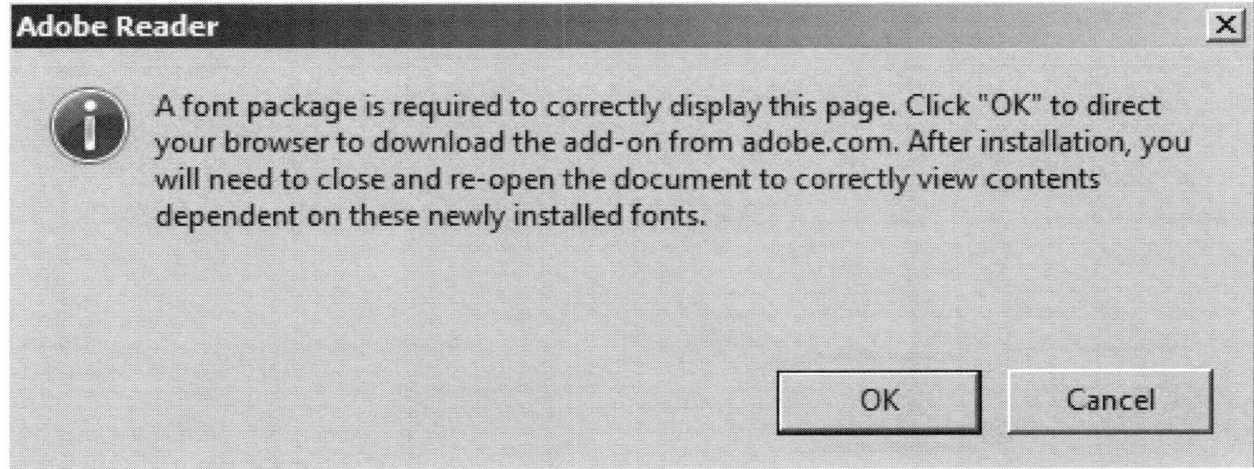

Fig. 2-3: **Font package warning**

Let's write some code to write the characters used for the word "Nippon", which means Japan. The characters we will use are Japanese kanji that were converted to Unicode. For this example, I just looked up a Unicode converter online and asked it to convert "Nippon" to Unicode. Here's the code:

```
# asian_font_demo.py

# Works with Python 2 and 3
from reportlab.lib.pagesizes import letter
from reportlab.pdfbase import pdfmetrics
from reportlab.pdfbase.cidfonts import UnicodeCIDFont
from reportlab.pdfgen import canvas


def asian_font_demo():
    my_canvas = canvas.Canvas("asian_font_demo.pdf",
                              pagesize=letter)

    # Set a Japanese font
```

Chapter 2 - ReportLab and Fonts

```
    pdfmetrics.registerFont(UnicodeCIDFont('HeiseiMin-W3'))
    my_canvas.setFont('HeiseiMin-W3', 16)

    # Find a word or phrase in Unicode to write out
    nippon = u'\u65e5\u672c'   # Nippon / Japan in Unicode

    my_canvas.drawString(25, 730, nippon)
    my_canvas.save()

if __name__ == '__main__':
    asian_font_demo()
```

When I ran this and tried to open the resulting PDF with Adobe Reader, I received the aforementioned dialog about needing to download a font package, **FontPack11009_XtdAlf_Lang.msi**, which ended up being a 52 MB download. If you don't install the font package, then the PDF will appear to be blank when opened. After installing the fonts, I got the following result:

Fig. 2-4: **Embedding an Asian font**

Since Python 3 supports Unicode out of the box, you don't have to use Unicode characters directly like we did in the example above. You can just use the actual Kanji! Just for fun, I went ahead and updated the example to use some actual Kanji:

Chapter 2 - ReportLab and Fonts

```python
# asian_font_demo2.py

from reportlab.lib.pagesizes import letter
from reportlab.pdfbase import pdfmetrics
from reportlab.pdfbase.cidfonts import UnicodeCIDFont
from reportlab.pdfgen import canvas


def asian_font_demo():
    my_canvas = canvas.Canvas("asian_font_demo2.pdf",
                              pagesize=letter)

    # Set a Japanese font
    pdfmetrics.registerFont(UnicodeCIDFont('HeiseiMin-W3'))
    my_canvas.setFont('HeiseiMin-W3', 16)

    # Find a word or phrase in Unicode to write out
    nippon = 'æ„›æƒ…'   # Love in Japanese

    my_canvas.drawString(25, 730, nippon)
    my_canvas.save()

if __name__ == '__main__':
    asian_font_demo()
```

You can also use TrueType fonts that have Asian characters. This is even easier to use than the **UnicodeCIDFont** that we had to use in the previous section. The ReportLab engineers did mention in their documentation that these kinds of fonts can take time to parse and that large subsets of the font will need to be embedded in your PDF for the characters to be displayed correctly. They also noted that ReportLab can also parse .ttc files, which is a variant of the TrueType extension, .ttf.

There are also the Noto and Source Han (Sans/Serif) fonts, which are both open source. Noto is from Google and aims to support all languages whereas Source Han Sans is a set of OpenType/CFF Pan-CJK fonts from Adobe.

Switching Between Fonts

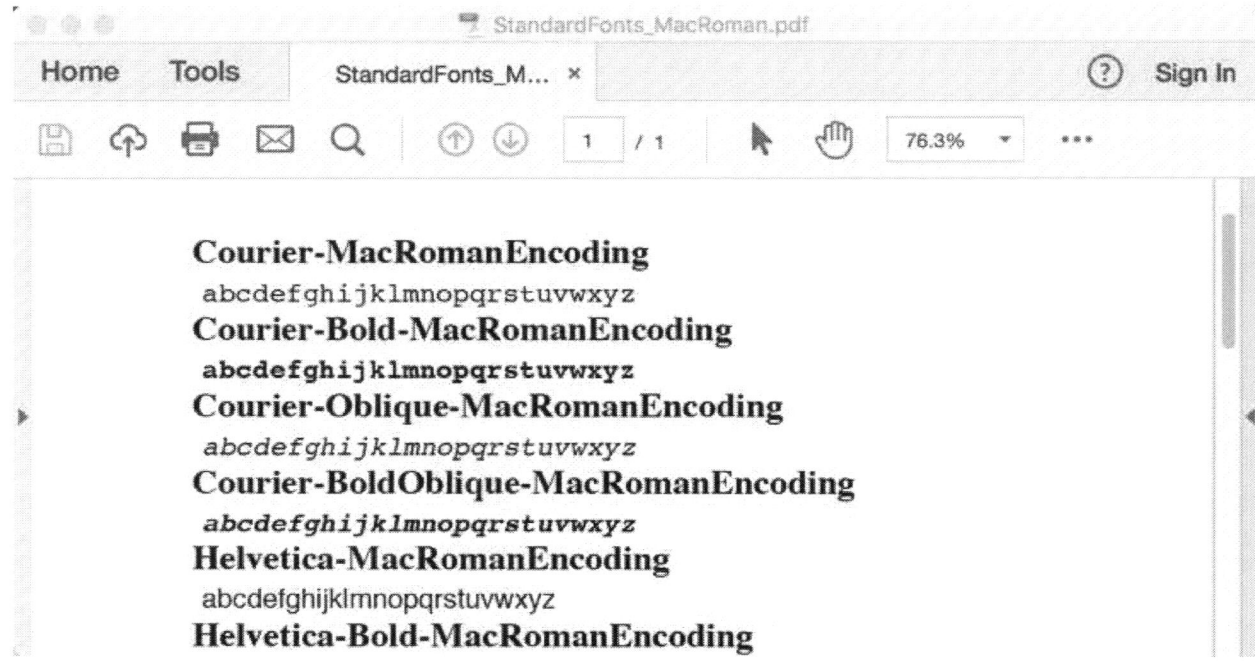

Fig. 2-5: Switching between fonts

We technically have already covered how to switch between fonts, but I didn't actually call it out in the previous examples. So I wanted to make sure my readers were quite clear on how to change fonts while generating their PDFs with ReportLab. Let's take a look at a simple demo:

```
# font_switching.py

import string
import sys

from reportlab.pdfbase import pdfmetrics
from reportlab.pdfgen import canvas


def standardFonts():
    """
    Create a PDF with all the standard fonts
    """
    for enc in ['MacRoman', 'WinAnsi']:
        canv = canvas.Canvas(
            'StandardFonts_%s.pdf' % enc,
```

```
            )
            canv.setPageCompression(0)

            x = 0
            y = 744
            for faceName in pdfmetrics.standardFonts:
                if faceName in ['Symbol', 'ZapfDingbats']:
                    encLabel = faceName+'Encoding'
                else:
                    encLabel = enc + 'Encoding'

                fontName = faceName + '-' + encLabel
                pdfmetrics.registerFont(pdfmetrics.Font(fontName,
                                            faceName,
                                            encLabel)
                                        )

                canv.setFont('Times-Bold', 18)
                canv.drawString(80, y, fontName)

                y -= 20

                alpha = "abcdefghijklmnopqrstuvwxyz"
                canv.setFont(fontName, 14)
                canv.drawString(x+85, y, alpha)

                y -= 20

        canv.save()

if __name__ == "__main__":
    standardFonts()
```

As mentioned earlier, Reportlab supports several fonts internally. You can think of them as standard or default fonts. The script above will create two PDFs: **StandardFonts_MacRoman.pdf** and **StandardFonts_WinAnsi.pdf**. As you can see, we just use a nested pair of for loops to extract the various fonts and register them with Reportlab. Then we called **setFont** with the selected font. From that point forward, ReportLab will use that font when it draws text. When you call **setFont** again, that will change your currently selected font to the one you specified and then that will be the font used. In other words, ReportLab always uses the last set font or the default until you explicitly set it to something else.

By the way, the difference between MacRoman and WinAnsi is that one was developed by Apple and the other became a Microsoft proprietary character set. While they are identical for some character (32 - 126 of ASCII), they each have different distinct sets of control characters.

Wrapping Up

In this chapter we covered how to embed Type-1 and TrueType fonts in our PDFs using ReportLab. We also covered ReportLab's Asian font support. You should take some time and play around with these examples to make sure you fully understand how to embed fonts in your PDF. This is quite handy when you need to give your documents a unique look or you need to support your Asian customers.

Chapter 3 - Intro to Page Layout

ReportLab has a neat concept that they call PLATYPUS, which stands for "Page Layout and Typography Using Scripts". It is a high level layout library that ReportLab provides that makes it easier to programmatically create complex layouts with a minimum of code. You can kind of think of PLATYPUS as analogous to SQLALchemy and SQL. It basically takes care of page breaking, layout and styling for you. In fact, you can kind of "theme" your document by applying templates.

The ReportLab engineers describe PLATYPUS as having several layers (from highest to lowest level):

- **DocTemplates** - the outermost container of your page
- **PageTemplates** - specifies the layout of your page
- **Frames** - kind of like a sizer in a desktop user interface. Basically it provides a region that contains other flowables
- **Flowables** - A text or graphic element that can be "flowed" across page boundaries, such as a paragraph of text. This does not include footers and headers.
- **pdfgen.Canvas** - The lowest level of ReportLab, and one that we have already covered. It will actually receive its instructions from one or more of the upper layers and "paint" your document accordingly.

We will be learning about flowables for the next few chapters. But for now, let's start learning the basics so you can get going with PLATYPUS!

The Basics of PLATYPUS

When I learn something new, I always find it helpful if I create a small runnable example. So to help us learn about ReportLab's PLATYPUS capabilities, we will create a couple of small runnable demos to help us learn. Let's create something that's really simple:

```python
# hello_platypus.py

from reportlab.lib.pagesizes import letter
from reportlab.platypus import SimpleDocTemplate, Paragraph
from reportlab.lib.styles import getSampleStyleSheet

def hello():
    doc = SimpleDocTemplate("hello_platypus.pdf",
                            pagesize=letter,
```

```
                            rightMargin=72,
                            leftMargin=72,
                            topMargin=72,
                            bottomMargin=18)
    styles = getSampleStyleSheet()

    flowables = []

    text = "Hello, I'm a Paragraph"
    para = Paragraph(text, style=styles["Normal"])
    flowables.append(para)

    doc.build(flowables)

if __name__ == '__main__':
    hello()
```

Let's start from the top. We have some new imports. The first two come from the **reportlab.platypus** submodule. Here we get **SimpleDocTemplate** and **Paragraph**. Then we import a style sheet from the **styles** submodule. Next we create a function called **hello** and create a template by instantiating an instance of **SimpleDocTemplate**. The only required argument here is the filename. But I went ahead and set the page size to letter and then I set the margins. As mentioned in chapter one, ReportLab uses the concept of points as a unit of measurement and this continues to be true in PLATYPUS. Next up, we get ReportLab's sample style sheet and we create an empty list called **flowables**. This list will contain all the flowable objects we want to draw in our PDF. Finally we create a **Paragraph**, which is a flowable that can format a block of text using the specified style sheet. We append this flowable object to our flowables list and then we call our template's **build** method. The build method will then construct our PDF.

Here is the output (cropped of course):

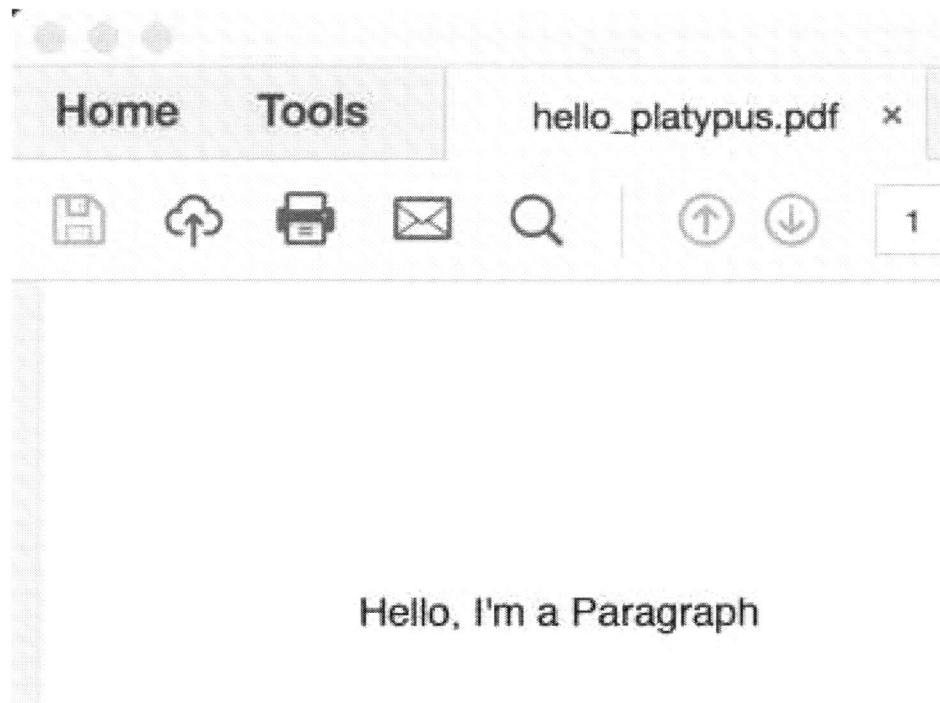

Fig. 3-1: Hello Platypus example

Now that was kind of a boring example, so let's create something a bit more complex.

```
# form_letter.py

import time
from reportlab.lib.enums import TA_JUSTIFY
from reportlab.lib.pagesizes import letter
from reportlab.platypus import SimpleDocTemplate, Paragraph, Spacer, Image
from reportlab.lib.styles import getSampleStyleSheet, ParagraphStyle
from reportlab.lib.units import inch

def form_letter():
    doc = SimpleDocTemplate("form_letter.pdf",
                            pagesize=letter,
                            rightMargin=72,
                            leftMargin=72,
                            topMargin=72,
                            bottomMargin=18)
    flowables = []
    logo = "python_logo.png"
    magName = "Pythonista"
    issueNum = 12
```

```python
    subPrice = "99.00"
    limitedDate = "03/05/2010"
    freeGift = "tin foil hat"

    formatted_time = time.ctime()
    full_name = "Mike Driscoll"
    address_parts = ["411 State St.", "Waterloo, IA 50158"]

    im = Image(logo, 2*inch, 2*inch)
    flowables.append(im)

    styles = getSampleStyleSheet()
    styles.add(ParagraphStyle(name='Justify', alignment=TA_JUSTIFY))
    ptext = '<font size=12>%s</font>' % formatted_time

    flowables.append(Paragraph(ptext, styles["Normal"]))
    flowables.append(Spacer(1, 12))

    # Create return address
    ptext = '<font size=12>%s</font>' % full_name
    flowables.append(Paragraph(ptext, styles["Normal"]))
    for part in address_parts:
        ptext = '<font size=12>%s</font>' % part.strip()
        flowables.append(Paragraph(ptext, styles["Normal"]))

    flowables.append(Spacer(1, 12))
    ptext = '<font size=12>Dear %s:</font>' % full_name.split()[0].strip()
    flowables.append(Paragraph(ptext, styles["Normal"]))
    flowables.append(Spacer(1, 12))

    ptext = '''
<font size=12>We would like to welcome you to our subscriber
base for {magName} Magazine! You will receive {issueNum} issues at
the excellent introductory price of ${subPrice}. Please respond by
{limitedDate} to start receiving your subscription and get the
following free gift: {freeGift}.</font>
'''.format(magName=magName,
           issueNum=issueNum,
           subPrice=subPrice,
           limitedDate=limitedDate,
           freeGift=freeGift)
    flowables.append(Paragraph(ptext, styles["Justify"]))
```

```
    flowables.append(Spacer(1, 12))
    
    ptext = '''<font size=12>Thank you very much and we look
    forward to serving you.</font>'''
    
    flowables.append(Paragraph(ptext, styles["Justify"]))
    flowables.append(Spacer(1, 12))
    ptext = '<font size=12>Sincerely,</font>'
    flowables.append(Paragraph(ptext, styles["Normal"]))
    flowables.append(Spacer(1, 48))
    ptext = '<font size=12>Ima Sucker</font>'
    flowables.append(Paragraph(ptext, styles["Normal"]))
    flowables.append(Spacer(1, 12))
    doc.build(flowables)

if __name__ == '__main__':
    form_letter()
```

Let's break this down a bit as it's a fairly lengthy example. You will note that this time we import a few new items from **platypus**: **Spacer** and **Image**. The Spacer class gives us a convenient way to add space between paragraphs or other flowables, while the Image class gives us a nice way to insert images into our document. We also import **ParagraphStyle**, which allows us to create a new style and add it to our styles list.

```
def form_letter():
    doc = SimpleDocTemplate("form_letter.pdf",
                            pagesize=letter,
                            rightMargin=72,
                            leftMargin=72,
                            topMargin=72,
                            bottomMargin=18)
    flowables = []
    logo = "python_logo.png"
    magName = "Pythonista"
    issueNum = 12
    subPrice = "99.00"
    limitedDate = "03/05/2010"
    freeGift = "tin foil hat"
    
    formatted_time = time.ctime()
    full_name = "Mike Driscoll"
    address_parts = ["411 State St.", "Waterloo, IA 50158"]
```

This chunk of code sets up our template object and our flowables list as before. We also set up a few variables that we will use later on in the code.

```
im = Image(logo, 2*inch, 2*inch)
flowables.append(im)

styles = getSampleStyleSheet()
# Modify the Normal Style
styles["Normal"].fontSize = 12
styles["Normal"].leading = 14

# Create a Justify style
styles.add(ParagraphStyle(name='Justify', alignment=TA_JUSTIFY))

flowables.append(Paragraph(formatted_time, styles["Normal"]))
flowables.append(Spacer(1, 12))

# Create return address
flowables.append(Paragraph(full_name, styles["Normal"]))
for part in address_parts:
    flowables.append(Paragraph(part.strip(), styles["Normal"]))

flowables.append(Spacer(1, 12))
ptext = 'Dear {}:'.format(full_name.split()[0].strip())
flowables.append(Paragraph(ptext, styles["Normal"]))
flowables.append(Spacer(1, 12))
```

Here we create our **Image** flowable. The first argument that we pass to it is the path to the image that we wish to insert. Then we tell the Image the what width and height to use. If you don't specify the width and height, then ReportLab will get the size from the image itself and use that. Next we get our style sheet and create a new style via **ParagraphStyle**. Note that it's name is **Justify**. After that we create some Paragraphs and Spacer objects and append them to our flowables list.

Note: If you dive into ReportLab's source code, you will find that the Normal style definition looks like this:

```
stylesheet.add(ParagraphStyle(name='Normal',
                              fontName=_baseFontName,
                              fontSize=10,
                              leading=12)
               )
```

The settings here mirror what is already the defaults in **ParagraphStyle**, so the Normal style is basically the default you get when you create an instance of **ParagraphStyle**. Thus when we create our Justify style, it is the same as Normal except for its alignment.

Now let's move on and look at the next part of the code:

```
ptext = '''
We would like to welcome you to our subscriber
base for {magName} Magazine! You will receive {issueNum} issues at
the excellent introductory price of ${subPrice}. Please respond by
{limitedDate} to start receiving your subscription and get the
following free gift: {freeGift}.
'''.format(magName=magName,
           issueNum=issueNum,
           subPrice=subPrice,
           limitedDate=limitedDate,
           freeGift=freeGift)
flowables.append(Paragraph(ptext, styles["Justify"]))
flowables.append(Spacer(1, 12))
```

This section of code is pretty similar to the previous one in that once again we create a series of Paragraphs and Spacers and add them to our flowables list. The part I want to highlight is that the last Paragraph that we create, we apply our **Justify** style to. Everything else used the **Normal** style.

```
ptext = '''Thank you very much and we look
forward to serving you.'''

flowables.append(Paragraph(ptext, styles["Justify"]))
flowables.append(Spacer(1, 12))
ptext = 'Sincerely,'
flowables.append(Paragraph(ptext, styles["Normal"]))
flowables.append(Spacer(1, 48))
ptext = 'Ima Sucker'
flowables.append(Paragraph(ptext, styles["Normal"]))
flowables.append(Spacer(1, 12))
doc.build(flowables)

    if __name__ == '__main__':
        form_letter()
```

This last chunk just finishes out the code by adding a few more flowables and then building the document. When you run the code, you should end up with something like this:

Fig. 3-2: A Form Letter in ReportLab

Let's move on and learn about a simple way to change static content across pages.

Chapter 3 - Intro to Page Layout

Changing Fixed Elements Across Pages

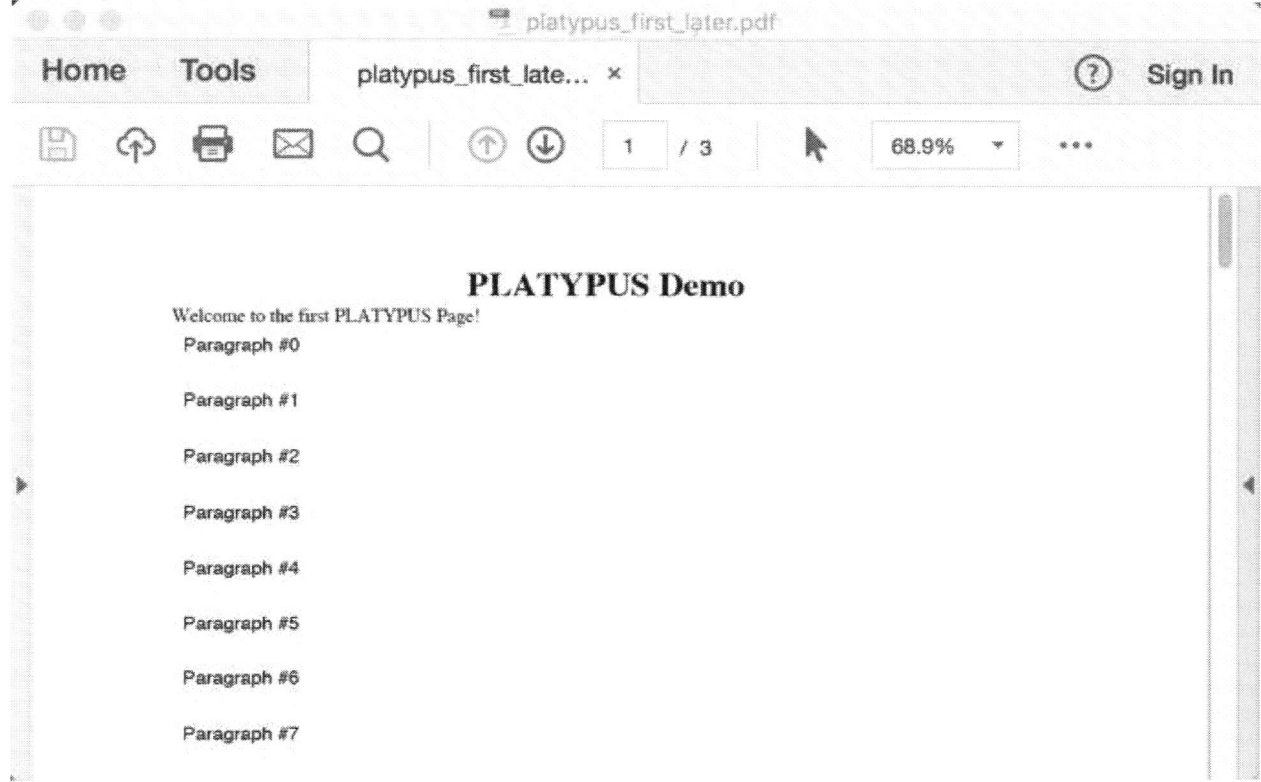

Fig. 3-3: Using a template to print alternate pages

One of the first examples in ReportLab's user guide on PLATYPUS talks about using some special parameters the template's **build** method that I think is often easily overlooked. When you call **build**, you can pass it 4 parameters: The flowables list, **onFirstPage**, **onLaterPages** and **canvasmaker**. The only required parameter is the flowables list. I won't be covering **canvasmaker** here, but we will look into that later on in the book.

The two that we want to focus on in this section are the **onFirstPage** and **onLaterPages** parameters. These parameters are supposed to be functions that the builder will call when creating your document. The **onFirstPage** function will annotate the first page of your PDF while the **onLaterPages** function will annotate all the pages after page one. You can use these functions to add page numbers, headers, footers, logos, etc.

For this example, we will create a script that adds a title and a string of text that will only appear on the first page. On all the subsequent pages, we will add a page number to the bottom of each page. Let's take a look:

```python
# alternating_text.py

from reportlab.lib.pagesizes import letter
from reportlab.lib.styles import getSampleStyleSheet
from reportlab.platypus import SimpleDocTemplate, Paragraph, Spacer
from reportlab.rl_config import defaultPageSize
from reportlab.lib.units import inch


def first_page(canvas, document):
    title = 'PLATYPUS Demo'
    PAGE_HEIGHT = defaultPageSize[1]
    PAGE_WIDTH = defaultPageSize[0]

    canvas.saveState()
    canvas.setFont('Times-Bold', 18)
    canvas.drawCentredString(PAGE_WIDTH/2.0, PAGE_HEIGHT-108, title)

    canvas.setFont('Times-Roman', 10)
    text = 'Welcome to the first PLATYPUS Page!'
    canvas.drawString(inch, 10*inch, text)
    canvas.restoreState()


def later_pages(canvas, document):
    canvas.saveState()
    canvas.setFont('Helvetica', 10)
    canvas.drawString(7*inch, 0.5*inch,
                      'Page {}'.format(document.page))
    canvas.restoreState()


def create_document():
    doc = SimpleDocTemplate("platypus_first_later.pdf",
                            pagesize=letter,
                            rightMargin=72,
                            leftMargin=72,
                            topMargin=72,
                            bottomMargin=18)
    styles = getSampleStyleSheet()
    flowables = []
    spacer = Spacer(1, 0.25*inch)
```

```
    # Create a lot of content to make a multipage PDF
    for i in range(50):
        text = 'Paragraph #{}'.format(i)
        para = Paragraph(text, styles["Normal"])
        flowables.append(para)
        flowables.append(spacer)

    doc.build(flowables, onFirstPage=first_page, onLaterPages=later_pages)

if __name__ == '__main__':
    create_document()
```

In this example, we create three functions. The first function will only get executed for the first page of the PDF. All it does is add a title to the page and centers it by calling **drawCentredString**. Note that this method call does require us to pass in and x and y coordinate. The x coordinate is used for positioning the string horizontally on the page while the y coordinate determines the text's position vertically on the page. We also draw some other text on the page in the first function to help differentiate it from function number two, **later_pages**.

The **later_pages** function gets called on all the pages after page one. So starting on page two, it will draw a page number on the page at the specified location. You will also note that in both of these functions, we call **saveState** and **restoreState**. These will save the current graphics state so that it will restore it back to what it was when the **restoreState** is reached. You cannot save the state from one page and restore it to another, for example.

Finally we have our main function, **create_document**, which is similar to what we've seen in our other code examples. The difference here is in the call to the template's **build** method, which actually calls our first two functions via the parameters **onFirstPage** and **onLaterPages**.

Note: If you'd like to see the margins for debugging purposes, you can do so by setting the document template's **showBoundary** argument to 1 or True.

This flexibility in generating your documents is extremely handy for complex PDFs.

Flowable Methods

We've been talking about flowables since the beginning of this chapter and it's high time we actually define what a flowable is in ReportLab. A Flowable is something that can be drawn and which has the following methods:

- draw
- wrap
- split (optionally)

ReportLab actually has a class named **Flowable** that is a Python abstract class and that you would normally use as a base class for your own custom flowable. Note that the Flowable class itself does *not* implelment **draw**. Instead the calling code should call **drawOn** which will call **draw** internally. The calling code should also make sure that the flowable object has a **pdfgen.Canvas** object on which it can draw and that said Canvas is in an state that can be drawn on. Here's a fairly simply example that uses **drawOn** and a method related to **wrap** called **wrapOn**:

```
# absolute_pos_flowable.py

from reportlab.lib.pagesizes import letter
from reportlab.pdfgen import canvas
from reportlab.platypus import SimpleDocTemplate, Paragraph
from reportlab.lib.styles import getSampleStyleSheet


def mixed():
    my_canvas = canvas.Canvas("mixed_flowables.pdf", pagesize=letter)
    styles = getSampleStyleSheet()
    width, height = letter

    text = "Hello, I'm a Paragraph"
    para = Paragraph(text, style=styles["Normal"])
    para.wrapOn(my_canvas, width, height)
    para.drawOn(my_canvas, 20, 760)

    my_canvas.save()

if __name__ == '__main__':
    mixed()
```

What this does it that it allows us to mix a flowable with the Canvas object itself. The drawOn method will allow you to render your flowable object on the canvas and translates the flowab'es position to the canvas coordinate. The **wrapOn** method is useful in that it will take the available width and available height and use that to calculate how to wrap the text in your paragraph based on that information.

The **split** function also also takes the available width and available height and use that information to know when to split the flowable should the flowable reach a frame boundary. A good flowable will split themselves and return a list of flowables. A stupid flowable will just return an empty list because they are unable to split.

If you need to find out what your vertical spacing is, then you can call **getSpaceAfter** or **getSpaceBefore** to find out. These methods will tell you how much space should follow or precede a flowable. Also all flowables have an **hAlign** property: ('LEFT', 'RIGHT', 'CENTER' or 'CENTRE'). Paragraphs ignore this property, but tables, images and other objects which are smaller than the width of the frame will use this property to determine their horizontal position.

Frame Basics

A **Frame** is a container that is itself contained within a **PageTemplate**. A Frame object has a location and size and will also maintain a concept of remaining drawable space. Here is the signature of the Frame class:

```
Frame(x1, y1, width, height, leftPadding=6, bottomPadding=6,
      rightPadding=6, topPadding=6, id=None, showBoundary=0)
```

There are quite a few arguments here. The first two are the x/y coordinates for the lower left-hand corner of the frame. Then you specify the width and height of the frame, respectively. Those first fours arguments are the only required ones. After that, you can add padding to each of the four sides of the frame. These padding arguments are positive values that are used to reduce the space available for drawing. The **id** argument is the identifier for your frame. It's actually usually a string that you can use to help you differentiate between the frames on your page, should you need to do so. Lastly, you have the **showBoundary** parameter, which if non-zero, will show the boundary of the frame. This can be useful for getting the padding right while you are creating your document.

Let's look at a quick demo that shows how you can use a Frame:

```python
# two_column_demo.py

from reportlab.lib.pagesizes import letter
from reportlab.lib.styles import getSampleStyleSheet
from reportlab.lib.units import inch
from reportlab.pdfgen.canvas import Canvas
from reportlab.platypus import Paragraph, Frame


def frame_demo():
    my_canvas = Canvas("frame_demo.pdf",
                       pagesize=letter)

    styles = getSampleStyleSheet()
    normal = styles['Normal']
    heading = styles['Heading1']
```

```python
    flowables = []
    flowables.append(Paragraph('Heading #1', heading))
    flowables.append(Paragraph('Paragraph #1', normal))

    right_flowables = []
    right_flowables.append(Paragraph('Heading #2', heading))
    right_flowables.append(Paragraph('ipsum lorem', normal))

    left_frame = Frame(inch, inch, width=3*inch, height=9*inch, showBoundary=1)
    right_frame = Frame(4*inch, inch, width=3*inch, height=9*inch)

    left_frame.addFromList(flowables, my_canvas)
    right_frame.addFromList(right_flowables, my_canvas)

    my_canvas.save()

if __name__ == '__main__':
    frame_demo()
```

Here we do our usual imports, but you will note that we also import the **Frame** class too. Then we create our little demo function and set up a Canvas object. Next we create a style object and extract a couple of different styles from said object. Then we create some flowables that we will place in each of our frame objects. You see, for this demo I wanted to create a page that had two columns of text, side-by-side, kind of like a newspaper. To do that, I need to create two lists of flowables and two Frames. Each frame is the same size, but you will note that one frame is pushed to the right by 4 inches. At the end of the code, we actually add the flowables to the frames by calling the **addFromList** method, which takes a list of flowables and the canvas that you want to draw on. According to the docstring for this function, if one of my flowables had been too large for the frame in which I put it, this method would raise an exception.

Anyway, then we save the document and the result should look something like this:

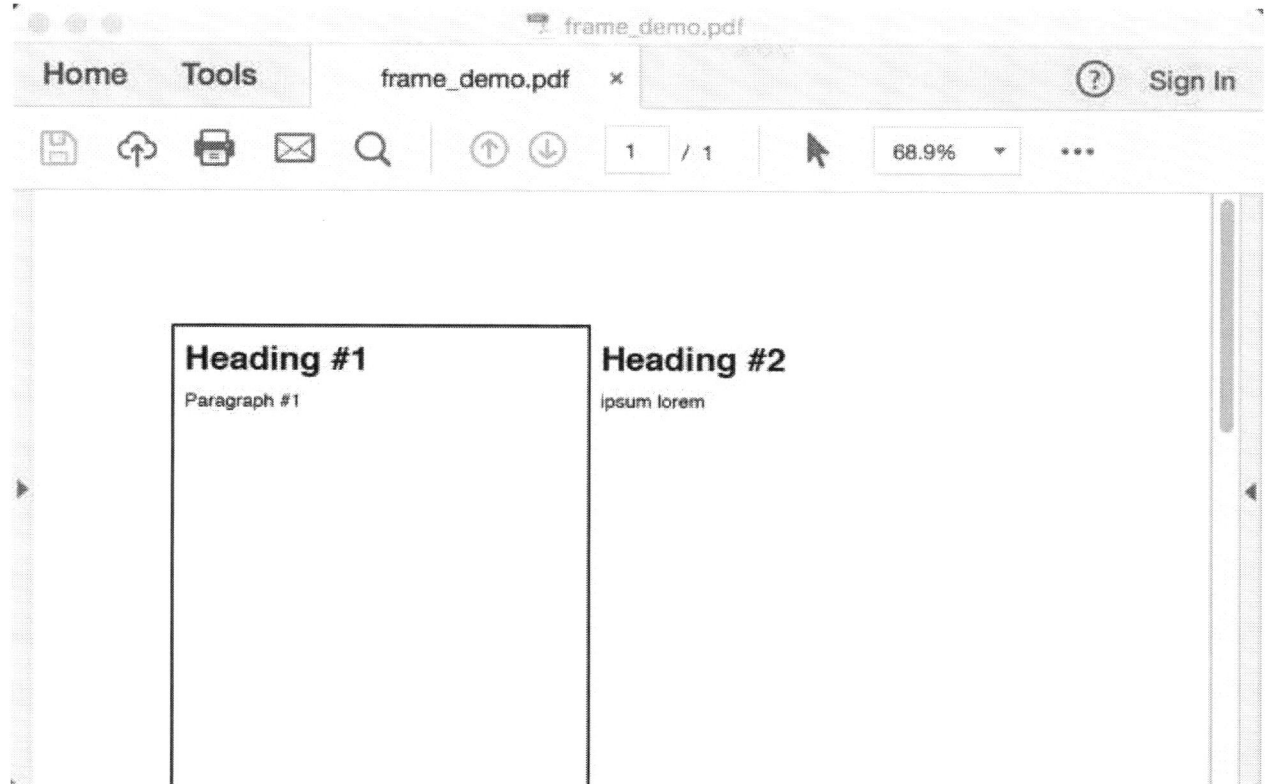

Fig. 3-4: **Using a template to print alternate pages**

Note that you don't usually need to use a Frame directly as other Flowables will do that work for you, unless you want to create a custom PageTemplate or other custom Flowable.

Now let's move on and learn a bit more about ReportLab's templates.

Templates

We have been using the **SimpleDocTemplate** up to this point for creating our multi-page PDFs. However the **SimpleDocTemplate** is actually a subclass of **BaseDocTemplate**, which implements the magic behind your document's formatting. When you create an instance of this class, it will contain one or more other **PageTemplates** that are a description of the layout of each of the pages of your document. When you call the **build** method of a template class, it will process the list of **Flowables** that we've been creating to create your PDF document.

Here is what a BaseDocTemplate code signature looks like:

```
BaseDocTemplate(self, filename,
    pagesize=defaultPageSize,
    pageTemplates=[],
    showBoundary=0,
    leftMargin=inch,
    rightMargin=inch,
    topMargin=inch,
    bottomMargin=inch,
    allowSplitting=1,
    title=None,
    author=None,
    _pageBreakQuick=1,
    encrypt=None)
```

The **filename** parameter is the only one required when creating an instance of the template. You can pass a string in for this parameter that can be the PDF's file name or an absolute path to said file. It can also be an object that implements a **write** method, such as **StringIO**, **BytesIO**, **file** or **socket** type.

The other methods are pretty obvious, but I will point out that there is a **showBoundary** parameter that you can use to turn on the boundaries of the frames in your document, should you have any.

The **allowSplitting** parameter tells ReportLab that it should try to split each Flowable across the Frames. There is also an **encrypt** parameter that defaults to **None**, that is unencrypted. If you pass in a string object, that will be the user's password to the document. Alternatively, you can pass an instance of **reportlab.lib.pdfencrypt.StandardEncryption** to encrypt your PDF, which will give you more control over the encryption settings.

There are a series of other methods that you can use with your templates. I won't be covering these here as I have never needed any of them. However if you need to do some serious custom layouts, then you will want to take a look at the documentation. The templates have event handlers that you can use as well to help you with complex or unusual layouts.

Flowable Orientation (Portrait vs. Landscape)

Back in chapter 1, we talked about how to set the orientation of your pages when using the **Canvas**. Flowables work a bit differently in that you need to modify the template you are working on slightly. In this case, you could do something as simple as the following to put the entire document in landscape rather than portrait (the default):

Chapter 3 - Intro to Page Layout

```python
from reportlab.lib.pagesizes import letter, landscape
from reportlab.platypus import SimpleDocTemplate

def landscape_orientation():
    doc = SimpleDocTemplate("orientations.pdf",
                            pagesize=landscape(letter),
                            rightMargin=72,
                            leftMargin=72,
                            topMargin=72,
                            bottomMargin=18)
```

You will notice that all we had to do here was set the **pagesize** parameter to equal **landscape(letter)**. The **landscape** function just takes a page size and sets it to landscape. Let's try to do something that's a bit more interesting though. Let's write some code that will alternate between portrait and landscape in the same document:

```python
# flowable_orientation.py

from reportlab.lib.pagesizes import letter, landscape
from reportlab.lib.styles import getSampleStyleSheet
from reportlab.lib.units import inch
from reportlab.platypus import SimpleDocTemplate, Paragraph, PageBreak
from reportlab.platypus import Frame, PageTemplate, NextPageTemplate, Spacer


def alternate_orientations():
    doc = SimpleDocTemplate("orientations.pdf",
                            pagesize=letter,
                            rightMargin=72,
                            leftMargin=72,
                            topMargin=72,
                            bottomMargin=18)
    styles = getSampleStyleSheet()
    normal = styles["Normal"]

    margin = 0.5 * inch
    frame = Frame(margin, margin, doc.width, doc.height,
                  id='frame')
    portrait_template = PageTemplate(id='portrait',
                                     frames=[frame],
                                     pagesize=letter)
    landscape_template = PageTemplate(id='landscape',
```

```python
                                    frames=[frame],
                                    pagesize=landscape(letter))
    doc.addPageTemplates([portrait_template, landscape_template])

    story = []
    story.append(Paragraph('This is a page in portrait orientation', normal))

    # Change to landscape orientation
    story.append(NextPageTemplate('landscape'))
    story.append(PageBreak())
    story.append(Spacer(inch, 2*inch))
    story.append(Paragraph('This is a page in landscape orientation', normal))

    # Change back to portrait
    story.append(NextPageTemplate('portrait'))
    story.append(PageBreak())
    story.append(Paragraph("Now we're back in portrait mode again", normal))

    doc.build(story)

if __name__ == '__main__':
    alternate_orientations()
```

Here we import a few new Flowables: **PageBreak**, **NextPageTemplate**, and **Spacer**. The **PageBreak** class inserts a page break in your document, the **NextPageTemplate** tells ReportLab what template to use starting on the next page while the **Spacer** class will add space between the flowables you are drawing. For this example, we create a frame that almost matches the size of the page itself. Then we create two **PageTemplates**, one that is in the portrait orientation and the other in landscape. Then we call our main template's **addPageTemplates()** method to add those other two templates to itself. This allows us to reference the templates we just created by name.

Now we just need to create a list of flowables! Here we just add a simple Paragraph and then call NextPageTemplate() to change to landscape on the second page. You will note that we didn't have to tell the first page what its orientation was as it defaults to portrait. After setting the landscape orientation, we insert a page break and add a spacer. The reason for the spacer is that now the page is shorter in height, so when we add the next Paragraph instance, we need a spacer to position it so that the text is on the page instead of off in the ether. Finally we call NextPageTemplate() again and set the orientation back to portrait, add a page break and add one more paragraph. When you run this code, you should get a 3-page document with the first and last pages in portrait and the middle page in landscape.

Wrapping Up

At this point, you should have a good understanding of how PLATYPUS works to layout your documents. In the next chapter, we will learn much more about one of the flowables that you will use a lot if you happen to use ReportLab for much of anything. The flowable that I am referring to is the **Paragraph**, which is one of the most important flowables in ReportLab.

Chapter 4 - Paragraphs

ReportLab has a **Paragraph** Flowable that you can import from **reportlab.platypus.Paragraph**. The Paragraph is one of the most flexible and useful of all the Flowables that ReportLab includes. You will most likely use it more than any other part of their PLATYPUS framework. The Paragraph can format text and allows the developer the ability to change font style and color inline using XML tags. You can also use the Paragraph to justify your text as well as set it to right, left or centered. Finally you can use your Paragraph to do subscripts or insert Greek characters.

Here is how you can create a Paragraph instance:

```
p = Paragraph(text, style, bulletText=None)
```

The **text** argument is just the string that you want to draw on your PDF. Any excess whitespace will be removed from the ends of the text. While this can be annoying when you want the whitespace for formatting, it does make it easy to use Python's triple-quoted text in your Paragraphs. Note that when you pass in your string, you can add some XML markup to format parts of the string. We will look at this later on the chapter though.

The **bulletText** parameter is used to provide text for the default bullet for a paragraph. We will talk more about bullets soon, but first let's look at paragraph styles as you will be using those much more frequently.

Paragraph Styles

The **style** argument to the Paragraph class has to be an instance of the **ParagraphStyle** class. You can import that like so:

```
from reportlab.lib.styles import ParagraphStyle
```

When you create a ParagraphStyle, you will note that it is basically just a Python dictionary of paragraph attributes that ReportLab calls a **StyleSheet**. In fact, you can get a sample style sheet from ReportLab by doing the following:

```
from reportlab.lib.styles import getSampleStyleSheet
```

What this allows you to do is to create a style sheet instance that you can then extract Paragraph-Styles from:

Chapter 4 - Paragraphs

```
styles = getSampleStyleSheet()
normal_style = styles['Normal']
```

This just grabs the **Normal** style from ReportLab's sample style sheet. If you want to get a listing of all their styles, you can do the following:

```
>>> from reportlab.lib.styles import getSampleStyleSheet
>>> styles = getSampleStyleSheet()
>>> styles.byName
{'BodyText': <ParagraphStyle 'BodyText'>,
 'Bullet': <ParagraphStyle 'Bullet'>,
 'Code': <ParagraphStyle 'Code'>,
 'Definition': <ParagraphStyle 'Definition'>,
 'Heading1': <ParagraphStyle 'Heading1'>,
 'Heading2': <ParagraphStyle 'Heading2'>,
 'Heading3': <ParagraphStyle 'Heading3'>,
 'Heading4': <ParagraphStyle 'Heading4'>,
 'Heading5': <ParagraphStyle 'Heading5'>,
 'Heading6': <ParagraphStyle 'Heading6'>,
 'Italic': <ParagraphStyle 'Italic'>,
 'Normal': <ParagraphStyle 'Normal'>,
 'OrderedList': <ListStyle 'OrderedList'>,
 'Title': <ParagraphStyle 'Title'>,
 'UnorderedList': <ListStyle 'UnorderedList'>}
```

You can call the **list** method on your style object to get a full listing of each of these styles. Here is just the Normal style's settings:

```
Normal None
    name = Normal
    parent = None
    alignment = 0
    allowOrphans = 0
    allowWidows = 1
    backColor = None
    borderColor = None
    borderPadding = 0
    borderRadius = None
    borderWidth = 0
    bulletAnchor = start
    bulletFontName = Helvetica
    bulletFontSize = 10
```

```
bulletIndent = 0
endDots = None
firstLineIndent = 0
fontName = Helvetica
fontSize = 10
justifyBreaks = 0
justifyLastLine = 0
leading = 12
leftIndent = 0
rightIndent = 0
spaceAfter = 0
spaceBefore = 0
spaceShrinkage = 0.05
splitLongWords = 1
textColor = Color(0,0,0,1)
textTransform = None
underlineProportion = 0.0
wordWrap = None
```

You can get the any of these settings from any of the styles whenever you like by doing the following:

```
>>> from reportlab.lib.styles import getSampleStyleSheet
>>> styles = getSampleStyleSheet()
>>> styles['Normal']['alignment']
>>> styles['Normal'].alignment
0
```

Changing a style's properties on the fly is also easy. All you need to do is this:

```
>>> styles['Normal'].leading
12
>>> styles['Normal'].leading = 14
>>> styles['Normal'].leading
14
```

Note that these changes will only be in effect from the point at which you change the style and also only if you keep a reference to that style. So I usually recommend just copying from one of the included styles and do your modifications on it if all you need is a simple change.

On the other hand if you'd like to create your own **ParagraphStyle**, then you should take a look at the source code

```
class ParagraphStyle(PropertySet):
    defaults = {
        'fontName':'Times-Roman',
        'fontSize':10,
        'leading':12,
        'leftIndent':0,
        'rightIndent':0,
        'firstLineIndent':0,
        'alignment':TA_LEFT,
        'spaceBefore':0,
        'spaceAfter':0,
        'bulletFontName':'Times-Roman',
        'bulletFontSize':10,
        'bulletIndent':0,
        'textColor': black,
        'backColor':None,
        'wordWrap':None,
        'borderWidth': 0,
        'borderPadding': 0,
        'borderColor': None,
        'borderRadius': None,
        'allowWidows': 1,
        'allowOrphans': 0,
        'textTransform':None,
        'endDots':None,
        'splitLongWords':1,
        'underlineProportion': _baseUnderlineProportion,
        'bulletAnchor': 'start',
        }
```

Now that we have that, we can easily see what the defaults are on a fresh paragraph style. Let's try creating our own paragraph style in Python's interpreter:

```
>>> from reportlab.lib.styles import ParagraphStyle
>>> p = ParagraphStyle('Test')
>>> p.name
'Test'
>>> p.leading
12
>>> p.leading = 14
```

Here we create a test style with the name of "Test". Then we check its default leading property, which turns out to be 12. So for fun, we set it to 14. But how do you subclass ParagraphStyle? Let's find out:

```python
# custom_style.py

from reportlab.lib.styles import ParagraphStyle

class TestStyle(ParagraphStyle):

    def __init__(self, name):
        self.name = name

        self.__dict__.update(self.defaults)
        self.leading = 14

if __name__ == '__main__':
    p = TestStyle('test')
    print(p.name)
    print(p.leading)
    print(p.fontSize)
```

This class is a bit weird, but it's based on ParagraphStyle's super class, which is called **PropertySet**. If you take a deep dive into the source, you will find that it uses Python's magic to update the class's property list by creating a dictionary of defaults and then calling **self.__dict__.update(self.defaults)**. So we replicate that here in our sub-class. But to set the **leading** property to something other than the default, we need to set it after we update the dictionary.

Paragraph Markup Tags

The Paragraph in ReportLab supports XML-like markup tags. You can use these tags to modify the paragraph style or to specify intra-paragraph formatting.

The Outermost Markup Tags

Here is a table that lists all the outermost markup tags that ReportLab supports:

Attribute	Synonyms
alignment	alignment, align
allowOrphans	alloworphans, allowOrphans
allowWidows	allowWidows, allowwidows
autoLeading	autoleading, autoLeading
backColor	bgcolor, backColor, backcolor, bg
borderColor	bordercolor, borderColor
borderRadius	borderRadius, borderradius
borderWidth	borderWidth, borderwidth
borderpadding	borderpadding
bulletAnchor	bulletanchor, banchor, bulletAnchor
bulletColor	bulletColor, bcolor, bulletcolor
bulletFontName	bulletFontName, bulletfontname, bfont
bulletFontSize	bulletfontsize, bulletFontSize, bfontsize
bulletIndent	bindent, bulletindent, bulletIndent
bulletOffsetY	boffsety, bulletoffsety, bulletOffsetY
endDots	endDots, enddots
firstLineIndent	findent, firstLineIndent, firstlineindent
fontName	font, fontname, fontName, face
fontSize	size, fontsize, fontSize
justifyBreaks	justifybreaks, justifyBreaks
justifyLastLine	justifyLastLine, justifylastline
leading	leading
leftIndent	leftIndent, lindent, leftindent
rightIndent	rightindent, rightIndent, rindent
spaceAfter	spacea, spaceafter, spaceAfter
spaceBefore	spaceb, spacebefore, spaceBefore
spaceShrinkage	spaceShrinkage, spaceshrinkage
splitLongWords	splitlongwords, splitLongWords
textColor	color, textColor, textcolor, fg
textTransform	texttransform, textTransform
underlineProportion	underlineProportion, underlineproportion
wordWrap	wordWrap, wordwrap

The **Attribute** column is a list of what I like to think of as the official tag name. The **Synonyms** column will also work and you will also notice that where possible, the ReportLab developers use equivalent names to the HTML standard wherever possible.

Note that you must use these tags in conjunction with the **<para>** tag. For example:

Chapter 4 - Paragraphs

```python
# para_tags.py

from reportlab.lib.pagesizes import letter
from reportlab.platypus import SimpleDocTemplate, Paragraph
from reportlab.lib.styles import getSampleStyleSheet

def paragraph_para_markup():
    doc = SimpleDocTemplate("para_tags.pdf",
                            pagesize=letter
                            )
    styles = getSampleStyleSheet()

    flowables = []

    text = "<para align=center>Hello, I'm a Paragraph</para>"
    para = Paragraph(text, style=styles["Normal"])
    flowables.append(para)

    doc.build(flowables)

if __name__ == '__main__':
    paragraph_para_markup()
```

Here we create a pretty simple demo using some code from earlier in the book. The main line you should pay attention to is line 15 where we actually use the **<para>** tag to center our text. If you run this code, you should end up with a PDF that has a single line of text centered at the top of the page.

A better method for centering text would be to create a custom **ParagraphStyle**. Here's an example:

```python
# para_tags2.py

from reportlab.lib.enums import TA_CENTER
from reportlab.lib.pagesizes import letter
from reportlab.platypus import SimpleDocTemplate, Paragraph
from reportlab.lib.styles import getSampleStyleSheet, ParagraphStyle

def paragraph_para_markup():
    doc = SimpleDocTemplate("para_tags2.pdf",
                            pagesize=letter
                            )
    styles = getSampleStyleSheet()
    styles.add(ParagraphStyle(name='Centered', alignment=TA_CENTER))
    print(styles)
```

```
    flowables = []
    
    text = "<para align=center>Hello, I'm a Paragraph</para>"
    para = Paragraph(text, style=styles["Centered"])
    flowables.append(para)
    
    doc.build(flowables)

if __name__ == '__main__':
    paragraph_para_markup()
```

Here we just add a ParagraphStyle object to our sample StyleSheet and set its alignment to **TA_-CENTER**.

Using Intra-Paragraph Markup

Personally I rarely use the <para> tags in my documents. Instead I almost always use the intra-paragraph tags:

- <b> or <strong> - bold
- <i> - italicize
- <u> - underline
- <a href> - Adding a link
- <a name> - Adding an anchor
- <strike> - Strike-through
-
 - line break

Let's take a look at how you might use these tags in your code:

```
# intra_paragraph_markup.py

from reportlab.lib.pagesizes import letter
from reportlab.platypus import SimpleDocTemplate, Paragraph
from reportlab.lib.styles import getSampleStyleSheet

def intra_tags():
    doc = SimpleDocTemplate("intra_paragraph_markup.pdf",
                            pagesize=letter
                            )
    styles = getSampleStyleSheet()
```

```
    flowables = []

    text = """
    This <b>text</b> is important,
    not <strong>strong</strong>.<br/><br/>

    A book title should be in <i>italics</i><br/><br/>

    You can also <u>underline</u> your text.<br/><br/>

    Bad text should be <strike>struck-through</strike>!<br/><br/>

    You can link to <a href="https://www.google.com" color="blue">Google</a>
    like this.
    """

    para = Paragraph(text, style=styles["Normal"])
    flowables.append(para)

    doc.build(flowables)

if __name__ == '__main__':
    intra_tags()
```

Here we create a pretty simple demo wherein we create a multi-line string using Python's triple-quotes. Within that string, we bold some text and use the **
** tag to add some line breaks between lines. If you do not add the **
** tag, then all the text will run together as the Paragraph class removes excess white space. You will also note that this example demonstrates almost all of the intra-paragraph tags mentioned at the beginning of this section except for adding an anchor. If you run this code, you should get something that looks like this:

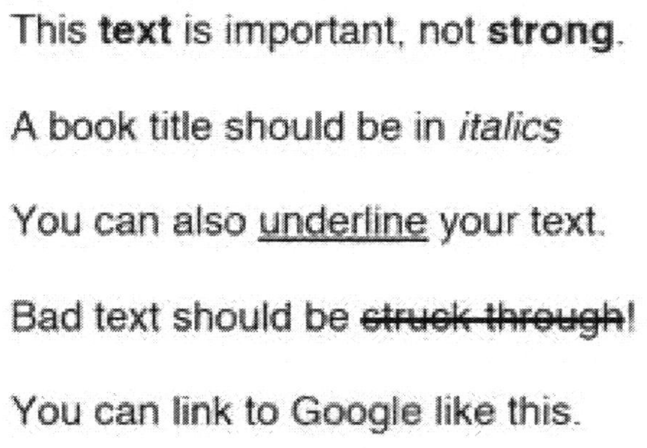

> This **text** is important, not **strong**.
>
> A book title should be in *italics*
>
> You can also underline your text.
>
> Bad text should be ~~struck through~~!
>
> You can link to Google like this.

Fig. 4-1: Intra-Paragraph markup results

If you need to control spacing between Paragraph flowables, you can edit the following Paragraph attributes: **spaceBefore** and **spaceAfter**. These are defaulted to zero in the **Normal** version of the StyleSheet. Here is an example:

```python
# paragraph_spacing.py

from reportlab.lib.pagesizes import letter
from reportlab.platypus import SimpleDocTemplate, Paragraph
from reportlab.lib.styles import getSampleStyleSheet

def paragraph_spacing():
    doc = SimpleDocTemplate("paragraph_spacing.pdf",
                            pagesize=letter
                            )
    styles = getSampleStyleSheet()
    styles["Normal"].spaceBefore = 10
    styles["Normal"].spaceAfter = 10

    flowables = []

    text = """
    This <b>text</b> is important,
    not <strong>strong</strong>.
    """
    para = Paragraph(text, style=styles["Normal"])
    flowables.append(para)
```

```python
    text = 'A book title should be in <i>italics</i>'
    para = Paragraph(text, style=styles["Normal"])
    flowables.append(para)


    text = 'You can also <u>underline</u> your text.'
    para = Paragraph(text, style=styles["Normal"])
    flowables.append(para)


    text = 'Bad text should be <strike>struck-through</strike>!'
    para = Paragraph(text, style=styles["Normal"])
    flowables.append(para)


    text = """
    You can link to <a href="https://www.google.com" color="blue">Google</a>
    like this.
    """
    para = Paragraph(text, style=styles["Normal"])
    flowables.append(para)

    doc.build(flowables)

if __name__ == '__main__':
    paragraph_spacing()
```

Of course, if you are dealing with just a single block of text, then you will be forced to use **
** tags for spacing since that text will not be inside separate Paragraph Flowables.

Now we're ready to learn about another intra-paragraph tag that controls fonts.

Working with Fonts

ReportLab also supports a **<font>** tag that you can use for formatting your text. It supports changing the font's name, size and color substring within your paragraph. You can use the following attributes in your font tag:

- face (or name)
- size

Chapter 4 - Paragraphs

- color (or fg)

The **name** (or **face**) attribute represents the font family name. You do not need to specify "bold" or "italic" suffixes when setting the font's name. Let's take a look:

```python
# paragraph_fonts.py

from reportlab.lib.pagesizes import letter
from reportlab.platypus import SimpleDocTemplate, Paragraph
from reportlab.lib.styles import getSampleStyleSheet

def paragraph_fonts():
    doc = SimpleDocTemplate("paragraph_fonts.pdf",
                            pagesize=letter
                            )
    styles = getSampleStyleSheet()

    flowables = []

    ptext = '<font name=helvetica size=12>Welcome to Reportlab! ' \
            '(helvetica)</font>'
    para = Paragraph(ptext, style=styles["Normal"])
    flowables.append(para)

    ptext = "<font face=courier size=14>Welcome to Reportlab! " \
            "(courier)</font>"
    para = Paragraph(ptext, style=styles["Normal"])
    flowables.append(para)

    ptext = "<font name=times-roman size=16>Welcome to Reportlab! " \
            "(times-roman)</font>"
    para = Paragraph(ptext, style=styles["Normal"])
    flowables.append(para)

    doc.build(flowables)

if __name__ == '__main__':
    paragraph_fonts()
```

Here we create the same string 3 times in 3 different fonts and 3 different sizes. When you run this code, you will get the following output in your PDF:

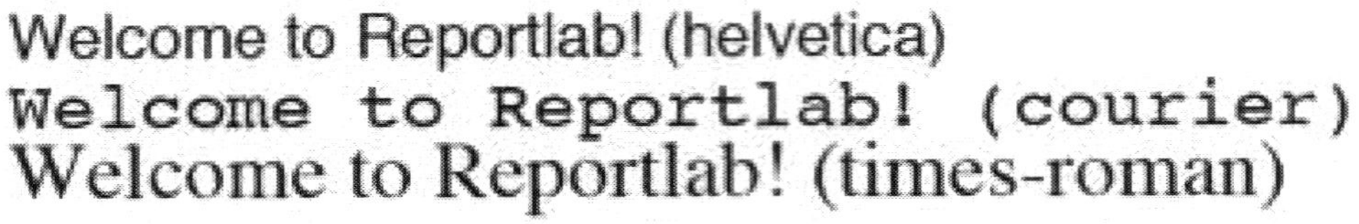

> # Welcome to Reportlab! (helvetica)
> # Welcome to Reportlab! (courier)
> # Welcome to Reportlab! (times-roman)

Fig. 4-2: Working with different fonts

You will note that in the code example above, we alternated specifying the font name by using the **name** and **face** attributes. These attributes can be used interchangeably in ReportLab.

I am no typography expert, however I want to point out that when you change font family and font size, you will likely need to change its leading value as well. **Leading** is a term used to describe the distance between the baselines of successive lines of text. Most word processors refer to this term as "line spacing" or "interline spacing". If this example used paragraphs of text instead of single lines, then you would see the difference in the text's leading and you would need to adjust it.

When you want to change the color of your text, you can use the **color** or **fg** attribute. The color attribute takes HTML color names or a hex string. For the latter, see *reportlab.lib.colors* for the formats that ReportLab supports. Here's a simple demo based on the previous example:

```
# paragraph_font_colors.py

from reportlab.lib.pagesizes import letter
from reportlab.platypus import SimpleDocTemplate, Paragraph
from reportlab.lib.styles import getSampleStyleSheet
import reportlab.lib.colors

def paragraph_font_colors():
    doc = SimpleDocTemplate("paragraph_font_colors.pdf",
                            pagesize=letter
                            )
    styles = getSampleStyleSheet()

    flowables = []

    ptext = """<font name=helvetica size=12 color=red>
    Welcome to Reportlab! (helvetica)</font>"""
    para = Paragraph(ptext, style=styles["Normal"])
    flowables.append(para)

    ptext = """<font name=courier fg=blue size=14>
    Welcome to Reportlab! (courier)</font>"""
```

```
    para = Paragraph(ptext, style=styles["Normal"])
    flowables.append(para)

    ptext = """<font name=times-roman size=16 color=#777215>
    Welcome to Reportlab! (times-roman)</font>"""
    para = Paragraph(ptext, style=styles["Normal"])
    flowables.append(para)

    doc.build(flowables)

if __name__ == '__main__':
    paragraph_font_colors()
```

Here we modify the strings from the last demo to contain the **color** or **fg** attribute, which allows us to specify the color of the text. You will note that we use the HTML names **red** and **blue** for the first two strings and a hex string (**#777215**) for the last string. When I ran this code, I got the following colors:

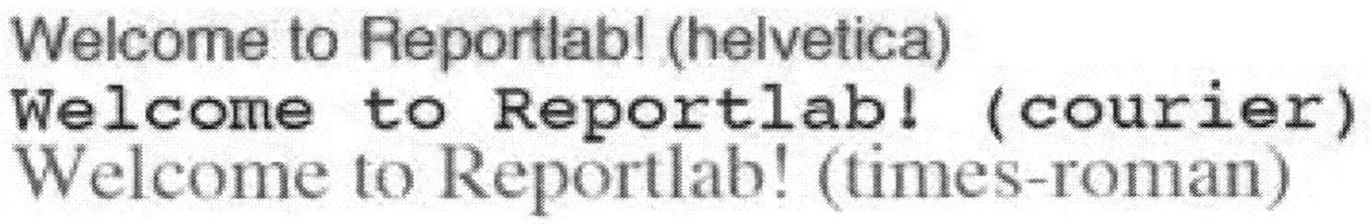

Fig. 4-3: Changing font colors in Paragraphs

That was pretty slick!

Here's something fun that you can try on your own. See if you can modify the code above to add color to the word "ReportLab" and nothing else.

Superscripts & Subscripts

The Paragraph class also supports special tags for controlling superscripts and subscripts as well as Greek letters. They are as follows:

- <super> - superscript
- <sub> - subscript
- <greek> - Greek letter

The **<super>** and **<sub>** tags also have a **rise** attribute that can be supplied. For example, you could do this:

```
text = "Use <super rise=12>Foobar</super> in your example"
```

While using rise gives you more control over the exact placement of your superscript or subscript, I personally think the default offset is fine. Here is a quick demo that shows how to use all three tags:

```python
# paragraph_scripting.py

from reportlab.lib.pagesizes import letter
from reportlab.platypus import SimpleDocTemplate, Paragraph, Spacer
from reportlab.lib.styles import getSampleStyleSheet
import reportlab.lib.colors

def paragraph_scripting():
    doc = SimpleDocTemplate("paragraph_scripting.pdf",
                            pagesize=letter
                            )
    styles = getSampleStyleSheet()

    flowables = []

    ptext = "Einstein says: E = mc<super>2</super>"
    para = Paragraph(ptext, style=styles["Normal"])
    flowables.append(para)

    flowables.append(Spacer(1, 15))

    ptext = "Reportlab <super rise=12>superscript</super> and <sub>subscript</su\
b>"
    para = Paragraph(ptext, style=styles["Normal"])
    flowables.append(para)

    flowables.append(Spacer(1, 15))

    ptext = "Reportlab Greek letter e: <greek>e</greek>"
    para = Paragraph(ptext, style=styles["Normal"])
    flowables.append(para)


    doc.build(flowables)

if __name__ == '__main__':
    paragraph_scripting()
```

Here we create a few silly strings with superscripts and subscripts applied. We also create a string that includes one Greek character. When you run this code, you should end up with a PDF that contains the following:

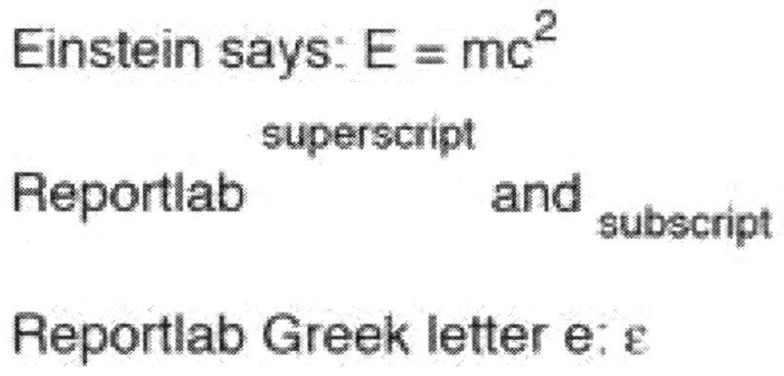

Einstein says: E = mc^2

Reportlab ^{superscript} and $_{subscript}$

Reportlab Greek letter e: ε

Fig. 4-4: Subscripts and superscripts

Personally, I think using the markup tags for the Paragraph to be a bit nicer to use than the canvas methods we looked at back in chapter 1.

Inserting Inline Images

Inline images weren't very popular until fairly recently. Probably the most popular use-case would be the insertion of emoji characters. ReportLab has support for inline images via the **<img>** tag. You can apply the following attributes to your inline image:

- src (required)
- width
- height
- valign

The **src** attribute takes a relative or absolute path to the image file that you want to insert. You can also set the **width** or **height** (or both) of the image. Note that if you just set the width or the height, ReportLab will not automatically scale your image. Finally you can set the alignment of the image to any of the following values:

- baseline
- sub
- super
- top
- text-top
- middle
- bottom
- text-bottom

You can also set the alignment to a numeric percentage or absolute value. For all of these attributes, you will need to surround the value in double quotes. Here is a very simple example:

```python
# paragraph_inline_images.py

from reportlab.lib.pagesizes import letter
from reportlab.platypus import SimpleDocTemplate, Paragraph
from reportlab.lib.styles import getSampleStyleSheet


def paragraph_inline_images():
    doc = SimpleDocTemplate("paragraph_inline_images.pdf",
                            pagesize=letter
                            )
    styles = getSampleStyleSheet()

    flowables = []

    ptext = '''Here is a picture:
    <img src="snakehead.jpg" width="50" height="50"/> in the
    middle of our text'''
    p = Paragraph(ptext, styles['Normal'])
    flowables.append(p)

    doc.build(flowables)

if __name__ == '__main__':
    paragraph_inline_images()
```

In this code, we create a string that sets its src to a file name. Then we set its width and height to a value of "50". We skip setting an explicit valign value. Then we build our flowable and save the document. The result looks like this:

Fig. 4-5: **Inline images**

If you have some free time, I recommend trying your hand at adding some valign values to the code above and re-running the code with different values to see how they work.

Numbering Paragraphs / Sections

ReportLab supports automatic numbering. You can automatically add section number, paragraph numbers or some other type of number to your document. All of this is done using the sequence tag: **<seq>**. ReportLab also supports using a **sequence template**. The following demo will show you how both of these concepts work:

```
# paragraph_numbering.py

from reportlab.lib.pagesizes import letter
from reportlab.platypus import SimpleDocTemplate, Paragraph
from reportlab.lib.styles import getSampleStyleSheet
from reportlab.lib.sequencer import getSequencer


def paragraph_numbering():
    doc = SimpleDocTemplate("paragraph_numbering.pdf",
                            pagesize=letter
                            )
    styles = getSampleStyleSheet()

    flowables = []

    for item in range(1, 4):
        ptext = '<seq id="test"> thing(s)'
        para = Paragraph(ptext, style=styles["Normal"])
        flowables.append(para)

    # templates
    seq = getSequencer()
    seq.setFormat('Section', '0')
    seq.setFormat('FigureNo', 'A')

    for item in range(4, 8):
        text = 'Fig. <seq template="%(Section)s-%(FigureNo+)s"/>'
        para = Paragraph(text, style=styles["Normal"])
        flowables.append(para)

    doc.build(flowables)

if __name__ == '__main__':
    paragraph_numbering()
```

Here we create a pretty simple string in the first **for** loop. In each iteration of the loop, ReportLab will replace the **<seq>** tag with a number that is incremented. For a sequence template, we need to create something new: a **sequencer** object! You can get this object by importing **getSequencer** from **reportlab.lib.sequencer**. Now that we have a sequencer object, we set the format for a couple of sections in your report. In this case, we set the Section's format to numeric starting with the number zero. Then we set a formatter for a string called "FigureNo" and tell it to start with "A". Next we use Python's old style string substitution syntax to insert the two different formatters into our string. You will note that for the FigureNo string, we added a "+" symbol. What this means is that it will increment each time. If you don't supply the plus symbol, then it won't increment that formatter's value.

If you run this code, you should end up with the following:

```
1 thing(s)
2 thing(s)
3 thing(s)
Fig. 0-A
Fig. 0-B
Fig. 0-C
Fig. 0-D
```

Fig. 4-6: Adding numbers to paragraphs

As you can see, the **Section** didn't increment at all while the **FigureNo** did.

Bullets

There are times when you will want to add bullet lists to your report. The ReportLab package supports this subject in several different ways. You can use the **Paragraph** class's **bulletText** argument to specify a custom bullet. Another way to create bullets is to use the **<bullet>** tag. Either way, the ReportLab guide says that you should try using the Unicode bullet first, which you can write in any of the following ways:

- `&bull;`
- `&\#x2022;`
- `\xe2\x80\xa2`

Let's create a demo that shows a couple of these variations:

Chapter 4 - Paragraphs

```python
# paragraph_bullets.py

from reportlab.lib.pagesizes import letter
from reportlab.platypus import SimpleDocTemplate, Paragraph
from reportlab.lib.styles import getSampleStyleSheet


def paragraph_bullets():
    doc = SimpleDocTemplate("paragraph_bullets.pdf",
                            pagesize=letter
                            )
    styles = getSampleStyleSheet()

    flowables = []

    ptext = "I'm a custom bulletted paragraph"
    para = Paragraph(ptext, style=styles["Normal"], bulletText='-')
    flowables.append(para)

    ptext = "This is a normal bullet"
    para = Paragraph(ptext, style=styles["Normal"], bulletText='\xe2\x80\xa2')
    flowables.append(para)

    ptext = "<bullet>&bull;</bullet>This text uses the bullet tag"
    para = Paragraph(ptext, style=styles["Normal"])
    flowables.append(para)

    doc.build(flowables)

if __name__ == '__main__':
    paragraph_bullets()
```

In our first example, we set the bullet to a simple dash (-) character. For the second example, we use the Unicode bullet character byte to create the bullet. Finally, in the last example we use the <bullet> tag. You will note that when you use the bullet tag, you need to tell it what to use for its bullet character as well. Also note that when you use the <bullet> tag it overrides the use of the **bulletText** parameter. You can modify some of the bullet's characteristics via the ParagraphStyle as well, such as its font name, size and indent level.

Here is the result of running the code:

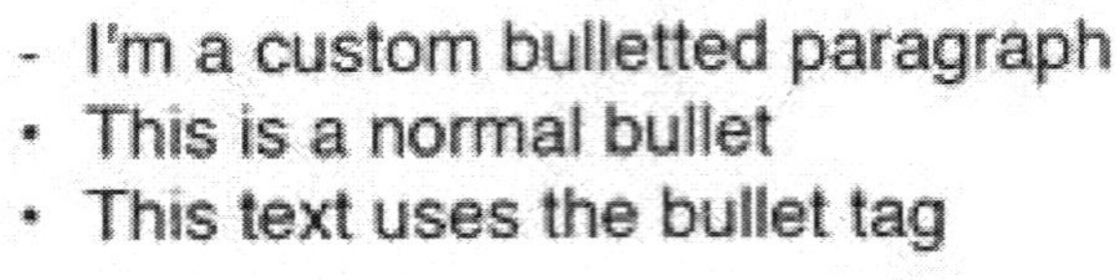

- I'm a custom bulletted paragraph
- This is a normal bullet
- This text uses the bullet tag

Fig. 4-7: **Adding bullets to paragraphs**

There is one other way to create bullets which is by using the **ListFlowable()**. We will be covering that flowable in a later chapter though.

Note that depending on the operating system you run this example on and the version of Python you use, you may have to experiment a bit to find a bullet type that will work for you. For example, `\xe2\x80\xa2` worked on Linux but I had to use the Unicode bullet to make it work on Mac OS.

Wrapping Up

I hope at this point you have a good idea of just how powerful and useful the **Paragraph** class is. You will be using it a lot in your reports and you'll even find it useful for formatting other ReportLab flowables, such as the **Table**'s cells. In this chapter we learned how to create and style our paragraphs. Then we learned about the many different kinds of markup tags we can use in the Paragraph. In ReportLab's Plus version (i.e. their commercial software), they have a **Report Markup Language** or RML that goes much farther than the tags that we can use in the open source version. However I have found the open source version of the software to be more than capable for formatting anything that I need to do.

Chapter 5 - Tables

ReportLab has a lovely class called **Table** that you can use for creating simple and complex tables out of your data. There is actually a **LongTable** class as well. The main difference between the two is that **LongTable** is a class that uses a "greedy algorithm" for calculating column widths that makes the creation of long tables faster. Anyway, a Table object's cells can hold anything that Python can convert to a string or you can insert ReportLab's **Flowables** or even lists of said Flowables.

Tables have the following features:

- They can contain anything you can turn into a Python string.
- They may contain flowables, including other tables
- A Table will calculate the row heights to fit your data if you don't provide an explicit row height
- Technically, a Table can also calculate the width of the columns if that is not provided, but it is recommended that you provide the width for faster drawing
- A Table can split across pages, just like a Paragraph can. See the **canSplit** attribute in the source code.
- You can specify the number of rows that should be repeated after a split. This is helpful when you want a header to be repeated over multiple pages.
- There is a simple "notation" that can be used for adding shading and grid-lines to your tables. This allows you to format rows in different ways even when you don't know how many rows of data will actually be displayed.
- The Table's style and its data are separate, so you can create your own custom styles to be applied to all your reports or a subset thereof.
- Table styles can inherit from other styles

Here is how you can create a Table object:

```
Table(data, colWidths=None, rowHeights=None, style=None, splitByRow=1,
      repeatRows=0, repeatCols=0, rowSplitRange=None, spaceBefore=None,
      spaceAfter=None)
```

The only required argument is the data that you want to load. However you can also pass in the column widths (**colWidths**), row heights (**rowHeights**) which are both sequences of numbers, normally Python lists. These lists will represent the width of the columns or the heights of rows. You can also pass **None** to these arguments, which means that the table will calculate the widths and heights itself.

The **style** argument is the initial TableStyle (or a list of tuples with the appropriate commands) that you want applied to the table.

The **splitByRow** argument is a bit unusual in that you only really need it for tables that are both too tall AND too wide to fit your page's dimensions. In these cases, the developer must choose whether they want the table to be "tiled" down and across or if they'd like it to go across and then down. This argument is a Boolean, so you can pass it 0 (False) or 1 (True). The default is 1. When setting it to 1 or True, you are telling the Table to split itself by row before attempting to split by column when there isn't enough space to draw the table. Interestingly, splitting a Table by column is currently not supported, so if you happen to try setting it to False, you will get a **NotImplementedError**.

The **repeatRows** argument tells the Table the number or tuple of leading rows that should be repeated when the Table is told to split. If you choose to pass in a tuple, then that tuple needs to specify which of the rows should be repeated.

The **repeatCols** argument does not do anything since splitting the Table by column is not implemented.

The **rowSplitRange** argument is used for controlling the splitting of the table to just a subset of the rows. According to the documentation, you might use this to prevent splitting from occurring too close to the beginning or end of the Table.

Finally the **spaceBefore** and **spaceAfter** argument are used as a kind of built-in Spacer. They allow you to specify the amount of extra space to be added before or after your Table.

Let's create a simple Table:.

```
# simple_table.py

from reportlab.lib.pagesizes import letter
from reportlab.platypus import SimpleDocTemplate, Table

def simple_table():
    doc = SimpleDocTemplate("simple_table.pdf", pagesize=letter)
    story = []

    data = [['col_{}'.format(x) for x in range(1, 6)],
            [str(x) for x in range(1, 6)],
            ['a', 'b', 'c', 'd', 'e']
            ]

    tbl = Table(data)
    story.append(tbl)

    doc.build(story)
```

```
if __name__ == '__main__':
    simple_table()
```

Here we create a template object and a flowable list as usual. Then we create a list of lists which we will use as the data that we load into our Table. Each list within the top-level list represents a row of data. Thus there should be 3 rows of data in our Table when we run this code. Finally we create our Table object by passing in our data structure, adding it to our flowable list (the story) and building the document. When you run this code, you should end up with the following:

col_1	col_2	col_3	col_4	col_5
1	2	3	4	5
a	b	c	d	e

Fig. 5-1: A simple table

That was easy. Now let's learn a bit about the Table's methods.

The Table's Methods

There aren't too many methods that you use when working with Tables. The main ones you are likely to use are the following:

- drawOn
- setStyle
- wrapOn

The **drawOn** and **wrapOn** methods are usually used when you are working with a Canvas object directly and you want to add a Table to your Canvas. When you do that, then you may need to handle the splitting of the Table itself if you want to use the Canvas to create a multi-page document. I think this is usually a bad idea as you are basically just re-inventing the wheel here. Just use your Table objects in PLATYPUS and you will do a lot better.

Applying Style to Your Table

The actual method you will use the most is **setStyle** because you will almost always want to set some kind of style on your Table. The **setStyle** method accepts a **TableStyle** object or a list of tuples as its sole argument. Here is how you create a TableStyle:

```
TableStyle(cmds=None, parent=None, **kw)
```

The **cmds** argument is just a list of tuples that define what cell formatting you want to apply. Here is an example cmd tuple:

```
('BACKGROUND', (0, 0), (-1, 0), colors.red)
```

The first element in the tuple is the **cell formatting command**. In this case, we want to apply a background color to the specified cells. The second and third elements define the cell coordinates that the formatting will apply to. The coordinates are (column, row), so in this example we want to apply the background color starting at column 0, row 0. The -1 in the second set of coordinates tells ReportLab that we want the formatting to extend across all the columns from left-to-right. When you use negative values for cell coordinates, you will basically count backwards from the other end of the table, exactly as you would if you use negative indices when working with lists or string slicing. So if you wanted to apply the cell formatting from the beginning column to the second from the last column, you could specify -2, for example.

Anyway, when you tell ReportLab to apply the formatting from (0, 0) to (-1, 0), what you are saying is that you want the formatting to apply to the entire first row of the table. In this example, we want to add a red background color to the first row. If you wanted to apply the formatting to the entire table, then you would say from (0, 0) to (-1, -1), which is top-left to bottom-right.

The last tuple element is the color to be applied to the cell formatting operation you want to complete.

The **parent** argument to the TableStyle class defaults to **None**, but you can pass in a **TableStyle** object here that your new TableStyle will inherit from.

Let's take a look at a small runnable example:

```python
# simple_table_with_style.py

from reportlab.lib import colors
from reportlab.lib.pagesizes import letter
from reportlab.platypus import SimpleDocTemplate, Table, TableStyle

def simple_table_with_style():
    doc = SimpleDocTemplate("simple_table_with_style.pdf", pagesize=letter)
    story = []
    
    data = [['col_{}'.format(x) for x in range(1, 6)],
            [str(x) for x in range(1, 6)],
            ['a', 'b', 'c', 'd', 'e']
            ]
```

```
    tblstyle = TableStyle([('BACKGROUND', (0, 0), (-1, 0), colors.red),
                           ('TEXTCOLOR', (0, 1), (-1, 1), colors.blue)
                           ])

    tbl = Table(data)
    tbl.setStyle(tblstyle)
    story.append(tbl)

    doc.build(story)

if __name__ == '__main__':
    simple_table_with_style()
```

Here we create a TableStyle that will make the first row's background color red. The second command we pass in is TEXTCOLOR, which will change the text's color to whatever we specify. In this case, we want the text to be blue. We also want to apply this to column zero, row one all the way across row one.

If you run this code, you should end up with the following table:

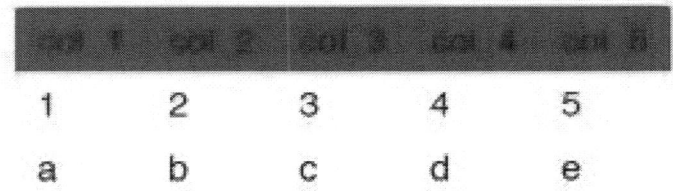

Fig. 5-2: A simple table with style applied

Let's learn what other types of formatting we can apply to our tables!

Cell Formatting

There are several cell formatting commands that you can use to format your Tables in ReportLab:

Chapter 5 - Tables

Command	Description
ALIGNMENT (or ALIGN)	LEFT, RIGHT, CENTRE/CENTER or DECIMAL
BACKGROUND	The cell's background color
FONT	The font name to be applied (optionally can add font size and leading)
FONTNAME (or FACE)	The font name
FONTSIZE (or SIZE)	The size of the font in points (leading will likely get out of sync)
LEADING	The leading space in points
TEXTCOLOR	The color name string or (R,G,B) tuple
LEFTPADDING	The amount of left padding as an integer (default: 6)
RIGHTPADDING	The amount of right padding as an integer (default: 6)
BOTTOMPADDING	The amount of bottom padding as an integer (default: 3)
TOPPADDING	The amount of top padding as an integer (default: 3)
COLBACKGROUNDS	A list of colors that ReportLab will cycle through
ROWBACKGROUNDS	A list of colors that ReportLab will cycle through
VALIGN	TOP, MIDDLE or the default of BOTTOM

The vast majority of these are explained by their descriptions, but I did want to add a little more information about the BACKGROUND command. It will actually take a ReportLab color from **reportlab.lib.colors**, a string name or a numeric tuple / list. If you go with the last one, then this tuple must contain the following information: (DIRECTION, startColor, endColor). The DIRECTION element needs to be either VERTICAL or HORIZONTAL. This will apply the color as a gradient.

Let's take a look at an example:

```python
# table_background_gradient.py

from reportlab.lib import colors
from reportlab.lib.pagesizes import letter
from reportlab.platypus import SimpleDocTemplate, Table, TableStyle

def table_background_gradient():
    doc = SimpleDocTemplate("table_background_gradient.pdf", pagesize=letter)
    story = []

    data = [['col_{}'.format(x) for x in range(1, 6)],
            [str(x) for x in range(1, 6)],
            ['a', 'b', 'c', 'd', 'e']
            ]

    tblstyle = TableStyle([('BACKGROUND', (0, 0), (-1, 0),
                           ["HORIZONTAL", colors.red, colors.blue]),
```

```
                    ('TEXTCOLOR', (0, 1), (-1, 1), colors.blue)
                    ])

    tbl = Table(data)
    tbl.setStyle(tblstyle)
    story.append(tbl)

    doc.build(story)

if __name__ == '__main__':
    table_background_gradient()
```

The code we care about here is the tblstyle code:

```
tblstyle = TableStyle([('BACKGROUND', (0, 0), (-1, 0),
                        ["HORIZONTAL", colors.red, colors.blue]),
                       ('TEXTCOLOR', (0, 1), (-1, 1), colors.blue)
                       ])
```

Here we are telling the Table to apply a style on the first row. That style will be applied **horizontally** and it will be a gradient that starts at red and goes to blue. The result ends up looking like this:

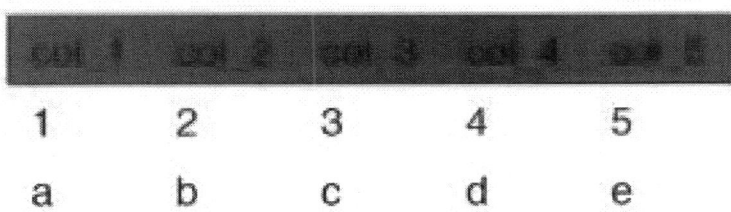

Fig. 5-3: Table with a gradient

Changing Fonts in Tables

There are several methods for working with fonts in Tables. The most straight-forward method is to use the **FONT** command in your **TableStyle**. You can use this command to change one or more of your cell's font face and size. Let's take a look:

```
# table_fonts.py

from reportlab.lib import colors
from reportlab.lib.pagesizes import letter
from reportlab.platypus import SimpleDocTemplate, Table, TableStyle

def table_fonts():
    doc = SimpleDocTemplate("table_fonts.pdf", pagesize=letter)
    story = []

    data = [['col_{}'.format(x) for x in range(1, 6)],
            [str(x) for x in range(1, 6)],
            ['a', 'b', 'c', 'd', 'e']
            ]

    tblstyle = TableStyle([('FONT', (0, 1), (-1, 1), 'Helvetica', 24)
                           ])

    tbl = Table(data)
    tbl.setStyle(tblstyle)
    story.append(tbl)

    doc.build(story)

if __name__ == '__main__':
    table_fonts()
```

The FONT command is actually a bit different from the commands we have looked at so far. It actually takes some additional elements that the others do not. In this case, we can add a font size and leading. For this example, we set the Font face to **Helvetica** and the font size to 24. When you run this code, you will see something like this:

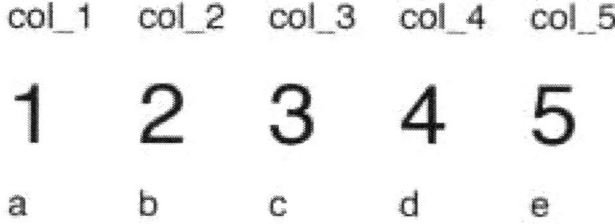

Fig. 5-4: A simple table with a FONT command

Now if you want to, you can use the **FONT** command and the **FONTSIZE** together. Let's try to reproduce the previous example by using both of these commands:

```python
# table_fonts_bad.py

from reportlab.lib import colors
from reportlab.lib.pagesizes import letter
from reportlab.platypus import SimpleDocTemplate, Table, TableStyle

def table_fonts_bad():
    doc = SimpleDocTemplate("table_font_bad.pdf", pagesize=letter)
    story = []

    data = [['col_{}'.format(x) for x in range(1, 6)],
            [str(x) for x in range(1, 6)],
            ['a', 'b', 'c', 'd', 'e']
            ]

    tblstyle = TableStyle([('FONT', (0, 1), (-1, 1), 'Helvetica'),
                           ('FONTSIZE', (0, 1), (-1, 1), 24)
                           ])

    tbl = Table(data)
    tbl.setStyle(tblstyle)
    story.append(tbl)

    doc.build(story)

if __name__ == '__main__':
    table_fonts_bad()
```

Here we set the Font to the same font face but we skip setting the font size. Then we try setting the font size by using the **FONTSIZE** command. If you run this, you should see something like the following:

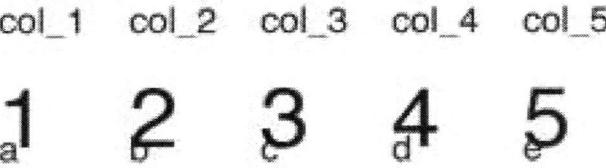

Fig. 5-5: Demo of FONT and FONTSIZE commands

Interestingly, these two examples look different. While the documentation doesn't really explain what is happening, if you look at the source code you will find that the **FONT** command has a built-in leading value or padding value that the **FONTSIZE** command does not.

Now let's take a look at how we might switch between fonts in our Table:

```python
# table_multiple_fonts.py

from reportlab.lib import colors
from reportlab.lib.pagesizes import letter
from reportlab.platypus import SimpleDocTemplate, Table, TableStyle

def table_multiple_fonts():
    doc = SimpleDocTemplate("table_multiple_fonts.pdf", pagesize=letter)
    story = []

    data = [['col_{}'.format(x) for x in range(1, 6)],
            [str(x) for x in range(1, 6)],
            ['a', 'b', 'c', 'd', 'e']
            ]

    tblstyle = TableStyle([('FONT', (0, 0), (-1, 0), 'Times-Roman'),
                           ('FONT', (0, 1), (-1, 1), 'Helvetica', 24),
                           ('FONT', (0, 2), (-1, 2), 'Courier', 12)
                           ])

    tbl = Table(data)
    tbl.setStyle(tblstyle)
    story.append(tbl)

    doc.build(story)

if __name__ == '__main__':
    table_multiple_fonts()
```

Here we change the font face in each row. You will note that we don't set the font size for the first row and just let it go to its default. The other two rows, we set the font size explicitly. Here is the result of running the code:

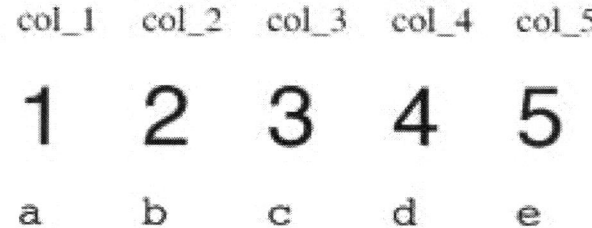

Fig. 5-6: A Table with multiple fonts applied

Now let's move on and learn how we can draw lines in our Table.

Line Commands

You might be wondering why a table doesn't have lines around its border or its cell's borders. I honestly don't know why they're off by default, but it's actually pretty easy to turn them on. In fact, ReportLab has several line commands you can use to add lines to your Tables. Here are the ones that are currently available:

- BOX
- GRID or OUTLINE
- INNERGRID
- LINEBELOW
- LINEABOVE
- LINEBEFORE
- LINEAFTER

The **GRID** line command is actually equivalent to applying the **BOX** and **INNERGRID** commands. Basically BOX will apply lines to the outside of the specified cells while INNERGRID will add lines inbetween the cells. The other line commands allow us to add lines above, below, before or after the specified cells. In other words, they allow you to add lines individually to each side of a cell or cells instead of creating multiple lines all at once.

Let's look at a simple example:

```python
# table_grids.py

from reportlab.lib import colors
from reportlab.lib.pagesizes import letter
from reportlab.platypus import SimpleDocTemplate, Table, TableStyle
from reportlab.platypus import Spacer

def table_grids():
    doc = SimpleDocTemplate("table_grids.pdf", pagesize=letter)
    story = []

    data = [['col_{}'.format(x) for x in range(1, 6)],
            [str(x) for x in range(1, 6)],
            ['a', 'b', 'c', 'd', 'e']
            ]

    tblstyle = TableStyle([('INNERGRID', (0,0), (-1,-1), 0.25, colors.red),
                           ('BOX', (0,0), (-1,-1), 0.25, colors.black),
                           ])

    tbl = Table(data)
    tbl.setStyle(tblstyle)
    story.append(tbl)

    story.append(Spacer(0, 25))

    tbl = Table(data, style=[
        ('GRID', (0,0), (-1,-1), 0.5, colors.blue)
    ])
    story.append(tbl)

    doc.build(story)

if __name__ == '__main__':
    table_grids()
```

Here we just create a simple table and add a box around the entire table. Then we also draw lines in-between all the cells. The result ends up looking like this:

Chapter 5 - Tables

col_1	col_2	col_3	col_4	col_5
1	2	3	4	5
a	b	c	d	e

col_1	col_2	col_3	col_4	col_5
1	2	3	4	5
a	b	c	d	e

Fig. 5-7: A Table with lines applied

You will note that you can apply a line width, which is the 4th element in the line command. In this example, we set it to 0.25, but you can set it to whatever you'd like to make the lines thicker or thinner.

Let's try changing line thickness and learn about the 4 other line commands using the following example:

```python
# table_cell_lines.py

from reportlab.lib import colors
from reportlab.lib.pagesizes import letter
from reportlab.platypus import SimpleDocTemplate, Table, TableStyle


def table_cell_lines():
    doc = SimpleDocTemplate("table_cell_lines.pdf", pagesize=letter)
    story = []

    data = [['col_{}'.format(x) for x in range(1, 6)],
            [str(x) for x in range(1, 6)],
            ['a', 'b', 'c', 'd', 'e'],
            ['F', 'G', 'H', 'I', 'J']
            ]

    tblstyle = TableStyle(
        [('LINEABOVE', (0, 0), (-1, 0), 0.5, colors.red),
```

```
        ('LINEBELOW', (0, 0), (-1, 0), 1.5, colors.blue),
        ('LINEBEFORE', (0, 0), (0, -1), 2.5, colors.orange),
        ('LINEAFTER', (-1, 0), (-1, -1), 3.5, colors.green),
        ])

    tbl = Table(data)
    tbl.setStyle(tblstyle)
    story.append(tbl)

    doc.build(story)

if __name__ == '__main__':
    table_cell_lines()
```

Here we use the **LINEABOVE**, **LINEBELOW**, **LINEBEFORE** and **LINEAFTER** commands to add lines to our Table in different colors and different line thicknesses. The first command, **LINEABOVE**, is applied to the first row in the color red with a line thickness of 0.5. Since it specifies the line should go *above* the cells, it appears at the top of row one. The next command, **LINEBELOW**, specifies that we want to add a line *below* the cells of row one. In this case, we add a blue line with a thickness of 1.5.

The third command, **LINEBEFORE**, is set to orange with a thickness of 2.5 and we tell it to be applied to the first column, so that means the line will appear on the far left side of our Table. To balance things out, we apply the **LINEAFTER** command to the last column of our table and set it to green with a thickness of 3.5. When you run this code, you should see a Table with the following lines:

col_1	col_2	col_3	col_4	col_5
1	2	3	4	5
a	b	c	d	e
F	G	H	I	J

Fig. 5-8: Table with line commands applied

Now let's learn how cell alignment works!

Cell Alignment

The examples we have looked at so far do not demonstrate that the cells default to being aligned to the bottom left of each cell. Let's create an example where we actually specify the column and row widths so we can see the default cell alignment:

Chapter 5 - Tables

```python
# table_default_cell_alignment.py

from reportlab.lib import colors
from reportlab.lib.pagesizes import letter
from reportlab.platypus import SimpleDocTemplate, Table, TableStyle


def table_default_cell_alignment():
    doc = SimpleDocTemplate("table_default_cell_alignment.pdf", pagesize=letter)
    story = []

    data = [['col_{}'.format(x) for x in range(1, 6)],
            [str(x) for x in range(1, 6)],
            ['a', 'b', 'c', 'd', 'e'],
            ['F', 'G', 'H', 'I', 'J']
            ]

    tblstyle = TableStyle([('INNERGRID', (0,0), (-1,-1), 0.25, colors.black),
                           ('BOX', (0,0), (-1,-1), 0.25, colors.black)
                           ])

    tbl = Table(data, colWidths=[55 for x in range(5)],
                rowHeights=[45 for x in range(len(data))]
                )
    tbl.setStyle(tblstyle)
    story.append(tbl)

    doc.build(story)

if __name__ == '__main__':
    table_default_cell_alignment()
```

The main difference to this code versus the ones we have seen previously is that when we create our Table, we pass in a list of **colWidths** and a list of **rowWidths**. When you run this example, your output should look something like this:

col_1	col_2	col_3	col_4	col_5
1	2	3	4	5
a	b	c	d	e
F	G	H	I	J

Fig. 5-9: Table default cell alignment

Now let's update our example to apply cell alignment to some of the columns using the **ALIGN** and **VALIGN** commands:

```
# table_cell_alignment.py

from reportlab.lib import colors
from reportlab.lib.pagesizes import letter
from reportlab.platypus import SimpleDocTemplate, Table, TableStyle


def table_cell_alignment():
    doc = SimpleDocTemplate("table_cell_alignment.pdf", pagesize=letter)
    story = []

    data = [['col_{}'.format(x) for x in range(1, 6)],
            [str(x) for x in range(1, 6)],
            ['a', 'b', 'c', 'd', 'e'],
            ['F', 'G', 'H', 'I', 'J']
            ]

    tblstyle = TableStyle([('INNERGRID', (0,0), (-1,-1), 0.25, colors.black),
```

```
                           ('BOX', (0,0), (-1,-1), 0.25, colors.black),
                           ('ALIGN', (0, 0), (0, -1), 'CENTER'),    # first column
                           ('VALIGN', (1, 0), (1, -1), 'MIDDLE'),   # second colu\
mn
                           ('ALIGN', (2, 0), (2, -1), 'CENTER'),    # middle colu\
mn
                           ('VALIGN', (2, 0), (2, -1), 'MIDDLE'),   # middle colu\
mn
                           ('ALIGN', (-1, 0), (-1, -1), 'RIGHT'),   # last column
                           ])

    tbl = Table(data, colWidths=[55 for x in range(5)],
                rowHeights=[45 for x in range(len(data))]
                )
    tbl.setStyle(tblstyle)
    story.append(tbl)

    doc.build(story)

if __name__ == '__main__':
    table_cell_alignment()
```

Here we tell our Table to center the cells in column one, which will result in the text being centered on the bottom of the cell. Next we tell the Table to put the second column's cells in the middle via the **VALIGN** command. What this does is put all the text in column two in the middle left. The next two commands tell the Table to ALIGN the third column's cells to the CENTER and to VALIGN them in the MIDDLE. This results in the text in those cells being in the exact center of the cells. We leave column four at its default position and apply ALIGN RIGHT to the final column, which puts the text on the bottom right of the cell.

Here is what it looks like in the PDF:

col_1	col_2	col_3	col_4	col_5
1	2	3	4	5
a	b	c	d	e
F	G	H	I	J

Fig. 5-10: Table custom cell alignment

Now we're ready to learn about alternating the background color of cells.

Alternating Background Colors

There are often cases where you will want your table to alternate the background colors in the rows or columns. This is especially true in financial reports where you will see a lot of reports that have white alternating with gray or occasionally, a light green. Let's learn how ReportLab makes this sort of thing trivial:

```
# table_alternating.py

from reportlab.lib import colors
from reportlab.lib.pagesizes import letter
from reportlab.platypus import SimpleDocTemplate, Table, TableStyle
from reportlab.platypus import Spacer

def table_alternating():
    doc = SimpleDocTemplate("table_alternating.pdf", pagesize=letter)
    story = []
```

```python
    data = [['col_{}'.format(x) for x in range(1, 6)],
            [str(x) for x in range(1, 6)],
            ['a', 'b', 'c', 'd', 'e'],
            ['f', 'g', 'h', 'i', 'j'],
            ]

    tblstyle = TableStyle([('ROWBACKGROUNDS', (0,0), (-1,-1), [colors.gray, colo\
rs.white]),
                          ('COLBACKGROUNDS', (0,0), (-1,-1),
                           [colors.red, colors.white, colors.blue])
                          ])

    tbl = Table(data)
    tbl.setStyle(tblstyle)
    story.append(tbl)

    story.append(Spacer(0, 25))

    tbl = Table(data, style=[
        ('GRID', (0,0), (-1,-1), 0.5, colors.blue)
    ])
    story.append(tbl)

    doc.build(story)

if __name__ == '__main__':
    table_alternating()
```

In this example, we use the **ROWBACKGROUNDS** and **COLBACKGROUNDS** commands to tell ReportLab how we want our Table formatting. For the rows, we tell ReportLab to alternate between gray and white. Then for the columns, we pass in red, white and blue. When you run this example, you will end up with something like this:

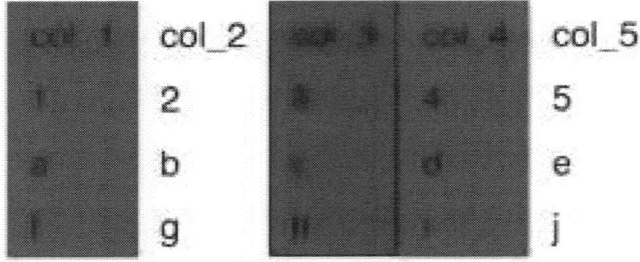

Fig. 5-11: A Table with alternating row/column colors

As you can see, changing row or column colors is quite easy with ReportLab.

Putting Paragraphs in Your Cells

One way to add some nice formatting to your Table's cells is to start using ReportLab's **Paragraph** flowable instead of just plain Python strings. Let's create a Paragraph with some formatting applied and add it to one row of cells:

```python
# table_paragraph.py

from reportlab.lib import colors
from reportlab.lib.pagesizes import letter
from reportlab.lib.styles import getSampleStyleSheet
from reportlab.platypus import SimpleDocTemplate, Table, TableStyle
from reportlab.platypus import Paragraph

def table_paragraph():
    doc = SimpleDocTemplate("table_paragraph.pdf", pagesize=letter)
    story = []
    styles = getSampleStyleSheet()
```

```
    ptext = 'This is some <font color=blue size=14>formatted</font> text'
    p = Paragraph(ptext, styles['Normal'])

    data = [['col_{}'.format(x) for x in range(1, 6)],
            [p for x in range(1, 6)],
            ['a', 'b', 'c', 'd', 'e']
            ]

    tblstyle = TableStyle([('INNERGRID', (0,0), (-1,-1), 0.25, colors.black),
                           ('BOX', (0,0), (-1,-1), 0.25, colors.black),
                           ])

    tbl = Table(data)
    tbl.setStyle(tblstyle)
    story.append(tbl)

    doc.build(story)

if __name__ == '__main__':
    table_paragraph()
```

Here we extend our previous example by adding some imports to get the Paragraph class and a paragraph style sheet. Then we format some text so that it has one word that is blue and in 14 point font. If you run this example, you should get this result:

col_1	col_2	col_3	col_4	col_5
This is some **formatted** text	This is some **formatted** text	This is some **formatted** text	This is some **formatted** text	This is some **formatted** text
a	b	c	d	e

Fig. 5-12: A Table with formatted Paragraphs in some cells

Now sometimes you want to also add images to your Tables. We will look at that next.

Adding Images to Cells

There are a couple of different ways to add an image to a Table cell. One method would be to insert an image into a Paragraph object and then add that Paragraph to a cell. When you do that, you will find that the Table's cells don't always automatically size themselves correctly to fit the image. Instead, the best way to insert an image into a Table cell is to use the **Image** flowable itself. Let's take a look:

```
# table_with_images.py

from reportlab.lib import colors
from reportlab.lib.pagesizes import letter
from reportlab.lib.styles import getSampleStyleSheet
from reportlab.platypus import SimpleDocTemplate, Table, TableStyle
from reportlab.platypus import Paragraph, Image

def table_with_images():
    doc = SimpleDocTemplate("table_with_images.pdf", pagesize=letter)
    story = []
    styles = getSampleStyleSheet()

    img = Image("snakehead.jpg", 50, 50)

    ptext = 'This is some <font color=blue size=14>formatted</font> text'
    p = Paragraph(ptext, styles['Normal'])

    data = [['col_{}'.format(x) for x in range(1, 6)],
            [p for x in range(1, 6)],
            [img, img, img, img, img]
            ]

    tblstyle = TableStyle([('INNERGRID', (0,0), (-1,-1), 0.25, colors.black),
                           ('BOX', (0,0), (-1,-1), 0.25, colors.black),
                           ])

    tbl = Table(data)
    tbl.setStyle(tblstyle)
    story.append(tbl)

    doc.build(story)

if __name__ == '__main__':
    table_with_images()
```

This example builds on the previous example by importing the **Image** flowable and then creating an image that we set to a height and width of 50 points. Then we add that object to row three 5 times so that we have an entire row of images. When I ran this code, I got this:

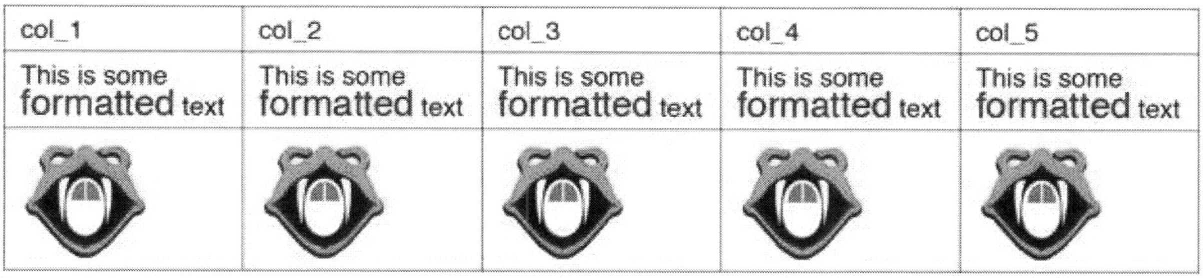

Chapter 5 - Tables

Fig. 5-13: A Table with Images in some cells

Feel free to try adding a Paragraph with an image inside of it to the cells to see how that differs.

Spanning

Any time you are dealing with tabular data you will find occasions where you want to combine cells in the Table. ReportLab's table implementation supports this via the **SPAN** command:

(SPAN, (begin_col, begin_row), (end_col, end, row))

For this command, we just tell ReportLab's Table that we want it to SPAN or combine the cells starting with (col, row) and ending with another (col, row) tuple. Here's a simple runnable example:

```python
# table_cell_spanning.py

from reportlab.lib import colors
from reportlab.lib.pagesizes import letter
from reportlab.platypus import SimpleDocTemplate, Table, TableStyle

def table_cell_spanning():
    doc = SimpleDocTemplate("table_cell_spanning.pdf", pagesize=letter)
    story = []

    data = [['col_{}'.format(x) for x in range(1, 6)],
            [str(x) for x in range(1, 6)],
            ['Bottom\nleft', '', '', '', '']
            ]

    tblstyle = TableStyle([('INNERGRID', (0,0), (-1,-1), 0.25, colors.black),
                           ('BOX', (0,0), (-1,-1), 0.25, colors.black),
                           ('SPAN', (0, -1), (1, -1))
                           ])
```

```
    tbl = Table(data)
    tbl.setStyle(tblstyle)
    story.append(tbl)

    doc.build(story)

if __name__ == '__main__':
    table_cell_spanning()
```

As with all of the commands we have looked at, you can always apply both positive and negative numbers. In this case, we add grid lines to make the cell combining more obvious. Then we call the SPAN command and tell it to start in column 0, and the last row (-1). Then we tell it to combine that cell with (column 1, last row). In other words, we want the bottom left two rows to combine or span. If you run this code, you should see the following:

col_1	col_2	col_3	col_4	col_5
1	2	3	4	5
Bottom left				

Fig. 5-14: A Table with cell spanning

While I don't think the SPAN command is particularly intuitive, it does work. Feel free to try it out with various other beginning and ending sets of coordinates.

Wrapping Up

We covered a lot of information about ReportLab's Table in this chapter. We learned how to create a basic table and then how to apply **TableStyles** to it. We learned how to change fonts and cell background colors. We also learned how to alternate colors in our rows and columns. Another topic we covered was how to create complex cell values by inserting other Flowables into our cells, such as a **Paragraph** or **Image** Flowable. Finally we learned how to combine or span cells within our Table.

Chapter 6 - Other Flowables

ReportLab has several other Flowables you can use besides the **Paragraph** and **Table** that we covered in the last couple of chapters. In this chapter we will look at the following Flowables:

- Preformatted
- XPreformatted
- Image
- Spacer
- PageBreak
- CondPageBreak
- KeepTogether
- TableOfContents
- SimpleIndex
- ListFlowable

Let's start learning about these other Flowables!

Preformatted

ReportLab has a couple of Flowables that are somewhat related called **Preformatted** and **XPreformatted**. The **Preformatted** Flowable is described as being kind of like the HTML <PRE> tag. According to ReportLab's docstring:

> It attempts to display text exactly as you typed it in a fixed width "typewriter" font. By default the line breaks are exactly where you put them, and it will not be wrapped. You can optionally define a maximum line length and the code will be wrapped; and extra characters to be inserted at the beginning of each wrapped line (e.g. '> ').

The class's instantiation looks like this:

```
Preformatted(text, style, bulletText=None,
    dedent=0, maxLineLength=None, splitChars=None,
    newLineChars=None)
```

This is quite similar to the Paragraph's instantiation, although Preformatted sub-classes from Flowable instead of Paragraph. As you can see, Preformatted requires **text** and a **Paragraph Style** for you to create an instance of this Flowable. You can also turn it into a bullet via the **bulletText** argument. The **dedent** defaults to **None**. If you happen to set dedent, then any common leading space will be removed. For example, if you were to set the dedent to 5, then it would dedent or delete 5 characters from the string.

The **maxLineLength** argument is used to define the maximum line length allowed in the Flowable. If your text happens to exceed the length that you define, the line will be automatically split. If you don't set a maximum line length and your line is too long for the page, then your line will just draw until it reaches the edge of the page and then basically get truncated. So it would behoove you to set a max line length if you think you will have long lines of text.

The **splitChars** argument tells ReportLab what character to split on. By default it will split on any of the following: space, colon, full stop, semi-colon, comma, hyphen, forward slash, back slash, left parenthesis, left square bracket and left curly brace. Of course, you can use a non-standard character by setting that explicitly.

If you would like new characters to be inserted when a new line is created, then you can set the **newLineChars** to insert those character.

Let's take a look at a simple example of using the **Preformatted** Flowable:

```python
# preformatted_paragraph.py

from reportlab.lib.pagesizes import letter
from reportlab.platypus import SimpleDocTemplate, Paragraph
from reportlab.platypus import Preformatted
from reportlab.lib.styles import getSampleStyleSheet


def preformatted_paragraph():
    doc = SimpleDocTemplate("preformatted_paragraph.pdf",
                            pagesize=letter
                            )
    styles = getSampleStyleSheet()

    flowables = []

    text = "<para align=center>Hello, I'm a Paragraph</para>"
    para = Paragraph(text, style=styles["Normal"])
    flowables.append(para)

    text = "<para align=center>Hello, I'm a Preformatted Paragraph</para>"
    para = Preformatted(text, style=styles["Code"])
```

```
        flowables.append(para)

        doc.build(flowables)

if __name__ == '__main__':
    preformatted_paragraph()
```

This example has a regular **Paragraph** and a **Preformatted** Flowable in it. Both have some XML tags in their text strings. When you run this, you will see the following:

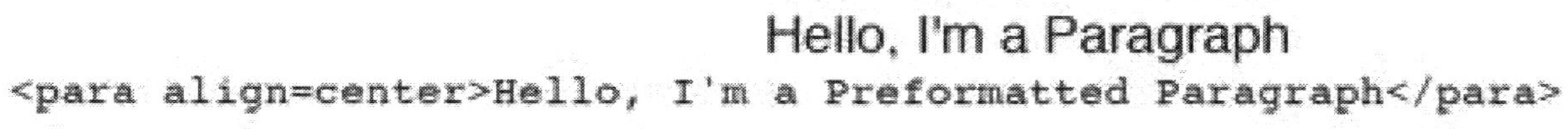

Hello, I'm a Paragraph
`<para align=center>Hello, I'm a Preformatted Paragraph</para>`

Fig. 6-1: A Preformatted paragraph

As you can see, the **Preformatted** Flowable doesn't use the Paragraph's XML tags, so they are completely visible and have no effect on the text.

XPreformatted

The **XPreformatted** Flowable is actually a sub-class of the **Paragraph** Flowable. According to the documentation, it is a "non rearranging form of the Paragraph class". It will actually work with XML tags in the same manner that they work with a regular Paragraph. To create an **XPreformatted** Flowable, you can just do the following:

```
XPreformatted(text, style, bulletText=None,
    dedent=0, frags=None)
```

The parameters here work the same way that they do when using a Paragraph or Preformatted Flowable.

```python
# xpreformatted_paragraph.py

from reportlab.lib.pagesizes import letter
from reportlab.platypus import SimpleDocTemplate, Paragraph
from reportlab.platypus import XPreformatted
from reportlab.lib.styles import getSampleStyleSheet


def xpreformatted_paragraph():
    doc = SimpleDocTemplate("xpreformatted_paragraph.pdf",
                            pagesize=letter
                            )
    styles = getSampleStyleSheet()

    flowables = []

    text = """<font color="blue">Hello, I'm a Paragraph</font>"""
    para = Paragraph(text, style=styles["Normal"])
    flowables.append(para)

    text = """Hello, I'm a <font color="red">XPreformatted Paragraph</font>"""
    para = XPreformatted(text, style=styles["Normal"])
    flowables.append(para)

    doc.build(flowables)

if __name__ == '__main__':
    xpreformatted_paragraph()
```

This Flowable works pretty much the same was as the **Preformatted** one. Frankly I personally use the **Paragraph** Flowable the most and unless you need one of these, I highly recommend sticking with it.

The Image Flowable

We have actually used the **Image** Flowable in previous chapters, but here we will go over it again in a bit more detail. Here is what it takes to create an **Image** in ReportLab:

```
Image(filename, width=None, height=None)
```

As you can see, the Image class takes 3 arguments: The filename, the width and the height of the image. The **filename** argument is required and can be a file path, a file-like object or an instance of

Chapter 6 - Other Flowables

reportlab.graphics.shapes.Drawing. Be default, ReportLab only supports the *jpeg* format. However if you have the **Pillow** (or PIL) package installed, then most other image types are also supported. The **width** and **height** parameters specify the dimensions of the image in *points*. If you do not specify one of the parameters, then ReportLab will just assume that the other dimension of the image is in points too and use it as is. What this means is that if you only specify one of the dimensions, the aspect ratio of the image will not be maintained and the image will be stretched.

Let's take a look at a simple demo of the Image Flowable:

```python
# image_demo.py

from reportlab.lib.pagesizes import letter
from reportlab.platypus import Image, SimpleDocTemplate

def full_size_image():
    doc = SimpleDocTemplate("image_full_size.pdf", pagesize=letter)
    story = []

    img = Image("snakehead.jpg")
    story.append(img)
    doc.build(story)


def no_scaling():
    doc = SimpleDocTemplate("image_no_scaling.pdf", pagesize=letter)
    story = []

    img = Image("snakehead.jpg", width=50)
    story.append(img)
    doc.build(story)


if __name__ == '__main__':
    full_size_image()
    no_scaling()
```

This demo will create two PDFs. The first one will create a PDF with the image as its default size since we do not specify either of its dimensions. Then in the **no_scaling** function, we just specify the width at 50 points. This will create the Image in a very squished-looking manner.

Here is what the first PDF looks like:

Fig. 6-2: A full size image

And here is the squished version:

Chapter 6 - Other Flowables

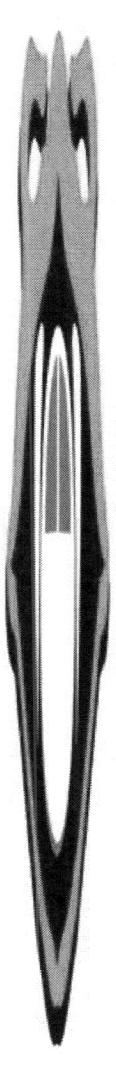

Fig. 6-3: An image with no scaling

Now let's create another script that can actually maintain the aspect ratio of the image:

```
# scaled_image.py

from reportlab.lib import utils
from reportlab.lib.pagesizes import letter
from reportlab.platypus import Image, SimpleDocTemplate

def scaled_image(desired_width):
    doc = SimpleDocTemplate("image_with_scaling.pdf", pagesize=letter)
    story = []

    img = utils.ImageReader('snakehead.jpg')
    img_width, img_height = img.getSize()
    aspect = img_height / float(img_width)

    img = Image("snakehead.jpg",
                width=desired_width,
                height=(desired_width * aspect))
    img.hAlign = 'CENTER'
    story.append(img)
    doc.build(story)

if __name__ == '__main__':
    scaled_image(50)
```

Here we import something new called **utils** from **reportlab.lib**. We then use the **ImageReader** class from the **utils** submodule to get an image object. It will use Pillow to get information about the image. Then we can call it's **getSize** method to get the image's width and height. Once we have that, we can use a simple calculation to get the aspect ration and apply it to whatever size of the image we want. In this case, we want the image to be 50 points wide. When you run this code, you should see something like the following:

Fig. 6-4: **An image with scaling**

You can also set the Image's horizontal alignment via it's **hAlign** attribute. We demonstrated that in our scaled demo above.

The Spacer Flowable

The Spacer Flowable has been mentioned in some of our previous chapters as well. Here is a reminder of how you can create one:

```
Spacer(width, height)
```

Note that the **width** parameter is ignored currently and has been for many years. The only use of the Spacer is for adding vertical space that is useful for positioning other Flowables on the page. Let's look at a simple example:

```python
# spacer_demo.py

from reportlab.lib.pagesizes import letter
from reportlab.platypus import SimpleDocTemplate, Paragraph, Spacer
from reportlab.lib.styles import getSampleStyleSheet


def no_spacers():
    doc = SimpleDocTemplate("no_spacers.pdf",
                            pagesize=letter
                            )
    styles = getSampleStyleSheet()

    flowables = []

    for p in range(3):
        text = "<para align=center>Hello, I'm a Paragraph</para>"
        para = Paragraph(text, style=styles["Normal"])
        flowables.append(para)

    doc.build(flowables)

def use_spacers():
    doc = SimpleDocTemplate("use_spacers.pdf",
                            pagesize=letter
                            )
    styles = getSampleStyleSheet()

    flowables = []

    for p in range(3):
```

```python
        text = "<para align=center>Hello, I'm a Paragraph</para>"
        para = Paragraph(text, style=styles["Normal"])
        flowables.append(para)
        spacer = Spacer(width=0, height=50)
        flowables.append(spacer)

    doc.build(flowables)


if __name__ == '__main__':
    no_spacers()
    use_spacers()
```

The first function creates 3 Paragraphs with no space between them, which looks like this:

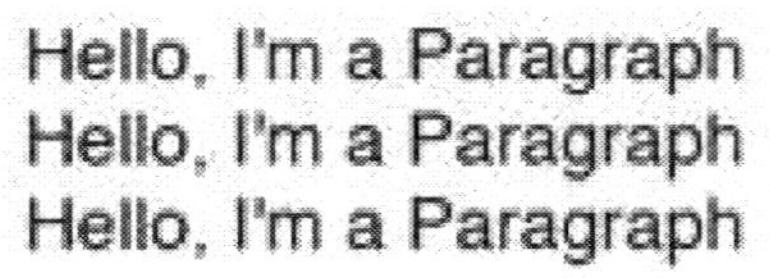

Hello, I'm a Paragraph
Hello, I'm a Paragraph
Hello, I'm a Paragraph

Fig. 6-5: **Paragraphs with no spacing**

Then in the second function, we add a Spacer with 50 points in height in-between each of the Paragraphs. This results in the following:

Hello, I'm a Paragraph

Hello, I'm a Paragraph

Hello, I'm a Paragraph

Fig. 6-6: **Paragraphs with spacing**

I believe you will find this simple Flowable very useful in your own code.

PageBreak

We mentioned the **PageBreak** Flowable back in chapter 3 and as its name implies, it will add a page break to your document by consuming all the vertical space left on the page. This will cause any other Flowables that are added after the PageBreak to appear on the following page. Note that this doesn't apply if you try to add a PageBreak to a Frame. In that case, ReportLab would detect that as a Frame break and the Flowable would continue in the next Frame, which could be on the same page. The **BaseDocTemplate** will detect PageBreaks though, so when using them in a template, they should work as expected.

Here is a simple example:

```
# page_break.py

from reportlab.lib.pagesizes import letter
from reportlab.platypus import SimpleDocTemplate, Paragraph, PageBreak
from reportlab.lib.styles import getSampleStyleSheet

def page_break():
    doc = SimpleDocTemplate("page_break.pdf")
    styles = getSampleStyleSheet()

    flowables = []

    text = "Hello, I'm a Paragraph"
    para = Paragraph(text, style=styles["Normal"])
    flowables.append(para)

    pagebreak = PageBreak()
    flowables.append(pagebreak)

    text = "Hello, I'm a Paragraph on page 2"
    para = Paragraph(text, style=styles["Normal"])
    flowables.append(para)

    doc.build(flowables)

if __name__ == '__main__':
    page_break()
```

All this code does is create two Paragraphs with a PageBreak between them. This will cause a two-page PDF to be generated with a Paragraph on each page.

CondPageBreak

The **CondPageBreak** is a Flowable that applies to Frames and will attempt to force a break in a Frame. In fact, the documentation says that this Flowable is poorly named and really ought to have been called **CondFrameBreak**.

Here is the typical signature for creating one:

```
CondPageBreak(height)
```

Personally I have never had the need for one of these nor seen one in the wild.

KeepTogether

The **KeepTogether** Flowable is a class that takes a list of other Flowables and will attempt to keep the entire list in the same **Frame**.

```
KeepTogether(flowables)
```

If the list of Flowables exceeds the height of the Frame in which they are contained, the a frame break will occur.

How to Add a Table of Contents

ReportLab has a neat Flowable called **TableOfContents** that will allow you to add a Table of Contents to your PDF. To create a **TableOfContents** instance, all you need to do is the following:

```
from reportlab.lib.styles import ParagraphStyle
from reportlab.platypus.tableofcontents import TableOfContents

toc = TableOfContents()
```

The **TableOfContents** Flowable has built-in styles, but from looking at the documentation, you will usually want to override those and replace them with your own. You can do that like this:

```
from reportlab.lib.styles import ParagraphStyle
from reportlab.platypus.tableofcontents import TableOfContents
toc = TableOfContents()

toc.levelStyles = [
    ParagraphStyle(name = 'Heading1',
                   fontSize = 16,
                   leading = 16),
    ParagraphStyle(name = 'Heading2',
                   fontSize = 12,
                   leading = 14),
]
```

As you can see, all you need to do is pass in some **ParagraphStyles** to add your styles. According to the documentation, you can use the **addEntry** or **AddEntries** methods to add Table of Contents entries manually. However after speaking with the ReportLab developers, these commands need to be done during the PDF rendering process, so using them directly is nigh impossible. Instead, the preferred method is to create a custom document template and override its **afterFlowable** method.

Let's take a look at an example that is based on one from ReportLab's user guide:

```
# toc_creator.py

from reportlab.lib.styles import ParagraphStyle
from reportlab.platypus import PageBreak
from reportlab.platypus.paragraph import Paragraph
from reportlab.platypus.doctemplate import PageTemplate, BaseDocTemplate
from reportlab.platypus.tableofcontents import TableOfContents
from reportlab.platypus.frames import Frame
from reportlab.lib.units import cm


class MyDocTemplate(BaseDocTemplate):
    def __init__(self, filename, **kw):
        self.allowSplitting = 0
        BaseDocTemplate.__init__(self, filename, **kw)
        template = PageTemplate('normal', [Frame(2.5*cm, 2.5*cm, 15*cm, 25*cm, i\
d='F1')])
        self.addPageTemplates(template)

    def afterFlowable(self, flowable):
        "Registers the Table Of Contents entries"
        if flowable.__class__.__name__ == 'Paragraph':
```

```python
            text = flowable.getPlainText()
            style = flowable.style.name
            if style == 'Heading1':
                self.notify('TOCEntry', (0, text, self.page))
            if style == 'Heading2':
                self.notify('TOCEntry', (1, text, self.page))

def main():
    heading1_style = ParagraphStyle(name = 'Heading1',
                                    fontSize = 16,
                                    leading = 16)
    heading2_style = ParagraphStyle(name = 'Heading2',
                                    fontSize = 12,
                                    leading = 14,
                                    )

    # create story and table of contents object
    story = []
    toc = TableOfContents()

    # Set the Paragraph styles in the Table of Contents
    toc.levelStyles = [heading1_style, heading2_style]
    story.append(toc)
    story.append(PageBreak())

    ipsum = '''Lorem ipsum dolor sit amet, consectetur adipiscing elit,
    sed do eiusmod tempor incididunt ut labore et dolore magna aliqua.
    Ut enim ad minim veniam, quis nostrud exercitation ullamco laboris
    nisi ut aliquip ex ea commodo consequat. Duis aute irure dolor in
    reprehenderit in voluptate velit esse cillum dolore eu fugiat nulla
    pariatur. Excepteur sint occaecat cupidatat non proident, sunt in
    culpa qui officia deserunt mollit anim id est laborum.'''

    story.append(Paragraph('Heading #1', heading1_style))
    story.append(Paragraph(ipsum, ParagraphStyle('body')))
    story.append(Paragraph('Sub-heading #1', heading2_style))
    story.append(Paragraph(ipsum, ParagraphStyle('body')))
    story.append(PageBreak())
    story.append(Paragraph('Sub-heading #2', heading2_style))
    story.append(Paragraph(ipsum, ParagraphStyle('body')))
    story.append(Paragraph('Heading #2', heading1_style))
```

```
    doc = MyDocTemplate('toc.pdf')
    doc.multiBuild(story)

if __name__ == '__main__':
    main()
```

The first thing we do is sub-class **BaseDocTemplate** and set up a few things in the **__init__**. Then we override the **afterFlowable** method. The key point here is that we call **self.notify** with a 'TOCEntry' notification string. This will tell our TableOfContents object that the template has detected an entry that should be added to the table of contents. In the notification, you will need to pass the entry text, page number and an optional destination key.

The destination key is a bookmark that should make those items that have it into clickable links. The rest of the code in this example lies in the **main** function where we create an instance of our custom template, add our TableOfContents and various Paragraphs and PageBreaks. You will note that we need to call the **multiBuild** method on our document template instance to actually create our TableOfContents. This is because ReportLab will need to make several passes over the document to generate your table of contents.

Here is what this code generated as a table of contents:

Heading #1 2
Sub-heading #1 2
Sub-heading #2 3
Heading #2 3

Fig. 6-7: Sample Table of Contents

SimpleIndex

ReportLab has basic support for adding an index to your PDFs as well. You can accomplish this via the **SimpleIndex** Flowable. To index a word in ReportLab, you will need to use the **<index>** tag along with the **item** attribute, like this:

```
ptext = """I'm a custom <index item="bulletted"/>bulletted paragraph"""
```

This will tell ReportLab that you would like to add an index for the word "bulletted". The other piece that is needed is to create a **SimpleIndex** instance and add it to the end of your flowables list. Let's take a look at a simple example:

```python
# simple_index.py

from reportlab.lib.pagesizes import letter
from reportlab.platypus import SimpleDocTemplate, Paragraph, PageBreak
from reportlab.platypus.tableofcontents import SimpleIndex
from reportlab.lib.styles import getSampleStyleSheet


def simple_index():
    doc = SimpleDocTemplate("simple_index.pdf",
                            pagesize=letter
                            )
    styles = getSampleStyleSheet()

    flowables = []

    ptext = """I'm a custom <index item="bulletted"/>bulletted paragraph"""
    para = Paragraph(ptext, style=styles["Normal"], bulletText='-')
    flowables.append(para)
    flowables.append(PageBreak())

    ptext = """<index item="Python"/>Python is an indexed word"""
    para = Paragraph(ptext, style=styles["Normal"], bulletText='-')
    flowables.append(para)

    index = SimpleIndex()
    flowables.append(PageBreak())
    flowables.append(index)


    doc.build(flowables, canvasmaker=index.getCanvasMaker())

if __name__ == '__main__':
    simple_index()
```

Here we create an index on two words, "bulletted" and "Python". Then we create our index object. Finally, to add the SimpleIndex you need to call the document template's **build** in a new way:

```
doc.build(flowables, canvasmaker=index.getCanvasMaker())
```

This will make the document builder use the index's canvas maker object. When you run this, you should end up with an index that looks like this:

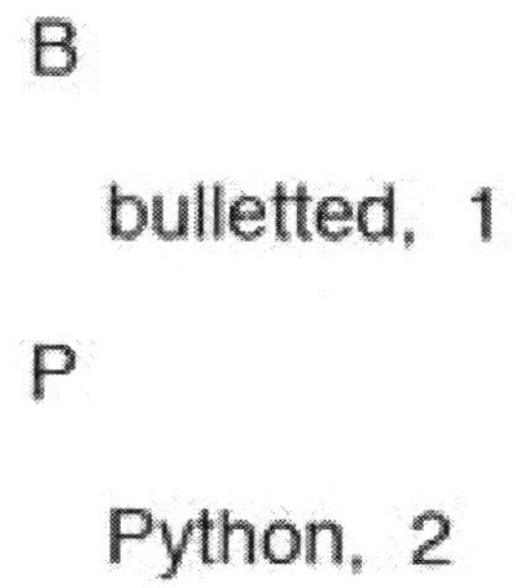

B

bulletted, 1

P

Python, 2

Fig. 6-8: A simple index

Note that you can supply some other items to the **SimpleIndex** constructor when you instantiate it, but the documentation doesn't really explain what it does. However you can kind of get a gist for how to use it if you look in the source code, specifically the SimpleIndex's **setup** method's docstring.

Looking at that and the user guide tells us that we could change the instantiation of the SimpleIndex object to the following:

```
index = SimpleIndex(dot='.')
```

If you do that then your index will now look like this:

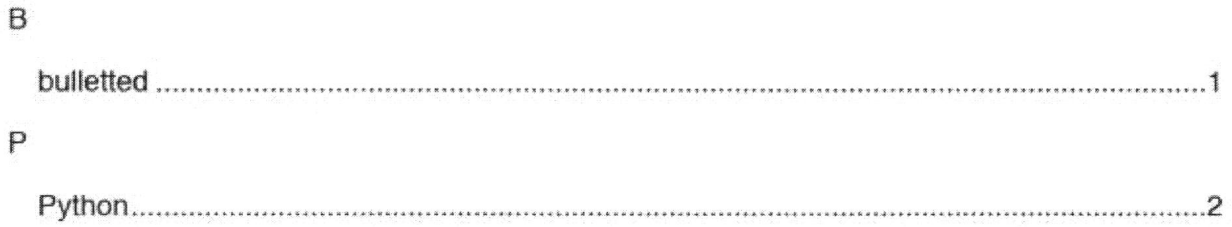

B

    bulletted 1

P

    Python 2

Fig. 6-9: A simple index with dots

I actually think this is more visually appealing than just using the defaults for SimpleIndex. You can also create an index that contains multiple levels by passing in a comma-separated list of items to index:

```
<index item="foo,bar,word"/>
```

The first term will be at the top-most level while the last will be at the lowest. If you have additional lists of indexed terms, they will appear at their appropriate levels as well.

One other thing of note is that if you happen to have the need to index a term that has a comma in it, then you will need to escape it by doubling the comma.

ListFlowable / ListItem

The last Flowables we will be covering in this chapter is the **ListFlowable** and its companion, the **ListItem**. These Flowables can be used to make ordered and unordered lists. You can also nest the lists. The cool thing about the **ListFlowable** is that it can contain any other Flowable and will use them to create the ordered list. You can also change the font, color, size, style and position of the list number or the bullets in unordered lists. You may also change the type of numbering applied to use lower or upper case letters or upper or lower Roman numerals via the **bulletType** property.

If you want the list to be unordered, then set **bulletType='bullet'**.

You can also change the default appearance of a ListFlowable by wrapping them in a ListItem and setting its properties.

Let's take a look at a simple example

```python
# list_flowable_demo.py

from reportlab.lib.pagesizes import letter
from reportlab.platypus import ListFlowable, ListItem
from reportlab.platypus import SimpleDocTemplate, Paragraph
from reportlab.lib.styles import getSampleStyleSheet

def list_flowable_demo():
    doc = SimpleDocTemplate("list_flowable_demo.pdf",
                            pagesize=letter
                            )
    styles = getSampleStyleSheet()
    normal = styles['Normal']
    story = []

    flowables = [
        Paragraph('Paragraph numero uno', normal),
        ListItem(Paragraph('Paragraph #2', normal),
                 bulletColor="blue", value=5),
        Paragraph('Paragraph #3', normal),
    ]

    lflow = ListFlowable(flowables)
    story.append(lflow)

    doc.build(story)
```

```python
if __name__ == '__main__':
    list_flowable_demo()
```

This will create an ordered list which some might call a numbered list. There are 3 items in the list. The first is a **Paragraph** object, followed by a **ListItem** that contains a Paragraph and the last item is also a regular **Paragraph**. You will note that in the ListItem, we change the "bullet" color to blue and the value to "5". What this means is that the ordered list will start at "1" but the second item will change to "5" because we wrapped it in a **ListItem** where we changed its value. Since the value got changed to a "5", the third item continues by incrementing to "6". Here is the result of running this code:

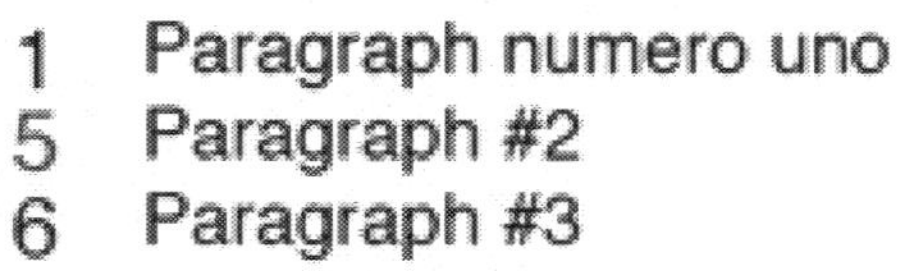

1 Paragraph numero uno
5 Paragraph #2
6 Paragraph #3

Fig. 6-10: An example of the ListFlowable

Now let's enhance the previous code so that we can add some sub-list items and learn more about formatting our lists:

```python
# list_flowable_squares.py

from reportlab.lib.pagesizes import letter
from reportlab.platypus import ListFlowable, ListItem
from reportlab.platypus import SimpleDocTemplate, Paragraph
from reportlab.lib.styles import getSampleStyleSheet

def list_flowable_squares():
    doc = SimpleDocTemplate("list_flowable_squares.pdf",
                            pagesize=letter
                            )
    styles = getSampleStyleSheet()
    normal = styles['Normal']
    story = []

    flowables = [
        Paragraph('Paragraph numero uno', normal),
        ListItem(Paragraph('Paragraph #2', normal),
                 bulletColor="blue"),
        Paragraph('Paragraph #3', normal),
        ]
```

```
        flowables.append(
            ListFlowable(
                [Paragraph("I'm a sublist item", normal),
                 ListItem(Paragraph("I'm another sublist item", normal),
                          bulletColor='blue'),
                 ListItem(Paragraph("I'm the last sublist item", normal),
                          bulletColor='red')
                ],
                bulletType='bullet',
                start='square'
            ))

        lflow = ListFlowable(flowables, bulletType='I')
        story.append(lflow)

        doc.build(story)

if __name__ == '__main__':
    list_flowable_squares()
```

The first half of the code is pretty much the same as we saw previously. The new piece is where we **append** a **ListFlowable** to our **flowables** list. Inside of this **ListFlowable** is a Paragraph and two ListItems. For this nested ListFlowable, we set its **bulletType** to 'bullet' and its shape to **square** by assigning **square** to the **start** keyword argument. Inside of the ListFlowable we change the **bulletColor** to various other colors to make the list items look different.

Here is the result:

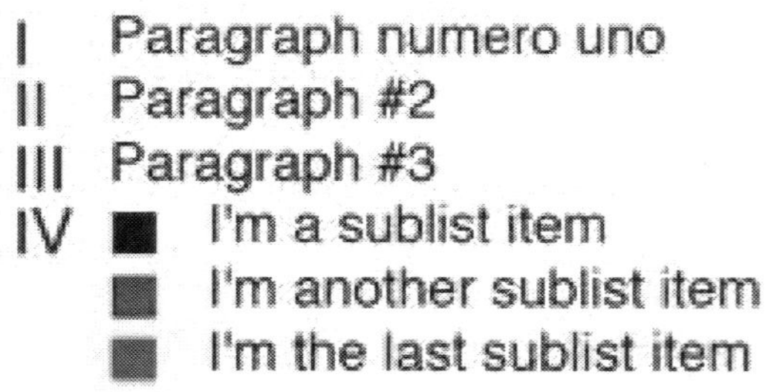

Fig. 6-11: An example of nested ListFlowables

For those that are curious, you can open up **flowables.py** in the ReportLab source code to get a listing of the available bullet names that you can use:

```
_bulletNames = dict(
            bulletchar=u'\u2022',   #usually a small circle
            circle=u'\u25cf',   #circle as high as the font
            square=u'\u25a0',
            disc=u'\u25cf',
            diamond=u'\u25c6',
            diamondwx=u'\u2756',
            rarrowhead=u'\u27a4',
            sparkle=u'\u2747',
            squarelrs=u'\u274f',
            blackstar=u'\u2605',
            )
```

As you can see, there 10 bullet names and the example we did only used the **square** bullet name. Feel free to edit the code and try running it with some of these other bullet names.

Wrapping Up

In this chapter we learned about how to create the following Flowables:

- Preformatted
- XPreformatted
- Image
- Spacer
- PageBreak
- CondPageBreak
- KeepTogether
- TableOfContents
- SimpleIndex
- ListFlowable

I personally believe that you will be using the **Image**, **Spacer**, and **PageBreak** Flowables the most. The rest are used primarily for very specific use cases that I don't believe happen all that often. However you should now know enough about each of these Flowables to be able to use them in your own code effectively.

Chapter 7 - Creating Your Own Flowables

The **Flowable** class is easy to sub-class so that you can create your own custom Flowables whenever you need to. You can look at the Flowables that are included with ReportLab for ideas. There is also a chapter in the ReportLab User Guide that has a fun example of creating a custom Flowable that looks like a hand. You might find some user contributed Flowables on ReportLab's website as well, although I haven't personally seen too many of these.

In this chapter we will look at how to create two very basic custom Flowables that should help you see how easy it is to create your own.

Creating a Line Flowable

Creating a line Flowable is actually quite simple. The first thing you need to do is sub-class ReportLab's **Flowable** class and then tell it to draw a line. Let's look at how we might put this together:

```
# line_flowable.py

from reportlab.platypus import Flowable


class MyLineFlowable(Flowable):
    """
    A Custom Line Flowable
    """

    def __init__(self, width, height=0):
        Flowable.__init__(self)
        self.width = width
        self.height = height

    def __repr__(self):
        return "Line(w=%s)" % self.width

    def draw(self):
```

```
    """
    draw the line
    """
    self.canv.line(0, self.height, self.width, self.height)
```

Here we create a pretty simply class. It accepts a **width** and a **height** as its sole arguments. Then we override the **__repr__** method to make the output from printing our instances of this Flowable more readable. Finally we override the **draw** method to just draw a line on the Flowable's **canvas** using the width and height that were passed in.

Now let's create some code that actually uses our custom Flowable:

```
# line_flowable_demo.py

from line_flowable import MyLineFlowable
from reportlab.lib.pagesizes import letter
from reportlab.lib.styles import getSampleStyleSheet
from reportlab.lib.units import inch
from reportlab.platypus import Paragraph, SimpleDocTemplate, Spacer


def create_line_flowable():
    """
    Create a pdf
    """
    story = []
    doc = SimpleDocTemplate("create_line_flowable.pdf", pagesize=letter)
    styles = getSampleStyleSheet()
    spacer = Spacer(0, 0.25*inch)

    ptext = '<font size=12>%s</font>' % "Section #1"
    story.append(Paragraph(ptext, styles["Normal"]))
    story.append(spacer)

    line = MyLineFlowable(500)
    story.append(line)
    story.append(spacer)

    ptext = '<font size=12>%s</font>' % "Section #2"
    story.append(Paragraph(ptext, styles["Normal"]))

    doc.build(story)
```

```
if __name__ == "__main__":
    create_line_flowable()
```

The first thing we do is import our custom Flowable. Then we import the various other bits and pieces we need from ReportLab itself. Next we create our **story** list, a document templates, a stylesheet and a Spacer object. Then we add a Paragraph and a spacer to our story list. Finally we get to the code that creates our Flowable:

```
line = MyLineFlowable(500)
```

This will draw a line that is 500 points long! We add it to our story list just like we did with our previous Flowables. Then we ad a spacer and another Paragraph before finally generating our PDF, which ends up looking like this:

Fig. 7-1: An example of our custom Line Flowable

This looks pretty good, but I think it's kind of a boring Flowable. So let's make something a bit more complicated!

Creating a Bordered Textbox + Line Flowable

During one of my jobs, I needed to create a text box with a border plus a line that went from the top of the box off to the right and I needed to be able to add it to my document as a Flowable. It kind of looked like this piece of ASCII art:

```
-----------------------------------------
| foobar |
----------
```

As you may have guessed, this custom Flowable is a little bit more complex than just creating a line. However it actually doesn't take up that much more code to create a really simple version. Let's take a look!

Chapter 7 - Creating Your Own Flowables

```
# boxy_line.py

from reportlab.lib.pagesizes import letter
from reportlab.platypus import Flowable, SimpleDocTemplate, Spacer
from reportlab.lib.units import inch


class BoxyLine(Flowable):
    """
    Draw a box + line + text

    -------------------------------------------
    | foobar |
    ---------

    """

    def __init__(self, x=0, y=-15, width=40, height=15, text=""):
        Flowable.__init__(self)
        self.x = x
        self.y = y
        self.width = width
        self.height = height
        self.text = text

    def draw(self):
        """
        Draw the shape, text, etc
        """
        self.canv.rect(self.x, self.y, self.width, self.height)
        self.canv.line(self.x, 0, 500, 0)
        self.canv.drawString(self.x+5, self.y+3, self.text)
```

This time when we create our class, we set it up to take five arguments: x, y, width, height and text. The x and y are for helping in positioning the Flowable's lines correctly. The width and height are for setting the rectangle's dimensions and the text is what will be displayed in the box. Now let's look at how we use this Flowable:

```python
# boxy_line_demo.py

from boxy_line import BoxyLine
from reportlab.lib.pagesizes import letter
from reportlab.platypus import SimpleDocTemplate, Spacer
from reportlab.lib.units import inch

def create_boxy_line_flowable():
    """
    Create a pdf
    """
    doc = SimpleDocTemplate("boxy_line_flowable.pdf",pagesize=letter)
    story=[]

    box = BoxyLine(text="foo")
    story.append(box)
    story.append(Spacer(0, 1*inch))
    box = BoxyLine(text="bar")
    story.append(box)

    doc.build(story)

if __name__ == "__main__":
    create_boxy_line_flowable()
```

Here we import our BoxyLine Flowable class and then we create two instances of it. We stick a Spacer object between them to give them some page real estate and then we build the story and generate the PDF. This is the result:

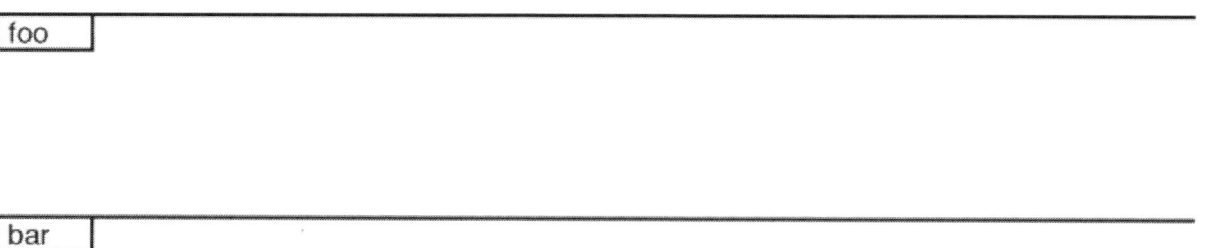

Fig. 7-2: **The Boxy Line Flowable**

I think it turned out pretty well. One of the immediate improvements you could make to this Flowable would be to calculate the width of the string that was passed into it and adjust the bounding rectangle accordingly. You could accomplish that fairly easily by using the **stringWidth** function from **reportlab.pdfbase.pdfmetrics**.

Modifying a Pre-Existing Flowable

Sometimes all you really want to do is make an existing Flowable behave in a way that the default version doesn't appear to do. You can easily subclass a pre-existing Flowable like the **Paragraph** or the **Image** and just override its methods to make it do something different.

Just take a look at the Flowable you would like to change and see what methods it has. Then you can make an educated guess which ones you will need to change to make your new Flowable work the way you want it to. The ReportLab User Guide has one example where they subclassed the **Image** class to make it draw all images at a 90 degree angle, for example.

Wrapping Up

At this point you should have a pretty good idea how to create your own Flowables and subclass a pre-existing one. This gives you a lot of power as a developer as you can create pretty much any kind of drawing with ReportLab and make it into a Flowable that is easy to add to your document generation process.

Chapter 8 - Intro to Graphics and Charts

The **reportlab.graphics** sub-package started off as a set of standalone programs. Today it fully integrated into the rest of the ReportLab Toolkit. The graphics sub-packages gives the developer a powerful set of features to create charts and graphics which will enhance your PDFs and programmatically generated reports.

What is a Drawing?

ReportLab's definition of a drawing is *a platform-independent description of a collection of shapes*. What this means is that a drawing is not actually associated with a file format, such as PDF or PostScript. On the plus side, most systems that create vector graphics have all followed the model that Postscript uses, so it is actually easy to describe a drawing. The reason that defining a drawing is important is that we need a way to describe what a shape is programmatically in an unambiguous way.

All drawings contain shapes. The ones you learned back in primary school (i.e. rectangles, lines, circles) can by used to create most other drawings. There is another shape that you will see in computer programs called a **Group**, which is a container of other shapes that you can manipulate via transforms. If you have ever used *Microsoft Publisher* or *Adobe Photoshop*, then you may have seen that you can group images and then manipulate them as a whole (i.e. resize the group, flip or turn them, etc). This is what I meant when I mentioned the word *transform*.

ReportLab's Renderers

ReportLab has several **Renderers** that you can use to draw your drawings. In other words, ReportLab can take your drawings and output them in different formats. As you might expect, ReportLab can output your drawings in PDF using the **renderPDF** renderer. You can also output Postscript via **renderPS** and bitmap via **renderPM**. The bitmap renderer is made possible via Raph Levien's *libart* rasterizer and Fredrik Lundh's *Python Imaging Library (PIL)*. Note however that you cannot install PIL in Python 3. Instead ReportLab uses Alex Clark's **Pillow** fork of PIL for that. In fact, you can use Pillow for Python 2.7 as well as it is "friendly fork" of the Python Imaging Library, which means that its API is the same as PIL's. There is also an experimental SVG renderer that utilizes Python's own built-in XML modules. What this all means is that if you have all of these extensions installed, then you should be able to generate the same drawings in several different formats.

The Drawings in ReportLab are also Flowables, so you can add them to your Platypus documents as you would any other Flowable. You can also draw your drawings directly in a ReportLab Canvas object if you need too. Another neat feature is that you can use a utility function to generate a one-page PDF of your drawing fast!

As an aside, the SVG renderer that I mentioned has not had any optimization applied to it and it can only use the drawing features that ReportLab Graphics supplies. What this means is that the SVG format that is in ReportLab is not full featured. You won't be able to do SVG animation, scripting, clipping, masking or gradient shapes.

The Coordinate System

The Graphics sub-package uses the same coordinate system that ReportLab defaults to which is that the Y-direction is from the bottom up. Some graphics models (i.e. SVG) use the opposite coordinate system where the Y-coordinate points down. The SVG renderer that ReportLab provides will flip things as necessary to make it look correct.

The X-coordinate is stil left-to-right just as it is in the rest of ReportLab.

A Simple Drawing

After all that information, you're probably starting to wonder if we would ever get to actually learning how to draw in ReportLab. You will be happy to know that that time is now. Let's create a simple drawing using ReportLab's **Graphics** sub-package!

```python
# simple_drawing.py

from reportlab.lib import colors
from reportlab.graphics import shapes, renderPDF


def simple_drawing():
    drawing = shapes.Drawing(400, 400)
    drawing.add(shapes.Circle(200, 200, 100, fillColor=colors.red))
    renderPDF.drawToFile(drawing, 'simple_drawing.pdf', msg='My Drawing')

if __name__ == '__main__':
    simple_drawing()
```

This will output the following in your PDF:

Fig. 8-1: An example drawing

Supported Outputs

Drawings support the following output formats:

- bmp
- eps
- gif
- jpeg
- jpg
- pct
- pdf
- pict
- png
- ps
- py
- svg
- tif
- tiff
- tiff1
- tiffl
- tiffp

You can change the code in the previous example to easily export PNG for example. All you need to do is import the **renderPM** renderer, which is for rendering pixmaps:

Chapter 8 - Intro to Graphics and Charts

```python
# simple_drawing2.py

from reportlab.lib import colors
from reportlab.graphics import shapes, renderPM


def simple_drawing():
    drawing = shapes.Drawing(400, 400)
    drawing.add(shapes.Circle(200, 200, 100, fillColor=colors.red))
    renderPM.drawToFile(drawing, 'simple_drawing.png', 'PNG')

if __name__ == '__main__':
    simple_drawing()
```

You will note that each renderer has a similar API. For example, if you are exporting to a file format, then the renderer will have a **drawToFile** method.

Verifying Attributes

ReportLab has some attribute verification built-in to their Graphics sub-package. The reason is because Python is a dynamic language where you can easily add an attribute to any of you objects that may or may not be intentional. Here is an example:

```
>>> class MyRect:
        pass
>>>
>>> rect = MyRect()
>>> rect.fullColor = 'green'
>>> rect.fullColor
'green'
```

To avoid runtime and logic errors, ReportLab will run a check on every object to check if there are any assignments to unknown attributes. For example:

```
>>> from reportlab.graphics import shapes
>>> reportlab_rect = shapes.Rect(5, 5, 100, 100)
>>> reportlab_rect.fullColor = 'red'
Traceback (most recent call last):
  Python Shell, prompt 16, line 1
  File "/usr/lib/python3/dist-packages/reportlab/graphics/shapes.py", line 361, \
in __setattr__
    validateSetattr(self,attr,value)     #from reportlab.lib.attrmap
  File "/usr/lib/python3/dist-packages/reportlab/lib/attrmap.py", line 115, in v\
alidateSetattr
    raise AttributeError("Illegal attribute '%s' in class %s" % (name, obj.__cla\
ss__.__name__))
builtins.AttributeError: Illegal attribute 'fullColor' in class Rect
```

This verification process does slow down the performance of generating graphics, so ReportLab will allow you to turn if off.

Here is how you can disable the attribute checking:

```
>>> import reportlab.rl_config
>>> reportlab.rl_config.shapeChecking = 0
```

According to the documentation, the performance only decreases by approximately 25% when creating batches of charts or graphs.

If you do happen to turn off attribute verification, then it is recommended that you call your drawing's **verify()** method in your tests to verify that your code is doing what you expect it to do.

Naming Shapes

When you add shapes to your **Drawing** or **Group** objects, you can give them a name. This makes it possible for the developer to easily access the shape after it was created and also allow you to change any of the elements thereof.

```
>>> from reportlab.graphics import shapes
>>> my_drawing = shapes.Drawing(width=400, height=200)
>>> circle = shapes.Circle(50, 50, 100)
>>> my_drawing.add(circle, name='my_circle')
>>> circle.cx
50
>>> my_drawing.my_circle.cx
50
```

The ReportLab guide points out that you can use the same shape instance in multiple locations of your code base and even use different names to refer to the same instance. If you make a change to the object, it will affect all the names since they all refer to the same thing. This is true of all Python objects, but it's something to be aware of as it can lead to subtle runtime errors.

Charts and Graphs

ReportLab supports creating several different types of charts and graphs via the **Graphics** sub-module. Here is a list of the types you can currently create:

- Bar charts
- Line charts
- Line plots
- Pie charts

These charts or plots are technically added to a **Drawing** object. However a chart itself is not a drawing object. This allows the developer to tell ReportLab where to put the plot on the page, add several copies of the same plot or even add annotations to the plot.

Each chart has two axes. These axes may be set to either **Value** or **Category**. Axes have a property called **Label** that you can use to configure all the text labels in your chart at once or individually change them. When it comes to charts, you will find that most of their configuration lies in the axis properties or the axis labels.

Anything in a chart that is required for it to function is handled through chart methods.

One other thing to note about charts is that they can be easily sub-classed just like other ReportLab Flowables as long as your actually implement the required methods and properties in your subclass.

Labels

The ReportLab Graphics sub-module provides a Label class that you can use to add Labels to your drawings as well as your charts. A Label is basically just a string of text. You may use a Label for axes, titles or data points. A Label may contain newline characters, but are limited to only one font.

Chapter 8 - Intro to Graphics and Charts

When creating a Label, you will typically set its parent object via Label methods. You can set properties of your Label (or labels) to change the label's position relative to its origin as well as a Label's formatting.

Here is an example of code that gets us a listing of the default properties we can change in our Label objects:

```
>>> from reportlab.graphics.charts.textlabels import Label
>>> label = Label()
>>> label.getProperties()
{'angle': 0,
 'bottomPadding': 0,
 'boxAnchor': 'c',
 'boxFillColor': None,
 'boxStrokeColor': None,
 'boxStrokeWidth': 0.5,
 'boxTarget': 'normal',
 'dx': 0,
 'dy': 0,
 'fillColor': Color(0,0,0,1),
 'fontName': 'Times-Roman',
 'fontSize': 10,
 'height': None,
 'leading': None,
 'leftPadding': 0,
 'maxWidth': None,
 'rightPadding': 0,
 'strokeColor': None,
 'strokeWidth': 0.1,
 'textAnchor': 'start',
 'topPadding': 0,
 'useAscentDescent': False,
 'visible': 1,
 'width': None,
 'x': 0,
 'y': 0}
```

Here is a table that describes the properties that are Label specific:

Chapter 8 - Intro to Graphics and Charts

Property	Meaning
dx	The x displacement of the label
dy	The y displacement of the label
angle	The angle of rotation (counterclockwise) applied to the label
boxAnchor	The label's box anchor, one of 'n', 'e', 'w', 's', 'ne', 'nw', 'se', 'sw'
textAnchor	The place where to anchor the label's text, one of 'start', 'middle', 'end'
boxFillColor	The fill color used in the label's box
boxStrokeColor	The stroke color used in the label's box
boxStrokeWidth	The line width of the label's box
fontName	The font name of the label
fontSize	The font size of the label
leading	The leading value of the label's text lines
x	The X-coordinate of the reference point
y	The Y-coordinate of the reference point
width	The label's width
height	The label's height

Let's take a look at a quick example of creating a Label:

```python
# simple_label.py

from reportlab.graphics import shapes, renderPDF
from reportlab.graphics.charts.textlabels import Label
from reportlab.lib import colors


def simple_label():
    drawing = shapes.Drawing(width=400, height=200)

    drawing.add(shapes.Rect(200, 100, 10, 10, fillColor=colors.red))

    x = 50
    angle = 0
    for item in range(3):
        label = Label()
        label.setOrigin(200, 100)
        label.boxAnchor = 'se'
        label.angle = angle
        #label.boxStrokeColor = colors.black
        label.setText('ReportLab label')
        drawing.add(label)
```

Chapter 8 - Intro to Graphics and Charts

```
        x += 25
        angle += 45

    renderPDF.drawToFile(drawing, 'simple_label.pdf')

if __name__ == '__main__':
    simple_label()
```

Here we create our Drawing object and then add a Rectangle via the **Rect** class. This rectangle will help us mark the origin point for our Label. Next we create 3 **Label** objects. For each Label, we set its origin to the same location and anchor them to *se*, or South-East. Then we set the angle for the Label and the Label's text value. Finally we add it to our Drawing. You will also note that we update the x-position by 25 points and the angle by 45 degrees each iteration. The result will look like this:

Fig. 8-2: An example label

There is also a line of code that was commented out: **label.boxStrokeColor = colors.black**. If you uncomment that, then you will see that ReportLab draws a rectangular box around each of the Labels. I thought this was less visually appealing for this example, so I commented it out.

Feel free to play around with any of these settings and see how it affects the resulting PDF.

Axes

Earlier in this chapter, we learned that ReportLab supports two kinds of axes: *Value* and *Category*. Each of these axes can be either horizontal or vertical. As always, if you need to do something custom, you can easily subclass an Axes.

ReportLab's Axes are used for the following purposes:

Chapter 8 - Intro to Graphics and Charts

- mapping the data to image coordinates
- transforming points on request
- drawing themselves
- drawing tickmarks, gridlines and the axis labels

Let's create a simple demo that shows how you can create some axes:

```
# axes_demo.py

from reportlab.graphics import shapes, renderPDF
from reportlab.graphics.charts.axes import XCategoryAxis, YValueAxis
from reportlab.lib import colors


def axes_demo():
    drawing = shapes.Drawing(width=500, height=300)

    data = [(5, 10, 15, 20),
            (10, 17, 25, 31)]

    x_axis = XCategoryAxis()
    x_axis.setPosition(100, 100, 350)
    x_axis.configure(data, barWidth=None)
    x_axis.categoryNames = ['Python', 'Ruby', 'C++', 'Haskell']
    x_axis.labels.boxAnchor = 'n'
    x_axis.labels[0].angle = 45
    x_axis.labels[0].fontName = 'Times-Bold'
    x_axis.labels[1].fontName = 'Courier'
    x_axis.labels[1].fontSize = 16
    drawing.add(x_axis)

    y_axis = YValueAxis()
    y_axis.setPosition(75, 75, 150)
    y_axis.configure(data)
    drawing.add(y_axis)

    renderPDF.drawToFile(drawing, 'axes_demo.pdf')

if __name__ == '__main__':
    axes_demo()
```

Here we import the **XCategoryAxis** and the **YValueAxis** from **reportlab.graphics.charts.axes**. Alternatively, you could replace those imports with **YCategoryAxis** and **XValueAxis** if you wanted to do something a bit different.

Next we create our **Drawing** object and then we create a list with two tuples in it. We will use these tuples to configure out axes. The first axis that we create is our **XCategoryAxis**. Here we set it's position, configure it with its data, set the category names and set the anchor for the labels. When you configure with the data, you are telling ReportLab to figure out how to position the axis's labels itself. The last few lines for the X axis shows how to configure the first and second labels. For the first label, we change its angle to 45 degrees and its font to **Times-Bold**. Then we set the second label to **Courier** with a font size of 16.

The next step is to create our **YValueAxis**. Then we set its position and configure it the same way we did for the X axis. When you run this example, you should end up with this:

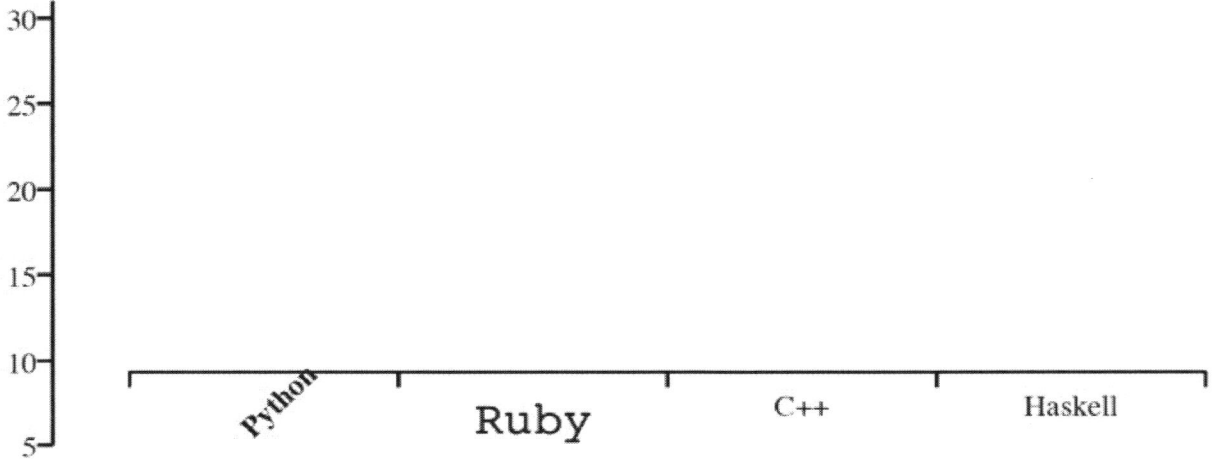

Fig. 8-3: Axes in action

Normally you do not create axes like this though. Instead, you will create a chart or plot and that widget will generate the axes for you.

The **XCategoryAxis** and the **YValueAxis** share some of the same properties. Here is a quick listing of the shared ones:

- **visible** - Display the axis. Occasionally this should be False to still allow the management of scaling the points
- **strokeColor** - The axis's color
- **strokeDashArray** - Determines if the axis should be drawn with a dash and, if so, the type of dash. Default: None
- **strokeWidth** - The axis's width in points
- **title** - An unimplemented property that should be like a Label
- **joinAxis** - Use this to join both axes when set to True
- **joinAxisMode** - The mode to use for connecting the axes ('bottom', 'top', 'left', 'right', 'value', 'points', None)
- **joinAxisPos** - The position to use to join the other axis

Chapter 8 - Intro to Graphics and Charts

The last three properties are all uses for joining the two axes together. ReportLab provides a nice sample of how to use these "joining" properties in *reportlab/graphics/axes.py*.

There is a **joinToAxis(otherAxis, mode, pos)** method that you can also use to join the first axis to the other axis. You will note that it contains **mode** and **pos** parameters that are the same as the ones you would use for **joinAxisMode** and **joinAxisPos** respectively.

Let's take a few minutes to learn a bit more about how each of these axes work specifically.

The XCategoryAxis

The Category Axis divides itself into equally sized "buckets" based on the amount of data given to it. It is a bit simpler to create than a Value axis is. You can set the location of a category axis by using the **setPosition** method that we looked at earlier. The chart you create can also use this method to do the same thing. The next step in creating a Category Axis is to give it some data by calling its **configure** method. You can set the axis's **reversed** attribute to 1 (or True) to tell it to reverse the categories. The **scale** method is used to tell the chart where a given category begins and ends.

Here is a list of the XCategoryAxis's editable properties:

- **tickUp** - Sets how far above the axis the tick marks should protrude. If you make this property equal to the chart's height, then you will have created a grid line
- **tickDown** - Sets how far below the axis the tick marks should protrude
- **categoryNames** - None or a list of strings which should be the same length as the data series
- **labels** - A collection (list, tuple) for the tick marks. Basically it's a list of lists or tuples. The text label defaults to the top center (or 'north'), 5 points down from the center of each of the categories on your axis. You can edit any property of the group of labels or any one label. If **categoryNames** is set to **None**, no labels are drawn.

Now let's learn about the **YValueAxis**.

The YValueAxis

The left axis in your charts is known as the **YValueAxis**. A Value Axis maps data to points along a y value (vertically) in chart space versus the Category Axis, which maps data along the x value plane (horizontally). The **YValueAxis** will configure itself with the data that you give to it. It will also convert Y values to points to help the chart plat correctly.

You can use the **setPosition** and **configure** methods of the Value Axis in the same way that you did for the Category Axis. If you don't set the max, min and tick interval, then when you call **configure()**, the axis will do that for your automatically.

You can use the **scale** method to convert y data values to your drawing space.

The default is that the largest data point will be at the top of the axis and the lowest will be at the bottom. The axis will choose "nice round numbers" to use for it tick marks. You can override any the following properties as you see fit:

- **tickLeft** - Sets how far to the left of the axis the tick marks should protrude. If you make this property equal to the chart's height, then you will have created a grid line
- **tickRight** - Sets how far to the right of the axis the tick marks should protrude
- **valueMin** - The y value that the axis's bottom should be set to. Default is None, which means that the axis sets the minimum to the lowest actual data point.
- **valueMax** - The y value that the axis's top should be set to. Default is None, which means that the axis sets the maximum to the highest actual data point.
- **valueStep** - The change in y between ticks. Defaults to None, so the axis will try to set the step to the best group of "round numbers" which are slightly wider than the **minimumTickSpacing**
- **valueSteps** - A Python list of numbers that describe where to place the tick marks
- **minimumTickSpacing** - Only used when the **valueStep** is set to None. It will be ignored if **valueStep** is set to anything else. You may use this to specify the minimum tick spacing in points.
- **labelTextFormat** - This property determines what will go into the labels. A Value Axis is supposed to use numbers while the Category Axis usually uses strings. You may provide a "format string" or a function that accepts a number and returns a string

Now we can move on and learn how to create charts in ReportLab!

Bar Charts

ReportLab supports several different bar charts. You can create the following:

- VerticalBarChart
- VerticalBarChart3D
- HorizontalBarChart
- HorizontalBarChart3D

Each of these bar charts utilize the Labels and Axes that we learned about in the previous few sections of this chapter. Let's take a look at a simple example:

Chapter 8 - Intro to Graphics and Charts

```python
# simple_bar_chart.py

from reportlab.lib.colors import PCMYKColor
from reportlab.graphics.shapes import Drawing
from reportlab.graphics.charts.barcharts import VerticalBarChart


def simple_bar_chart():
    d = Drawing(280, 250)
    bar = VerticalBarChart()
    bar.x = 50
    bar.y = 85
    data = [[1, 2, 3, None, None, None, 5],
            [10, 5, 2, 6, 8, 3, 5],
            [5, 7, 2, 8, 8, 2, 5],
            [2, 10, 2, 1, 8, 9, 5],
            ]
    bar.data = data
    bar.categoryAxis.categoryNames = ['Year1', 'Year2', 'Year3',
                                      'Year4', 'Year5', 'Year6',
                                      'Year7']

    bar.bars[0].fillColor = PCMYKColor(0,100,100,40,alpha=85)
    bar.bars[1].fillColor = PCMYKColor(23,51,0,4,alpha=85)

    d.add(bar, '')

    d.save(formats=['pdf'], outDir='.', fnRoot='simple_bar_chart')

if __name__ == '__main__':
    simple_bar_chart()
```

Here we import a type of color, **PCMYKColor**, the **Drawing** class and the **VerticalBarChart**. Next we create our Drawing and then instantiate the VerticalBarChart. The rest of the code is pretty much the same as what we learned about in the Label and Axes sections of this chapter. That is until we reach the end, where we see the following:

```python
d.save(formats=['pdf'], outDir='.', fnRoot='simple_bar_chart')
```

Here we just call the Drawing's **save** command and tell it we want to save in PDF format. We also tell it to save it to the folder that the code is run from and we give it a name via the **fnRoot** parameter. If you run this code, you should see the following:

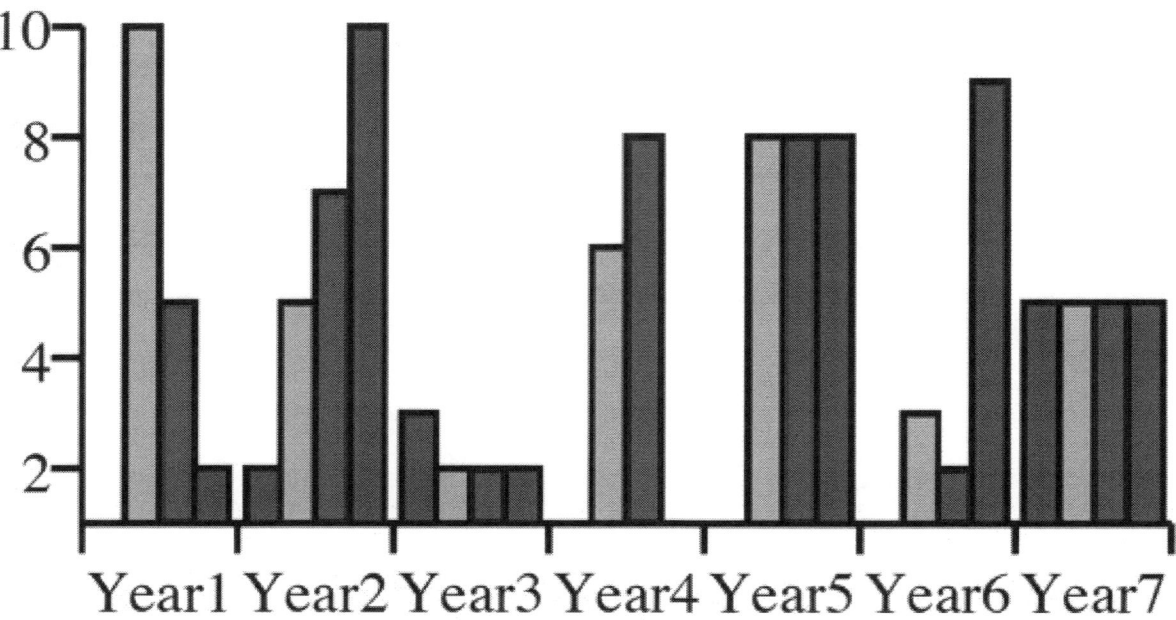

Fig. 8-4: A simple bar chart

You could import the **renderPDF** module and use that instead like this:

```
from reportlab.graphics import renderPDF
renderPDF.drawToFile(d, 'simple_bar_chart.pdf')
```

Or you could just add the chart to a list of Flowables and use a document template to generate your PDF. Here's an example:

```
# simple_bar_chart_flowable.py

from reportlab.lib.colors import PCMYKColor
from reportlab.graphics.shapes import Drawing
from reportlab.graphics.charts.barcharts import VerticalBarChart
from reportlab.platypus import SimpleDocTemplate


def simple_bar_chart_flowable():
    d = Drawing(280, 250)
    bar = VerticalBarChart()
    bar.x = 50
    bar.y = 85
    data = [[1, 2, 3, None, None, None, 5],
```

```
              [10, 5, 2, 6, 8, 3, 5],
              [5, 7, 2, 8, 8, 2, 5],
              [2, 10, 2, 1, 8, 9, 5],
              ]
    bar.data = data
    bar.categoryAxis.categoryNames = ['Year1', 'Year2', 'Year3',
                                      'Year4', 'Year5', 'Year6',
                                      'Year7']

    bar.bars[0].fillColor = PCMYKColor(0,100,100,40,alpha=85)
    bar.bars[1].fillColor = PCMYKColor(23,51,0,4,alpha=85)

    d.add(bar, '')

    doc = SimpleDocTemplate("simple_bar_chart_flowable.pdf"
                            )
    story = []
    story.append(d)
    doc.build(story)

if __name__ == '__main__':
    simple_bar_chart_flowable()
```

Each of these methods is valid. If you want to use a renderer directly, then you may need to adjust the Drawing object's size a bit to better fit your chart.

The **VerticalBarChart** has several top-level properties of its own that deserve some time in the spotlight:

- **data** - A Python list of lists of number or a list of tuples of numbers.
- **x, y, width, height** - These four properties define the "chart rectangle". You must place your chart in your drawing so that it has enough room for its axis labels and ticks.
- **strokeColor** - Used to draw a border around the chart rectangle. Typically used for debugging. Default: None
- **fillColor** - Fill your chart rectangle with a solid color. Default: None
- **useAbsolute** - Defaults to 0. If set to 1, the **barWidth**, **groupSpacing** and **barSpacing** are absolute values in points. When set to 0, these properties use relative quantities and will use proportional widths
- **barWidth** - The width of the bar. Default: 10
- **groupSpacing** - The space between each group of bars. Default: 5. If you have only one series of data, use this property to split them up instead of **barSpacing**
- **barSpacing** - The space between bars in each group. Default: 0

- **barLabelFormat** - Follows the same format as the YValueAxis property. You can use a function or format string for the labels. Defaults to None
- **barLabels** - A collection of labels used for bar's labels. You can use it to apply formatting to all labels.
- **valueAxis** - The value axis (see previous section for formatting information)
- **categoryAxis** - The category axis (see previous section for formatting information)
- **title** - Not implemented

Let's try updating the code a bit so that the chart's labels are angled and the bars are spaced out a bit:

```
# simple_bar_chart_angled_labels.py

from reportlab.lib import colors
from reportlab.graphics.shapes import Drawing
from reportlab.graphics.charts.barcharts import VerticalBarChart
from reportlab.platypus import SimpleDocTemplate


def simple_bar_chart_angled_labels():
    d = Drawing(280, 250)
    bar = VerticalBarChart()
    bar.x = 50
    bar.y = 85
    data = [[1, 2, 3, None, None, None, 5],
            [10, 5, 2, 6, 8, 3, 5],
            [5, 7, 2, 8, 8, 2, 5],
            [2, 10, 2, 1, 8, 9, 5],
            ]
    bar.data = data
    bar.categoryAxis.categoryNames = ['Year1', 'Year2', 'Year3',
                                      'Year4', 'Year5', 'Year6',
                                      'Year7']

    bar.bars[0].fillColor = colors.green
    bar.bars[1].fillColor = colors.blue
    bar.bars[2].fillColor = colors.red
    bar.bars[3].fillColor = colors.purple
    bar.categoryAxis.labels.angle = 45
    bar.categoryAxis.labels.dy = -15
    bar.groupSpacing = 12
    bar.barSpacing = 2
```

Chapter 8 - Intro to Graphics and Charts

```
    d.add(bar, '')

    doc = SimpleDocTemplate('simple_bar_chart_angled_labels.pdf')
    story = []
    story.append(d)
    doc.build(story)

if __name__ == '__main__':
    simple_bar_chart_angled_labels()
```

Here we set all the labels in the chart to a 45 degree angle and we set it's y displacement at -15 points to move the labels away from the axis. You will note that we also updated the bar chart's colors to use just named colors from ReportLab's color module rather than continuing to use **PCMYKColor**. We also update the bar and group spacing via the **barSpacing** and **groupSpacing** properties. When you run this example, your new bar chart should look like this:

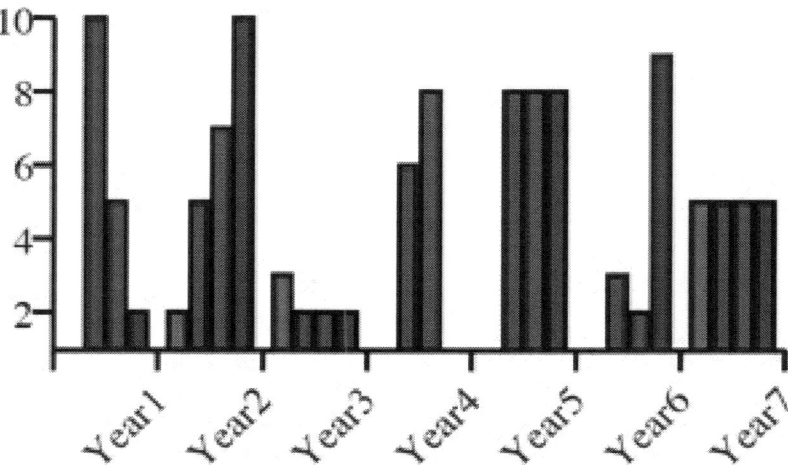

Fig. 8-5: A simple bar chart with angled labels

A bar chart's labels are automatically shown for negative numbers below the lower end of bar and for positive values above the upper end. You can add stacked bars by setting the **categoryAxis**'s **style** attribute to "stacked". Here is some example code:

```python
# simple_stacked_bar_chart.py

from reportlab.lib import colors
from reportlab.graphics.shapes import Drawing
from reportlab.graphics.charts.barcharts import VerticalBarChart
from reportlab.platypus import SimpleDocTemplate


def simple_stacked_bar_chart():
    """
    Creates a bar chart in a PDF
    """
    d = Drawing(280, 250)
    bar = VerticalBarChart()
    bar.x = 50
    bar.y = 85
    data = [[1, 2, 3, None, None, None, 5],
            [10, 5, 2, 6, 8, 3, 5]
            ]
    bar.data = data
    bar.categoryAxis.categoryNames = ['Year1', 'Year2', 'Year3',
                                      'Year4', 'Year5', 'Year6',
                                      'Year7']

    bar.bars[0].fillColor = colors.green
    bar.bars[1].fillColor = colors.blue
    bar.categoryAxis.labels.angle = 45
    bar.categoryAxis.labels.dy = -15
    bar.categoryAxis.style = 'stacked'

    d.add(bar, '')

    doc = SimpleDocTemplate('simple_stacked_bar_chart.pdf')
    story = []
    story.append(d)
    doc.build(story)

if __name__ == '__main__':
    simple_stacked_bar_chart()
```

When you run this code, you should see the following:

Chapter 8 - Intro to Graphics and Charts

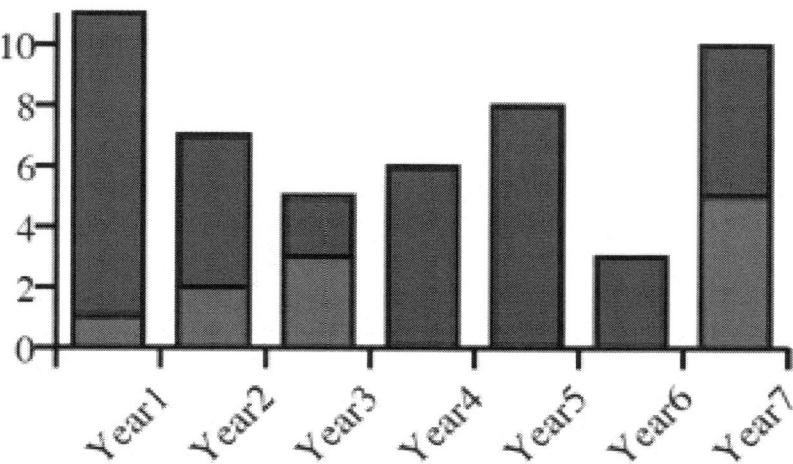

Fig. 8-6: A simple stacked bar chart

Now let's write some code that uses a **VerticalBarChart3D** instead of a **VerticalBarChart** object:

```
# simple_vertical_3d_bar_chart.py

from reportlab.lib import colors
from reportlab.graphics.shapes import Drawing
from reportlab.graphics.charts.barcharts import VerticalBarChart3D
from reportlab.platypus import SimpleDocTemplate


def simple_vertical_3d_bar_chart():
    d = Drawing(280, 250)
    bar = VerticalBarChart3D()
    bar.x = 50
    bar.y = 85
    bar.height = 225
    bar.width = 350
    data = [[1, 2, 3, None, None],
            [10, 5, 2, 6, 8],
            [5, 7, 2, 8, 8],
            [2, 10, 2, 1, 8],
            ]
    bar.data = data
    bar.categoryAxis.categoryNames = ['Year1', 'Year2', 'Year3',
                                      'Year4', 'Year5', 'Year6',
                                      'Year7']
```

```
    bar.bars[0].fillColor = colors.green
    bar.bars[1].fillColor = colors.blue
    bar.bars[2].fillColor = colors.red
    bar.bars[3].fillColor = colors.purple

    bar.categoryAxis.labels.angle = 45
    bar.categoryAxis.labels.dy = -15

    d.add(bar, '')

    doc = SimpleDocTemplate('simple_vertical_3d_bar_chart.pdf')
    story = []
    story.append(d)
    doc.build(story)

if __name__ == '__main__':
    simple_vertical_3d_bar_chart()
```

This code is virtually the same as the last with the exception of switching to a different chart type and updating the chart's width and height. Here is the output:

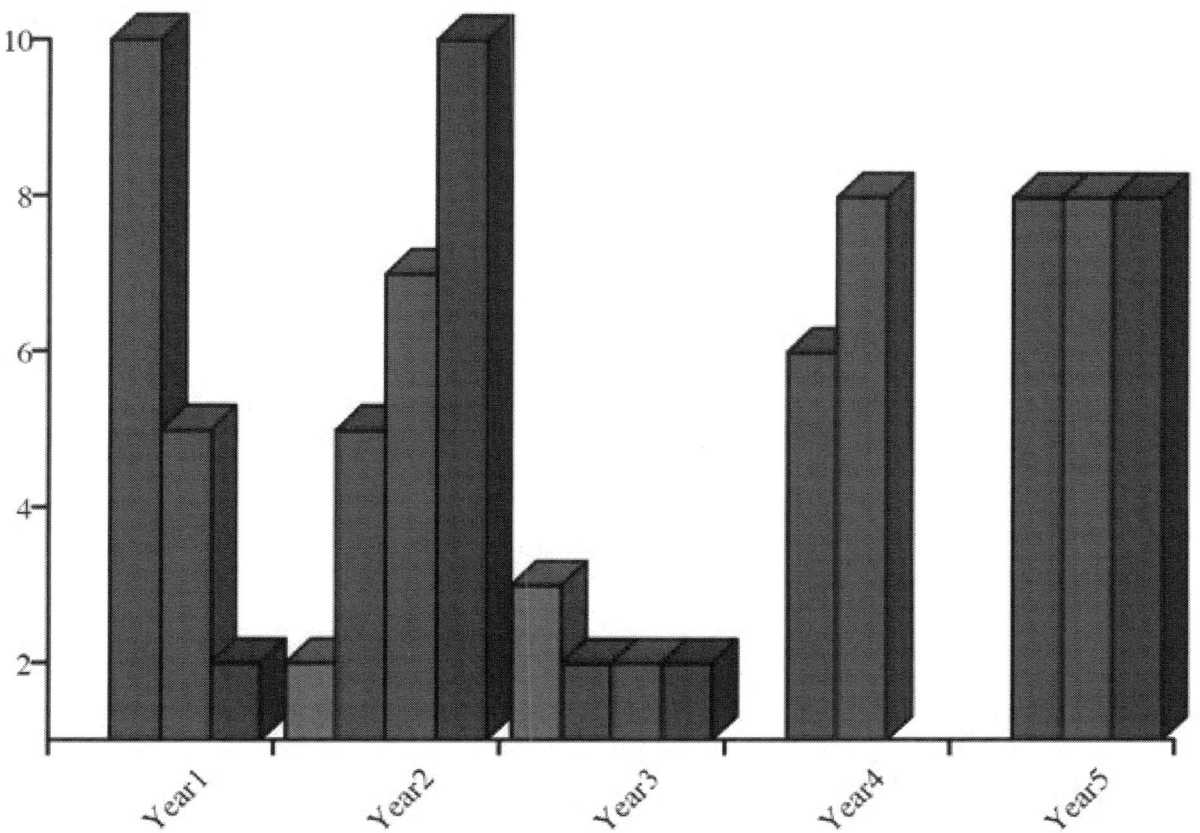

Fig. 8-7: A simple vertical 3D bar chart

Now let's try swapping out the **VerticalBarChart3D** for a **HorizontalBarChart** so we can see how that might look:

```
# simple_horizontal_bar_chart.py

from reportlab.lib import colors
from reportlab.graphics.shapes import Drawing
from reportlab.graphics.charts.barcharts import HorizontalBarChart
from reportlab.platypus import SimpleDocTemplate


def simple_horizontal_bar_chart():
    d = Drawing(280, 250)
    bar = HorizontalBarChart()
    bar.x = 50
    bar.y = 85
    bar.height = 225
```

```python
        bar.width = 250
        data = [[1, 2, 3, None, None],
                [10, 5, 2, 6, 8],
                [5, 7, 2, 8, 8],
                [2, 10, 2, 1, 8],
                ]
        bar.data = data
        bar.categoryAxis.categoryNames = ['Year1', 'Year2', 'Year3',
                                          'Year4', 'Year5', 'Year6',
                                          'Year7']

        bar.bars[0].fillColor = colors.green
        bar.bars[1].fillColor = colors.blue
        bar.bars[2].fillColor = colors.red
        bar.bars[3].fillColor = colors.purple

        bar.categoryAxis.labels.angle = 45
        bar.categoryAxis.labels.dx = -15

        d.add(bar, '')

        doc = SimpleDocTemplate('simple_horizontal_bar_chart.pdf')
        story = []
        story.append(d)
        doc.build(story)

if __name__ == '__main__':
    simple_horizontal_bar_chart()
```

The primary difference between a **HorizontalBarChart** and a **VerticalBarChart** is the orientation of the chart. Otherwise they are basically the same. Here's the new chart:

Chapter 8 - Intro to Graphics and Charts

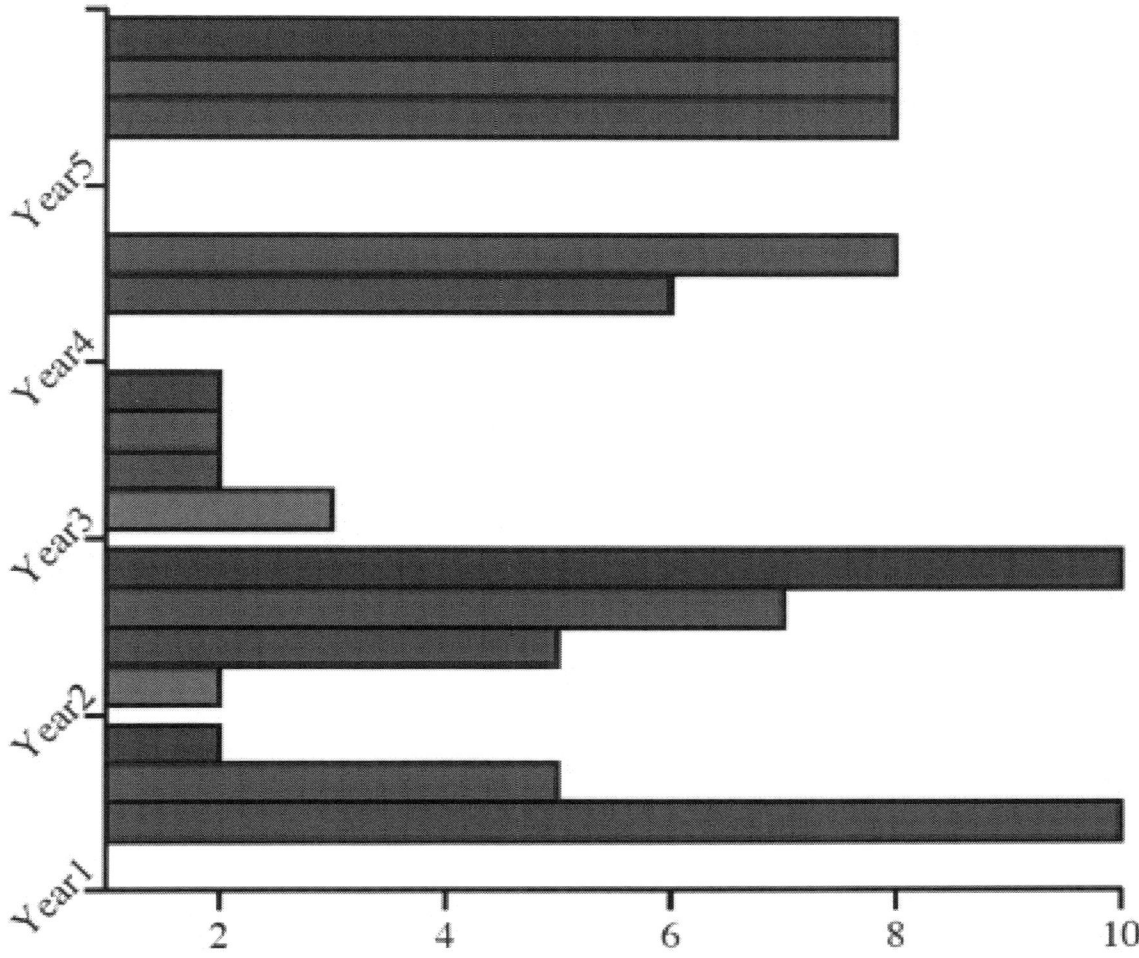

Fig. 8-8: A simple horizontal bar chart

Now let's learn how we can create a line chart.

Line Charts

A Line Chart in ReportLab is basically the same as their Bar Chart except that they are drawn with lines. The Line and Bar charts both use Category and Value axes whereas Line Plots use two *Value* axes. You can modify the following properties of a Line Chart:

Property	Meaning
data	The data to be plotted (list of lists of numbers)
x, y, width, height	The rectangle around the line chart. Note: x/y specify the bottom left corner
valueAxis	The value axis (see axes section)
categoryAxis	The category axis (see axes section)
strokeColor	If set, it will draw a border around the plot. Default is None. Axes will overwrite this
fillColor	If set, it will fill the plot's rectangle with a solid color. Default is None
lines.strokeColor	The color of the line
lines.strokeWidth	The width of the line
lineLabels	A collection (i.e. 2-dimensional array) of labels used for formatting
lineLabelFormat	Default is None. You may supply a function or format string to format the labels. You may also pass it "values" to display the array you supply to **lineLabelArray**
lineLabelArray	An explicit list of line label values that must match the size of the data provided. Only shown if **lineLabelFormat** is set to "values"

Let's try creating our own Line Chart by using the **HorizontalLineChart** class:

```
# simple_line_chart.py

from reportlab.lib import colors
from reportlab.graphics.shapes import Drawing
from reportlab.graphics.charts.linecharts import HorizontalLineChart
from reportlab.platypus import SimpleDocTemplate


def simple_line_chart():
    d = Drawing(280, 250)
    line = HorizontalLineChart()
    line.x = 50
    line.y = 85
    line.height = 150
    line.width = 250

    data = [[1, 2, 3, None, None, None, 5],
```

```
            [10, 5, 2, 6, 8, 3, 5]
            ]
    line.data = data
    line.categoryAxis.categoryNames = [
        'Dogs', 'Cats', 'Mice', 'Hamsters',
        'Parakeets', 'Gerbils', 'Fish'
    ]

    line.lines[0].strokeColor = colors.green
    line.lines[1].strokeColor = colors.blue
    line.lines[0].strokeWidth = 3
    line.categoryAxis.labels.angle = 45
    line.categoryAxis.labels.dy = -15

    d.add(line, '')

    doc = SimpleDocTemplate('simple_line_chart.pdf')
    story = []
    story.append(d)
    doc.build(story)

if __name__ == '__main__':
    simple_line_chart()
```

Here we import a **HorizontalLineChart** from **reportlab.graphics.charts.linecharts**. Most of the code is the same as what we saw in our Bar Chart examples. The main differences here is that when we want to set the line colors, we need to set **strokeColor** as **fillColor** doesn't exist for a line in a Line Chart. We can also set out **strokeWidth**, which will change the width of the line that it is applied to. This is the chart we end up with:

Chapter 8 - Intro to Graphics and Charts   170

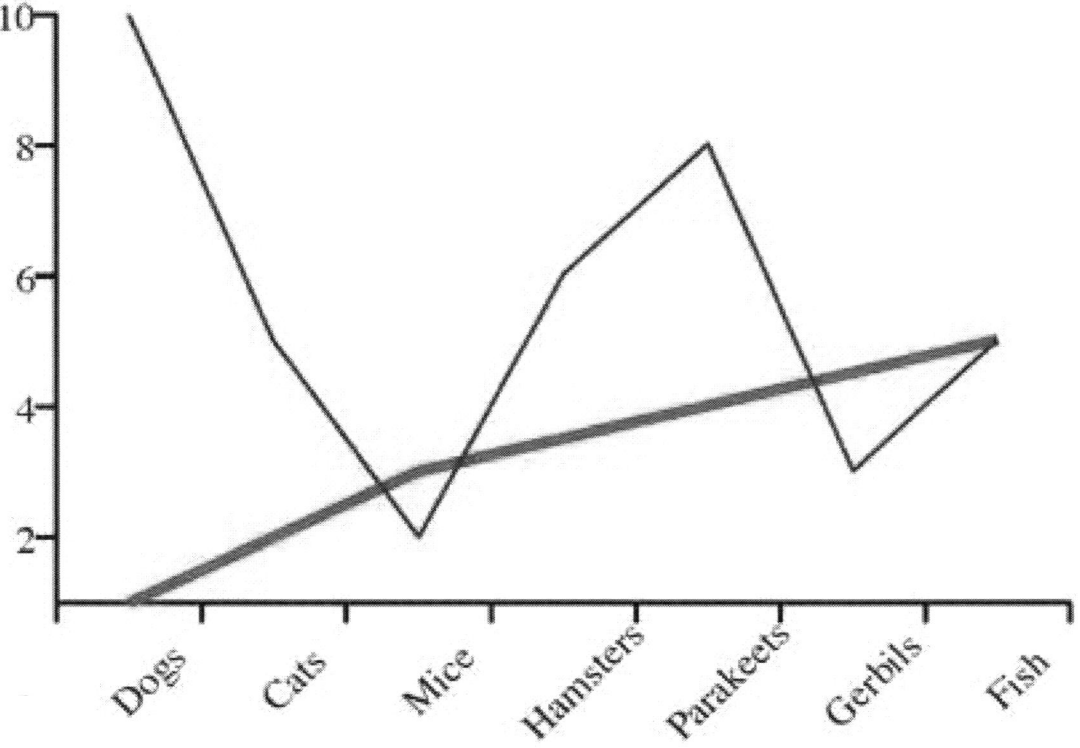

Fig. 8-9: A simple line chart

The other Line Chart that you might want to create is the 3D version of the above. To do that, just import **HorizontalLineChart3D** and use that instead of **HorizontalLineChart**. If you do that, then the result would look like this:

Chapter 8 - Intro to Graphics and Charts

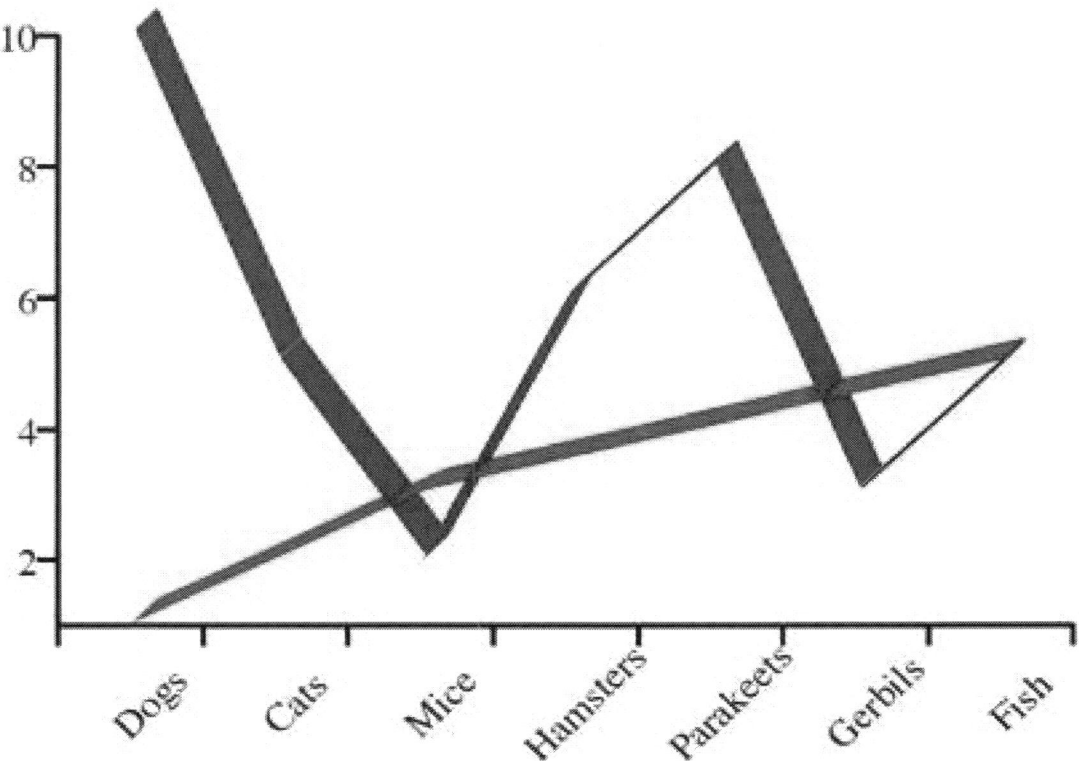

Fig. 8-10: A simple 3D line chart

There are some sample charts you can also import and play around with from the following:

- **reportlab.graphics.charts.linecharts**

There is also a **VerticalLineChart** sub-class, but it appears to be a stub and doesn't actually work when instantiated directly.

Line Plots

A Line Plot is slightly different than a Line Chart. It has two Value Axes instead of a Value Axis and a Category Axis, for example. They also have an "experimental" feature in that you can place line markers at each data point on the plot. Here is a listing of the various properties you can edit in your Line Plots:

Property	Meaning
data	The data to be plotted (list of lists of numbers)
x, y, width, height	The rectangle around the line chart. Note: x/y specify the bottom left corner
xValueAxis	The vertical value axis which can be formatted as seen in the axes section
yValueAxis	The vertical value axis which can be formatted as seen in the axes section
strokeColor	If set, it will draw a border around the plot. Default is None. Axes will overwrite this
strokeWidth	If set, this will be the width of the plot's border
fillColor	If set, it will fill the plot's rectangle with a solid color. Default is None
lines.strokeColor	The color of the line
lines.strokeWidth	The width of the line
lines.symbol	The marker used for each point in the line. You can create a marker via **makeMarker()**
lineLabels	A collection (i.e. 2-dimensional array) of labels used for formatting
lineLabelFormat	Default is None. You may supply a function or format string to format the labels. You may also pass it "values" to display the array you supply to **lineLabelArray**
lineLabelArray	An explicit list of line label values that must match the size of the data provided. Only shown if **lineLabelFormat** is set to "values"

Now let's try actually creating a Line Plot so we can visually see how they differ from a Line Chart:

```
# line_plot_demo.py

from reportlab.lib import colors
from reportlab.graphics.shapes import Drawing
from reportlab.graphics.charts.lineplots import LinePlot
from reportlab.graphics.widgets.markers import makeMarker


def line_plot_demo():
    d = Drawing(400, 400)
    line = LinePlot()
    line.x = 50
```

```python
    line.y = 85
    line.height = 150
    line.width = 250
    line.lineLabelFormat = '%2.0f'

    data = [
        ((1,1), (2,2), (2.5,1), (3,3), (4,5)),
        ((1,2), (2,3), (2.5,2), (3.5,5), (4,6))
    ]
    line.data = data

    line.lines[0].strokeColor = colors.green
    line.lines[1].strokeColor = colors.blue
    line.lines[0].strokeWidth = 3

    line.lines[0].symbol = makeMarker('Circle')
    line.lines[1].symbol = makeMarker('Hexagon')

    line.xValueAxis.valueMin = 0
    line.xValueAxis.valueMax = 10
    line.xValueAxis.valueSteps = [1, 2, 4]
    line.xValueAxis.labelTextFormat = '%2.1f'

    line.yValueAxis.valueMin = 0
    line.yValueAxis.valueMax = 12

    d.add(line, '')
    d.save(formats=['pdf'], outDir='.', fnRoot='line_plot_demo')


if __name__ == '__main__':
    line_plot_demo()
```

When you run this code, you will see the following output:

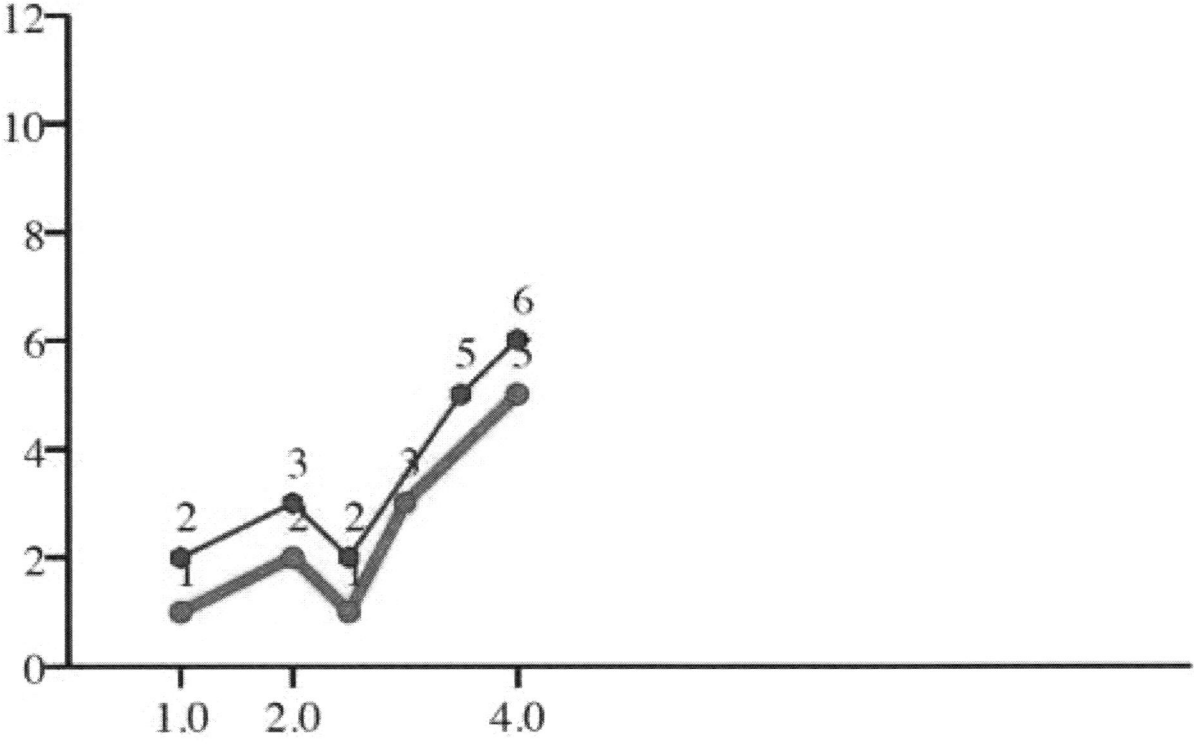

Fig. 8-11: A simple line plot

As you can see, this plot has markers (i.e. dots) that mark each data point on the plot. If you look closely, you will notice that the green line had circle markers while the blue line has hexagon shaped markers. You can set your marker shape to any of the following values:

'Square', 'Diamond', 'Circle', 'Cross', 'Triangle', 'StarSix', 'Pentagon', 'Hexagon', 'Heptagon', 'Octagon', 'StarFive', 'FilledSquare', 'FilledCircle', 'FilledDiamond', 'FilledCross', 'FilledTriangle','FilledStarSix', 'FilledPentagon', 'FilledHexagon', 'FilledHeptagon', 'FilledOctagon', 'FilledStarFive', 'Smiley','ArrowHead', 'FilledArrowHead'

Now let's move on and learn about making pie charts!

Pie Charts

ReportLab also supports the creation of Pie charts. Personally I find their pie charts to be the most fun of the bunch. Let's start off with a pie property list. You will notice that this table also shows what properties you can edit for the pie slices too:

Property	Meaning
data	A list or tuple of numbers that will go in your chart
x, y, width, height	The rectangle around the pie chart. Note: x/y specify the bottom left corner Note: The width and height do not have to be the same. Pies may be elliptical
labels	None or a list of strings. It is recommended that you leave this set to None and put the labels in a Legend object instead for readability
startAngle	The start angle of the first pie slice. Default is 90 or twelve o'clock
direction	The direction the pie slices progress in. Default is 'clockwise'
sideLabels	This will create a chart with labels in two columns, one per side
sideLabelsOffset	A fraction of the width of the pie that determines the horizontal distance between the pie itself and the column of labels
simpleLabels	Defaults to 1. Set to 0 if you want to enable custom labels and properties
slices	A collection of wedges that allows you to customize each slice
slices.strokeWidth	The border width of a slice
slices.strokeColor	The color of the border of a slice
slices.strokeDashArray	Solid a dashed lines
slices.popout	Distance that the slice(s) stick out from the pie's center. Default is 0
slices.fontName	The slice label's font name
slices.fontSize	The slice label's font size
slices.fontColor	The slice label's font color
slices.labelRadius	The anchor point for the slice's text label. This is a fraction of the radius of the pie

These should be pretty self-explanatory. Let's create a super simple pie chart so you can see how easy they are to create:

```
# simple_pie_chart.py

from reportlab.graphics.charts.piecharts import Pie
from reportlab.graphics.shapes import Drawing

def simple_pie_chart():
    data = [10, 20, 30, 40]
    drawing = Drawing()
    pie = Pie()

    pie.x = 150
    pie.y = 65
    pie.data = data
    pie.labels = [letter for letter in 'abcd']
    pie.slices.strokeWidth = 0.5
    pie.slices[3].popout = 20
    pie.slices[3].strokeDashArray = [1,1]
    drawing.add(pie)
    drawing.save(formats=['pdf'], outDir='.', fnRoot='simple_pie_chart')

if __name__ == '__main__':
    simple_pie_chart()
```

Here we import the **Pie** class from **reportlab.graphics.charts.piecharts**. Then we set its position and add some data. Next we set the labels for each wedge of the pie. Then we set the wedge's **strokeWidth** and which wedge will be "popped out", which in this case is the 4th slice. You will note that to access slices, we have to use the **slices** property. Finally we set the **strokeDashArray**, add the chart to our drawing and then save it to disk. You should end up with the following chart:

Chapter 8 - Intro to Graphics and Charts

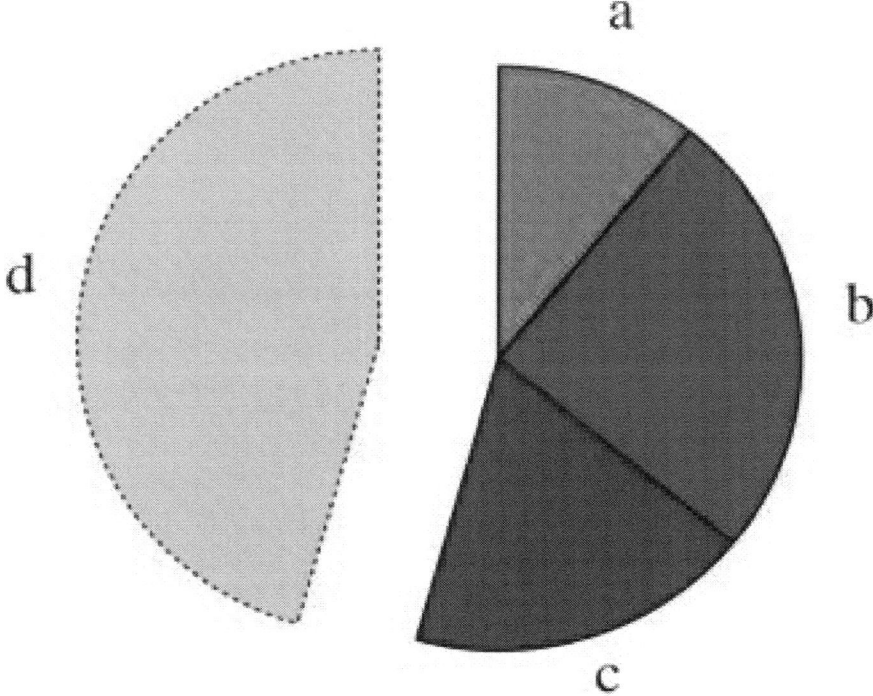

Fig. 8-12: A simple pie chart

Customizing Pie Chart Labels

ReportLab allows you to customize a pie chart's labels. If you want to enable customization of said labels, then you must set your pie instance's **simplesLabels** to zero:

```
pie.simpleLabels = 0
```

Now let's look at an example that does some minor label customization:

```
# simple_pie_chart_label_customization.py

from reportlab.graphics.charts.piecharts import Pie
from reportlab.graphics.shapes import Drawing

def simple_pie_chart_label_customization():
    data = [10, 20, 30, 40]
    drawing = Drawing()
    pie = Pie()
```

```python
    pie.x = 150
    pie.y = 65
    pie.data = data
    pie.labels = [letter for letter in 'abcd']

    # enable label customization
    pie.simpleLabels = 0

    # add some customization
    pie.slices[0].label_angle = 45
    pie.slices[0].label_text = 'foobar'

    # normal pie properties
    pie.slices.strokeWidth = 0.5
    pie.slices[3].popout = 20
    pie.slices[3].strokeDashArray = [1,1]
    drawing.add(pie)
    drawing.save(formats=['pdf'], outDir='.',
                 fnRoot='simple_pie_chart_label_customization')

if __name__ == '__main__':
    simple_pie_chart_label_customization()
```

This will change the first label to have a 45 degree angle and it will also change its text to "foobar". When you run this example, you will see that our new pie chart looks like this:

Chapter 8 - Intro to Graphics and Charts

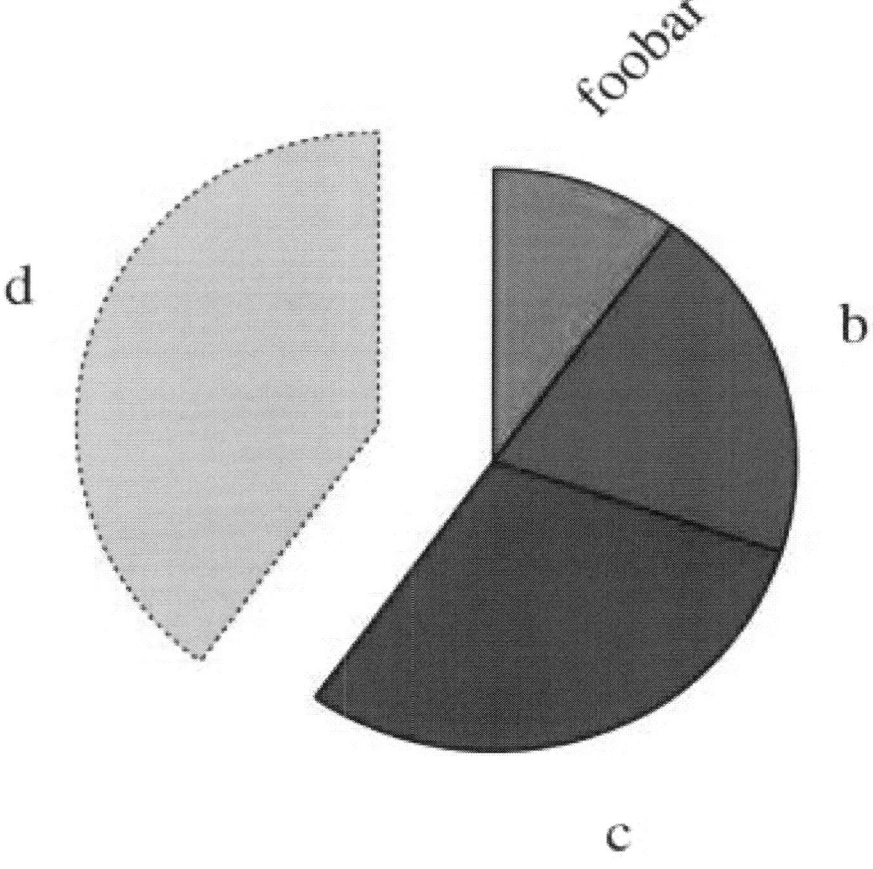

Fig. 8-13: **A simple pie chart with label customization**

Here is a listing of all the properties you can change for the labels:

Property	Meaning
label_dx	The X offset of the label
label_dy	The Y offset of the label
label_angle	The angle of the label. Default is 0 (horizontal), 90 is vertical and 180 is upside down
label_boxAnchor	The label's anchor point
label_boxStrokeColor	The label box's border color
label_boxStrokeWidth	The label box's border width
label_boxFillColor	The label box's filling color
label_strokeColor	The label's border color
label_strokeWidth	The label's border width

Property	Meaning
label_text	The label's text
label_width	The label's width
label_maxWidth	The label's maximum width that it can grow into
label_height	The label's height
label_textAnchor	The label's maximum height that it can grow into
label_visible	Whether or not the label will be drawn (visible)
label_topPadding	The top padding of the box
label_leftPadding	The left padding of the box
label_rightPadding	The right padding of the box
label_bottomPadding	The bottom padding of the box
label_simple_pointer	Enables simple pointers if set to 1
label_pointer_strokeColor	The color of the indicator line
label_pointer_strokeWidth	The width of the indicator line

Pie Chart Side Labels

ReportLab pie charts also have the concept of "side labels". These are labels that have a line drawn from the label to the slice that they correspond to. You can enable side labels like this:

```
pie.sideLabels = True
```

The anchor for the side label's right hand side is set to "start" while the label's left hand side is set to "end". The distance from the pie's edge to the label can be set via the **sideLabelsOffset** attribute. It is a fraction of the width of the pie. Finally, you can change the **xradius** in such a way that the pie overlaps the labels, so it is recommended that you just set xradius to **None**.

Let's modify our previous pie chart example to add some side labels:

Chapter 8 - Intro to Graphics and Charts

```python
# simple_pie_chart_side_labels.py

from reportlab.graphics.charts.piecharts import Pie
from reportlab.graphics.shapes import Drawing

def simple_pie_chart_side_labels():
    data = list(range(15, 105, 15))
    drawing = Drawing()
    pie = Pie()
    pie.sideLabels = True

    pie.x = 150
    pie.y = 65

    pie.data = data
    pie.labels = [letter for letter in 'abcdefg']
    pie.slices.strokeWidth = 0.5
    drawing.add(pie)
    drawing.save(formats=['pdf'], outDir='.',
                 fnRoot='simple_pie_chart_side_labels')

if __name__ == '__main__':
    simple_pie_chart_side_labels()
```

Here we set the **sideLabels** property to **True** and increase the amount of data and labels. Then we run the code and we get this:

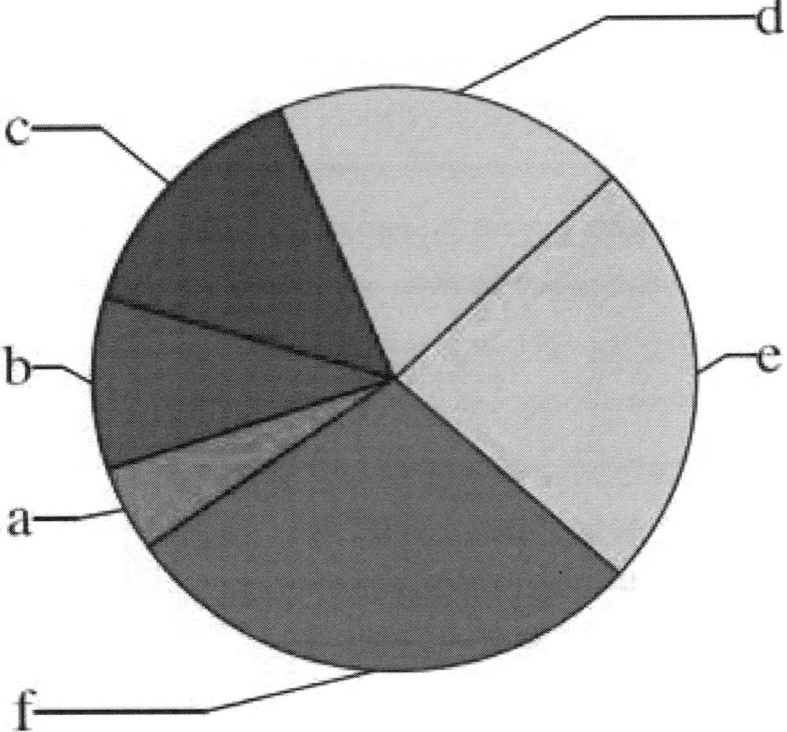

Fig. 8-14: **A simple pie chart with side labels**

This looks pretty good. However there are some known issues with using side labels. The main two mentioned in the ReportLab user guide is that if you have too many slices in your pie chart, the side label's pointers will cross over each other and become difficult to follow. The other issue is that labels can also overlap each other, making them difficult to read, even if you have the **checkLabelOverlap** set.

Adding Titles and Legends

There are a couple of items missing from our charts: a title and a legend. We could easily add a title using the String class from **reportlab.graphics.shapes**. Let's take a look:

Chapter 8 - Intro to Graphics and Charts

```python
# simple_pie_chart_with_title.py

from reportlab.graphics.charts.piecharts import Pie
from reportlab.graphics.shapes import Drawing, String

def simple_pie_chart_with_title():
    data = list(range(15, 105, 15))
    drawing = Drawing(width=400, height=200)
    my_title = String(170, 40, 'My Pie Chart', fontSize=14)
    pie = Pie()
    pie.sideLabels = True

    pie.x = 150
    pie.y = 65

    pie.data = data
    pie.labels = [letter for letter in 'abcdefg']
    pie.slices.strokeWidth = 0.5
    drawing.add(my_title)
    drawing.add(pie)
    drawing.save(formats=['pdf'], outDir='.',
                 fnRoot='simple_pie_chart_with_title')

if __name__ == '__main__':
    simple_pie_chart_with_title()
```

Here we import the String class and instantiate it. The rest is pretty much the same as our previous pie chart code. When you run this, you get the following:

Chapter 8 - Intro to Graphics and Charts

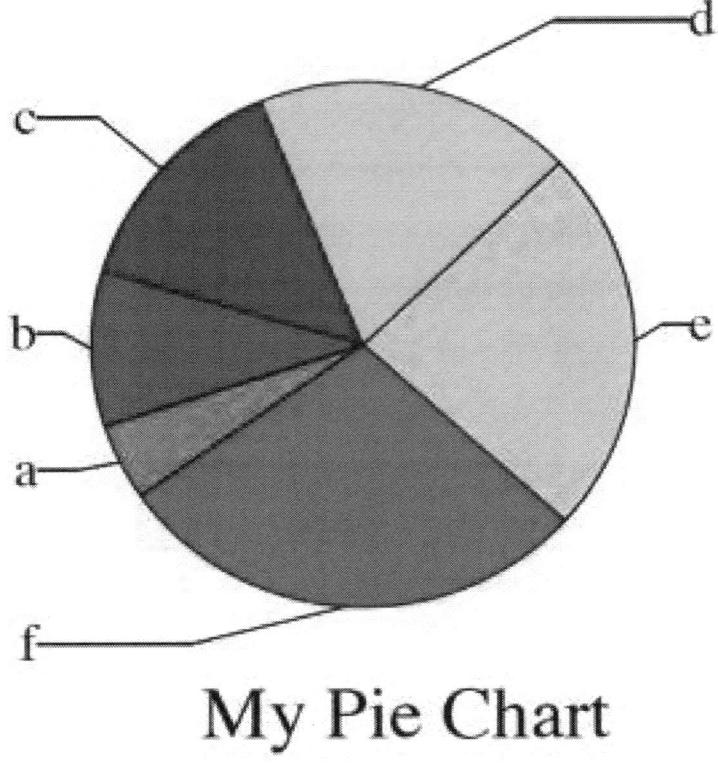

Fig. 8-15: A simple pie chart with a title

If you'd like to add a Legend, then you will want to import it from the **reportlab.graphics.charts.legends** sub-module. Let's take a look:

```
# pie_chart_with_legend.py

from reportlab.lib.validators import Auto
from reportlab.graphics.charts.legends import Legend
from reportlab.graphics.charts.piecharts import Pie
from reportlab.graphics.shapes import Drawing, String


def pie_chart_with_legend():
    data = list(range(15, 105, 15))
    drawing = Drawing(width=400, height=200)
    my_title = String(170, 40, 'My Pie Chart', fontSize=14)
    pie = Pie()
    pie.sideLabels = True

    pie.x = 150
```

Chapter 8 - Intro to Graphics and Charts

```python
        pie.y = 65

        pie.data = data
        pie.labels = [letter for letter in 'abcdefg']
        pie.slices.strokeWidth = 0.5
        drawing.add(my_title)
        drawing.add(pie)
        add_legend(drawing, pie, data)
        drawing.save(formats=['pdf'], outDir='.',
                     fnRoot='pie_chart_with_legend')


def add_legend(draw_obj, chart, data):
    legend = Legend()
    legend.alignment = 'right'
    legend.x = 10
    legend.y = 70
    legend.colorNamePairs = Auto(obj=chart)
    draw_obj.add(legend)


if __name__ == '__main__':
    pie_chart_with_legend()
```

Here we use the same code we were using before with some minor modifications The big one is that we now have an **add_legend** function that takes a Drawing object, the Chart object and the data we populated the chart with. In said function, we instantiate the Legend, set its alignment and its position. We also set up the **colorNamePairs**, which basically just syncs up the colors of the chart with the Legend via the **Auto** validator. Here is what it looks like:

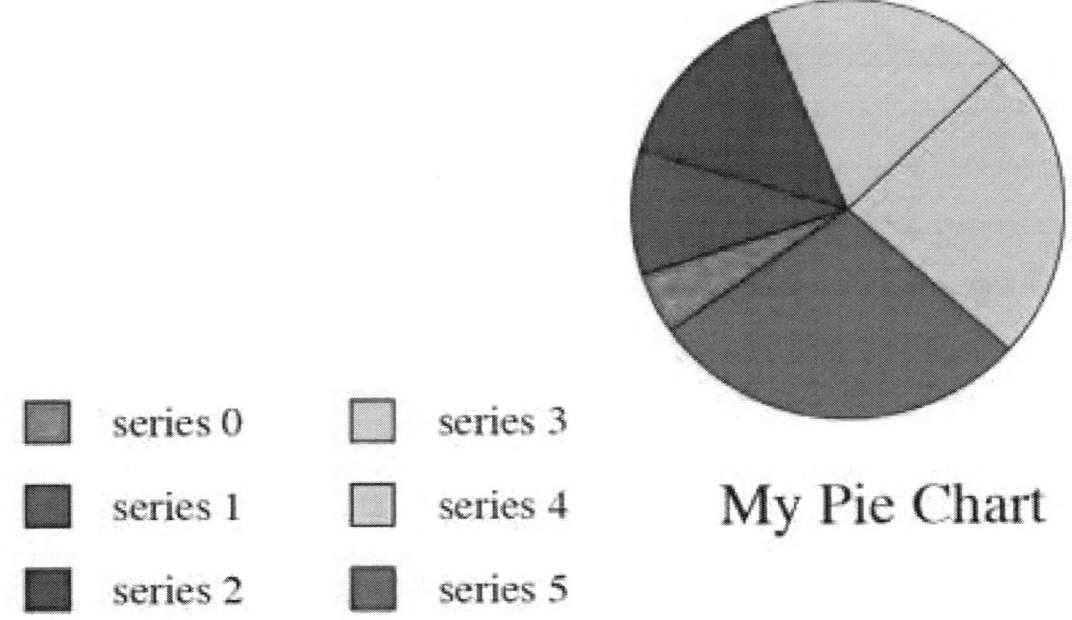

Fig. 8-16: A simple pie chart with a title and legend

According to the documentation, there is still a lot of work to be done to the Legend class to make it support all the charts correctly. There are also some issues with color specification.

Odds and Ends

While ReportLab doesn't currently support X-Y Plots out of the box, they do seem confident that you can use the tools in the Graphics module to create your own. They also provide the tools you need to generate your own markers and custom shapes such that you could create your own chart widget fairly easily.

You can also combine charts in the same drawing, creating fairly complex charts.

There are several other chart classes that are not covered in this chapter. In fact, the Graphics sub module is in flux so the best way to see a full list is to run **graphdoc.py**. You can run this utility with the **-h** flag to learn how to use it to.

Wrapping Up

This chapter covered a lot of ground. You should now have the knowledge to create your drawings as well as create basic charts. We learned how to create Labels, Axes, and Legends as well as how to modify each of them. We also learned how to generate bar charts, line charts, line plots and pie charts.

If you need other types of charts that ReportLab does not, you can generate a lot of other graphs using matplotlib, Bokeh, pygal or one of the other many 3rd party visualization libraries.

Chapter 9 - Other Graphics

There are some other modules in the Graphics sub-module that I think are also worth learning about. While we won't dive into every single facet within the Graphics sub-module, I want to make sure that you know about as much of the Graphics sub-library can be reasonably covered. With that said, in this chapter we will be learning about the following:

- Shapes
- Widgets
- Bar codes

Let's get started!

Shapes

Shapes are the building blocks that we use to create any output from ReportLab's Graphics library. Each Drawing that you create is generated using shapes. You can create anything that you can imagine just by taking the primitive shapes and combining them in different ways. This is actually how the charts that we created in the previous chapter are created. If you open up **shapes.py** in the ReportLab source code, you can see what primitive shapes are available for your use. Here's a listing:

- Circle
- Group
- Ellipse
- Line
- PolyLine
- Polygon
- Rect
- String
- Wedge (pie slice)

We actually showed how to use a couple of these in the previous chapter. The following example is a demonstration of how to create solid shapes:

Chapter 9 - Other Graphics

 # solid_shapes.py

```python
from reportlab.lib import colors
from reportlab.graphics.shapes import Drawing
from reportlab.graphics.shapes import Rect, Ellipse, Circle
from reportlab.graphics.shapes import Wedge, Polygon

def solid_shapes():
    drawing = Drawing(width=400, height=200)

    rectangle = Rect(10, 10, 100, 100)
    rectangle.fillColor = colors.blue
    drawing.add(rectangle)

    ellipse = Ellipse(100, 50, 50, 25)
    ellipse.fillColor = colors.red
    drawing.add(ellipse)

    circle = Circle(50, 170, 25)
    circle.fillColor = colors.green
    drawing.add(circle)

    wedge = Wedge(150, 150, 65,
                  startangledegrees=0,
                  endangledegrees=45)
    wedge.fillColor = colors.yellow
    drawing.add(wedge)

    poly = Polygon(points=[250, 150,
                           280, 150,
                           280, 100,
                           250, 100
                           ])
    poly.fillColor = colors.purple
    drawing.add(poly)

    drawing.save(formats=['pdf'], outDir='.', fnRoot='solid_shapes')

if __name__ == '__main__':
    solid_shapes()
```

Here we create a circle, ellipse, polygon, rectangle and wedge. The **Rect** class requires x and y coordinates as well as width and height. The **Ellipse** takes arguments called cx, cy, rx and ry. The cx/cy values are the x and y positions of the center of the ellipse. The rx/ry values are the x and y radius respectively. The **Circle** is similar to the Ellipse in that it also has cx/cy values, but only requires one radius argument, which is the 3rd one.

The **Wedge** class takes an x, y and radius for its first three parameters. Then we also set the beginning and ending angles of the wedge in degrees. Finally we get to our **Polygon**. It just takes a series of points where the total must be an even amount. The reason is that this is a series of x and y coordinates, which I tried to make more obvious using whitespace in the example above. In this case, we drew a rectangle, but you could draw any number of points to create whatever polygon you want to.

Here is the result of running the code:

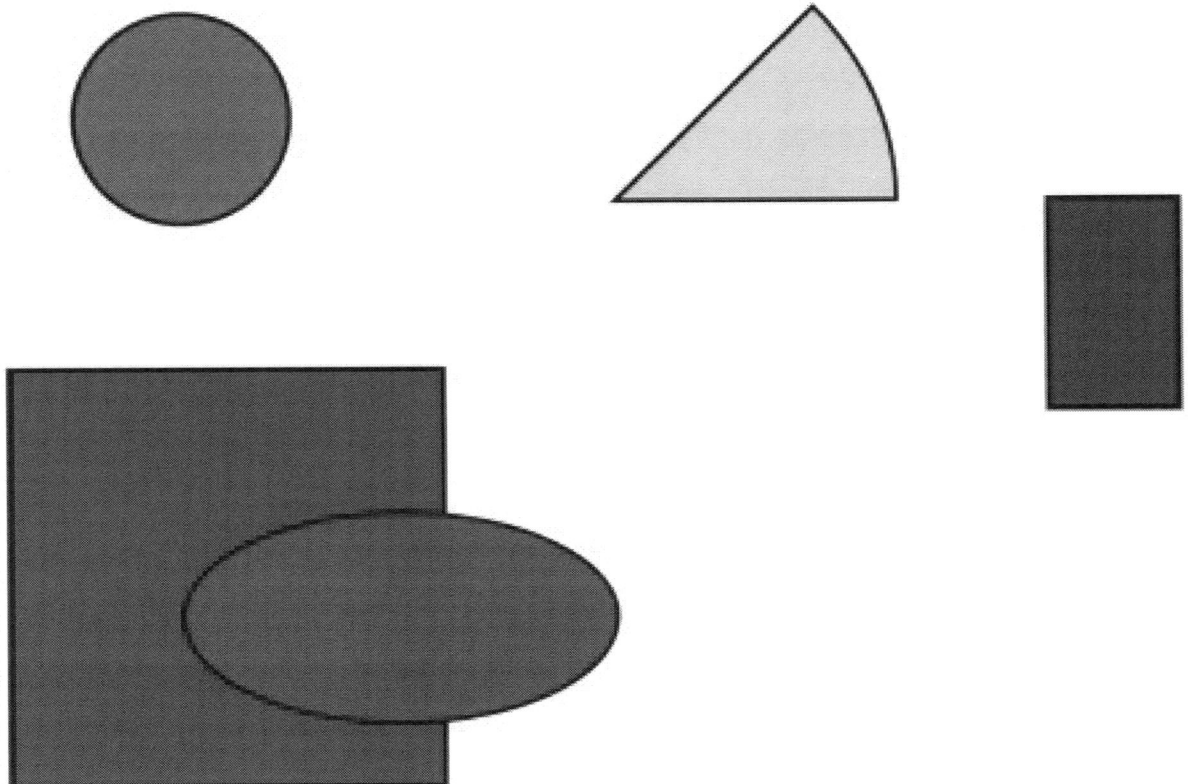

Fig. 9-1: Solid shapes

Now let's learn a bit more about the properties of your shapes.

Properties of a Shape

All shapes have two kinds of properties: those that define their geometry and those that define their style.

Chapter 9 - Other Graphics

Most shapes have some required geometric properties that you have to set for the shape to be drawn. For example, if you want to draw a **Circle**, then you must set the circle's center x/y coordinates and its radius. For a **Rect**, you need to set its x/y start position, which is the bottom left position that it should start at. You must also define a Rect's width and height.

The other properties can be set either on separate lines in your code or as optional arguments when instantiating the shape. The optional properties come with good defaults, so it's not a problem if you end up not setting some of them.

The style properties are as follows:

- fillColor - what color to fill the shape with
- stroke - the edge of the shape (i.e. border)
- strokeColor - the color of the stroke (border)
- strokeWidth - the width of the stroke

Let's take a look at a quick example:

```python
# circle_demo.py

from reportlab.graphics.shapes import Circle, Drawing
from reportlab.lib import colors


def create_circle():
    drawing = Drawing(width=400, height=200)
    circle = Circle(50, 170, 25)
    circle.fillColor = colors.green
    circle.strokeColor = colors.red
    circle.strokeWidth = 5
    drawing.add(circle)

    drawing.save(formats=['pdf'], outDir='.', fnRoot='circle')

if __name__ == '__main__':
    create_circle()
```

When you run this code, you should get the following:

Fig. 9-2: Circle properties

If you would like to see a full listing of the properties that you can change, then you can call the shape's **dumpProperties** method. Here is an example:

```
>>> from reportlab.graphics.shapes import Circle
>>> circle = Circle(10, 10, 100)
>>> circle.dumpProperties()
cx = 10
cy = 10
fillColor = Color(0,0,0,1)
fillOpacity = None
r = 100
strokeColor = Color(0,0,0,1)
strokeDashArray = None
strokeLineCap = 0
strokeLineJoin = 0
strokeMiterLimit = 0
strokeOpacity = None
strokeWidth = 1
```

There are some other properties, like setting a dash pattern or a feature you can use to tell ReportLab what should happen when a line turns a corner, but these properties are used less often or rarely. All of the solid shapes have the same style properties.

Lines

ReportLab gives you the ability to draw Lines and PolyLines. These Line classes have all the **stroke** properties that the other shapes have, but since they are lines, they do not have the **fillColor** property.

Let's take a look at how we can use these classes:

```python
# line_demo.py

from reportlab.graphics.shapes import Line, PolyLine
from reportlab.graphics.shapes import Drawing
from reportlab.lib import colors


def line_demo():
    drawing = Drawing(width=400, height=200)
    line = Line(25, 25, 150, 150)
    line.strokeColor = colors.red
    line.strokeWidth = 5
    drawing.add(line)

    points = [25,50, 35,100, 100,50, 150,150]
    poly = PolyLine(points=points,
                    strokeWidth=3,
                    strokeColor=colors.blue)
    drawing.add(poly)

    drawing.save(formats=['pdf'], outDir='.', fnRoot='line_demo')

if __name__ == '__main__':
    line_demo()
```

As you might have guessed, for a Line you just need to pass in the first x/y coordinate and a second x/y coordinate and then ReportLab will connect the dots. We also set the color of the line along with its width.

Next we create a PolyLine, which uses a series of x/y coordinates in the same manner than the Polygon class did. In this example, we set the width and the color as parameters, but you could have set those properties the same way that we did for the Line example. The result of running this example looks like this:

Fig. 9-3: A Line and a PolyLine

Strings

The Graphics package does not have robust support for fancy text layout. However you can easily add strings anywhere in your drawing using x/y coordinates and you can align the text to the right, left or center. We actually used a String shape near the end of the previous chapter to create a title for our charts.

Here is a simple example that creates a String object and then dumps the properties so we can see what we can edit:

```
>>> from reportlab.graphics.shapes import String
>>> my_string = String(50, 50, "Python is amazing!")
>>> my_string.dumpProperties()
fillColor = Color(0,0,0,1)
fontName = Times-Roman
fontSize = 10
text = Python is amazing!
textAnchor = start
x = 50
y = 50
```

This shows us that there is a **textAnchor** property that we can set. The valid values are 'start', 'middle' and 'end'. What this means is that if you set it to 'start', then the x and y will relate to where the string starts. You can use the anchor to align your text, in other words.

Chapter 9 - Other Graphics

The font standard for strings is Type 1 fonts. If you remember way back in chapter 2, we talked about the 14 fonts that ReportLab supports by default. These fonts have accurate metrics associated with them that makes anchoring and editing them easier. There is also support for other Type 1 fonts though. Just follow the process we used in chapter 2 to register a Type 1 font and you will be able to use them in your String classes too.

Let's take a look at another string demo that's loosely based on one from the ReportLab user guide:

```python
# string_demo.py

from reportlab.graphics.shapes import String, Drawing
from reportlab.lib import colors


def string_demo():
    drawing = Drawing(width=400, height=200)

    for size in range(10, 32, 4):
        x = 15 + size * 1.5
        y = 15 + size * 1.5
        my_string = String(x, y, 'Python rocks!')
        my_string.fontName = 'Courier'
        my_string.fontSize = size
        drawing.add(my_string)

    other_string = String(200, 150, 'Centered Text')
    other_string.fontName = 'Times-Roman'
    other_string.fontSize = 40
    other_string.fillColor = colors.red
    other_string.textAnchor = 'middle'
    drawing.add(other_string)

    drawing.save(formats=['pdf'], outDir='.', fnRoot='string_demo')

if __name__ == '__main__':
    string_demo()
```

The first thing we do is create a loop that loops over different font sizes. Through each iteration, we set different x/y coordinates, create the String with those coordinates and set a few of its properties before adding it to our drawing. Then we create another string that we try to center using the **textAnchor** property. We also demonstrate how to change the text's color. This is the result:

Fig. 9-4: **Different strings**

Postscript Paths

According to the ReportLab user guide, Postscript paths are a widely known concept. While ReportLab plans to support them at some point, at the time of writing, this particular shape is currently not implemented.

Groups

Group objects are basically containers for other shapes. They also allow you to apply transformations on the group of shapes, such as rotating, scaling or shifting. If you have a mathematical background, then you can set the transform directly. If you do not, then use the convenience functions themselves. Let's look at a simple example:

```
# group_demo.py

from reportlab.lib import colors
from reportlab.graphics.shapes import Drawing
from reportlab.graphics.shapes import Group
from reportlab.graphics.shapes import Circle, String


def group_demo():
    drawing = Drawing(width=400, height=200)
    radius = 25
```

```
    circles = Group(
        Circle(50, 40, radius, fillColor=colors.blue),
        Circle(75, 40, radius, fillColor=colors.red),
        Circle(100, 40, radius, fillColor=colors.green),
        Circle(125, 40, radius, fillColor=colors.yellow),
        String(75, 5, 'Circles')
    )
    drawing.add(circles)

    more_circles = Group(circles)
    more_circles.translate(75, 55)
    more_circles.rotate(35)
    drawing.add(more_circles)

    drawing.save(formats=['pdf'], outDir='.', fnRoot='group_demo')

if __name__ == '__main__':
    group_demo()
```

For this demo, we create a group that contains four Circles and a String. Then we put them into a second Group object. For the second group, we apply both translate and rotate methods. The result is that we have the same group drawn in difference locations on our drawing and at different angles. Here is a screenshot:

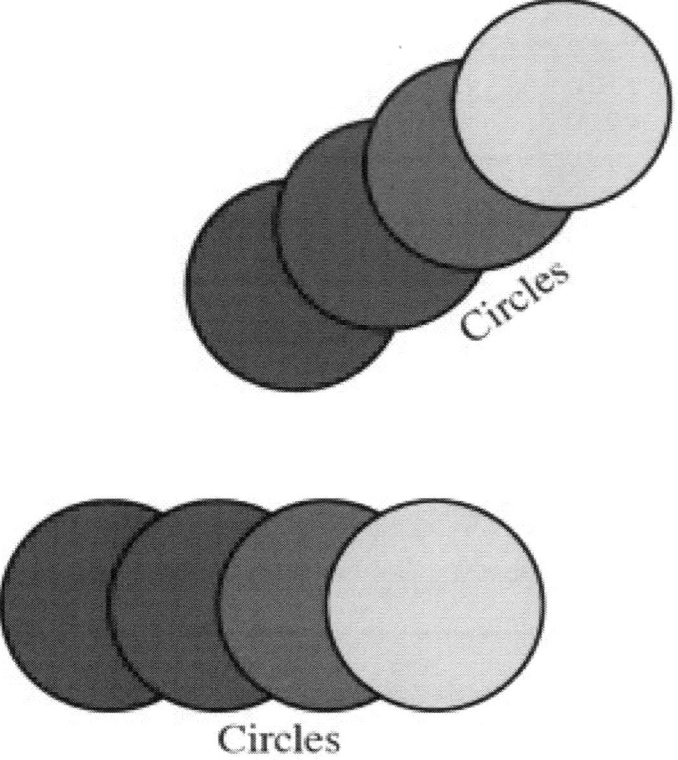

Fig. 9-5: Group transforms

This can give you a lot of flexibility for moving around lots of shapes at once or applying other transforms across a series of shapes.

Widgets

ReportLab also has the concept of **Widgets**. In fact, in the previous chapter you were using Widgets without even realizing it. The Charts that we created were all ultimately sub-classed from a Widget class. A Widget in ReportLab is a reusable graphic object. Basically it's a Group of shapes that have their own properties and methods that you can use to enhance your widget. The founding idea behind all of this is that it is just a drawing with primitive shapes which makes the renderer simpler and more portable.

Widgets are built on top of the **shapes** sub-module. You can create your own widgets and build up your own custom library of widgets just as you could with custom charts. A Widget will support the **getProperties()** and **setProperties()** methods, which will allow you to inspect and edit your widgets as well as intrinsically document your Widget.

Here is a list of items that a fully fleshed out Widget should be able to do:

- It is a reusable shape

Chapter 9 - Other Graphics

- You can initialize the Widget with no arguments
- When you call its **draw()** method it will create a primitive shape or group
- It can have whatever parameters that you desire, but you will be responsible for making those properties draw itself correctly
- A **demo()** method must be provided that will return a drawing of the widget in a 200x100 rectangle. This is a documentation feature of your widget

A Widget isn't just a group of shapes because it has its own unique code. But it can convert itself into shapes. A Widget may have other Widgets nested inside of it. During the rendering process, all the widgets will be reduced to their primitive underpinnings and drawn out.

ReportLab comes with some other pre-build widgets that we can play around with. One of their sillier ones is the **Face** class. Let's take a look:

```
# face_demo.py

from reportlab.lib import colors
from reportlab.graphics import widgetbase
from reportlab.graphics.shapes import Drawing, String


def face_demo():
    drawing = Drawing(width=400, height=200)

    sad_face = widgetbase.Face()
    sad_face.skinColor = colors.blue
    sad_face.mood = 'sad'
    drawing.add(sad_face)

    ok_face = widgetbase.Face()
    ok_face.skinColor = colors.beige
    ok_face.mood = 'ok'
    ok_face.x = 110
    drawing.add(ok_face)

    happy_face = widgetbase.Face()
    happy_face.skinColor = colors.yellow
    happy_face.mood = 'happy'
    happy_face.x = 215
    drawing.add(happy_face)

    drawing.save(formats=['pdf'], outDir='.', fnRoot='face_demo')
```

```
if __name__ == '__main__':
    face_demo()
```

Here we create a "Face" widget. You can make the face's **mood** 'happy', 'sad' or 'ok'. You can also set its **skinColor** and various other properties. Just for fun, this demo creates all three moods with different skin colors:

Fig. 9-6: Face demo

Another demo Widget that is available is the **flags** module. It can create a couple of dozen country flags. Here's an example piece of code that will create six flags:

```
# flag_demo.py

from reportlab.lib import colors
from reportlab.graphics.widgets import flags
from reportlab.graphics.shapes import Drawing, String


def flag_demo():
    drawing = Drawing(width=612, height=792)
    y = 692

    flag = flags.Flag(kind='USA')
    flag.y = y
    drawing.add(flag)
    label = String(95, y-15, 'USA', fontSize=14,
                   textAnchor='middle')
    drawing.add(label)

    countries = flag.availableFlagNames()
    countries.pop(1)
```

```
    country = 1
    for flag in range(5):
        flag = flags.Flag()
        flag.kind = countries[country]

        flag.y = y - 125
        drawing.add(flag)

        label = String(95, flag.y-15, countries[country],
                       fontSize=14, textAnchor='middle')
        drawing.add(label)

        country += 1
        y -= 125

    drawing.save(formats=['pdf'], outDir='.', fnRoot='flag_demo')

if __name__ == '__main__':
    flag_demo()
```

When you run this, you will see something like this (truncated for brevity):

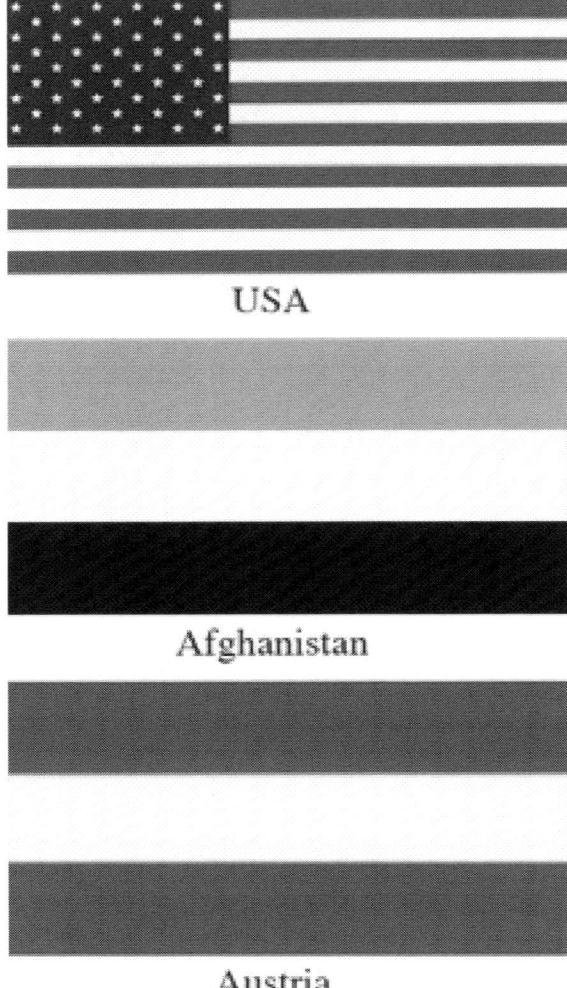

Fig. 9-6: **Flag demo**

There are several other modules inside the **widgets** module that you can look at too for inspiration. I won't be going into all of them, so feel free to explore them to get ideas of what you can do with your own custom ReportLab Widgets.

Bar Codes

ReportLab's Graphics library has a **barcodes** sub-module that you can use to add bar codes to your PDFs or just generate them as images. Here is a listing of the currently supported bar code types"

- code39 (code 3 of 9)
- code93
- code128

- EANBC
- QR
- USPS Postnet

Underneath some of these types, there are sub-types such as Standard, Extended or MultiWidth. I won't be going into these in-depth. This section is just to get you familiar enough with this sub-module to be able to use it effectively.

Code39

The Code 39 barcode is a very common barcode type that is used for inventory, name badges and industrial applications. The barcode's symbols represents the numbers 0-9, upper-case letters A-Z, the space character and the following special characters: - . $ / + %. If you look at the code39 module, you will note that ReportLab also supports the Extended Code 39 Barcode Font Information, which means that you can also encode lowercase letters and most of the other characters on a standard keyboard.

Code 39 is also known as the Alpha39, Code 3 of 9, Code 3/9, Type 39, USS Code 39, or USD-3. There are several standards for how a Code 39 bar code should be printed and several of these standards require a checksum character. ReportLab also supports adding a checksum character, which is on by default.

Here is a table that explains how a Code 39 barcode is typically organized:

Start Character	Data	Optional Checksum	Stop Character
*	Code 39	P	*

The asterisk character is typically used as the start and the stop character. You should not use it within the barcode. If you are using the extended character set, then the exclamation and parantheses characters can also be used for start and stop characters, which would allow you to put asterisks in the barcode itself if need be.

If you need more information, please see Wikipedia as they have a really good specification of everything you would need to know. There are plenty of other websites to choose from that contain similar information too.

Let's look at how we can generate a Code 39 barcode:

code39_demo.py

```python
from reportlab.graphics.barcode import code39
from reportlab.platypus import SimpleDocTemplate, Spacer
from reportlab.platypus import Paragraph
from reportlab.lib.styles import getSampleStyleSheet


def code39_demo(barcode_value):
    doc = SimpleDocTemplate('code39_demo.pdf')
    styles = getSampleStyleSheet()
    flowables = []

    flowables.append(Paragraph('Code 39 Standard:',
                               style=styles['Normal']))
    barcode39Std = code39.Standard39(
        barcode_value, barHeight=20, stop=1)
    flowables.append(barcode39Std)

    flowables.append(Spacer(0, 25))

    flowables.append(Paragraph('Code 39 Extended:',
                               style=styles['Normal']))
    barcode39 = code39.Extended39(barcode_value)
    flowables.append(barcode39)


    doc.build(flowables)

if __name__ == "__main__":
    code39_demo('ReportLab')
```

In this example, we import the **code39** module from the **barcode** sub-module. Then we create a standard Code 39 barcode as well as an Extended Code 39 bar code. You will note that the standard version of the bar code has its **barHeight** set as well as its **stop** character. When you run this code, you should see something like this:

Chapter 9 - Other Graphics

Fig. 9-7: Code 39 demo

Code93

Code 93 is basically a higher density version of Code 39 that also includes some data security enhancements. It is used primarily by the Canada Post as a way to encode supplementary delivery information. A code 93 barcode is nine modules wide and always consists of three bars and three spaces. Also, each bar and space may be 1 to 4 modules wide.

You may use the following characters in a Code 93 barcode:

- A B C D E F G H I J K L M N O P Q R S T U V W X Y Z
- 0 1 2 3 4 5 6 7 8 9
- − . $ / + % SPACE

There are also 5 special characters that can be combined with the above to represent all 128 characters in ASCII.

The structure of a Code 93 bar code is as follows:

- The start character: *
- The encoded text
- The first and second modulo-47 check characters, "C" and "K"
- A stop character: *
- The termination bar

Let's try creating a Code 93 bar code in ReportLab:

```python
# code93_demo.py

from reportlab.graphics.barcode import code93
from reportlab.platypus import SimpleDocTemplate, Spacer
from reportlab.platypus import Paragraph
from reportlab.lib.styles import getSampleStyleSheet


def code93_demo(barcode_value):
    doc = SimpleDocTemplate('code93_demo.pdf')
    styles = getSampleStyleSheet()
    flowables = []

    flowables.append(Paragraph('Code 93 Standard:',
                               style=styles['Normal']))
    barcode93Std = code93.Standard93()
    flowables.append(barcode93Std)

    flowables.append(Spacer(0, 25))

    flowables.append(Paragraph('Code 93 Extended:',
                               style=styles['Normal']))
    barcode93 = code93.Extended93(barcode_value)
    flowables.append(barcode93)

    doc.build(flowables)

if __name__ == "__main__":
    code93_demo('123456789')
```

Here we just import **code93** instead of **code39**. Then we create the standard and extender versions of the bar code. This is what you end up with:

Fig. 9-8: Code 93 demo

The API for this module appears to be the same as the previous one, so you can edit the the bar's width and height here too. There are also properties for the stop character and the quiet zones. Admittedly, Code 93 doesn't have a checksum, ratio or bearers properties as far as I can tell.

Code128

The Code 128 bar code is very compact and can encode all 128 characters in ASCII, as well as 4 special control codes called FNC1-FNC4. According to the module's docstring, it can encode digits at double density (2 per byte) and has a mandatory checksum. It also mentions that this bar code is well supported and commonly used. One example use-case would be for generating labels for the United Parcel Service (UPS). The docstring for this module has a lot more information and is actually one of the better documented of the bunch.

Let's look at an example:

```python
# code128_demo.py

from reportlab.graphics.barcode import code128
from reportlab.platypus import SimpleDocTemplate
from reportlab.platypus import Paragraph
from reportlab.lib.styles import getSampleStyleSheet


def code128_demo(barcode_value):
    doc = SimpleDocTemplate('code128_demo.pdf')
    styles = getSampleStyleSheet()
    flowables = []
```

```
        flowables.append(Paragraph('Code 128:',
                                   style=styles['Normal']))
        barcode128 = code128.Code128(barcode_value)
        flowables.append(barcode128)

        doc.build(flowables)

if __name__ == "__main__":
    code128_demo('123456789')
```

Here we import the **code128** sub-module and then create an instance of it via the **Code128** class. When you run this example, you will see the following bar code:

Fig. 9-9: Code 128 demo

The docstring has a bunch of URLs in it that you can follow for additional information on this bar code. Wikipedia also has a decent write up on it.

EANBC

The EANBC bar code is a bit of a misnomer. This appears to actually be the International Article Number or European Article Number module. It contains the EAN-13 bar code class, which is used for generating certain types of Universal Product Codes (UPC). If you look at the source code, you will find that there are ways to set which country you want. This module also supports EAN-8 and EAN-5. While the code does not mention this, I assume that it supports the Global Trade Item Number standard as well.

Unfortunately, this class does not implement the **getKeepWithNext** attribute, so we currently have to draw the bar code to the canvas directly. What this means is that you can't currently use this bar code in a document template easily.

Let's take a look at an example:

```
# eanbc_demo.py

from reportlab.graphics import renderPDF
from reportlab.graphics.barcode import eanbc
from reportlab.graphics.shapes import Drawing
from reportlab.pdfgen import canvas


def eanbc_demo(barcode_value):
    c = canvas.Canvas('eanbc_demo.pdf')

    barcode_eanbc8 = eanbc.Ean8BarcodeWidget(barcode_value)
    d = Drawing(50, 10)
    d.add(barcode_eanbc8)
    renderPDF.draw(d, c, 15, 555)

    # draw the eanbc13 code
    barcode_eanbc13 = eanbc.Ean13BarcodeWidget(barcode_value)
    d = Drawing(50, 10)
    d.add(barcode_eanbc13)
    renderPDF.draw(d, c, 15, 465)
    c.save()

if __name__ == "__main__":
    eanbc_demo('12345678')
```

In this example, we create a **Ean8BarcodeWidget** instance and an **Ean13BarcodeWidget** instance. Here is what you will see when you run this code:

Fig. 9-10: EANBC demo

As you can see, these are pretty recognizable.

QR Codes

A Quick Response or QR Code is a trademark for a type of matrix barcode that was originally designed for Japanese auto industry. It became popular because of its fast readability and because it had more storage capacity than traditional barcodes. There are four encoding modes:

- numeric
- alphanumeric
- byte / binary
- kanji

You may also use extensions with QR Codes. A QR Code is made up of black squares inside of a square grid on a white background.

You can use most cell phone cameras to read QR Codes. They use the "Reed-Solomon error correction" method to interpret the code.

Let's create a simple script that generates a QR code that will go to my blog:

```python
# qr_code_demo.py

from reportlab.graphics import renderPDF
from reportlab.graphics.barcode import qr
from reportlab.graphics.shapes import Drawing
from reportlab.pdfgen import canvas


def qr_code_demo(barcode_value):
    c = canvas.Canvas('qr_code_demo.pdf')

    qr_code = qr.QrCodeWidget(barcode_value)
    qr_code.barWidth = 145
    qr_code.barHeight = 145
    qr_code.qrVersion = 1
    bounds = qr_code.getBounds()
    width = bounds[2] - bounds[0]
    height = bounds[3] - bounds[1]
    d = Drawing()
    d.add(qr_code)
    renderPDF.draw(d, c, 15, 405)

    c.save()

if __name__ == "__main__":
    qr_code_demo('www.mousevspython.com')
```

As you can see, ReportLab's QR code also does not support adding them to a doctemplate, so you will have to draw them on your canvas directly, as we did with the EAN bar codes in the previous section. Here is the result:

Fig. 9-11: QR Code demo

If you scan this with your cell phone, it should take you to my blog. If you want, you can also try the **qrcode** Python package:

- https://pypi.python.org/pypi/qrcode/

You can generate a QR code much more simply using that library, but if you want to add it to your PDF in ReportLab, then you will want to insert it using ReportLab's **Image** Flowable. Let's take a look at how this would work with an external package:

```python
# qr_code_demo2.py

import qrcode

from reportlab.platypus import SimpleDocTemplate
from reportlab.platypus import Image


def qr_code_demo(barcode_value):
    doc = SimpleDocTemplate('qr_code_demo2.pdf')
    flowables = []

    qr_img = qrcode.make(barcode_value)
    qr_img.save('test.png')
    flowables.append(Image('test.png'))

    doc.build(flowables)

if __name__ == "__main__":
    qr_code_demo('www.mousevspython.com')
```

Chapter 9 - Other Graphics

Here we just generate our QR code using the **qrcode** Python package and save it to disk. Then we create an instance of the Image class and add it to our flowable list. Here is the result:

Fig. 9-12: QR Code demo #2

If you'd like to give this code a try, then you will need to install qrcode using pip:

```
pip install qrcode
```

Check out its documentation for details on creating the various versions of the QR Code specification.

USPS Postnet

ReportLab supports two different types of bar codes related to the United State Postal Service: POSTNET and FIM. POSTNET is used for encoding the zip code. It supports 5, 9, and 11 digit codes. You will see these bar codes along the bottom of the envelopes. You should use the 9 or 11 digit versions.

The FIM (Facing ID Marks) bar code is used for encoding a single letter. According to the docstring for the FIM class, there are four types defined:

- A - used for courtest reply mail with pre-printed POSTNET
- B - business reply mail without pre-printed
- POSTNET C - Business reply with pre-printed
- POSTNET D - OCR readable mail without pre-printed

Let's take a look at a simple example of creating a POSTNET bar code:

```
# usps_demo.py

from reportlab.graphics.barcode import usps
from reportlab.platypus import SimpleDocTemplate
from reportlab.platypus import Paragraph
from reportlab.lib.styles import getSampleStyleSheet


def usps_demo(barcode_value):
    doc = SimpleDocTemplate('usps_demo.pdf')
    styles = getSampleStyleSheet()
    flowables = []

    flowables.append(Paragraph('USPS POSTNET:',
                               style=styles['Normal']))
    barcode128 = usps.POSTNET(barcode_value)
    flowables.append(barcode128)

    doc.build(flowables)

if __name__ == "__main__":
    usps_demo('50158-9999')
```

Here we create a bar code using one from Iowa. You should end up with something like this:

Fig. 9-13: USPS POSTNET demo

Wrapping Up

We covered a diverse set of topics in this chapter. First we learned about **Shapes**. This helped us get the understanding we needed when we moved on to **Widgets**. The Widget classes are built on top of the Shapes and are used for the charts we looked at in the last chapter.

To wrap up the chapter, we learned about ReportLab's support for creating bar codes. You can create several different types of bar codes with ReportLab including code 39, code 93, EAN, QR and USPS.

You can generate bar codes with other Python libraries and insert them in your ReportLab documents if the library supports outputting the bar codes as an image, such as PNG or JPG.

Feel free to play around with the examples and see how you can change them. It is also worth your time to take a dive into the source code of ReportLab's Graphics module as there are other sub-modules in there that are not covered here.

Chapter 10 - Creating Special Features in Your PDF

There are several special features that you can utilize with ReportLab when generating a PDF. We will be covering the following topics in this chapter:

- File Annotations
- Bookmarks
- Page Transitions
- Encryption
- Interactive Forms

Let's start by learning about how you can annotate your PDF with ReportLab.

File Annotations

You can add metadata to your PDF with ReportLab as well. This is accomplished by calling the following self-explanatory canvas methods:

- setAuthor()
- setTitle()
- setSubject()

File annotations are invisible. You can only view them by opening up the **Document Properties** dialog, which can be found in the File –> Properties menu item in Adobe Reader. This is a great way to provide simple standard information about the document to archiving software or other software that might need to consume your PDFs.

Let's look at a simple demo:

```
# annotations.py

from reportlab.pdfgen import canvas

def annotations():
    my_canvas = canvas.Canvas('annotations.pdf')

    my_canvas.drawString(10, 700, 'Annotations demo')

    my_canvas.setAuthor('Mike Driscoll')
    my_canvas.setTitle('ReportLab: PDF Processing with Python')
    my_canvas.setSubject('Use Python to create PDFs')

    my_canvas.save()

if __name__ == '__main__':
    annotations()
```

All this does is set the author, title and subject of the PDF. If you open up the PDF in Adobe Reader and go to File -> Properties, you should see something like this:

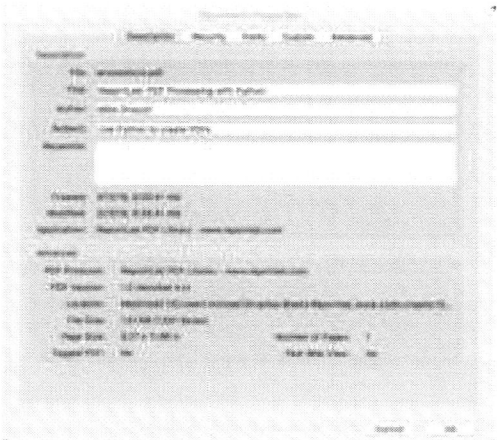

Fig. 10-1: PDF File Annotations

Bookmarks

ReportLab has support for adding Bookmarks to your PDFs. A bookmark is an internal hyperlink that you can click on to navigate the document. ReportLab just supports the ability to jump from one part of the document to another part. You can also control the zoom level in the document reader after the jump. To add a bookmark to your document, you will need to use the **bookmarkPage** canvas method.

To make the bookmark visible to be clicked on, you will also need to call the **addOutlineEntry** method.

The **bookmarkPage** canvas method signature looks like this:

```
canvas.bookmarkPage(name,
                fit="Fit",
                left=None,
                top=None,
                bottom=None,
                right=None,
                zoom
                )
```

The default of the **bookmarkPage** canvas method is for it to define the page itself as the destination to jump to. It will also scale the entire page to fit the screen by default.

Here is a table that explains the various ways that the **fit** argument can be set:

Fit	Parameters Required	Description
Fit		The entire page will fit in the window (default)
FitH	top	The top coord at the top of the window with the width scaled to fit
FitV	left	The left coord at the left of the window with the height scaled to fit
FitR	left bottom right top	Scales the window to fit the specified rectangle
XYZ	left top zoom	Fine grained control. If a parameter is omitted, the PDF interprets that as "leave as is"

The **Parameters Required** column describes which of the other parameters for the **bookmarkPage** will need to be set for that version of the **fit** argument to work correctly.

Let's look at a simple example of creating a bookmark:

```python
# bookmark_demo.py

from reportlab.pdfgen import canvas

def bookmark_demo():
    my_canvas = canvas.Canvas('bookmarks.pdf')
    
    my_canvas.drawString(10, 700, 'Page 1')
    my_canvas.bookmarkPage('page1')
```

Chapter 10 - Creating Special Features in Your PDF

```
    my_canvas.showPage()

    my_canvas.drawString(10, 700, 'Page 2')
    my_canvas.bookmarkPage('page2')

    my_canvas.addOutlineEntry('Page 1', 'page1')
    my_canvas.addOutlineEntry('Page 2', 'page2')

    my_canvas.save()

if __name__ == '__main__':
    bookmark_demo()
```

Here we create our canvas object and draw a string. Then we add a bookmark and call the **showPage** method. This will effectively create a pagebreak so that any other drawing calls made to the canvas will be made on the next page. Thus we draw a new string on page 2 and add another bookmark. Finally we add the bookmarks to the PDF's outline via the aforementioned **addOutlineEntry** method. The **addOutlineEntry** method signature is as follows:

```
canvas.addOutlineEntry(self, title, key, level=0, closed=None)
```

In our example, we pass in just the title and the key. The key must match the name of the bookmark that we added earlier in the document. When you run this code, you will see something like the following in your PDF's navigation sidebar:

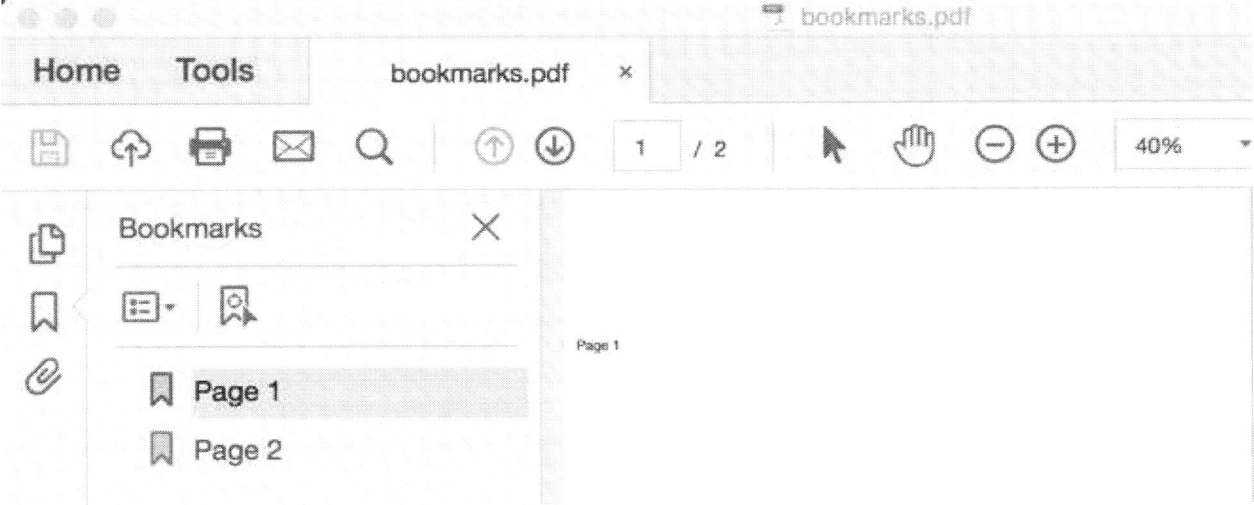

Fig. 10-2: PDF Bookmarks in the outline tree

Note: There are two other bookmark related methods in ReportLab called **bookmarkHorizontalAbsolute** and **bookmarkHorizontal**. They are both deprecated in favor of **bookmarkPage**.

The Outline Tree

ReportLab calls the navigation sidebar an **Outline Tree**. When you want to add an outline entry to the outline tree, you need to use the previously mentioned **addOutlineEntry** method. A lot of users like navigating their documents using the sidebar, so knowing how to add entries to that sidebar can be valuable.

As we learned just a bit ago, there are four arguments that you can pass to the **addOutlineEntry** method: title, key, level, and closed. The **title** argument is the caption that will appear in your navigation pane. The **key** is a unique string within the document that you used when creating a bookmark. The **level** argument defaults to zero, which is the uppermost level. You may only go down one level at a time. If you try to do go down more than one level, an error will be raised. Lastly, the **closed** argument tells the navigation pane whether or not the bookmark should be closed or opened.

Page Transitions

ReportLab supports the concept of **Page Transitions**, which is kind of a limited form of the transitions you can add to Microsoft Powerpoint when switching between slides. In this case, the transitions appear to only be activated in Adobe Reader when you have it set to fullscreen mode. Here is a listing of the transitions that you can apply:

```
PageTransitionEffects = {
    'Split': [direction_arg, motion_arg],
    'Blinds': [dimension_arg],
    'Box': [motion_arg],
    'Wipe' : [direction_arg],
    'Dissolve' : [],
    'Glitter':[direction_arg]
    }
```

As you can see, you have six to choose from. You can apply a direction argument or a motion argument or both, as is shown above. Here is a listing from the ReportLab documentation that shows valid values for these arguments:

```
direction_arg = [0,90,180,270]
dimension_arg = ['H', 'V']
```

If you would like to add a transition effect to your PDF, then you will need to call the **setPageTransition** canvas method, which looks like this:

```
canvas.setPageTransition(self, effectname=None, duration=1,
    direction=0, dimension='H', motion='I')
```

Let's create a simple example:

```python
# transition_demo.py

from reportlab.pdfgen import canvas

def transition_demo():
    my_canvas = canvas.Canvas('transition_demo.pdf')

    my_canvas.drawString(20, 750, 'This is page one')
    my_canvas.showPage()

    my_canvas.setPageTransition(
        effectname='Blinds', duration=1, direction=0,
        dimension='H',
        motion='I')
    my_canvas.drawString(20, 750, 'This is a transitional page')
    my_canvas.drawImage('snakehead.png', 30, 600,
                        width=100, height=100)

    my_canvas.save()


if __name__ == '__main__':
    transition_demo()
```

In the code above, we create a two page document. The first page just has a single line of text painted onto it. The second page has a string and an image in it. This page also has a transition set to use the "Blinds" transition for 1 seconds in the Horizontal dimension. After running this code, open up the PDF in Adobe Reader and make it full screen. Then navigate to the second page to see the effect in action. Now you can go back and edit the code to try out one of the other effects!

Encryption

Adobe's implementation of the PDF specification allows you to encrypt your PDFs. You may do any of the following things when encrypting your PDFs:

- Password protect the document

- Encrypt the contents of the file
- Control the ability to print, copy and paste or edit the document in the viewer

Note that an encrypted PDF does not require a password, but when you do password protect your PDF, it is encrypted automatically. When the user enters their password, the PDF will open the document, decrypt it and then display it for the user to read. There are two different types of passwords:

- The "owner" password - Basically gives you administrator privileges
- The "user" password - Allows you to open the document for viewing

If you have the "owner" password, you can print, copy/paste and change the password itself. When you use the "user" password, your options may be restricted. The following describes what permissions you can set:

- Modification of the document
- Copying text / graphics
- Adding / modifying annotations or form fields
- Printing

If you set the user password to a blank string, then Adobe will not prompt you for a password. If you only set the owner password, then the PDF will open without a prompt. Finally, if you set the password for the owner and the user to the same string, then the PDF will only open in restricted mode with whatever privileges you have set. You will not be able to modify any of those settings in this case. Always set the owner and the user password to different strings.

When the PDF is encrypted, the encryption will apply to all the strings and streams in the file. This will prevent nefarious people from trying to find the password in a text or hex editor and changing it. According to ReportLab's documentation, PDF's use an MD5 hash and the RC4 encryption algorithm for encrypting the PDF. RC4 is a symmetric stream cipher that uses the same mechanic for encrypting and decrypting your file without changing the length of the data.

Now we are ready to learn how to actually encrypt a PDF using ReportLab. You will need to import **pdfencrypt** from **reportlab.pdfgen**. Then to encrypt the document, you will create an instance of the **StandardEncryption** class. It __init__() looks like this:

```
def __init__(self, userPassword,
    ownerPassword=None,
    canPrint=1,
    canModify=1,
    canCopy=1,
    canAnnotate=1,
    strength=40):
```

Everything is set to a default except for the **userPassword** argument. The **ownerPassword** is just set to None. The next four arguments set various privileges on the PDF document itself. The last is the encryption strength. Looking at the source, it looks like the only valid values are 40 and 128 with the default being the weakest security.

Here is a full example:

```
# encryption_demo.py

from reportlab.lib import pdfencrypt
from reportlab.pdfgen import canvas


def encryption_demo(userPassword, ownerPassword,
                    canPrint=1, canModify=1, canCopy=1, canAnnotate=1):
    encrypt = pdfencrypt.StandardEncryption(
        userPassword=userPassword,
        ownerPassword=ownerPassword,
        canPrint=canPrint,
        canModify=canModify,
        canCopy=canCopy,
        canAnnotate=canAnnotate,
        strength=40)

    my_canvas = canvas.Canvas('encryption_demo.pdf', encrypt=encrypt)

    my_canvas.drawString(20, 750, 'This is page one')

    my_canvas.save()


if __name__ == '__main__':
    encryption_demo(userPassword='bad_password',
                    ownerPassword='b3Tt3R_P@$$W0Rd')
```

When you run this code, you should end up with a PDF document that prompts you for a password.

Interactive Forms

ReportLab also allows you to create interactive fillable forms using their toolkit. The PDF standard actually has a fairly rich set of interactive elements. ReportLab doesn't support all of these elements, but it does cover most of them. In this section, we will look at the following widgets:

- checkbox
- radio
- choice
- listbox
- textfield

All of these widgets are created by calling various methods on the *canvas.acroform* property. Note that you can only have one form per document. Let's take a look at the widgets that ReportLab supports!

Checkbox

The **checkbox** widget is exactly what it sounds like. It's a little box that you can check. ReportLab supports several different "check" styles though, so when the checkbox is checked, it can look different depending on the style that you set. Here are all the parameters that you can set for a checkbox:

Parameter	Meaning	Default
name	The parameter's name	None
x	The horizontal absolute coordinate position	0
y	The vertical absolute coordinate position	0
size	The outline dimensions (size x size)	20
checked	If True, the checkbox is checked	False
buttonStyle	The checkbox's style (see below for more information)	'check'
shape	The outline of the widget (see below for more information)	'square'
fillColor	The color filling the widget	None
textColor	The color of the text / symbol	None
borderWidth	The width of the border	1
borderColor	The border color	None
borderStyle	The border style name	'solid'
tooltip	The text to show when hovering over the widget	None
annotationFlags	Space separated string of flags for annotation	'print'
fieldFlags	Space separated string of field flags	'required'
forceBorder	When True, a border is drawn	False
relative	When True, obey the current canvas transform setting	False
dashLen	The dashline to be used if the borderStyle=='dashed'	3

Now let's write up a simple example that demonstrates how some of these arguments behave:

```python
# simple_checkboxes.py

from reportlab.pdfgen import canvas
from reportlab.pdfbase import pdfform
from reportlab.lib.colors import magenta, pink, blue, green

def create_simple_checkboxes():
    c = canvas.Canvas('simple_checkboxes.pdf')

    c.setFont("Courier", 20)
    c.drawCentredString(300, 700, 'Pets')
    c.setFont("Courier", 14)
    form = c.acroForm

    c.drawString(10, 650, 'Dog:')
    form.checkbox(name='cb1', tooltip='Field cb1',
                  x=110, y=645, buttonStyle='check',
                  borderColor=magenta, fillColor=pink,
                  textColor=blue, forceBorder=True)

    c.drawString(10, 600, 'Cat:')
    form.checkbox(name='cb2', tooltip='Field cb2',
                  x=110, y=595, buttonStyle='cross',
                  borderWidth=2, forceBorder=True)

    c.drawString(10, 550, 'Pony:')
    form.checkbox(name='cb3', tooltip='Field cb3',
                  x=110, y=545, buttonStyle='star',
                  borderWidth=1, forceBorder=True)

    c.drawString(10, 500, 'Python:')
    form.checkbox(name='cb4', tooltip='Field cb4',
                  x=110, y=495, buttonStyle='circle',
                  borderWidth=3, forceBorder=True)

    c.drawString(10, 450, 'Hamster:')
    form.checkbox(name='cb5', tooltip='Field cb5',
                  x=110, y=445, buttonStyle='diamond',
                  borderWidth=None,
                  checked=True,
                  forceBorder=True)
```

```
    c.save()

if __name__ == '__main__':
    create_simple_checkboxes()
```

As you can see, we set up the name and set the tooltip to basically match the name of the widget. Then we set its position and a few other things. You can play around with the width of the checkbox's border or turn the border off. If you turn it off though, the checkbox may become invisible, so you might want to set its background color via fillColor if you do that. I set the buttonStyle to something different for each of the checkboxes. Here is what I get when I run the code:

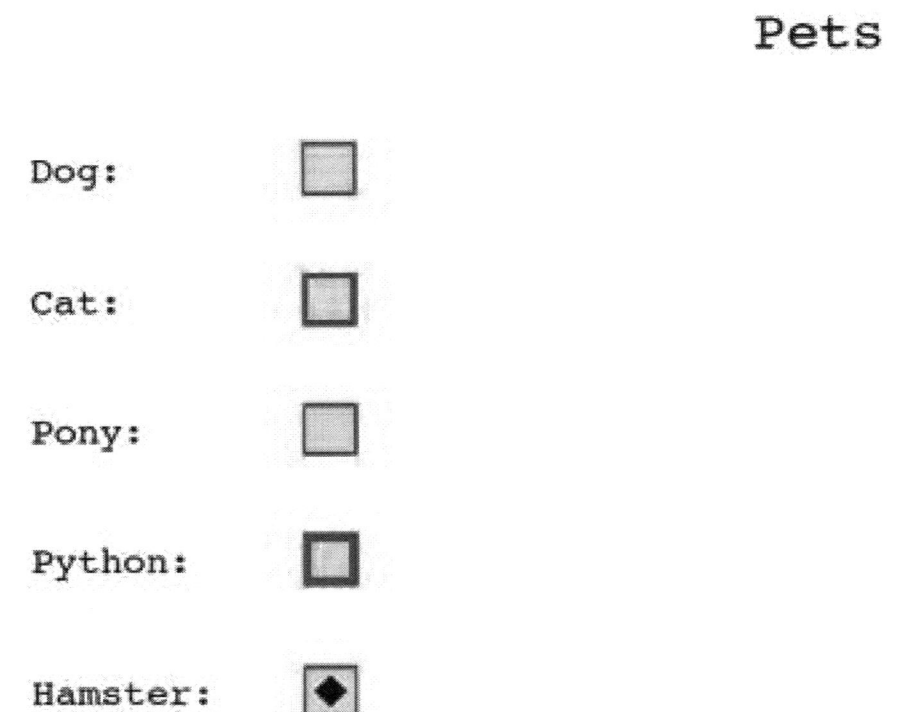

Fig. 10-3: Checkboxes in an interactive form

If you open up the document and check all of the checkboxes, you will end up with them looking like this:

Fig. 10-4: Checked checkboxes

Now let's learn about the radio widget!

Radio

Radio widgets are kind of like checkboxes except that usually you put radio buttons into a group where only one radio button can be selected. Checkboxes are rarely limited to just allowing one checkbox per group. ReportLab does not appear to have a way to explicitly group a set of radio boxes as being together. This appears to only happen implicitly. In other words, if you create a series of radios one after the other, they will be grouped together.

Anyway, here is a listing of the parameters you can use when creating a radio widget:

Parameter	Meaning	Default
name	The radio group's (parameter) name	None
value	The radio group's name	None
x	The horizontal absolute coordinate position	0
y	The vertical absolute coordinate position	0
size	The outline dimensions (size x size)	20
selected	If True, this radio is the selected one in the group	False
buttonStyle	The checkbox's style (see below for more information)	'check'
shape	The outline of the widget (see below for more information)	'square'
fillColor	The color filling the widget	None
textColor	The color of the text / symbol	None
borderWidth	The width of the border	1
borderColor	The border color	None
borderStyle	The border style name	'solid'
tooltip	The text to show when hovering over the widget	None
annotationFlags	Space separated string of flags for annotation	'print'
fieldFlags	Space separated string of field flags	'noToggleToOff required radio'
forceBorder	When True, a border is drawn	False
relative	When True, obey the current canvas transform setting	False
dashLen	The dashline to be used if the borderStyle=='dashed'	3

Now let's take a moment and create a simple demo of the radio widgets:

```
# simple_radios.py

from reportlab.pdfgen import canvas
from reportlab.pdfbase import pdfform
from reportlab.lib.colors import magenta, pink, blue, green

def create_simple_radios():
    c = canvas.Canvas('simple_radios.pdf')

    c.setFont("Courier", 20)
    c.drawCentredString(300, 700, 'Radio demo')
```

```
c.setFont("Courier", 14)
form = c.acroForm

c.drawString(10, 650, 'Dog:')
form.radio(name='radio1', tooltip='Field radio1',
           value='value1', selected=False,
           x=110, y=645, buttonStyle='check',
           borderStyle='solid', shape='square',
           borderColor=magenta, fillColor=pink,
           textColor=blue, forceBorder=True)
form.radio(name='radio1', tooltip='Field radio1',
           value='value2', selected=True,
           x=110, y=645, buttonStyle='check',
           borderStyle='solid', shape='square',
           borderColor=magenta, fillColor=pink,
           textColor=blue, forceBorder=True)

c.drawString(10, 600, 'Cat:')
form.radio(name='radio2', tooltip='Field radio2',
           value='value1', selected=True,
           x=110, y=595, buttonStyle='cross',
           borderStyle='solid', shape='circle',
           borderColor=green, fillColor=blue,
           borderWidth=2,
           textColor=pink, forceBorder=True)
form.radio(name='radio2', tooltip='Field radio2',
           value='value2', selected=False,
           x=110, y=595, buttonStyle='cross',
           borderStyle='solid', shape='circle',
           borderColor=green, fillColor=blue,
           borderWidth=2,
           textColor=pink, forceBorder=True)

c.drawString(10, 550, 'Pony:')
form.radio(name='radio3', tooltip='Field radio3',
           value='value1', selected=False,
           x=110, y=545, buttonStyle='star',
           borderStyle='bevelled', shape='square',
           borderColor=blue, fillColor=green,
           borderWidth=2,
           textColor=magenta, forceBorder=False)
form.radio(name='radio3', tooltip='Field radio3',
```

```
                value='value2', selected=True,
                x=110, y=545, buttonStyle='star',
                borderStyle='bevelled', shape='circle',
                borderColor=blue, fillColor=green,
                borderWidth=2,
                textColor=magenta, forceBorder=True)

    c.save()

if __name__ == '__main__':
    create_simple_radios()
```

When you run this code, you will notice that you only get 3 radios. This is because you are required to create two instances of each radio button with the same name, but with different values and sections. The documentation does not state why, but I assume this is done to help ReportLab track the "selected" state of the widget. This also allows you to change the appearance of the radio when it is selected or deselected.

Here is an example of what this code generates:

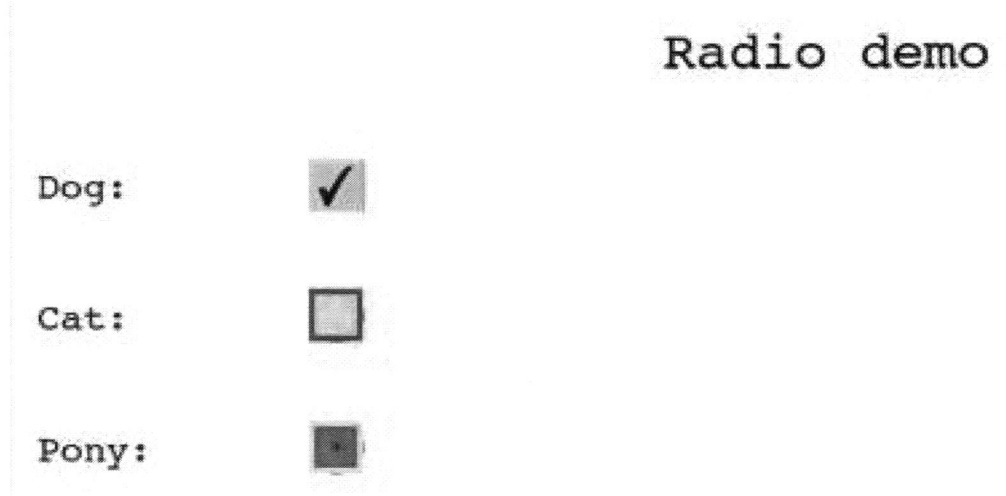

Fig. 10-5: Radios in an interactive form

Now let's discover how to create a choice widget!

Choice

The **choice** widget is basically a combobox that displays a dropdown when the user clicks on it. This allows the user to pick one or more options from the drop-down list, depending on the **fieldFlags** you have set. If you add **edit** to the **fieldFlags**, then the user can edit item in the choice widget.

Here is a listing of the various arguments you can use when creating this widget:

Parameter	Meaning	Default
name	The radio group's (parameter) name	None
options	A Python list or tuple of available options	[]
value	A singleton or list of strings of the selected options	[]
x	The horizontal absolute coordinate position	0
y	The vertical absolute coordinate position	0
width	The widget's width	120
height	The widget's height	36
fontName	The name of the Type 1 font	'Helvetica'
fontSize	The size of the font	12
fillColor	The color filling the widget	None
textColor	The color of the text / symbol	None
borderWidth	The width of the border	1
borderColor	The border color	None
borderStyle	The border style name	'solid'
tooltip	The text to show when hovering over the widget	None
annotationFlags	Space separated string of flags for annotation	'print'
fieldFlags	Space separated string of field flags	'combo'
forceBorder	When True, a border is drawn	False
relative	When True, obey the current canvas transform setting	False
dashLen	The dashline to be used if the borderStyle=='dashed'	3
maxlen	None or the max length of the widget's value	None

Let's take a moment to create a couple of choice widgets in a PDF document:

```
# simple_choices.py

from reportlab.pdfgen import canvas
from reportlab.pdfbase import pdfform
from reportlab.lib.colors import magenta, pink, blue, green, red

def create_simple_choices():
    c = canvas.Canvas('simple_choices.pdf')

    c.setFont("Courier", 20)
    c.drawCentredString(300, 700, 'Choices')
    c.setFont("Courier", 14)
    form = c.acroForm

    c.drawString(10, 650, 'Choose a letter:')
    options = [('A','Av'),'B',('C','Cv'),('D','Dv'),'E',('F',),('G','Gv')]
    form.choice(name='choice1', tooltip='Field choice1',
```

```
                value='A',
                x=165, y=645, width=72, height=20,
                borderColor=magenta, fillColor=pink,
                textColor=blue, forceBorder=True, options=options)

    c.drawString(10, 600, 'Choose an animal:')
    options = [('Cat', 'cat'), ('Dog', 'dog'), ('Pig', 'pig')]
    form.choice(name='choice2', tooltip='Field choice2',
                value='Cat',
                options=options,
                x=165, y=595, width=72, height=20,
                borderStyle='solid', borderWidth=1,
                forceBorder=True)

    c.save()

if __name__ == '__main__':
    create_simple_choices()
```

In this example, we create two choice widgets with slightly different styles applied. While I couldn't find it anywhere in the documentation, the **value** argument appears to be required. If you do not include it, you will get a rather bizarre error that doesn't say anything about that argument being missing. Anyway, when you run this code, you will find that it generates something like this:

Fig. 10-6: Choice widgets in an interactive form

Now let's learn about the listbox!

Listbox

The **listbox** widget is kind of like the choice widget except that a listbox is a scrollable box instead of a combobox. You can use the **fieldFlags** argument to allow the user to select one or more items

Chapter 10 - Creating Special Features in Your PDF

from the listbox.

Here is a listing of all the arguments you can use when creating a listbox:

Parameter	Meaning	Default
name	The radio group's (parameter) name	None
options	A Python list or tuple of available options	[]
value	A singleton or list of strings of the selected options	[]
x	The horizontal absolute coordinate position	0
y	The vertical absolute coordinate position	0
width	The widget's width	120
height	The widget's height	36
fontName	The name of the Type 1 font	'Helvetica'
fontSize	The size of the font	12
fillColor	The color filling the widget	None
textColor	The color of the text / symbol	None
borderWidth	The width of the border	1
borderColor	The border color	None
borderStyle	The border style name	'solid'
tooltip	The text to show when hovering over the widget	None
annotationFlags	Space separated string of flags for annotation	'print'
fieldFlags	Space separated string of field flags	''
forceBorder	When True, a border is drawn	False
relative	When True, obey the current canvas transform setting	False
dashLen	The dashline to be used if the borderStyle=='dashed'	3

Now let's write up a quick demo so we can see how you might create one of these widgets:

```
# simple_listboxes.py

from reportlab.pdfgen import canvas
from reportlab.pdfbase import pdfform
from reportlab.lib.colors import magenta, pink, blue, green, red

def create_simple_listboxes():
    c = canvas.Canvas('simple_listboxes.pdf')

    c.setFont("Courier", 20)
    c.drawCentredString(300, 700, 'Listboxes')
    c.setFont("Courier", 14)
    form = c.acroForm
```

```
    c.drawString(10, 650, 'Choose a letter:')
    options = [('A','Av'),'B',('C','Cv'),('D','Dv'),'E',('F',),('G','Gv')]
    form.listbox(name='listbox1', value='A',
              x=165, y=590, width=72, height=72,
              borderColor=magenta, fillColor=pink,
              textColor=blue, forceBorder=True, options=options,
              fieldFlags='multiSelect')

    c.drawString(10, 500, 'Choose an animal:')
    options = [('Cat', 'cat'), ('Dog', 'dog'), ('Pig', 'pig')]
    form.listbox(name='choice2', tooltip='Field choice2',
              value='Cat',
              options=options,
              x=165, y=440, width=72, height=72,
              borderStyle='solid', borderWidth=1,
              forceBorder=True)

    c.save()

if __name__ == '__main__':
    create_simple_listboxes()
```

This example is actually pretty similar to the previous one where we created the **choice** widget. The main difference here is the look of the listbox widget versus the choice widget. Otherwise, they are pretty much the same. Following is a screenshot of what this code generates:

Chapter 10 - Creating Special Features in Your PDF

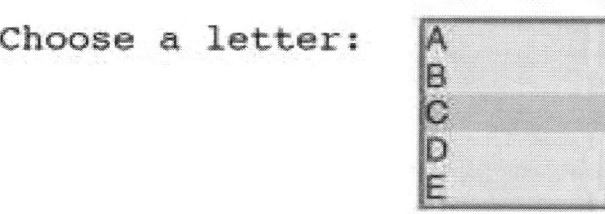

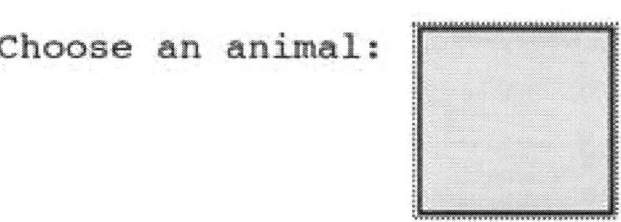

Fig. 10-7: Listbox widgets in an interactive form

Now let's learn about the textfield widget!

Textfield

The **textfield** is a text entry widget. You will see these in forms for entering your name and address. Most of the arguments for the textfield are the same as the ones you've seen in the previous widgets:

Parameter	Meaning	Default
name	The radio group's (parameter) name	None
value	A singleton or list of strings of the selected options	''
x	The horizontal absolute coordinate position	0
y	The vertical absolute coordinate position	0
width	The widget's width	120
height	The widget's height	36
fontName	The name of the Type 1 font	'Helvetica'
fontSize	The size of the font	12
fillColor	The color filling the widget	None
textColor	The color of the text / symbol	None
borderWidth	The width of the border	1
borderColor	The border color	None

Parameter	Meaning	Default
borderStyle	The border style name	'solid'
tooltip	The text to show when hovering over the widget	None
annotationFlags	Space separated string of flags for annotation	'print'
fieldFlags	Space separated string of field flags	''
forceBorder	When True, a border is drawn	False
relative	When True, obey the current canvas transform setting	False
dashLen	The dashline to be used if the borderStyle=='dashed'	3
maxlen	None or the max length of the widget's value	100

As usual, we will spend a little time writing up a small example in code so you can see how you might use this widget:

```python
# simple_form.py

from reportlab.pdfgen import canvas
from reportlab.pdfbase import pdfform
from reportlab.lib.colors import magenta, pink, blue, green

def create_simple_form():
    c = canvas.Canvas('simple_form.pdf')

    c.setFont("Courier", 20)
    c.drawCentredString(300, 700, 'Employment Form')
    c.setFont("Courier", 14)
    form = c.acroForm

    c.drawString(10, 650, 'First Name:')
    form.textfield(name='fname', tooltip='First Name',
                   x=110, y=635, borderStyle='inset',
                   borderColor=magenta, fillColor=pink,
                   width=300,
                   textColor=blue, forceBorder=True)

    c.drawString(10, 600, 'Last Name:')
    form.textfield(name='lname', tooltip='Last Name',
                   x=110, y=585, borderStyle='inset',
                   borderColor=green, fillColor=magenta,
                   width=300,
                   textColor=blue, forceBorder=True)
```

```
    c.drawString(10, 550, 'Address:')
    form.textfield(name='address', tooltip='Address',
                   x=110, y=535, borderStyle='inset',
                   width=400, forceBorder=True)

    c.drawString(10, 500, 'City:')
    form.textfield(name='city', tooltip='City',
                   x=110, y=485, borderStyle='inset',
                   forceBorder=True)

    c.drawString(250, 500, 'State:')
    form.textfield(name='state', tooltip='State',
                   x=350, y=485, borderStyle='inset',
                   forceBorder=True)

    c.drawString(10, 450, 'Zip Code:')
    form.textfield(name='zip_code', tooltip='Zip Code',
                   x=110, y=435, borderStyle='inset',
                   forceBorder=True)

    c.save()

if __name__ == '__main__':
    create_simple_form()
```

Here we create a series of textfields with different settings applied to them. As you can see, we changed the border and background color on several of the fields. Then we just added some fairly standard ones. We also used the **width** parameter to change how wide the textfield is.

Here is what this code ended up generating for me:

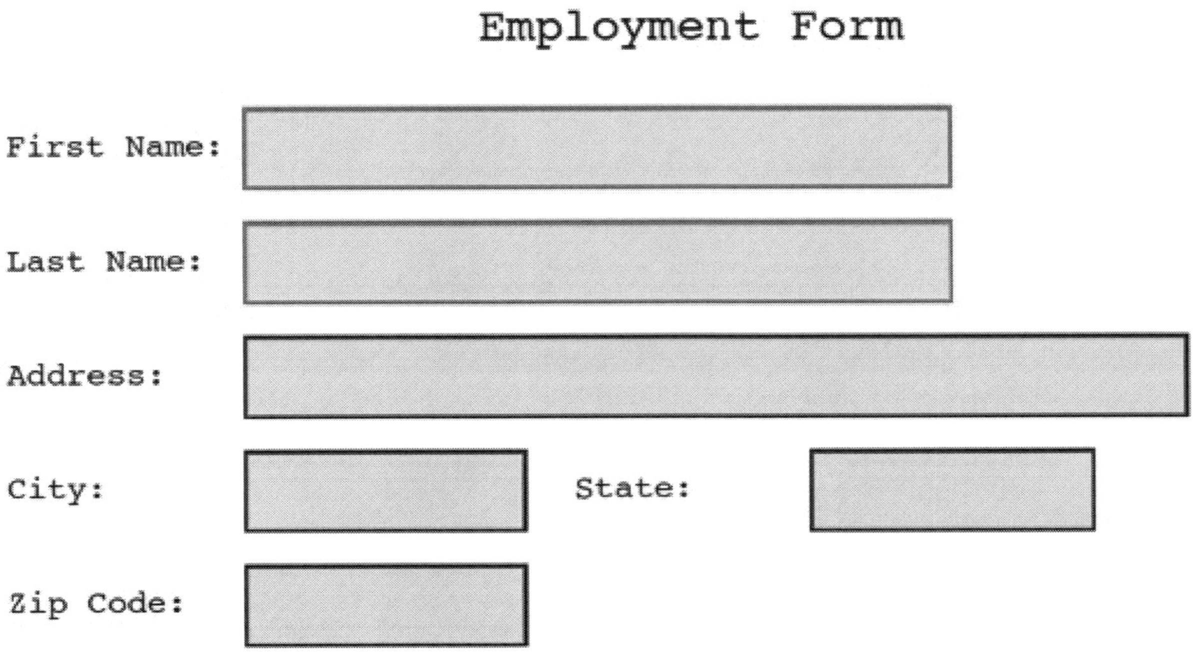

```
Employment Form
```

First Name: [   ]

Last Name: [   ]

Address: [   ]

City: [   ]   State: [   ]

Zip Code: [   ]

Fig. 10-8: Textfield widgets in an interactive form

Now let's learn about the various styles and shapes that we can use with some of these widgets!

Button Styles

There are actually several different button styles that ReportLab supports. You can use these styles to indicate to ReportLab what style or symbol should appear when the widget is selected. Here are the current choices:

- check
- circle
- cross
- diamond
- star

There is a note in ReportLab's documentation that states that the document renderer may render the symbols incorrectly for their intended application. For example, Acrobat Reader will prefer to use its own rendering over what the actual specification states should be shown.

Widget Shapes

ReportLab supports two different widget shapes. These shapes apply to the checkbox and radio widgets. You may use either of the following:

- circle
- square

Once again, the renderer may override your setting. For example, according to ReportLab's documentation, Acrobat Reader will usually render radios with circles instead of squares.

Border Styles

The **borderStyle** argument is used by the widget to change its 3D appearance. There are five settings to choose from. Here is a list of your options:

- bevelled
- dashed
- inset
- solid
- underlined

Now let's learn about flags!

fieldFlags

ReportLab supports a lot of different **fieldFlags** that you can use to modify the behavior of your widgets. All the widgets that ReportLab supports can use **fieldFlags**. A flag can be an integer or a string that contains blank (or space) separated values.

Let's take a look at all the different kinds of **fieldFlags** that can be applied:

Token	Meaning	Value
readOnly	This widget is read-only	1<<0
required	This widget is required	1<<1
noExport	Do not export the value of the widget	1<<2
noToggleToOff	Only one radio must be on	1<<14
radio	Added for the radio method	1<<15
pushButton	Determines if the button is a push button type	1<<16
radiosInUnison	Radios with the same value will toggle together	1<<25
multiline	Make the textfield widget multiline	1<<12
password	Turns the textfield into a password field	1<<13
fileSelect	Turns the widget into a file select widget	1<<20
doNotSpellCheck	Do not spell check this widget	1<<22
doNotScroll	The textfield will not scroll	1<<23
comb	Creates a comb style text based on the maxlen value	1<<24
richText	Toggles rich text on	1<<25

Token	Meaning	Value
combo	Used for choice fields	1<<17
edit	Makes the choice editable	1<<18
sort	Sorts the values	1<<19
multiSelect	Allows multi-selection	1<<21
commitOnSelChange	not used by ReportLab	1<<26

There is another type of flags that we can use with our widgets. We will look at that next.

annotationFlags

ReportLab's widgets are technically known as annotations. So they can also have special **annotationFlags** applied to them in addition to the **fieldFlags**. Let's take a look:

Token	Meaning	Value
invisible	This widget is not shown	1<<0
hidden	This widget is hidden	1<<1
print	This widget is printable	1<<2
nozoom	The annotation will not scale with the page	1<<3
norotate	The widget will not rotate with the page	1<<4
noview	Do not render the widget	1<<5
readonly	The widget cannot be interacted with by the user	1<<6
locked	The widget cannot be changed	1<<7
togglenoview	The widget can only be viewed after some events	1<<8
lockedcontents	The widget's contents are locked / fixed	1<<9

Wrapping Up

In this chapter we learned how to add simple annotations to our PDF. We also learned how to add bookmarks to our outline tree. This is quite useful for generating a professional looking document. Next we learned about adding basic page transitional effects, which are useful for presentation purposes. We also learned how to encrypt our PDF and set various privileges upon it. Finally, we learned about ReportLab's support for interactive forms. You should now spend some time working through the examples and modifying them to learn how they work before moving on.

Part II - Tutorials and How-Tos

Welcome to Part II. At this point in the book, you should be well versed in how to use the ReportLab toolkit. This section of the book will go over a few use-cases where you will create reports or partial reports using ReportLab. You will also learn about other Python packages that you can use to work with PDFs.

Here is the chapter line-up:

- Chapter 11 - Turning XML into PDFs
- Chapter 12 - Custom Headers and Footers
- Chapter 13 - Creating a Custom PDF Generation Module
- Chapter 14 - The PyPDF2 Package
- Chapter 15 - The pdfrw Package
- Chapter 16 - Exporting Data from PDFs
- Chapter 17 - Populating PDF Fillable Forms
- Chapter 18 - Turning Markup into PDFs
- Chapter 19 - The PyFPDF Package

By the time you finish this part of the book, you should be to generate PDFs from various data sources, split PDFs up and merge them back together. You will learn how to create custom headers and footers. You will discover how to fill out PDF fillable forms using Python. You will also learn how to export data from a PDF into another format.

There is a lot of information to cover in this chapter. Let's get started!

Chapter 11 - Turning Data into PDFs

One major use-case for using ReportLab involves consuming a data file and turning it into a report or a series of reports. There are many common data file types such as XML, JSON, CSV, fixed width file formats, etc. In this chapter, we will look at how to take an XML data file and turn it into a report. I found a neat looking report that is actually kind of similar to other reports that I have created in the past. It was an explanation of benefits (EOB) from AETNA. I will focus on page two of the document as I think it will be more instructive. Here's a link so you can see what I am talking about:

- https://ctmirror.org/2014/09/02/what-is-this-form-the-explanation-of-benefits/

We will be trying to copy that document's layout with ReportLab. By the end of this chapter, you will be able to generate a PDF using ReportLab that looks similar to this:

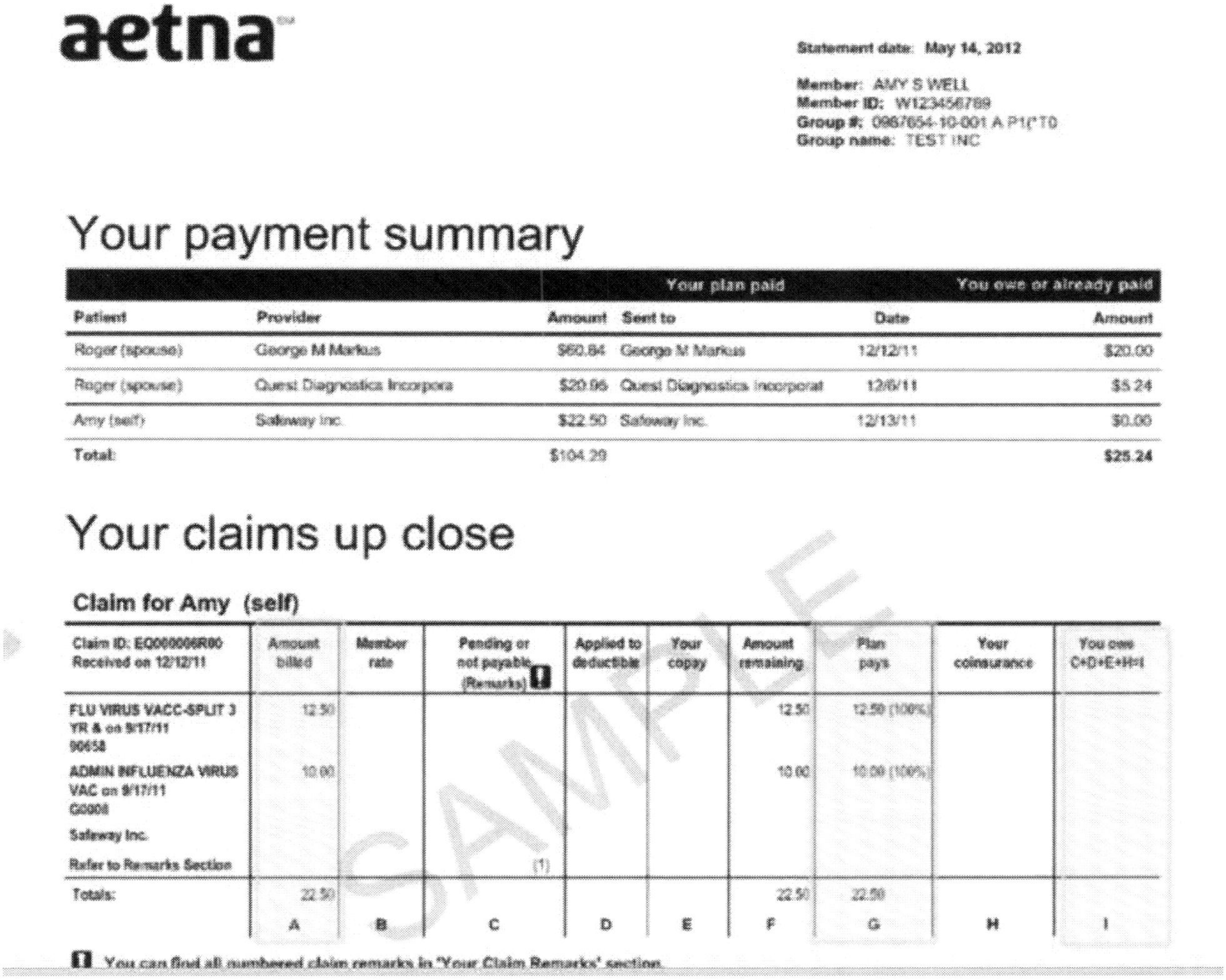

Chapter 11 - Turning Data into PDFs

Fig. 11-1: An Example EOB from AETNA

The code you will create will support generating multi-page reports based on the amount of data in the XML data file. Let's find out how!

Getting Started

Usually a client will give you a data file and the output that they expect you to generate from that file. Occasionally, you will get to design your own specification that the client will have to use, but I have rarely had that happen. The first thing to do when receiving a data file and a report is to identify where the various pieces of data fit on the report. In this case, the pieces will be in XML tags, so they will actually be labeled. That makes things a lot easier, especially if the XML has good tag names. Fixed width data files are more difficult because they don't have named fields that you can figure out at a glance.

Once you have identified all the pieces on the pre-existing document, then you are ready to start creating some code. Every developer is different. You could start by writing a parser for the XML at this point. Or you could try to layout the document using some hard-coded values. It doesn't really matter all that much which is done first as the parser and layout code should be in separate modules.

Creating the Base Template Class

Let's start the design of the report by creating a base class that we can use. We will stub out some of the methods that we think we will need as well. Save the following code to a file named **eob.py**:

```python
# eob.py

from reportlab.lib.pagesizes import letter
from reportlab.lib.styles import getSampleStyleSheet
from reportlab.pdfgen import canvas
from reportlab.platypus import SimpleDocTemplate, Paragraph, Table
from reportlab.lib.units import inch, mm


class EOB:
    """
    Explanation of Benefits PDF Class
    """

    def __init__(self, pdf_file):
        """"""
        self.canvas = canvas.Canvas(pdf_file, pagesize=letter)
        self.styles = getSampleStyleSheet()
        self.width, self.height = letter

    def coord(self, x, y, unit=1):
        x, y = x * unit, self.height - y * unit
        return x, y

    def create_header(self):
        """"""
        pass

    def create_payment_summary(self):
        """"""
        pass
```

```python
    def create_claims(self):
        """ """
        pass

    def save(self):
        """ """
        self.canvas.save()


def main(pdf_file):
    """ """
    eob = EOB(pdf_file)
    eob.save()


if __name__ == '__main__':
    pdf_file = 'eob.pdf'
    main(pdf_file)
```

You will note that for our first attempt at generating an Explanation of Benefits (EOB), we use ReportLab's **canvas** module. You could start with **platypus** too, but for simplicity, we will start with the canvas and then update it to use platypus when we need to. The __init__ method is where we create our **canvas** instance. We also create some class properties that define the page's width and height. You will also note that we created a style sheet, which we will use for styling our Paragraphs.

The next method that we create is called **coord**. We will use this method to help us position elements on the page eventually.

Next we create three stubbed methods: **create_header**, **create_payment_summary** and **create_claims**. These methods do not do anything right now. The last method is our **save** method, which just saves the PDF to disk.

Finally we have the **main** function. Here we create our **EOB** instance and tell it to save. This code will generate an empty PDF, which isn't all that interesting. So let's make our code do something useful by updating the **create_header** method:

```python
def create_header(self):
    """ """
    ptext = '<font size=10><b>Statement Date: {}' \
        '</b></font>'.format('01/01/2017')
    p = Paragraph(ptext, self.styles["Normal"])
    p.wrapOn(self.canvas, self.width, self.height)
    p.drawOn(self.canvas, *self.coord(145, 17, mm))

    ptext = '''<font size=10>
    <b>Member:</b> {member}<br/>
    <b>Member ID:</b> {member_id}<br/>
    <b>Group #:</b> {group_num}<br/>
    <b>Group name:</b> {group_name}<br/>
    </font>
    '''.format(member='MIKE D',
              member_id='X123456',
              group_num=789456-1235,
              group_name='PYTHON CORP'
              )
    p = Paragraph(ptext, self.styles["Normal"])
    p.wrapOn(self.canvas, self.width, self.height)
    p.drawOn(self.canvas, *self.coord(145, 35, mm))
```

Here we create some formatted text and add it to a **Paragraph** that we draw in a fixed position on the canvas. Then we create some more text that we add to a second Paragraph and draw it as well. Don't forget to update the **main()** method to call your **create_header** method:

```python
def main(pdf_file):
    """ """
    eob = EOB(pdf_file)
    eob.create_header()
    eob.save()
```

Save this code as **eob2.py** and then run the script. If everything works correctly, you should end up with a PDF that looks like this:

Chapter 11 - Turning Data into PDFs

Fig. 11-2: Adding a simple header

Adding the Summary Section

Let's move on and update another method in our **EOB** class. This time, we will fill out the **create_-payment_summary** method:

```
def create_payment_summary(self):
    """ """
    ptext = '<font size=26>Your payment summary</font>'
    p = Paragraph(ptext, self.styles["Normal"])
    p.wrapOn(self.canvas, self.width, self.height)
    p.drawOn(self.canvas, *self.coord(15, 47, mm))

    colWidths = [75, 125, 50, 125, 50, 150]

    data = [['', '', '', '', '', ''],
            [self.create_bold_text('Patient'),
             self.create_bold_text('Provider'),
             self.create_bold_text('Amount'),
             self.create_bold_text('Sent to'),
             self.create_bold_text('Date'),
             self.create_bold_text('Amount'),
             ]]
    table = Table(data, colWidths=colWidths)
    table.wrapOn(self.canvas, self.width, self.height)
    table.drawOn(self.canvas, 20, 600)
```

Here we create another **Paragraph** object with some text and we also create a **Table**. The table will hold the summary of the payment. You will note that we call another method here named **create_bold_text**. Let's create that method now:

```
def create_bold_text(self, text, size=8):
    """"""
    return Paragraph('''<font size={size}><b>
    {text}</b></font>
    '''.format(size=size, text=text),
       self.styles['Normal'])
```

This is just a helper method that will take a string and a font size as its arguments. Then it will return a Paragraph object that bolds the text. For this version of the code, let's save it as **eob3.py**. Note that you will also need to update the **main()** function so that it calls your newly defined method:

```
def main(pdf_file):
    """"""
    eob = EOB(pdf_file)
    eob.create_header()
    eob.create_payment_summary()
    eob.save()
```

Save this code as **eob3.py**. When you run this updated code, you will see that the result now looks like the following:

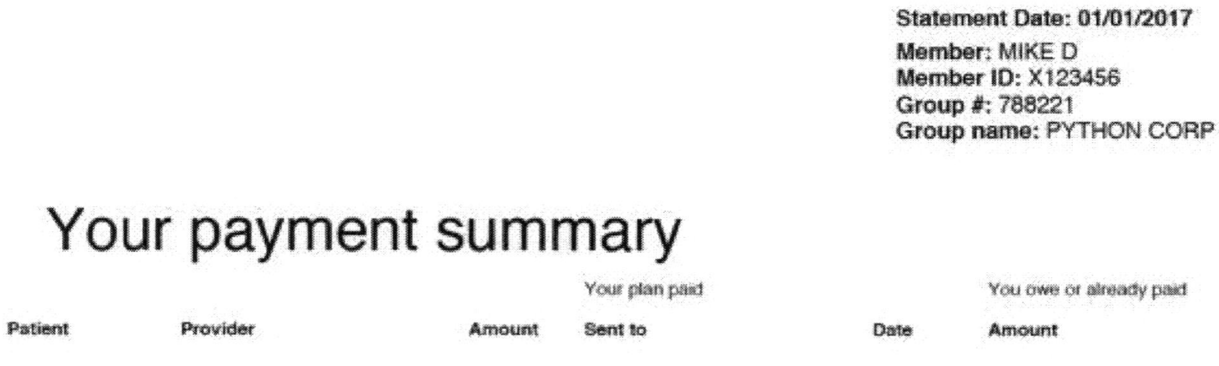
Statement Date: 01/01/2017
Member: MIKE D
Member ID: X123456
Group #: 788221
Group name: PYTHON CORP

Your payment summary

Patient	Provider	Amount	Your plan paid Sent to	Date	You owe or already paid Amount

Fig. 11-3: Adding the payment summary

Adding the Claims Section

The next method we need to create is the **create_claims** method in our EOB class. This method is a bit longer than any of the other methods we have looked at as of yet. Let's take a look though:

Chapter 11 - Turning Data into PDFs

```python
def create_claims(self):
    """"""
    fsize = 8

    ptext = '<font size=26>Your claims up close</font>'
    p = Paragraph(ptext, self.styles["Normal"])
    p.wrapOn(self.canvas, self.width, self.height)
    p.drawOn(self.canvas, *self.coord(10, 100, mm))

    claim = Paragraph('''<font size={0}>
        Claim ID {1}<br/>
        Received on 12/12/16<br/></font>
        '''.format(fsize, 'ER123456789'),
            self.styles["Normal"])
    billed = Paragraph(
        '<font size={}>Amount<br/>billed</font>'.format(fsize),
        self.styles["Normal"])
    member_rate = Paragraph(
        '<font size={}>Member<br/>rate</font>'.format(fsize),
        self.styles["Normal"])
    pending = Paragraph(
        '<font size={}>Pending or<br/>not payable<br/>(Remarks)</font>'
        .format(fsize),
        self.styles["Normal"])
    applied = Paragraph(
        '<font size={}>Applied to<br/>deductible</font>'.format(fsize),
        self.styles["Normal"])
    copay = Paragraph(
        '<font size={}>Your<br/>copay</font>'.format(fsize),
        self.styles["Normal"])
    remaining = Paragraph(
        '<font size={}>Amount<br/>remaining</font>'.format(fsize),
        self.styles["Normal"])
    plan_pays = Paragraph(
        '<font size={}>Plan<br/>pays</font>'.format(fsize),
        self.styles["Normal"])
    coins = Paragraph(
        '<font size={}>Your<br/>coinsurance</font>'.format(fsize),
        self.styles["Normal"])
    owe = Paragraph(
        '<font size={}>You owe<br/>C+D+E+H=I</font>'.format(fsize),
        self.styles["Normal"])
```

```
    data = [[claim, billed, member_rate, pending, applied,
             remaining, plan_pays, coins, owe],
            ]
    colWidths = [110, 50, 50, 60, 50, 50, 50, 70, 60]
    table = Table(data, colWidths=colWidths)
    table.wrapOn(self.canvas, self.width, self.height)
    table.drawOn(self.canvas, 20, 450)
```

In this method, we create a series of Paragraphs and end this method with another Table object. We use the Paragraphs to format the text the way we want. The Table doesn't really have any formatting applied to it at this time. As you've probably gathered by now, you will want to update the **main()** function to reflect our changes:

```
def main(pdf_file):
    """"""
    eob = EOB(pdf_file)
    eob.create_header()
    eob.create_payment_summary()
    eob.create_claims()
    eob.save()
```

To continue to keep our iterations separate, you can edit the previous example and then save it as **eob4.py**. When you run this example, the result should look something like this:

Fig. 11-4: Adding the claims

It's kind of annoying needing to update the **main()** function all the time. Now is a good time to refactor the class and switch over to using Flowables rather than continuing to use Canvas methods.

Refactoring the EOB Class

The first thing we need to do is update our imports a bit. Here is how I would like you to update the imports at the top of your new **eob_flow.py** file:

```
# eob_flow.py

import time
from reportlab.lib.enums import TA_JUSTIFY
from reportlab.lib.pagesizes import letter
from reportlab.lib.styles import getSampleStyleSheet, ParagraphStyle
from reportlab.lib.units import inch, mm
from reportlab.pdfgen import canvas
from reportlab.platypus import SimpleDocTemplate, Paragraph, Spacer, Image
from reportlab.platypus import Flowable, Indenter, Table
```

Now let's create a custom **Header** Flowable to hold our page header. This will allow us to easily update the header and we can also move the Header class into its own module if we want to. Here's the code:

```python
class Header(Flowable):

    def __init__(self, width=150, height=50):
        Flowable.__init__(self)
        self.width = width
        self.height = height
        self.styles = getSampleStyleSheet()

    def coord(self, x, y, unit=1):
        x, y = x * unit, self.height -  y * unit
        return x, y

    def draw(self):
        ptext = '<font size=10><b>Statement Date: {}' \
                '</b></font>'.format('01/01/2017')

        p = Paragraph(ptext, self.styles["Normal"])
        p.wrapOn(self.canv, self.width, self.height)
        p.drawOn(self.canv, *self.coord(110, 14, mm))

        ptext = '''<font size=10>
        <b>Member:</b> {member}<br/>
        <b>Member ID:</b> {member_id}<br/>
        <b>Group #:</b> {group_num}<br/>
        <b>Group name:</b> {group_name}<br/>
        </font>
        '''.format(member='MIKE D',
                   member_id='X123456',
                   group_num=789456-1235,
                   group_name='PYTHON CORP'
                   )
        p = Paragraph(ptext, self.styles["Normal"])
        p.wrapOn(self.canv, self.width, self.height)
        p.drawOn(self.canv, *self.coord(110, 35, mm))
```

This class is just a subclass of ReportLab's **Flowable** class. We allow the developer to set the width and height of the Flowable. Then we create the **coord** method that we talked about earlier in the chapter and override the **draw** method of the Flowable class. This allows us to draw our header where we want it to go. Now we need to update the **EOB** class to call our new **Header** class.

```python
class EOB:
    """
    Explanation of Benefits PDF Class
    """

    def __init__(self, pdf_file):
        """"""
        self.doc = SimpleDocTemplate(
            pdf_file, pagesize=letter,
            rightMargin=72, leftMargin=36,
            topMargin=36, bottomMargin=18)
        self.elements = []
        self.styles = getSampleStyleSheet()
        self.width, self.height = letter

    def create_header(self):
        """"""
        header = Header()
        self.elements.append(header)
        self.elements.append(Spacer(1, 50))
```

Here we update the **__init__()** method to create an instance of **SimpleDocTemplate** instead of **canvas.Canvas**. We set up the page size and the margins in our document template while we are at it. We also create a Flowables list that we call **elements** and we create a stylesheet. Finally we save off the width and height of the page for use later on in the class.

Next we update the **create_header** method so that it creates an instance of the Header class. Then we append our Header to the Flowables list and add a Spacer object too.

To make things a bit simpler, I decided to replace the **create_bold_text** method with a more generic **create_text** method:

```python
def create_text(self, text, size=8, bold=False):
    """"""
    if bold:
        return Paragraph('''<font size={size}><b>
        {text}</b></font>
        '''.format(size=size, text=text),
            self.styles['Normal'])

    return Paragraph('''<font size={size}>
    {text}</font>
    '''.format(size=size, text=text),
        self.styles['Normal'])
```

This method will only bold the text if the **bold** parameter is set. Otherwise it just sets the font size and returns a Paragraph object. The next update needs to happen to the **create_payment_summary** method. Let's take a look:

```
def create_payment_summary(self):
    """ """
    ptext = '<font size=26>Your payment summary</font>'
    p = Paragraph(ptext, self.styles["Normal"])
    self.elements.append(p)
    self.elements.append(Spacer(1, 20))

    colWidths = [75, 125, 50, 125, 50, 150]

    data = [['', '', '', '', '', ''],
            [self.create_text('Patient', bold=True),
             self.create_text('Provider', bold=True),
             self.create_text('Amount', bold=True),
             self.create_text('Sent to', bold=True),
             self.create_text('Date', bold=True),
             self.create_text('Amount', bold=True),
            ]]
    self.elements.append(Indenter(left=60))
    table = Table(data, colWidths=colWidths)
    self.elements.append(table)
    self.elements.append(Indenter(left=-60))
```

Here we create some Paragraphs and a Spacer. You will note that we have updated the table's data to call our **create_text** method. This allows us to format the table's content because we are now using Paragraphs instead of just plain strings.

The next method we need to update is also the largest. It is the **create_claims** method:

```
def create_claims(self):
    """ """
    fsize = 8

    ptext = '<font size=26>Your claims up close</font>'
    p = Paragraph(ptext, self.styles["Normal"])
    self.elements.append(p)
    self.elements.append(Spacer(1, 20))

    claim = Paragraph('''<font size={0}>
        Claim ID {1}<br/>
```

```
            Received on 12/12/16<br/></font>
    '''.format(fsize, 'ER123456789'),
        self.styles["Normal"])
billed = Paragraph(
    '<font size={}>Amount<br/>billed</font>'.format(fsize),
    self.styles["Normal"])
member_rate = Paragraph(
    '<font size={}>Member<br/>rate</font>'.format(fsize),
    self.styles["Normal"])
pending = Paragraph(
    '<font size={}>Pending or<br/>not payable<br/>(Remarks)</font>'
    .format(fsize),
    self.styles["Normal"])
applied = Paragraph(
    '<font size={}>Applied to<br/>deductible</font>'.format(fsize),
    self.styles["Normal"])
copay = Paragraph(
    '<font size={}>Your<br/>copay</font>'.format(fsize),
    self.styles["Normal"])
remaining = Paragraph(
    '<font size={}>Amount<br/>remaining</font>'.format(fsize),
    self.styles["Normal"])
plan_pays = Paragraph(
    '<font size={}>Plan<br/>pays</font>'.format(fsize),
    self.styles["Normal"])
coins = Paragraph(
    '<font size={}>Your<br/>coinsurance</font>'.format(fsize),
     self.styles["Normal"])
owe = Paragraph(
    '<font size={}>You owe<br/>C+D+E+H=I</font>'.format(fsize),
    self.styles["Normal"])

claim_one = [
    self.create_text('FLU VIRUS VACC-SPLIT 3 YR & on 9/12/16'),
    self.create_text('12.50'),
    '', '', '', '',
    self.create_text('12.50'),
    self.create_text('12.50 (100%)'),
    '', ''
]

data = [[claim, billed, member_rate, pending, applied,
```

```
            copay, remaining, plan_pays, coins, owe],
        ]
for item in range(50):
    data.append(claim_one)

colWidths = [110, 50, 50, 60, 50, 50, 50, 40, 60, 60]
table = Table(data, colWidths=colWidths)

self.elements.append(Indenter(left=60))
self.elements.append(table)
self.elements.append(Indenter(left=-60))
```

This one is pretty similar to the previous method updates that we have looked at. We do use a bit more in-line XML formatting of the Paragraphs here though. There is also a couple of examples of using the **Indenter** flowable, which you can use to indent another Flowable. In this case, we want to indent our Table 60 points from the left hand side of the page. Then we add the table. You will note that we also need to dedent or unindent the Flowable after adding the Table so that if we add anything after the Table, it won't get indented too.

I personally like to have a method that controls most of the rest of the script. We were using a **main** function earlier and we could keep doing so if we wanted to. But I decided to put all that logic into the class and added the following **create** method instead:

```
def create(self):
    """"""
    self.create_header()
    self.create_payment_summary()
    self.create_claims()
    self.save()
```

This method will create the various pieces of the document and then call the **save** method. One good reason to encapsulate all this logic into a class's method is that now you can import the module and run it more easily rather than trying to guess which of the functions you need to call to create a complete document. It's kind of like a demo, in other words.

Anyway, the save method also needs an update since we are now working with a document template instead of the Canvas:

```
def save(self):
    """"""
    self.doc.build(self.elements)
```

This should look familiar. We have to call the **build** method and pass in the list of flowables to have the PDF generated correctly.

Finally we can just remove the **main** function entirely and put all the logic into the following:

Chapter 11 - Turning Data into PDFs

```
if __name__ == '__main__':
    pdf_file = "eob_flow.pdf"
    eob = EOB(pdf_file)
    eob.create()
```

That was a lot of changes, but I think you will find that this code is much more flexible now. Feel free to stop and download the full version of the code from Github.

Now that you have the code, let's try running it. When you do, you will find that the result is pretty similar to the canvas code from the previous section.

Creating a Multipage Document

We have successfully updated all the code so that it uses Flowables instead of the Canvas. What this means is that we should be able to theoretically create a multipage document easily. To test that theory out, let's change the **create_claims** method so that it generates 50 rows of data. The following is the only snippet you need to change:

```
# Add these imports to the top of the file:
from reportlab.lib import colors
from reportlab.platypus import TableStyle

claim_one = [
        self.create_text('FLU VIRUS VACC-SPLIT 3 YR & on 9/12/16'),
        self.create_text('12.50'),
        '', '', '', '',
        self.create_text('12.50'),
        self.create_text('12.50 (100%)'),
        '', ''
    ]

data = [[claim, billed, member_rate, pending, applied,
        copay, remaining, plan_pays, coins, owe],
        ]

for item in range(50):
    data.append(claim_one)

# NEW CODE STARTS HERE
colWidths = [110, 50, 40, 60, 50, 40, 50, 40, 55, 60]
table_style = TableStyle(
    [('INNERGRID', (0,0), (-1,-1), 0.25, colors.black),  # Add grid to cells
```

Chapter 11 - Turning Data into PDFs

```
        ('BOX', (0,0), (-1,-1), 0.25, colors.black),  # add outer border
        ('BACKGROUND', (1,0), (1, -1), colors.lightgoldenrodyellow),
        ('BACKGROUND', (7,0), (7, -1), colors.lightgoldenrodyellow)
        ])

table = Table(data, colWidths=colWidths)
table.setStyle(table_style)
# NEW CODE ENDS HERE

self.elements.append(Indenter(left=40))
self.elements.append(table)
self.elements.append(Indenter(left=-40))
```

I left in the **claim_one** and the **data** variables for context. The real change starts at the loop, where we append the claim we created at the beginning of this snippet to our data list 50 times. Then we create a TableStyle instance to style the rows in our table. Finally we add the data to the Table and apply the table style. Then we get back to the original code again.

If you re-run the code with this update, you should now have a multipage document!

Fig. 11-5: **Making a multipage document**

Using Real Data

Now we have a decent piece of code, but it's only good at creating the same document over and over again. That's because everything is hard-coded in the code that we have created up until this point. We need to update our code so it can read an XML file and generate a report from it. Let's start by looking at a piece of example XML:

```xml
<?xml version="1.0" ?>
<patient>
    <claim_id>ER123456789</claim_id>
    <member_name>Mike D</member_name>
    <member_id>X123456</member_id>
    <group_num>788221</group_num>
    <group_name>Python Corp</group_name>
    <amount_owed>525.25</amount_owed>
    <sent_to></sent_to>
    <date>01/01/2018</date>
    <amount_paid></amount_paid>
    <received_date>12/20/2017</received_date>
    <claims>
        <claim>
            <description>FLU VIRUS VACC-SPLIT 3 YR and on 9/12/16</description>
            <amount_billed>12.50</amount_billed>
            <member_rate></member_rate>
            <pending></pending>
            <deductible></deductible>
            <copay></copay>
            <amount_remaining>12.50</amount_remaining>
            <plan_pays>12.50</plan_pays>
            <coinsurance></coinsurance>
            <total_owed>0.00</total_owed>
            <received_date>12/20/2017</received_date>
        </claim>
    </claims>
</patient>
```

We should be able to take this XML and use it for the data that we feed to our ReportLab module. This particular piece of XML will only create a table with two rows though, so we won't be able to generate a multipage document with it. However, this is a good place to start with. Note that in real data, you would have several claims per patient and multiple patients per XML file. In fact, when I used to consume XML like this, it wasn't uncommon to have thousands patients with dozens (or occasionally, over a hundred) claims per patient.

When you have files like that, you might not want to load the entire file into memory. Instead, what I would do is write a pre-parser (or pre-processor) script that would split out each patient into its own self-contained XML file. Then each file would be fed to the report generating module.

We don't need to do the pre-processing part of it here. We just need to figure out how to parse a self-contained XML file.

Python comes with several XML modules built into the standard library. My favorite of those is **ElementTree**. However, I actually prefer a third party XML package called **lxml**, so we will use it instead. You can install lxml with the following command:

```
pip install lxml
```

Once you have that installed, we will need to update the code so it can consume XML!

Consuming XML

I am going to create a copy of the last script we wrote and call it **eob_flow_consumer.py**. Feel free to download the full code from Github so you can follow along.

The first step to consume XML in our report module is to update the imports in our code:

```python
# eob_flow_consumer.py

import os
import time

from lxml import objectify
from reportlab.lib import colors
from reportlab.lib.enums import TA_JUSTIFY
from reportlab.lib.pagesizes import letter
from reportlab.lib.styles import getSampleStyleSheet, ParagraphStyle
from reportlab.lib.units import inch, mm
from reportlab.pdfgen import canvas
from reportlab.platypus import SimpleDocTemplate, Paragraph, Spacer, Image
from reportlab.platypus import Flowable, Indenter, Table, TableStyle
```

Here we import **objectify**, which is a sub-module within the **lxml** package. The **objectify** module allows us to turn our XML into a Python object.

The first thing we will need to do is modify the **Header** class so that it accepts the XML object:

```python
class Header(Flowable):

    def __init__(self, xml_data, width=150, height=50):
        Flowable.__init__(self)
        self.xml_data = xml_data
        self.width = width
        self.height = height
        self.styles = getSampleStyleSheet()

    def coord(self, x, y, unit=1):
        x, y = x * unit, self.height -  y * unit
        return x, y

    def draw(self):
        ptext = '<font size=10><b>Statement Date: {}' \
            '</b></font>'.format('01/01/2017')

        p = Paragraph(ptext, self.styles["Normal"])
        p.wrapOn(self.canv, self.width, self.height)
        p.drawOn(self.canv, *self.coord(110, 14, mm))

        ptext = '''<font size=10>
        <b>Member:</b> {member}<br/>
        <b>Member ID:</b> {member_id}<br/>
        <b>Group #:</b> {group_num}<br/>
        <b>Group name:</b> {group_name}<br/>
        </font>
        '''.format(member=self.xml_data.member_name,
                   member_id=self.xml_data.member_id,
                   group_num=self.xml_data.group_num,
                   group_name=self.xml_data.group_name
                   )
        p = Paragraph(ptext, self.styles["Normal"])
        p.wrapOn(self.canv, self.width, self.height)
        p.drawOn(self.canv, *self.coord(110, 35, mm))
```

Here we insert a new parameter called **xml_data** that is required. Then we create an instance attribute with the same name. Finally we need to update the Header's **draw** method so that it uses the XML object that we passed in to replace the Member and Group information in our header with whatever is in the XML object.

Now we are ready to move on and update the **EOB** class. However, I will only focus on the methods that need updating. The first thing we need to do is modify the **__init__** method:

```python
class EOB:
    """
    Explanation of Benefits PDF Class
    """

    def __init__(self, xml_file, pdf_file='eob.pdf'):
        """"""
        if not os.path.exists(xml_file):
            raise RuntimeError('XML file ({}) does not exist!'.format(xml_file))

        self.xml = self.parse_xml(xml_file)

        self.doc = SimpleDocTemplate(
            pdf_file, pagesize=letter,
            rightMargin=72, leftMargin=36,
            topMargin=36, bottomMargin=18)
        self.elements = []
        self.styles = getSampleStyleSheet()
        self.width, self.height = letter
```

Here we add a new parameter for accepting the XML file path and we also default the name of the PDF. Next we verify that the XML file path that we passed in exists. If not, we raise a **RuntimeError**. Finally, we create an instance variable called **self.xml** by calling a function called **parse_xml** with the XML file path as its argument. Let's create that new method now:

```python
def parse_xml(self, xml_file):
    with open(xml_file) as f:
        xml = f.read()

    root = objectify.fromstring(xml)
    return root
```

All this method does is read the XML file's contents into memory. Then we pass the file's contents to lxml using the **objectify.fromstring** method. This will turn our XML into a Python object that we can then use throughout the rest of our EOB class.

Next up, we need to modify the **create_header** method slightly so it can pass the XML object to the Header class:

Chapter 11 - Turning Data into PDFs

```
def create_header(self):
    """"""
    header = Header(self.xml)
    self.elements.append(header)
    self.elements.append(Spacer(1, 50))
```

That was pretty straight-forward, eh?

There are a couple of methods in the EOB class that we don't even need to change. They are the following two methods:

- create_text
- create_payment_summary

These methods do not depend on the XML in any way, so we don't need to reproduce them again here. In fact, most of the changes will occur in the **create_claims** method. Let's break that method up a bit to make the changes more obvious:

```
def create_claims(self):
    """"""
    fsize = 7.5

    ptext = '<font size=26>Your claims up close</font>'
    p = Paragraph(ptext, self.styles["Normal"])
    self.elements.append(p)
    self.elements.append(Spacer(1, 20))

    claim = Paragraph('''<font size={fsize}>
        Claim ID {claim_id}<br/>
        Received on {received_date}<br/></font>
        '''.format(fsize=fsize,
                   claim_id=self.xml.claim_id,
                   received_date=self.xml.received_date),
        self.styles["Normal"])
```

Here we change the **claim** variable so that the Paragraph instance is created using values from the XML rather than using the hard-coded one we had used earlier. The next portion of the code is required, but no changes were done to it:

```
billed = Paragraph(
    '<font size={}>Amount<br/>billed</font>'.format(fsize),
    self.styles["Normal"])
member_rate = Paragraph(
    '<font size={}>Member<br/>rate</font>'.format(fsize),
    self.styles["Normal"])
pending = Paragraph(
    '<font size={}>Pending or<br/>not payable<br/>(Remarks)</font>'.format(fsize\
),
    self.styles["Normal"])
applied = Paragraph(
    '<font size={}>Applied to<br/>deductible</font>'.format(fsize),
    self.styles["Normal"])
copay = Paragraph(
    '<font size={}>Your<br/>copay</font>'.format(fsize), self.styles["Normal"])
remaining = Paragraph(
    '<font size={}>Amount<br/>remaining</font>'.format(fsize), self.styles["Norm\
al"])
plan_pays = Paragraph(
    '<font size={}>Plan<br/>pays</font>'.format(fsize), self.styles["Normal"])
coins = Paragraph(
    '<font size={}>Your<br/>coinsurance</font>'.format(fsize), self.styles["Norm\
al"])
owe = Paragraph(
    '<font size={}>You owe<br/>C+D+E+H=I</font>'.format(fsize), self.styles["Nor\
mal"])

data = [[claim, billed, member_rate, pending, applied,
        copay, remaining, plan_pays, coins, owe],
        ]
```

All this code does is set up the rest of the header columns for the Table. The major change is this next bit:

```
for claim in self.xml.claims.getchildren():
    data.append([
        self.create_text(claim.description),
        self.create_text(claim.amount_billed.text),
        self.create_text(claim.member_rate),
        self.create_text(claim.pending),
        self.create_text(claim.deductible),
        self.create_text(claim.copay),
        self.create_text(claim.amount_remaining.text),
        self.create_text(claim.plan_pays.text),
        self.create_text(claim.coinsurance),
        self.create_text(claim.total_owed.text)
    ])
```

Here we actually loop over the children of the **claims** XML tag. In this example, the **claims** tag only has one child. But when we update the XML to have additional claims, this code will happily loop over all of them. It then extracts the values from the XML. One thing I want to point out is that when you use lxml to extract floats from XML, it will truncate the second significant digit, thus making 12.50 into 12.5. While this is normal Python behavior, it doesn't look correct in a report. This is why you will see that when I am dealing with floats, I access the raw value by accessing the **text** attribute above. Another way to get around this would be to just format the text using Python's **.2f** string formatter syntax.

This code actually has an intentional bug in it in that I don't access that **text** attribute in all the places that I should. Try updating the XML for the deductible or copay fields and you might end up seeing how the truncating looks.

Anyway, the rest of the **create_claims** method remains unchanged:

```
colWidths = [110, 50, 40, 60, 50, 40, 50, 40, 55, 60]
table_style = TableStyle(
    [('INNERGRID', (0,0), (-1,-1), 0.25, colors.black),   # Add grid to cells
     ('BOX', (0,0), (-1,-1), 0.25, colors.black),   # add outer border
     ('BACKGROUND', (1,0), (1, -1), colors.lightgoldenrodyellow),
     ('BACKGROUND', (7,0), (7, -1), colors.lightgoldenrodyellow)
    ])

table = Table(data, colWidths=colWidths)
table.setStyle(table_style)

self.elements.append(Indenter(left=40))
self.elements.append(table)
self.elements.append(Indenter(left=-40))
```

You also do not need to update the **create** or the **save** methods since they do not have anything to do with XML either. However, you do need to update the last few lines of code to pass in the XML file itself:

```
if __name__ == '__main__':
    eob = EOB(xml_file='eob.xml')
    eob.create()
```

Now if you run this updated code, you will find that it generates the report using real data instead of the hard-coded values. In the Github repository, I have added an extra XML file with 50 claims in it so you can create a multipage document using this code as well. Give that a try and see how it works.

Wrapping Up

This chapter is based on some of my personal experiences writing parsers for XML and other data formats and then taking the parsed data and turning it into PDFs. The nice thing about working with XML is that you already have good libraries or packages like Python's ElementTree or lxml to turn the XML into objects. But if your data is JSON, CSV or some other format, then you will need to find some other way to use that data.

My favorite method is to create a class that parses out the data I need and basically creates an object much like the one that is generated by lxml's **objectify** module. Then I can just pass an object to my report module that I can just use attribute access on for filling out the report. In the next chapter, we will learn how to generate custom headers and footers.

In the meantime, feel free to play around with the XML examples provided for this chapter on Github. Try changing some of the values in the tags and re-running the code a few times to see how thing change.

Chapter 12 - Custom Headers and Footers

There are many documents and reports that require you to have a header on the first page or on every page. For example, if you are generating a report for a lawyer or judge, then you will almost certainly need the partnership information on all the pages. The same is true when generating reports in most medical offices or hospitals. Their stationary is required to look a certain way.

Most of the time, these headers will contain the following fields:

- Date
- Name or names of people (like all the doctors in the practice)
- Address
- Phone / Fax
- Website
- Logo

Some documents have other information. For example:

- document number
- page number
- page number with total number of pages
- ID numbers

The header can really have an infinite number of fields when you think about it. I can think of many others. Just open up some mail from your financial institutions or your insurance company and you will see other fields that they put in their headers. This kind of thing can also apply to footers. However footers usually don't have as many fields. They tend to have page numbers most of the time, although I have seen some that include some type of contact information.

In this chapter we will learn how to do the following to our headers:

- Create a general header / footer template
- Add page numbers
- Add page numbers with a total number of pages
- Add logos
- Add other fields

This information will also apply to footers. We will be creating several different templates that we can use in generating our headers. Let's start by looking at the one we created in the previous chapter.

A Naive Header

When you are writing code, you usually want to create your own reusable modules. So let's try to do that with our report generating code. In this case, we will create a simple header class using the one from the previous chapter. We will call this module **header.py**. Here's the code:

```python
# header.py

from reportlab.lib.units import mm
from reportlab.lib.styles import getSampleStyleSheet
from reportlab.platypus import Flowable, Paragraph

class Header(Flowable):

    def __init__(self, xml_data, width=150, height=50):
        Flowable.__init__(self)
        self.xml_data = xml_data
        self.width = width
        self.height = height
        self.styles = getSampleStyleSheet()

    def coord(self, x, y, unit=1):
        x, y = x * unit, self.height -  y * unit
        return x, y

    def draw(self):
        ptext = '<font size=10><b>Statement Date: {}' \
            '</b></font>'.format('01/01/2017')

        p = Paragraph(ptext, self.styles["Normal"])
        p.wrapOn(self.canv, self.width, self.height)
        p.drawOn(self.canv, *self.coord(110, 14, mm))

        ptext = '''<font size=10>
        <b>Member:</b> {member}<br/>
        <b>Member ID:</b> {member_id}<br/>
        <b>Group #:</b> {group_num}<br/>
        <b>Group name:</b> {group_name}<br/>
        </font>
        '''.format(member=self.xml_data.member_name,
                   member_id=self.xml_data.member_id,
                   group_num=self.xml_data.group_num,
```

```
                    group_name=self.xml_data.group_name
                    )
        p = Paragraph(ptext, self.styles["Normal"])
        p.wrapOn(self.canv, self.width, self.height)
        p.drawOn(self.canv, *self.coord(110, 35, mm))
```

Now we just need to write some code that can use our new header module. Create a new file called **main.py** and add the following code:

```
# main.py

from header import Header
from lxml import objectify
from reportlab.platypus import SimpleDocTemplate


def parse_xml(xml_file):
    with open(xml_file) as f:
        xml = f.read()

    root = objectify.fromstring(xml)
    return root


def main(pdf_file, xml_file):
    doc = SimpleDocTemplate(
        pdf_file,
        rightMargin=72, leftMargin=36,
        topMargin=36, bottomMargin=18)

    xml = parse_xml(xml_file)

    elements = []

    header = Header(xml)
    elements.append(header)
    doc.build(elements)

if __name__ == '__main__':
    main(pdf_file='header.pdf', xml_file='eob.xml')
```

All this code does is import our **Header** class from our **header** module, create an instance of it and add it to our list of flowables before generating the report. The result of running this second example looks like this:

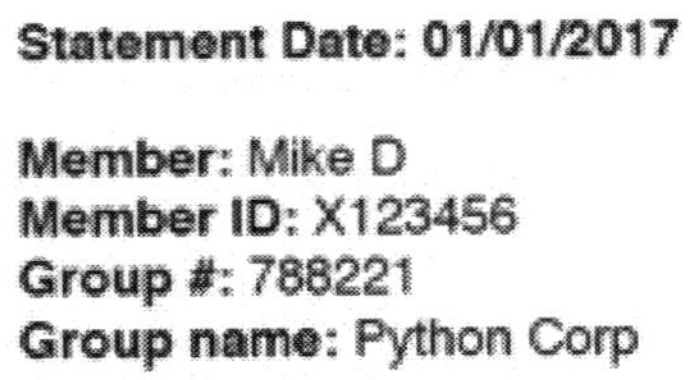

Statement Date: 01/01/2017

Member: Mike D
Member ID: X123456
Group #: 788221
Group name: Python Corp

Fig. 12-1: A Simple Header Example

This looks nice and all, but it's not a true header. It is just a flowable. When you create a header using this method, you will have to manually add it each time you create a new page, which can be difficult to calculate on the fly. So let's learn how to make this work the right way!

Putting the Header on Every Page

When you build a document, you have a couple of extra special arguments that you can use to control what happens on the first page as well as what happens on all the subsequent pages. These arguments are called **onFirstPage** and **onLaterPages**. You can use this knowledge to craft custom headers and footers and then just adjust the document template's margins to account for them.

Let's start by creating a new header module that we will call **header2.py**. Here is what it should look like:

```
# header2.py

from reportlab.lib.styles import getSampleStyleSheet
from reportlab.platypus import Paragraph


def header(canvas, doc):
    width, height = doc.pagesize

    styles = getSampleStyleSheet()

    ptext = '<font size=10><b>Statement Date: {}' \
        '</b></font>'.format('01/01/2017')

    p = Paragraph(ptext, styles["Normal"])
    p.wrapOn(canvas, width, height)
    p.drawOn(canvas, 400, 800)
```

```
    ptext = '''<font size=10>
<b>Member:</b> {member}<br/>
<b>Member ID:</b> {member_id}<br/>
<b>Group #:</b> {group_num}<br/>
<b>Group name:</b> {group_name}<br/>
</font>
'''.format(member=doc.xml.member_name,
           member_id=doc.xml.member_id,
           group_num=doc.xml.group_num,
           group_name=doc.xml.group_name
           )
    p = Paragraph(ptext, styles["Normal"])
    p.wrapOn(canvas, width, height)
    p.drawOn(canvas, 400, 730)
```

This code only needs two imports, where we grab the sample style sheet that we can use with Paragraphs and the Paragraph class itself. Then we create the **header** function, which takes a **canvas** and a **DocumentTemplate** object as its sole arguments. Next we grab the document's width and height and create a sample style sheet. The rest of the function is just using absolute positioning to get the various bits and pieces of text where we want it.

The next thing we need to do is create a new entry point for our code. For this task, we will create a file called **main2.py** and save the following to it:

```
# main2.py

from header2 import header
from lxml import objectify
from reportlab.lib.styles import getSampleStyleSheet
from reportlab.platypus import SimpleDocTemplate
from reportlab.platypus import Paragraph


def parse_xml(xml_file):
    with open(xml_file) as f:
        xml = f.read()

    root = objectify.fromstring(xml)
    return root

def main(pdf_file, xml_file):
    doc = SimpleDocTemplate(
```

```
            pdf_file,
            rightMargin=72, leftMargin=36,
            topMargin=125, bottomMargin=18)

    xml = parse_xml(xml_file)

    elements = []

    txt = 'Lorem ipsum dolor sit amet, consectetur adipiscing elit,'
    styles = getSampleStyleSheet()
    for line in range(150):
        paragraph = Paragraph(txt, styles["Normal"])
        elements.append(paragraph)

    doc.xml = xml

    doc.build(elements, onFirstPage=header, onLaterPages=header)

if __name__ == '__main__':
    main(pdf_file='main2.pdf', xml_file='eob.xml')
```

The only new import here is our new **header** function. We don't need to update our **parse_xml** function at all. So let's move on to our **main** function. Here we just need to create a new attribute on our **doc** object to hold our XML object. Then we call **doc.build** and pass in our list of Flowables and set the **onFirstPage** argument to our **header** function. The purpose of the **onFirstPage** argument is to tell ReportLab to do something special on just the first page of your document, which in this case is adding a header. It will implicitly pass that function a canvas object and our document template object.

The **onLaterPages** argument is similar. It also takes a function that should be of the same format as the onFirstPage argument. This function will be called on all pages after the first page but NOT on the first page itself. This is useful for those times when you want a header on the first page but not on any of the others. Instead you might add a footer or some page numbers instead.

One other note that I'd like to bring up is that you will need to set your **topMargin** argument to an amount that takes the header's width into account. This usually takes a bit of experimentation. As you can see, I ended up using 125 points for the top margin in this example. You will need to something similar for the **bottomMargin** argument is you happen to add a footer.

Now let's move on to making our header look more professional by adding a logo!

Adding a Logo

Most headers you see will include some kind of logo on the page. Logos are important branding for most businesses, so being able to add a logo to your report is a must.

Let's update our **header** module so that we can add a logo. Make sure you name this module **header3.py**:

```
# header3.py

from reportlab.lib.styles import getSampleStyleSheet
from reportlab.platypus import Paragraph, Image


def header(canvas, doc):
    width, height = doc.pagesize

    styles = getSampleStyleSheet()

    ptext = '<font size=10><b>Statement Date: {}' \
        '</b></font>'.format('01/01/2017')

    img = Image(doc.logo_path, width=76.2, height=76.2)
    img.wrapOn(canvas, width, height)
    img.drawOn(canvas, 100, 725)

    p = Paragraph(ptext, styles["Normal"])
    p.wrapOn(canvas, width, height)
    p.drawOn(canvas, 400, 800)

    ptext = '''<font size=10>
    <b>Member:</b> {member}<br/>
    <b>Member ID:</b> {member_id}<br/>
    <b>Group #:</b> {group_num}<br/>
    <b>Group name:</b> {group_name}<br/>
    </font>
    '''.format(member=doc.xml.member_name,
               member_id=doc.xml.member_id,
               group_num=doc.xml.group_num,
               group_name=doc.xml.group_name
               )
    p = Paragraph(ptext, styles["Normal"])
```

```
    p.wrapOn(canvas, width, height)
    p.drawOn(canvas, 400, 730)
```

Here we add an import for the **Image** flowable. Then we set the size of the image to be 76.2 x 76.2 points and we draw the image in the upper left side of the header.

An obvious future improvement would be to only pass in images that are already at the correct size as you do not want to hard code the dimensions of the image if the logos you will be inserting might vary in width. For example, I have written code where we just set the height of the image but the width can be variable. As long the width of the logo isn't too much, this can greatly simplify your code.

The final step is to update our main script, which we will rename **main3.py**:

```
# main3.py

from header3 import header
from lxml import objectify
from reportlab.lib.styles import getSampleStyleSheet
from reportlab.platypus import SimpleDocTemplate
from reportlab.platypus import Paragraph


def parse_xml(xml_file):
    with open(xml_file) as f:
        xml = f.read()

    root = objectify.fromstring(xml)
    return root

def main(pdf_file, xml_file, logo):
    doc = SimpleDocTemplate(
        pdf_file,
        rightMargin=72, leftMargin=36,
        topMargin=125, bottomMargin=18)

    xml = parse_xml(xml_file)

    elements = []

    txt = 'Lorem ipsum dolor sit amet, consectetur adipiscing elit,'
    styles = getSampleStyleSheet()
    paragraph = Paragraph(txt, styles["Normal"])
```

Chapter 12 - Custom Headers and Footers

```
    elements.append(paragraph)

    doc.xml = xml
    doc.logo_path = logo

    doc.build(elements, onFirstPage=header)

if __name__ == '__main__':
    main(pdf_file='main3.pdf', xml_file='eob.xml',
         logo='snakehead.jpg')
```

Here we update the import to use the new header module we created. Then we add a new attribute to our document template object called **logo_path** and set it to the passed in path. Finally we hard code in a "path" to the logo that we want to add to our header. When you run this code, the result should look like this:

Fig. 12-2: Header using a canvas + flowables

That looks pretty good, but it's not very flexible. Let's learn some different ways to make our code load different logos on command!

Configurable Logos

There are a lot of different ways that we can tell our code that we want to load a file. Here is just a few:

- Hard code the file path
- Pass it in as an argument (argparse)
- Read a config file
- Read it from the data file
- Load the logo from a database

In this section, we will look at how to pass the file path to our script using Python's **argparse** library. We will also look at how we could read the logo's file path using a config file and Python's **configparser** library.

Using Command Line Arguments

Python's standard library includes the **argparse** library, which is a pretty simple and straightforward way to add argument parsing to your applications. Technically, you could also use Python's **sys** module too. Let's take a look at how that would work first:

```python
# main4.py

import sys

from header3 import header
from lxml import objectify
from reportlab.lib.styles import getSampleStyleSheet
from reportlab.platypus import SimpleDocTemplate
from reportlab.platypus import Paragraph


def parse_xml(xml_file):
    with open(xml_file) as f:
        xml = f.read()

    root = objectify.fromstring(xml)
    return root

def main(pdf_file, xml_file, logo):
    doc = SimpleDocTemplate(
        pdf_file,
        rightMargin=72, leftMargin=36,
        topMargin=125, bottomMargin=18)

    xml = parse_xml(xml_file)

    elements = []

    txt = 'Lorem ipsum dolor sit amet, consectetur adipiscing elit,'
    styles = getSampleStyleSheet()
    paragraph = Paragraph(txt, styles["Normal"])
    elements.append(paragraph)
```

```
    doc.xml = xml
    doc.logo_path = logo

    doc.build(elements, onFirstPage=header)

if __name__ == '__main__':
    logo_path = sys.argv[1]
    main(pdf_file='main4.pdf', xml_file='eob.xml',
         logo=logo_path)
```

Here we add an import of the **sys** library. The other change is in the **if** statement at the bottom of the code. You can access all the arguments that are passed to your script via **sys.argv**, which returns a Python list. The first element in the list is always the path to your application or script. The other elements are the arguments passed to your script on the command line in the order that they were passed.

To run this script on the command line, you will need to do the following:

```
python3 main4.py /path/to/logo.jpg
```

When you run this example, you should see something similar to the previous example. However, there is a problem with this last piece of code though. If you don't pass in the path to the logo, you will receive an **IndexError** as the list that is returned from **sys.argv** contains only one element and we are trying to access element two.

A better version of that part of the code could go like this:

```
if __name__ == '__main__':
    if len(sys.argv) > 1:
        logo_path = sys.argv[1]
        main(pdf_file='main3.pdf', xml_file='eob.xml', logo=logo_path)
    else:
        raise RuntimeError('Logo path is a required argument!')
```

Now if we don't pass in the logo path, we raise a **RuntimeError** that explains the problem. You could go one better if you also add a check that verifies that the logo path is valid, but I will leave that to the reader.

Most of the time, I don't really recommend handling command line arguments this way. It's great for a prototype, but you will inevitably want to add other arguments. When you do that, it can become difficult to know what the order of the arguments should be. This is why I recommend that you use Python's **argparse** as it gives you a lot more flexibility when it comes to argument parsing.

There are also several other 3rd party argument parsing libraries that are good too, such as **docopt** or **python-fire**.

For this book, we will stick with **argparse** so you don't need to install anything else though. Feel free to check out some of those other projects though.

Let's take a few moments to update our code again so that it can utilize **argparse**. Here's the first part:

```
# main5.py

import argparse

from header3 import header
from lxml import objectify
from reportlab.lib.styles import getSampleStyleSheet
from reportlab.platypus import SimpleDocTemplate
from reportlab.platypus import Paragraph


def get_args():
    parser = argparse.ArgumentParser(
        description="Custom PDF Header with Logos")
    parser.add_argument('-l', '-logo', '--logo',
                        action='store',
                        required=True,
                        help="The logo's file path",
                        dest='logo')
    arguments = parser.parse_args()

    return arguments
```

Here we import the **argparse** library. You will also notice that we removed the **sys** library as we no longer need it. Next we create a **get_args** function. This creates our argument parser. When we create the parser, we give it a simple description. We also add an argument, which is one of the following: -l, -**logo** or –**logo**. We tell argparse that we want to save off the value and that it is a required argument. We store the argument in the "logo" attribute. Finally we parse the arguments that are passed in and return our object, which is an instance of **argparse.Namespace**.

Now we need to modify the rest of our new main script:

```python
def parse_xml(xml_file):
    with open(xml_file) as f:
        xml = f.read()

    root = objectify.fromstring(xml)
    return root


def main(pdf_file, xml_file):
    arguments = get_args()
    doc = SimpleDocTemplate(
        pdf_file,
        rightMargin=72, leftMargin=36,
        topMargin=125, bottomMargin=18)

    xml = parse_xml(xml_file)

    elements = []

    txt = 'Lorem ipsum dolor sit amet, consectetur adipiscing elit,'
    styles = getSampleStyleSheet()
    paragraph = Paragraph(txt, styles["Normal"])
    elements.append(paragraph)

    doc.xml = xml
    doc.logo_path = arguments.logo

    doc.build(elements, onFirstPage=header)

if __name__ == '__main__':
    main(pdf_file='main5.pdf', xml_file='eob.xml')
```

In this section, we only need to modify the **main** function. We call our **get_args*** function right away and then the rest of the code is pretty much the same. The only other difference is when we instantiate our **Header** class. Here we just pass in **arguments.logo** as our **logo** argument.

Let's try to run our new code without arguments:

```
python3 main5.py
```

When I ran this, I ended up with the following output:

```
usage: main5.py [-h] -l LOGO
main4.py: error: argument -l/-logo/--logo is required
```

That tells me that the "-l" argument is required. But it also mentions that I can pass a "-h" argument, which is something that we didn't even add. Let's see what happens when we do that:

```
python3 main5.py -h
```

Running it with the "-h" argument will give you this:

```
usage: main5.py [-h] -l LOGO

Custom PDF Header with Logos

optional arguments:
  -h, --help            show this help message and exit
  -l LOGO, -logo LOGO, --logo LOGO
                        The logo's file path
```

That is pretty helpful. Now we know that **argparse** automatically creates a help option. Now we can call our script the right way:

```
python main5.py -l snakehead.jpg
```

Remember when I said that you will often want to add new command line arguments? Well most of the time, your user will want to enter the PDF's name themselves and they should probably be able to pass in whatever XML data file that they want to as well. Let's make that possible in **main6.py**:

```
# main6.py

import argparse

from header3 import header
from lxml import objectify
from reportlab.lib.styles import getSampleStyleSheet
from reportlab.platypus import Paragraph
from reportlab.platypus import SimpleDocTemplate

def get_args():
    parser = argparse.ArgumentParser(
        description="Custom PDF Header with Logos")
```

```
    parser.add_argument('-l', '-logo', '--logo',
                        action='store',
                        required=True,
                        help="The logo's file path",
                        dest='logo')
    parser.add_argument('-d', '--data_file',
                        action='store',
                        required=True,
                        help="The data file path",
                        dest='data_file')
    parser.add_argument('-f', '-filepath', '--filepath',
                        action='store',
                        required=True,
                        help="The file path",
                        dest='path')
    arguments = parser.parse_args()

    return arguments
```

The first thing we need to do is update our **get_args** function. Here we add two new arguments to our argument parser: "-d" and "-f". We make both of these arguments required and we save off the values into our argparse object.

Now we can simplify our **main** function a bit:

```
def parse_xml(xml_file):
    with open(xml_file) as f:
        xml = f.read()

    root = objectify.fromstring(xml)
    return root


def main():
    arguments = get_args()
    doc = SimpleDocTemplate(
        arguments.path,
        rightMargin=72, leftMargin=36,
        topMargin=125, bottomMargin=18)

    xml = parse_xml(arguments.data_file)

    elements = []
```

```
    txt = 'Lorem ipsum dolor sit amet, consectetur adipiscing elit,'
    styles = getSampleStyleSheet()
    paragraph = Paragraph(txt, styles["Normal"])
    elements.append(paragraph)

    doc.xml = xml
    doc.logo_path = arguments.logo

    doc.build(elements, onFirstPage=header)

if __name__ == '__main__':
    main()
```

In this example, we update our instantiation of the **SimpleDocTemplate** so that it accesses our argparse object for the file path of the PDF. Then we update the call to the **parse_xml** function so it uses our argparse object as well for its data file. We also remove the arguments that were originally required for our **main** function to run. Otherwise, the code remains the same.

When you go to run your code now, you will be required to pass in all three arguments:

```
python main6.py -l snakehead.jpg -f main6.pdf -d eob.xml
```

The argparse library will allow you to pass these arguments in whatever order you want to. It will also prevent you from passing in two few or two many arguments. Go ahead and give the code a spin to see what happens when you don't pass in all the arguments. You can also try passing in an undefined argument.

Reading from a Config File

There are easier ways to tell your application what logo to use. One popular method is to put the path into a user modifiable config file. This gives the user the ability to change how a program works without needing to access the code, much like using the previous method of passing in paths on the command line. The nice thing about config files over command line arguments is that you can just set them and forget them.

Python has a decent config related library called **configparser**. If you are running Python 2, then the library is called **ConfigParser**. Note the difference in capitalization. Since we are using Python 3, we will be using the **configparser** version.

Let's create a new file called **main_config.py** and copy the last example into it. Now we are ready to add some modifications!

```python
# main_config.py

import configparser
import os

from header3 import header
from lxml import objectify
from reportlab.lib.styles import getSampleStyleSheet
from reportlab.platypus import Paragraph
from reportlab.platypus import SimpleDocTemplate

def get_logo_from_config():
    cfg_path = 'config.ini'
    if os.path.exists(cfg_path):
        config = configparser.ConfigParser()
        config.read(cfg_path)
        logo_path = config.get('General', 'logo_path')
        return logo_path
    else:
        return None

def parse_xml(xml_file):
    with open(xml_file) as f:
        xml = f.read()

    root = objectify.fromstring(xml)
    return root


def main(pdf_file, xml_file):
    doc = SimpleDocTemplate(
        pdf_file,
        rightMargin=72, leftMargin=36,
        topMargin=125, bottomMargin=18)

    xml = parse_xml(xml_file)

    doc.xml = xml
    doc.logo_path = get_logo_from_config()

    elements = []
```

```
    txt = 'Lorem ipsum dolor sit amet, consectetur adipiscing elit,'
    styles = getSampleStyleSheet()
    paragraph = Paragraph(txt, styles["Normal"])
    elements.append(paragraph)

    doc.build(elements, onFirstPage=header)

if __name__ == '__main__':
    main(pdf_file='main_config.pdf', xml_file='eob.xml')
```

The first thing we needed to do was import **configparser** and the **os** module. We also removed **argparse** to keep this example simpler. Feel free to take this example and the previous one and combine them so they use both though.

The next step is to create the new **get_logo_from_config** function. It is hard-coded to read from a local file called **config.ini**. If that files exists, we read it and try to extract the logo's file path from a section of the config file that is called "General". The other modification to our main script is where we instantiate the **Header** class near the end of the **main** function. Here we just call our **get_logo_from_config** function as a keyword argument.

If you run this code without creating the config file, it should work without any issues. You just won't have a logo in your header. Let's go ahead and create the **config.ini** file and enter the following into it:

```
[General]
logo_path = snakehead.jpg
```

Now re-run the code and you should now have a logo, assuming you entered a valid file path for the logo.

Adding Page Numbers

A lot of documents contain page numbers, so this is a worthy add-on feature that we should probably cover. Adding page numbers in ReportLab is actually pretty easy to do. Add we need to do is modify our header module again. This will be our fourth revision, so we will call it **header4.py**:

```python
# header4.py

from reportlab.lib.styles import getSampleStyleSheet
from reportlab.lib.units import mm

from reportlab.platypus import Paragraph


def header(canvas, doc):
    width, height = doc.pagesize

    styles = getSampleStyleSheet()

    ptext = '<font size=10><b>Statement Date: {}' \
        '</b></font>'.format('01/01/2017')

    p = Paragraph(ptext, styles["Normal"])
    p.wrapOn(canvas, width, height)
    p.drawOn(canvas, 400, 800)

    ptext = '''<font size=10>
<b>Member:</b> {member}<br/>
<b>Member ID:</b> {member_id}<br/>
<b>Group #:</b> {group_num}<br/>
<b>Group name:</b> {group_name}<br/>
</font>
'''.format(member=doc.xml.member_name,
           member_id=doc.xml.member_id,
           group_num=doc.xml.group_num,
           group_name=doc.xml.group_name
           )
    p = Paragraph(ptext, styles["Normal"])
    p.wrapOn(canvas, width, height)
    p.drawOn(canvas, 400, 730)

    # Add page number
    page_num = canvas.getPageNumber()
    text = "Page #%s" % page_num
    canvas.drawRightString(200*mm, 20*mm, text)
```

All we needed to do to add the page number is call the canvas's **getPageNumber** method. Then we draw it on the canvas via the **drawRightString** method. In this case, we draw the page number on the bottom right of each page.

You only need to update one line in our main module's code, which happens to be the import. We also rename the file to **page_number_main.py** so we can keep all these different versions separate:

```
# page_number_main.py

from header4 import header
```

The rest of the main module should be the same since the major code change happened in our header module.

Adding a Page Number of Total

When working with page numbers, it can be useful to have a running total of pages on each page (i.e. Page # of Total). To get this to work correctly, we need to subclass **canvas.Canvas** and use **doc.build**'s **canvasmaker** argument. There isn't a whole lot of information about what you use the **canvasmaker** argument for. But from my experience, it appears to be especially useful for those times when you need complete control over the placement of certain elements that will appear on each page.

To start off, we need to create a subclass of **canvas.Canvas**. Save the following code to a file named **custom_canvas.py**:

```
# custom_canvas.py

from reportlab.lib.units import mm
from reportlab.pdfgen import canvas


class PageNumCanvas(canvas.Canvas):

    def __init__(self, *args, **kwargs):
        """Constructor"""
        canvas.Canvas.__init__(self, *args, **kwargs)
        self.pages = []

    def showPage(self):
        """
        On a page break, add information to the list
        """
        self.pages.append(dict(self.__dict__))
        self._startPage()
```

```python
    def save(self):
        """
        Add the page number to each page (page x of y)
        """
        page_count = len(self.pages)
        
        for page in self.pages:
            self.__dict__.update(page)
            self.draw_page_number(page_count)
            canvas.Canvas.showPage(self)
        
        canvas.Canvas.save(self)
    
    def draw_page_number(self, page_count):
        """
        Add the page number
        """
        page = "Page %s of %s" % (self._pageNumber, page_count)
        self.setFont("Helvetica", 9)
        self.drawRightString(200*mm, 20*mm, page)
```

Here we set up a custom Canvas class. We add an instance attribute called **self.pages** to our **__init__** method that is assigned an empty list. Then we override the canvas's **showPage** method. This method gets called whenever a new page is created. This allows us to add each new page to our list of pages.

Next we override the **save** method. This allows us to loop through each of the pages in the document and draw a page number along with the total number of pages. As we loop through, we also call **showPage**, which tells the canvas to close the current page and potentially start a new one. The save method calls our own custom method, **draw_page_number**, which takes the total page count as its sole argument. This is the method that actually draws our page number information to each page.

Now we need to create a **page_number_total_main.py** script that we can use to call our custom canvas class.

```python
# page_number_total_main.py

from custom_canvas import PageNumCanvas
from header3 import header
from lxml import objectify
from reportlab.lib.styles import getSampleStyleSheet
from reportlab.lib.units import mm
from reportlab.platypus import SimpleDocTemplate
from reportlab.platypus import Paragraph, Spacer


def parse_xml(xml_file):
    with open(xml_file) as f:
        xml = f.read()

    root = objectify.fromstring(xml)
    return root


def main(pdf_file, xml_file, logo):
    doc = SimpleDocTemplate(
        pdf_file,
        rightMargin=72, leftMargin=36,
        topMargin=125, bottomMargin=36)

    xml = parse_xml(xml_file)

    doc.xml = xml
    doc.logo_path = logo

    elements = []

    txt = 'Lorem ipsum dolor sit amet, consectetur adipiscing elit,'
    styles = getSampleStyleSheet()
    for line in range(150):
        paragraph = Paragraph(txt, styles["Normal"])
        elements.append(paragraph)

    doc.build(elements, onFirstPage=header,
              onLaterPages=header,
              canvasmaker=PageNumCanvas)
```

```
if __name__ == '__main__':
    main(pdf_file='page_number_total_main.pdf',
         xml_file='eob.xml',
         logo='snakehead.jpg')
```

There are really only a couple of new things in this main module. We import our custom canvas at the top of the code. Then we add a new argument to the **doc.build** call at the end of the **main** function. You will note that we can still call our header function too using the **onFirstPage** and **onLaterPages** arguments.

Headers + Footers

This chapter wouldn't be complete without a quick example of a document that has a custom header and a custom footer. Let's take the **header4.py** script we wrote earlier and save it as **header_and_footer.py**. Keep all the original code in there so you still have a **header** function. Now add the following function to the bottom of the file:

```
# header_and_footer.py

def footer(canvas, doc):
    """
    Create a footer
    """
    width, height = doc.pagesize

    styles = getSampleStyleSheet()

    ptext = '<font size=10><b>This is a custom footer' \
        '</b></font>'

    p = Paragraph(ptext, styles["Normal"])
    p.wrapOn(canvas, width, height)
    p.drawOn(canvas, 250, 35)
```

All this function does is accept the same arguments as the header function and then it draws a single line of text that identifies itself as the footer.

The next step you can take is to take the code from **page_number_total_main.py** and copy it and save it as **header_and_footer_main.py**. Then remove the reference to **PageNumCanvas** since we won't need it for this example. Update the code to import from our new **header_and_footer** module and you'll almost be done:

```python
# header_and_footer_main.py

from header_and_footer import header, footer
from lxml import objectify
from reportlab.lib.styles import getSampleStyleSheet
from reportlab.platypus import SimpleDocTemplate
from reportlab.platypus import Paragraph


def parse_xml(xml_file):
    with open(xml_file) as f:
        xml = f.read()

    root = objectify.fromstring(xml)
    return root


def main(pdf_file, xml_file, logo):
    doc = SimpleDocTemplate(
        pdf_file,
        rightMargin=72, leftMargin=36,
        topMargin=125, bottomMargin=36)

    xml = parse_xml(xml_file)

    doc.xml = xml
    doc.logo_path = logo

    elements = []

    txt = 'Lorem ipsum dolor sit amet, consectetur adipiscing elit,'
    styles = getSampleStyleSheet()
    for line in range(150):
        paragraph = Paragraph(txt, styles["Normal"])
        elements.append(paragraph)

    doc.build(elements, onFirstPage=header,
              onLaterPages=footer)

if __name__ == '__main__':
    main(pdf_file='header_and_footer_main.pdf',
         xml_file='eob.xml',
```

```
                logo='snakehead.jpg')
```

The final change to make this work is to update the **onLaterPages** argument to call the **footer** we imported. This will cause the footer to appear on every page except the first one. Of course, this also prevents us from having the header on any page but the first one, which might not be what you want. To fix that issue, let's add one more simple helper function to our **header_and_footer.py** module:

```
def header_and_footer(canvas, doc):
    """
    Add the header and footer to each page
    """
    header(canvas, doc)
    footer(canvas, doc)
```

All this new function does is call both the header and the footer with the appropriate arguments. To use it, you will need to update our main function in the other file to use it. To do that, you will just need to update the **doc.build** command as follows:

```
doc.build(elements, onFirstPage=header_and_footer,
          onLaterPages=header_and_footer)
```

Now you should have a header and footer on every page.

Wrapping Up

At this point you should know how to add custom headers and footers that can draw pretty much anything on demand. You have also learned how to add page numbers to each page as well as how to add a page number with the total number of pages. The main takeaway from this is that when you are working with headers and footers, you will need to make sure you set the margins correctly in your document template so that they take your header and footer's height into consideration.

Feel free to play around with the examples and try adding different logos or other lines of text. You may want to refer to chapter 2 if you'd like to apply different fonts to your text.

Chapter 13 - Creating a PDF Library

We learned how to take data and turn it into a PDF in chapter 11. Then we learned how to create custom headers and footers in the last chapter. For this chapter, we will take what we have learned from the previous two and expand on it a bit. The idea here is that we will create a little reusable PDF library. We will craft it so that it remains modular and easy to extend. Here is a list of what we will learn about in this chapter:

- How to take in different data formats
- Creating and using custom stylesheets
- Expand what the configuration file can do
- Create a simple cross-platform user interface

The idea behind creating a module for creating PDFs is that it allows you to enforce standards in regards to how the PDF is generated. For example, you can define in your module if headers and footers are added and how much space they take up. You can also define the fonts, margins, page size, page numbering and many other variables that control how your PDF will look.

To keep things organized, we will be putting all the files into folders labeled **version_1**, **version_2**, etc. I will be sure to mention when we switch to a new version in the section that that occurs in.

Let's get started!

Accepting Different Data Formats

The first item on our list of updates is to make our PDF library accept different data formats. We will go with the simplest approach here. For this chapter, we will update our code so that we can accept data files in XML or JSON formats. To do that, we will simply look at the extension of the file that is passed in to our application. If you want Python to attempt to figure out the file's type itself, you might be interested in a 3rd party package called **python-magic** that you can find here: https://github.com/ahupp/python-magic

Anyway, let's update our code a bit so that it checks what the file extension is and parses the file accordingly. We will take the **main6.py** from chapter 12 and save it as **main.py** for this chapter. We will be saving all our changes to a folder called **version_1**, or you can just check that out of the book's Github repository if you don't want to write code yourself.

Now, let's take a look at the changes we need to make:

Chapter 13 - Creating a PDF Library

```python
# main.py

import argparse
import os

from header import header
from lxml import objectify
from parsers import parse_json
from reportlab.lib.styles import getSampleStyleSheet
from reportlab.platypus import Paragraph
from reportlab.platypus import SimpleDocTemplate


def get_args():
    parser = argparse.ArgumentParser(
            description="Custom PDF Header with Logos")
    parser.add_argument('-l', '-logo', '--logo',
                        action='store',
                        required=True,
                        help="The logo's file path",
                        dest='logo')
    parser.add_argument('-d', '--data_file',
                        action='store',
                        required=True,
                        help="The data file path",
                        dest='data_file')
    parser.add_argument('-f', '-filepath', '--filepath',
                        action='store',
                        required=True,
                        help="The file path",
                        dest='path')
    arguments = parser.parse_args()

    return arguments


def parse_xml(xml_file):
    with open(xml_file) as f:
        xml = f.read()

    root = objectify.fromstring(xml)
    return root
```

The first thing we need to do is import the **os** module. We will use it to help us figure out the file extension shortly. We also import something new from a **parsers** module called **parse_json**. We will use that to parse JSON data files. Other than that, we really don't need to do any updates to the **get_args** or **parse_xml** functions at this time. So let's move on to our **main** function instead:

```
def main():
    arguments = get_args()
    supported_ext_types = ['.json', '.xml']

    # Get the file extension
    _, ext = os.path.splitext(arguments.data_file)

    if ext not in supported_ext_types:
        msg = 'PDF Creator only accepts the following file types: ' \
        '{}. Got {}'
        raise RuntimeError(msg.format(str(supported_ext_types, ext)))

    doc = SimpleDocTemplate(
        arguments.path,
        rightMargin=72, leftMargin=36,
        topMargin=125, bottomMargin=18)

    if ext == '.xml':
        data = parse_xml(arguments.data_file)
    elif ext == '.json':
        data = parse_json(arguments.data_file)

    elements = []

    txt = 'Lorem ipsum dolor sit amet, consectetur adipiscing elit,'
    styles = getSampleStyleSheet()
    paragraph = Paragraph(txt, styles["Normal"])
    elements.append(paragraph)

    doc.data = data
    doc.logo_path = arguments.logo

    doc.build(elements, onFirstPage=header)

if __name__ == '__main__':
    main()
```

Here we create a list of support extension types, which in this case are JSON and XML file types. Then we extract the file extension using **os.path.splitext**, which will return a tuple of the file path and

Chapter 13 - Creating a PDF Library

the extension itself. Since we don't care about the file path here, we just assign it to the underscore character, which is a conventional way to just throwaway data. Next we check if the extension we extracted is in the supported extension list we created. If not, we raise a **RuntimeError** with a custom error message to tell the user what went wrong.

The last change is to check what the extension is and call the appropriate function. So if we passed in an XML file, we want to call **parse_xml** and if we pass in a JSON file, then we want to call **parse_json**. You will also note that we changed the **doc** object to use **doc.data** instead of **doc.xml** like we did in the previous chapter.

The one thing we are missing here is the **parse_json** function that we imported from **parsers**, so let's write that next! Open up a new file and save it as **parsers.py**. Then add the following code:

```python
# parsers.py

import json


class JSON:
    """
    A way to "objectify" a json object to match
    the API we get from lxml.objectify
    """

    def __init__(self, data):
        self.member_name = data['patient']['member_name']
        self.member_id = data['patient']['member_id']
        self.group_num = data['patient']['group_num']
        self.group_name = data['patient']['group_name']


def parse_json(json_file):
    """
    Opens a JSON file and turns it into an object
    """
    with open(json_file) as f:
        data = json.load(f)

    return JSON(data)
```

Here we import Python's **json** library and then we create a class called **JSON**. This reason we create a class is that we want to turn the JSON encoded data into an object that has the same API as **lxml.objectify** does. This abstracts away some of the complexities of writing code for different data types. The main application doesn't need to do the conversion itself. It relies on the **parsers** module to do that for it. In fact, we could (and probably should) add the XML parsing code to this parser module. Anyway, the last piece of code here is the **parse_json** function, which just opens the JSON file and turns it into a JSON object which it then returns.

The last piece of code that we need to update is our **header.py** script:

```python
# header.py

from reportlab.lib.styles import getSampleStyleSheet
from reportlab.platypus import Paragraph, Image


def header(canvas, doc):
    width, height = doc.pagesize

    styles = getSampleStyleSheet()

    ptext = '<font size=10><b>Statement Date: {}' \
        '</b></font>'.format('01/01/2017')

    img = Image(doc.logo_path, width=76.2, height=76.2)
    img.wrapOn(canvas, width, height)
    img.drawOn(canvas, 100, 725)

    p = Paragraph(ptext, styles["Normal"])
    p.wrapOn(canvas, width, height)
    p.drawOn(canvas, 400, 800)

    ptext = '''<font size=10>
    <b>Member:</b> {member}<br/>
    <b>Member ID:</b> {member_id}<br/>
    <b>Group #:</b> {group_num}<br/>
    <b>Group name:</b> {group_name}<br/>
    </font>
    '''.format(member=doc.data.member_name,
               member_id=doc.data.member_id,
               group_num=doc.data.group_num,
               group_name=doc.data.group_name
               )
    p = Paragraph(ptext, styles["Normal"])
    p.wrapOn(canvas, width, height)
    p.drawOn(canvas, 400, 730)
```

Chapter 13 - Creating a PDF Library

If you compare this version to the one from the previous chapter, you will note that we are now referring to **doc.data** instead of **doc.xml**. That is the only change that we needed to make. The rest is the same.

To run this code, all you need to do is the following:

```
python main.py -l snakehead.jpg -d eob.xml -f output.pdf
```

Multipage Data Files

You may not have noticed this, but the code we looked at in the previous section doesn't read everything in the XML. So we need to update the code so that it can read everything. We also need to add a table for the claim data in the EOB data file. That way if we have a lot of claims, our PDF library will create a multipage document automatically. The effort to change this into a multipage capable set of scripts is a bit big as there will be a lot of refactoring going on. So we will copy all the files in **version_1** and paste them in a new folder called **version_2**.

We are going to make the code much more modular in this step, so the first thing we want to do is reduce all the things that **main.py** does. Let's take a look:

```python
# main.py

import argparse
import os
import pdf_creator

from parsers import parse_json, parse_xml


def get_args():
    parser = argparse.ArgumentParser(
            description="Custom PDF Header with Logos")
    parser.add_argument('-l', '-logo', '--logo',
                        action='store',
                        required=True,
                        help="The logo's file path",
                        dest='logo')
    parser.add_argument('-d', '--data_file',
                        action='store',
                        required=True,
                        help="The data file path",
                        dest='data_file')
```

```python
    parser.add_argument('-f', '-filepath', '--filepath',
                        action='store',
                        required=True,
                        help="The output file path",
                        dest='path')
    arguments = parser.parse_args()

    return arguments


def main():
    arguments = get_args()
    supported_ext_types = ['.json', '.xml']

    # Get the file extension
    _, ext = os.path.splitext(arguments.data_file)

    if ext not in supported_ext_types:
        msg = 'PDF Creator only accepts the following file types: ' \
              '{}. Got {}'
        raise RuntimeError(msg.format(str(supported_ext_types, ext)))

    if ext == '.xml':
        data = parse_xml(arguments.data_file)
    elif ext == '.json':
        data = parse_json(arguments.data_file)

    eob = pdf_creator.EOB(data,
                          pdf_file=arguments.path,
                          logo=arguments.logo)
    eob.save()

if __name__ == '__main__':
    main()
```

As you can see, we moved the **parse_xml** function out and into the **parsers** module. We also removed all the ReportLab related code from main and put it into another module called **pdf_creator**. This reduces the number of imports needed in main by quite a margin. Now all that main does is call the parsing logic and then creates the PDF document via the pdf_creator module. We could simplify this even more by putting the calls to the parser into the pdf_creator module and by moving the argument parsing into its own module. If you want to attempt to do that, feel free to do so.

Let's create the **pdf_creator.py** script next. We will be using the **EOB** class that we created in chapter

Chapter 13 - Creating a PDF Library

11 and modifying it slightly for this example. Here is the first part of the class:

```python
# pdf_creator.py

from header import header
from reportlab.lib import colors
from reportlab.lib.pagesizes import letter
from reportlab.lib.styles import getSampleStyleSheet
from reportlab.platypus import Indenter, Paragraph, Spacer
from reportlab.platypus import SimpleDocTemplate
from reportlab.platypus import Table, TableStyle

class EOB:
    """
    Explanation of Benefits PDF Class
    """

    def __init__(self, data, pdf_file='eob.pdf', logo=None):
        """"""
        self.data = data

        self.doc = SimpleDocTemplate(
                    pdf_file, pagesize=letter,
                    rightMargin=72, leftMargin=36,
                    topMargin=125, bottomMargin=18)
        self.doc.logo_path = logo
        self.doc.data = self.data

        self.elements = []
        self.styles = getSampleStyleSheet()
        self.width, self.height = letter
        self.create()
```

Here we just do all the imports that we need to create our PDF. You will note that we also import our **header** module here, so we do separate out a little of our PDF creation into a separate module. Anyway, the main takeaware here is that we are passing in the **data** object, the name of the output PDF (**pdf_file**) and the **logo** path. This code is pretty self-explanatory, so I won't go into it in depth here.

The next two methods that we need to make are **create** and **create_text**:

```python
def create(self):
    """
    Create the PDF
    """
    self.create_claims()

def create_text(self, text, size=8, bold=False):
    """
    Create formatted Paragraphs
    """
    if bold:
        return Paragraph('''<font size={size}><b>
        {text}</b></font>
        '''.format(size=size, text=text),
            self.styles['Normal'])

    return Paragraph('''<font size={size}>
    {text}</font>
    '''.format(size=size, text=text),
        self.styles['Normal'])
```

The create method is where you would put all the main calls of your program. You could have it save the PDF too if you wanted. In this case, we only want it to create the claims table. The **create_text** method is just a helper method for creating styled ReportLab Paragraphs.

The **create_claims** is pretty long, but here it is anyway:

```python
def create_claims(self):
    """"""
    fsize = 7.5

    ptext = '<font size=26>Your claims up close</font>'
    p = Paragraph(ptext, self.styles["Heading1"])
    self.elements.append(p)
    self.elements.append(Spacer(1, 20))

    claim = Paragraph('''<font size={fsize}>
        Claim ID {claim_id}<br/>
        Received on {received_date}<br/></font>
        '''.format(fsize=fsize,
                claim_id=self.data.claim_id,
                received_date=self.data.received_date),
            self.styles["Normal"])
```

```python
        billed = Paragraph(
            '<font size={}>Amount<br/>billed</font>'.format(fsize),
                self.styles["Normal"])
        member_rate = Paragraph(
            '<font size={}>Member<br/>rate</font>'.format(fsize),
            self.styles["Normal"])
        pending = Paragraph(
            '<font size={}>Pending or<br/>not payable<br/>(Remarks)</font>'
            .format(fsize),
            self.styles["Normal"])
        applied = Paragraph(
            '<font size={}>Applied to<br/>deductible</font>'.format(fsize),
            self.styles["Normal"])
        copay = Paragraph(
            '<font size={}>Your<br/>copay</font>'.format(fsize),
            self.styles["Normal"])
        remaining = Paragraph(
            '<font size={}>Amount<br/>remaining</font>'.format(fsize),
            self.styles["Normal"])
        plan_pays = Paragraph(
            '<font size={}>Plan<br/>pays</font>'.format(fsize),
            self.styles["Normal"])
        coins = Paragraph(
            '<font size={}>Your<br/>coinsurance</font>'.format(fsize),
            self.styles["Normal"])
        owe = Paragraph(
            '<font size={}>You owe<br/>C+D+E+H=I</font>'.format(fsize),
            self.styles["Normal"])

        data = [[claim, billed, member_rate, pending, applied,
                copay, remaining, plan_pays, coins, owe],
                ]

        for claim in self.data.claims.getchildren():
            data.append([
                self.create_text(claim.description),
                self.create_text(claim.amount_billed.text),
                self.create_text(claim.member_rate),
                self.create_text(claim.pending),
                self.create_text(claim.deductible),
                self.create_text(claim.copay),
```

```
                    self.create_text(claim.amount_remaining.text),
                    self.create_text(claim.plan_pays.text),
                    self.create_text(claim.coinsurance),
                    self.create_text(claim.total_owed.text)
            ])

        colWidths = [110, 50, 40, 60, 50, 40, 50, 40, 55, 60]
        table_style = TableStyle(
            [('INNERGRID', (0,0), (-1,-1), 0.25, colors.black),  # Add grid to cells
             ('BOX', (0,0), (-1,-1), 0.25, colors.black),  # add outer border
             ('BACKGROUND', (1,0), (1, -1), colors.lightgoldenrodyellow),
             ('BACKGROUND', (7,0), (7, -1), colors.lightgoldenrodyellow)
             ])

        table = Table(data, colWidths=colWidths)
        table.setStyle(table_style)

        self.elements.append(Indenter(left=40))
        self.elements.append(table)
        self.elements.append(Indenter(left=-40))
```

For a full explanation, I recommend flipping back to chapter 11. The main thing we changed here was updating it to refer to **self.data** instead of **self.xml**. This was done because we are supporting other data file formats.

The last method we need to make to complete this class is our **save** method:

```
def save(self):
    """
    Save the PDF
    """
    self.doc.build(self.elements, onFirstPage=header)
```

Note that this save method will build our document and apply our header to the first page and the first page only! Now we are ready to update our **parsers.py** script. This is a fairly extensive change as we want it to fully support JSON whether it has a single claim or many claims in it.

Chapter 13 - Creating a PDF Library

```python
# parsers.py

import json

from lxml import objectify

class String(str):
    """
    Custom string sub-class to emulate the "strings"
    returned from lxml
    """

    @property
    def text(self):
        """
        Return the str
        """
        return self

class Claim:
    """
    Represents the data that makes up a claim
    """

    def __init__(self, data):
        self.amount_billed = String(data['amount_billed'])
        self.amount_remaining = String(data['amount_remaining'])
        self.coinsurance = String(data['coinsurance'])
        self.copay = String(data['copay'])
        self.deductible = String(data['deductible'])
        self.description = String(data['description'])
        self.member_rate = String(data['member_rate'])
        self.pending = String(data['pending'])
        self.plan_pays = String(data['plan_pays'])
        self.received_date = String(data['received_date'])
        self.total_owed = String(data['total_owed'])
```

The first change here is that we now import **lxml** because we moved the XML "parser" into this function. But the next few changes are what's really interesting. The first class you will see is one named **String** that subclasses Python's built-in **str** type. We do that because in our **pdf_creator** script you will see that we have some calls to a **.text** attribute and so we need to emulate that for our JSON parser.

Chapter 13 - Creating a PDF Library

The next piece is that we need to create a **Claim** class. This class will represent all the elements that make up a claim. Since **lxml.objectify** turns the XML tree into a series of objects, we need to do the same with our JSON parser. Now we need to create a **Claims** class:

```
class Claims:
    """
    Represents a series of Claim objects
    """

    def __init__(self, data):
        """
        Accepts a data dictionary and turns it into a
        claim object
        """
        self.data = data

    def getchildren(self):
        """
        Return all the children claim
        """
        data_claims = self.data['patient']['claims']['claim']
        claims = []
        if isinstance(data_claims, dict):
            # only a single claim exists
            claim = Claim(data_claims)
            claims.append(claim)
        else:
            # claims is a list
            for claim in data_claims:
                claims.append(Claim(claim))
        return claims
```

The Claims class is basically a container object for all our Claim objects. We implement a **getchildren** method so that it matches **lxml.objectify**'s **getchildren** method. All this method does is check to see if the JSON has one or more elements. Depending on which it is, it will then create either a list that contains one claim or a list that contains many claims.

Here is the rest of **parsers.py**:

```python
class JSON:
    """
    A way to "objectify" a json object to match
    the API we get from lxml.objectify
    """

    def __init__(self, data):
        self.member_name = data['patient']['member_name']
        self.member_id = data['patient']['member_id']
        self.group_num = data['patient']['group_num']
        self.group_name = data['patient']['group_name']
        self.claim_id = data['patient']['claim_id']
        self.date = data['patient']['date']
        self.received_date = data['patient']['received_date']
        self.sent_to = data['patient']['sent_to']
        self.amount_owed = data['patient']['amount_owed']
        self.amount_paid = data['patient']['amount_paid']

        self.claims = Claims(data)


def parse_json(json_file):
    """
    Opens a JSON file and turns it into an object
    """
    with open(json_file) as f:
        data = json.load(f)

    return JSON(data)


def parse_xml(xml_file):
    """
    Opens an XML file and turns it into an lxml.objectify object
    """
    with open(xml_file) as f:
        xml = f.read()

    root = objectify.fromstring(xml)
    return root
```

The only change here is that we added a couple more attributes, including one that creates an instance of the **Claims** class.

The next item in our list of changes is the **header.py** script. All it needs is one slight adjustment that is actually optional:

```
# header.py

from reportlab.lib.styles import getSampleStyleSheet
from reportlab.platypus import Paragraph, Image


def header(canvas, doc):
    width, height = doc.pagesize

    styles = getSampleStyleSheet()

    if doc.logo_path:
        img = Image(doc.logo_path, width=76.2, height=76.2)
        img.wrapOn(canvas, width, height)
        img.drawOn(canvas, 100, 700)

    ptext = '<b>Statement Date: {}</b>'.format('01/01/2017')
    p = Paragraph(ptext, styles["Normal"])
    p.wrapOn(canvas, width, height)
    p.drawOn(canvas, 400, 700)

    ptext = '''
    <b>Member:</b> {member}<br/>
    <b>Member ID:</b> {member_id}<br/>
    <b>Group #:</b> {group_num}<br/>
    <b>Group name:</b> {group_name}<br/>
    '''.format(member=doc.data.member_name,
               member_id=doc.data.member_id,
               group_num=doc.data.group_num,
               group_name=doc.data.group_name
               )
    p = Paragraph(ptext, styles["Normal"])
    p.wrapOn(canvas, width, height)
    p.drawOn(canvas, 400, 730)
```

All that was added here was to check if the **logo_path** wasn't set to **None**, since that is the default in the **pdf_creator** script. If it's not None, then we attempt to add the logo. We should add a check to the **main.py** script that verifies the input logo and data files exist, but that can wait for the next version.

At this point, you should be able to run the code the same way as before:

```
python main.py -l snakehead.jpg -d eob.xml -f output.pdf
```

And if we want to test the json parser, so we run the command a second time:

```
python main.py -l snakehead.jpg -d eob.json -f output.pdf
```

I have also included a file called **eob2.xml** and a **eob2.json** file that you can use to create a multipage document if you want to try that.

Custom Stylesheets

Another way to control the look and feel of your PDF is by creating your own **StyleSheet**. The nice thing about using a template is that you can easily change the entire look of all the text in your document by just changing the stylesheet.

Let's take a few moments and write our own stylesheet. Create a new directory called **version_3** and copy in all the files from the **version_2** folder we created in the last section. Then open up your favorite Python editor and create a new file named **custom_stylesheet.py** and save it to the newly created **version_3** folder. Now enter the following code:

```python
# custom_stylesheet.py

from reportlab.lib.colors import blue
from reportlab.lib.enums import TA_LEFT, TA_CENTER
from reportlab.lib.fonts import tt2ps
from reportlab.lib.styles import StyleSheet1, ParagraphStyle
from reportlab.rl_config import canvas_basefontname as _baseFontName

_baseFontNameB = tt2ps(_baseFontName,1,0)
_baseFontNameI = tt2ps(_baseFontName,0,1)
_baseFontNameBI = tt2ps(_baseFontName,1,1)


def get_custom_stylesheet_1():
    """
    Create and return a custom stylesheet
    """
    stylesheet = StyleSheet1()

    stylesheet.add(ParagraphStyle(name='Normal',
                                  fontName=_baseFontName,
```

```
                                    fontSize=12,
                                    leading=14,
                                    textColor=blue)
               )

    stylesheet.add(ParagraphStyle(name='BodyText',
                                  parent=stylesheet['Normal'],
                                  spaceBefore=6)
               )

    stylesheet.add(ParagraphStyle(name='Italic',
                                  parent=stylesheet['BodyText'],
                                  fontName = _baseFontNameI)
               )

    stylesheet.add(ParagraphStyle(name='Bold',
                                  parent=stylesheet['BodyText'],
                                  fontName = _baseFontNameB)
               )

    stylesheet.add(ParagraphStyle(name='Heading1',
                                  parent=stylesheet['Normal'],
                                  fontName = _baseFontNameB,
                                  fontSize=20,
                                  leading=24,
                                  spaceAfter=6),
                   alias='h1')

    return stylesheet
```

Here we import a bunch of required bits and pieces from ReportLab. This file is actually based on ReportLab's own **styles.py** file that you can find in its **lib** folder. Anyway, we create five styles. The Normal style is used as the parent for the **BodyText** and **Heading** styles whereas **BodyText** is the parent for the **Italic** and **Bold** styles. We append each of these **ParagraphStyles** to our StyleSheet1 instance.

To actually use the stylesheet, we will need to modify the **pdf_creator.py** script and the **header.py** script. Let's start by changing **pdf_creator.py**. I will only show the part of the script that we need to change:

Chapter 13 - Creating a PDF Library

```python
# pdf_creator.py

from custom_stylesheet import get_custom_stylesheet_1
from header import header
from reportlab.lib import colors
from reportlab.lib.pagesizes import letter
from reportlab.platypus import Indenter, Paragraph, Spacer
from reportlab.platypus import SimpleDocTemplate
from reportlab.platypus import Table, TableStyle


class EOB:
    """
    Explanation of Benefits PDF Class
    """

    def __init__(self, data, pdf_file='eob.pdf', logo=None):
        """"""
        self.data = data

        self.doc = SimpleDocTemplate(
                    pdf_file, pagesize=letter,
                    rightMargin=72, leftMargin=36,
                    topMargin=125, bottomMargin=18)
        self.doc.logo_path = logo
        self.doc.data = self.data

        self.elements = []
        self.styles = get_custom_stylesheet_1()
        self.width, self.height = letter
        self.create()
```

The first thing we do is import our new custom stylesheet. We also delete the line that used to import **getSampleStyleSheet** from **reportlab.lib.styles** because we no longer need it. Then we just create our new stylesheet and the rest of our **EOB** class will use it.

Now let's change the **header** script:

```
# header.py

from custom_stylesheet import get_custom_stylesheet_1
from reportlab.platypus import Paragraph, Image


def header(canvas, doc):
    width, height = doc.pagesize

    styles = get_custom_stylesheet_1()

    if doc.logo_path:
        img = Image(doc.logo_path, width=76.2, height=76.2)
        img.wrapOn(canvas, width, height)
        img.drawOn(canvas, 100, 700)

    ptext = 'Statement Date: {}'.format('01/01/2017')
    p = Paragraph(ptext, styles["Bold"])
    p.wrapOn(canvas, width, height)
    p.drawOn(canvas, 400, 700)

    ptext = '''
    <b>Member:</b> {member}<br/>
    <b>Member ID:</b> {member_id}<br/>
    <b>Group #:</b> {group_num}<br/>
    <b>Group name:</b> {group_name}<br/>
    '''.format(member=doc.data.member_name,
               member_id=doc.data.member_id,
               group_num=doc.data.group_num,
               group_name=doc.data.group_name
               )
    p = Paragraph(ptext, styles["Normal"])
    p.wrapOn(canvas, width, height)
    p.drawOn(canvas, 400, 730)
```

Once again we import our new stylesheet and replace **getSampleStyleSheet** with **get_custom_-stylesheet_1**. If you were paying close attention to the stylesheet code, you will note that we changed the font color for our new stylesheet to blue. So when you run the **main** script, the main difference you will see is that the text color will be blue instead of black. However the font size of some of the elements will also be larger in our new stylesheet by a couple of points, so if you look at the header of the table or the block of text in the upper right hand corner, you might notice that the font size is larger in our new version.

You can use the custom stylesheet to apply various settings to various parts of your document or to the entire document. You can set the font size, family, and color here as well as many other stylistic settings.

Configuring Your Application

There are several popular file formats used for configuring applications. One of the most popular that we've mentioned before is the INI file. Another popular configuration file type is YAML. You can use whatever format you are most comfortable using. For this chapter, we will focus on using an INI type file. This will allow us to continue to use Python's **configparser** library. You can configure anything about your application that you want to in the config file. For this example, we will just create a small sample of the settings you could configure.

Let's create a **version_4** folder and copy the contents of the **version_3** folder into it. Then create a file named **config.ini** in your new folder with the following contents:

```
[General]
logo_path = snakehead.jpg
left_margin = 36
right_margin = 72
top_margin = 125
bottom_margin = 18
style = customer_1_stylesheet
output_dir = output
```

This config file allows us to configure the logo's file path so we won't need to pass it in any more on the command line. It also allows us to set the margins of the page. Since we just set up a stylesheet in the previous section, I thought it would be fun to add a **style** parameter so we could tell our code what stylesheet to use. Finally we set the output directory which is the folder our PDF will get saved to.

Let's start by renaming **custom_stylesheet.py** to **customer_1_stylesheet.py**. Now create a folder inside your **version_4** folder called **stylesheets** and move your stylesheet Python file in there.

Now let's create a generic **default_stylsheet.py** file in that same folder. Once that is created, add the following code:

```
# default_stylesheet.py


from reportlab.lib.fonts import tt2ps
from reportlab.lib.styles import ParagraphStyle, getSampleStyleSheet
from reportlab.rl_config import canvas_basefontname as _baseFontName

_baseFontNameB = tt2ps(_baseFontName,1,0)
_baseFontNameI = tt2ps(_baseFontName,0,1)
_baseFontNameBI = tt2ps(_baseFontName,1,1)


def get_stylesheet():
    """
    Create and return a custom default stylesheet
    """
    stylesheet = getSampleStyleSheet()

    stylesheet.add(ParagraphStyle(name='Bold',
                                  parent=stylesheet['BodyText'],
                                  fontName = _baseFontNameB)
                  )
    return stylesheet
```

The reason we want to have a default stylesheet is that we want to be able to fall back on something if someone mistypes the style name in the config file. Since our custom style has a **Bold** sub-style, we also need the default stylesheet to have one too. Otherwise it just inherits everything that it does from ReportLab's default stylesheet.

There is one other item we need to do while we are in the **stylesheets** folder and that is creating an **__init__.py** file there. We do this because we want to be able to import our modules from the stylesheets folder. Inside of your brand new **__init__.py** file, enter the following code:

```
from . import default_stylesheet
```

The next thing we need to do is create some kind of utility module. Let's call it **util.py** and put it in the **version_4** folder. We will add a class in this module for reading the config file:

```python
# util.py

import configparser
import importlib
import os

from stylesheets import default_stylesheet


class ConfigObj:
    """
    Create a configuration object
    """

    def __init__(self):
        cfg_path = 'config.ini'
        # Set some defaults
        self.logo_path = None
        self.right_margin = 36
        self.left_margin = 36
        self.top_margin = 18
        self.bottom_margin = 18
        self.style = None
        self.output_dir = None

        if os.path.exists(cfg_path):
            config = configparser.ConfigParser()
            config.read(cfg_path)
            self.logo_path = config.get('General', 'logo_path')
            self.right_margin = int(config.get('General', 'right_margin'))
            self.left_margin = int(config.get('General', 'left_margin'))
            self.top_margin = int(config.get('General', 'top_margin'))
            self.bottom_margin = int(config.get('General', 'bottom_margin'))
            self.style = config.get('General', 'style')
            self.output_dir = config.get('General', 'output_dir')
```

This code attempts to read the config file and basically turn it into an object. If the config file doesn't exist, then we also have some defaults set so that our PDF library should still work, although it won't look right without the correct margins applied. We could actually simplify this code a lot by using Michael Foord's config parsing library, **configobj** as it already turns config files into objects. It hasn't been updated in a while though, but it is well worth a look if you don't like **configparser**.

The next piece that we want to add to our **util.py** module is some code to load up our custom

Chapter 13 - Creating a PDF Library

stylesheet. Add the following function to your module:

```
def get_stylesheet():
    """
    Returns the stylesheet object
    """
    config = ConfigObj()

    try:
        path = os.path.abspath(os.path.join('stylesheets',
                                           '{}.py'.format(config.style)))
        spec = importlib.util.spec_from_file_location(config.style, path)
        stylesheet =  importlib.util.module_from_spec(spec)
        spec.loader.exec_module(stylesheet)
        getSampleStyleSheet = stylesheet.get_stylesheet
    except (ImportError, FileNotFoundError):
        getSampleStyleSheet = default_stylesheet.get_stylesheet

    return getSampleStyleSheet()
```

Here we use Python's **importlib** module to attempt to dynamically load whatever style was put into the config file. If we run into an issue attempting to load the style, then we fall back to using our default stylesheet. You could replace the code in the **except** block with the following if you prefer to continue using **importlib**:

```
path = os.path.abspath(os.path.join('stylesheets',
                                    'default_stylesheet.py'))
spec = importlib.util.spec_from_file_location(config.style, path)
stylesheet =  importlib.util.module_from_spec(spec)
spec.loader.exec_module(stylesheet)
getSampleStyleSheet = stylesheet.get_stylesheet
```

While I think importlib is pretty neat, I prefer just turning the **stylesheets** folder into an importable sub-module.

Now we need to update the **pdf_creator.py** file to use our utility module. I will only show the portion of the code that we need to change to make this work in the **pdf_creator.py** file rather than showing you the entire module again:

Chapter 13 - Creating a PDF Library   315

```python
# pdf_creator.py

import os

from header import header
from reportlab.lib import colors
from reportlab.lib.pagesizes import letter
from reportlab.platypus import Indenter, Paragraph, Spacer
from reportlab.platypus import SimpleDocTemplate
from reportlab.platypus import Table, TableStyle
from util import ConfigObj, get_stylesheet


class EOB:
    """
    Explanation of Benefits PDF Class
    """

    def __init__(self, data, pdf_file='eob.pdf'):
        """"""
        config = ConfigObj()
        self.data = data

        self.doc = SimpleDocTemplate(
                    pdf_file, pagesize=letter,
                    rightMargin=config.right_margin,
                    leftMargin=config.left_margin,
                    topMargin=config.top_margin,
                    bottomMargin=config.bottom_margin)
        self.doc.logo_path = config.logo_path
        self.doc.data = self.data

        self.elements = []

        self.styles = get_stylesheet()
        self.width, self.height = letter
        self.create()
```

The new code here is where we import **ConfigObj** and **get_stylesheet** from our **util** module. Then we create an instance of our ConfigObj() class and use that object to set out margins and the logo's path. Finally we call **get_stylesheet** to set up our styles. That's all we need to do in this module to make it work.

We also need to update **header.py** to use our utility module too as it also relies on our new custom stylesheet infrastructure. Here are the first 11 lines of code from the header module:

```
# header.py

import os

from reportlab.platypus import Paragraph, Image
from util import get_stylesheet

def header(canvas, doc):
    width, height = doc.pagesize

    styles = get_stylesheet()
```

You will notice that we import our **get_stylesheet** function here and then we use it in the **header** function itself. Other than that, the rest of the module stays the same.

Adding a Graphical User Interface

Most end users prefer using a graphical user interface (GUI) with buttons and other widgets to interact with their software over using a terminal. In fact, a lot of users don't understand terminals or why you would use them. Python has several choices for creating graphical user interfaces. Probably the most popular are tkinter, wxPython and PyQt or one of its variants. I will be using **wxPython** for this example. The wxPython toolkit has been around for many years and works on Linux, Mac and Windows. You can use pip to install wxPython 4 like this:

```
python -m pip install wxPython
```

Note that you may need to have a compiler installed on Linux or Mac for this to succeed successfully. Linux may also require that you install webkit and one or two other dependencies. Most of the time, the errors that you will see will be quite obvious and you can just install the dependency and then retry installing wxPython. I haven't had any issues getting wxPython to install on Windows or Mac. Also note that versions of wxPython prior to version 4 were **not** pip installable!

Once you have it installed, we can get started. The first thing we will want to create is the main user interface. We want to be able to do the following:

- Choose an input data file
- Choose where the output PDF is saved
- Edit the config file via a user interface

Chapter 13 - Creating a PDF Library

- Generate the PDF

You might find it helpful to sketch out what the user interface should look like. In my mind, this sounds like we need to have something that looks like this:

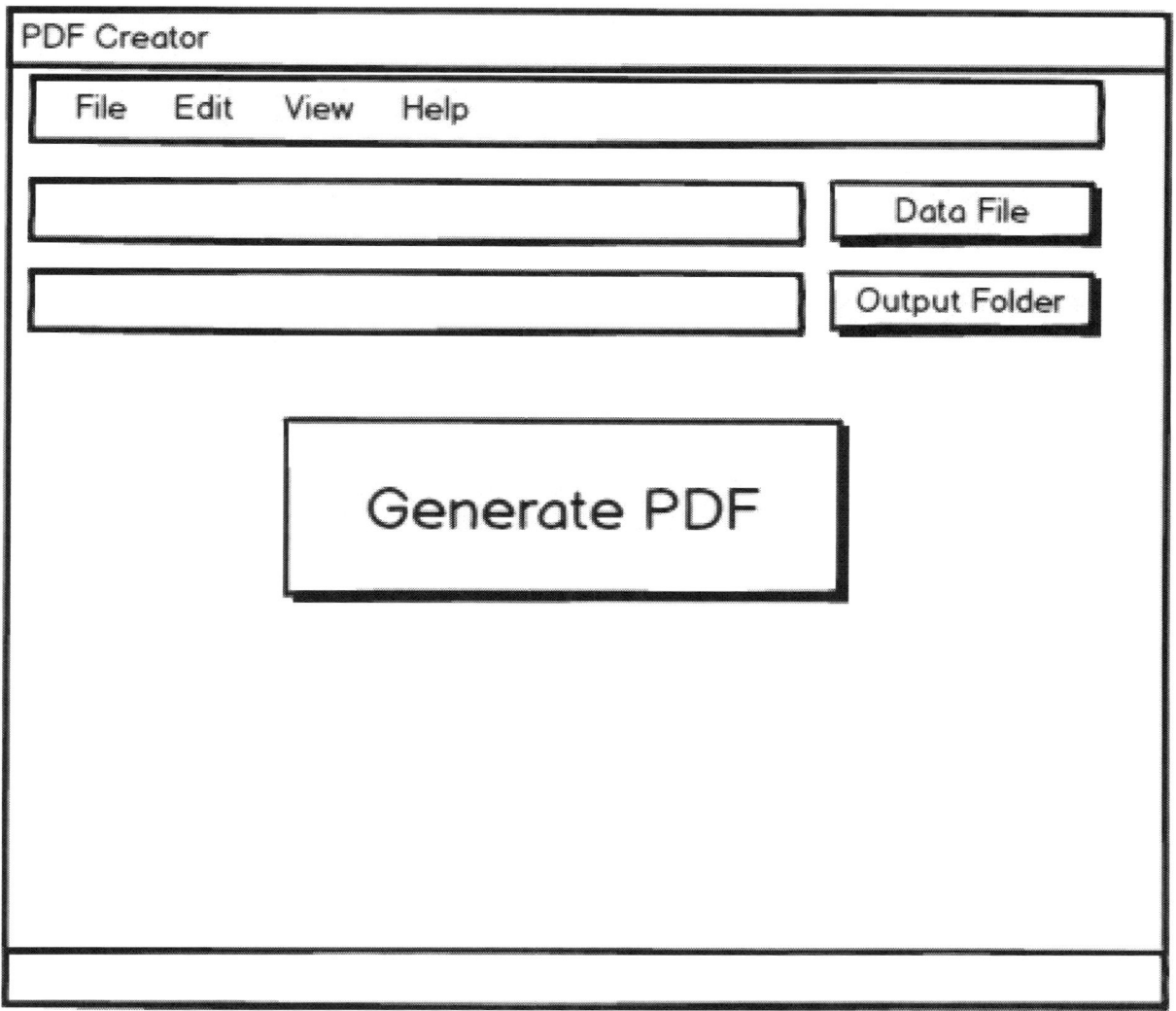

Fig. 13-1: Mock-up of our PDF Creator

Let's try to create a user interface that looks something like our mock-up! For the first iteration, we will need to create a new file. Since we already have a **main.py** for our command line interface, let's create a file called **gui.py** for our graphical user interface.

We will be going over this piece by piece because the code is fairly complex. Feel free to just download the code if you think that would make it easier to follow along.

Here is the beginning of **gui.py**:

```
# gui.py

import os
import pdf_creator
import wx

from parsers import parse_json, parse_xml

wildcard = ("XML (*.xml)|*.xml|"
            "JSON (*.json)|*.json|"
            "All files (*.*)|*.*")


class PDFPanel(wx.Panel):
    """
    Panel container for holding the PDF generation
    widgets
    """
```

This code imports the pieces that we need for the GUI to create the PDF. You will note that we have imported our custom **pdf_creator** module and our two parsers. We also set up a **wildcard** variable that we will be using when we go to choose our data file later on in the code. Finally we create a class called **PDFPanel** which subclasses **wx.Panel**. A Panel in wxPython is just a container for other widgets. It can be given a different background color and other panels can also be put into it.

Now let's initialize our Panel:

```
def __init__(self, parent):
    wx.Panel.__init__(self, parent)
    self.main_sizer = wx.BoxSizer(wx.VERTICAL)
    self.std_paths = wx.StandardPaths.Get()

    self.data_file = wx.TextCtrl(self, style=wx.TE_READONLY)
    data_file_btn = wx.Button(self, label='Data File')
    data_file_btn.Bind(wx.EVT_BUTTON, self.get_data_file)
    self.layout(self.data_file, data_file_btn)

    self.output_path = wx.TextCtrl(self, style=wx.TE_READONLY)
    output_btn = wx.Button(self, label='Output Folder')
    output_btn.Bind(wx.EVT_BUTTON, self.get_output_path)
    self.layout(self.output_path, output_btn)

    generate_btn = wx.Button(self, label='Generate PDF')
```

```
        generate_btn.Bind(wx.EVT_BUTTON, self.generate_pdf)
        self.main_sizer.Add(generate_btn, 0, wx.ALL|wx.CENTER, 5)

        self.SetSizer(self.main_sizer)
```

Panels almost always have a parent widget, so we pass one in here. Then we create a sizer, which allows you to layout your widgets without setting an absolute position. This gives the user the ability to resize the window and have the widgets resize accordingly, depending on how you add the widgets to the sizer.

Anyway, in this example, we add a series of **wx.TextCtrl** and **wx.Button** widgets. You will note that our text entry control widgets are set to read only. This prevents the user from messing up the path to the files. We bind the buttons to **wx.EVT_BUTTON**, which tells wxPython that when the button is clicked, it should call the associated function that it is bound to. The other item I want to point out here is the 3rd line in the **__init__**, which basically creates a special paths object from which you can get various standard paths in a cross-platform way. This allows me to query wxPython for the user's App Data folder, desktop, documents and much more.

As you may have noticed, in the code above we are calling a method called **layout**. So we should probably look at that next:

```
def layout(self, txt, btn):
    """
    Layout the text control and related button
    """
    hsizer = wx.BoxSizer(wx.HORIZONTAL)
    hsizer.Add(txt, 1, wx.ALL, 5)
    hsizer.Add(btn, 0, wx.ALL, 5)
    self.main_sizer.Add(hsizer, 0, wx.EXPAND)
```

This is what I call a "helper" method. You pass in a couple of widgets and it adds them to a sizer for you. The reason I am doing it this way is to prevent writing the same sizer code repeatedly. There are several other types of sizers available in wxPython that we could use here, but I find that nesting **BoxSizers** is a powerful way to layout my widgets.

```python
def get_data_file(self, event):
    """
    Get the data file path
    """
    dlg = wx.FileDialog(
        self, message='Choose a data file',
        defaultDir=self.std_paths.GetDocumentsDir(),
        defaultFile="",
        wildcard=wildcard,
        style=wx.FD_OPEN | wx.FD_MULTIPLE | wx.FD_CHANGE_DIR
        )
    if dlg.ShowModal() == wx.ID_OK:
        path = dlg.GetPath()
        self.data_file.SetValue(path)
        dlg.Destroy()
```

The **get_data_file** method is called when the user presses the "Get Data" button. It will open a file dialog and allow the user to choose a JSON or XML file or any file using that **wildcard** we set earlier. If the user presses the OK button, then we grab the path to the file that they chose and put that path in the text control. Then we destroy the file dialog as it is no longer needed.

```python
def get_output_path(self, event):
    """
    Get the output folder
    """
    dlg = wx.FileDialog(
        self, message="Save file",
        defaultDir=self.std_paths.GetDocumentsDir(),
        defaultFile="",
        wildcard="PDF (*.pdf)|*.pdf",
        style=wx.FD_SAVE
        )
    if dlg.ShowModal() == wx.ID_OK:
        path = dlg.GetPath()
        name, ext = os.path.splitext(path)
        if not ext:
            path += '.pdf'
        self.output_path.SetValue(path)
    dlg.Destroy()
```

The **get_output_path** method is called when the user presses the "Output Folder" button. Instead of opening an Open File Dialog, it instead opens a Save File dialog. They are slightly different in that

Chapter 13 - Creating a PDF Library

the Open File dialog allows you to select a file for opening while the Save File dialog allows you to choose a location to save the file and also give the saved file a name.

In this example, we only allow the user to save files in the PDF format. If the user doesn't set an extension, then we add the ".pdf" extension to it. Note that the user could enter the wrong extension and this code will not detect that and will save the PDF with the wrong extension. Feel free to try to correct this error on your own.

Now it's time to learn what happens when the user presses the "Generate PDF" button:

```
def generate_pdf(self, event):
    """
    Create the PDF
    """
    supported_ext_types = ['.json', '.xml']

    data_file = self.data_file.GetValue()
    output_path = self.output_path.GetValue()
    _, ext = os.path.splitext(data_file)

    if not data_file:
        self.show_error_msg('A data file is required')
        return

    if ext not in supported_ext_types:
        msg = 'PDF Creator only accepts the following file types: {}'
        self.show_error_msg(msg.format(supported_ext_types))
        return

    if not output_path:
        self.show_error_msg('You must choose an output folder')
        return

    if ext == '.xml':
        data = parse_xml(data_file)
    elif ext == '.json':
        data = parse_json(data_file)

    eob = pdf_creator.EOB(data,
                          pdf_file=output_path)
    eob.save()

    dlg = wx.MessageDialog(
        parent=None,
```

```
                message='PDF saved to {}'.format(self.output_path.GetValue()),
                caption='PDF Saved',
                style=wx.OK|wx.ICON_INFORMATION
            )
        dlg.ShowModal()
        dlg.Destroy()
```

Here we set up some code that should look kind of familiar. We create a list of supported extension types and then we grab the data file path and the save location. Next we grab the extension of the data file. The next three **if** statements check if we actually have paths to use and that the extension type is correct. If any of these return False, then we display an error dialog and do nothing.

If the user has filled out our GUI correctly, then we call our **pdf_creator** module and have it generate the PDF. If that is successful, then we show a dialog that says as much and also tells the user where we saved the PDF.

Now let's learn how we are displaying the error messages:

```
def show_error_msg(self, msg):
    """
    Display an error message
    """
    dlg = wx.MessageDialog(parent=None,
                           message=msg,
                           caption='Error',
                           style=wx.OK|wx.ICON_ERROR)
    dlg.ShowModal()
    dlg.Destroy()
```

This code is very similar to the code we used to tell the user that the PDF saved successfully. All we are doing is creating a **MessageDialog** and displaying it to the user.

The last bit of code that we need to look at is for creating the top level widget, which in this case is a **wx.Frame** class. This is the parent widget that we pass to our **wx.Panel**. Here's the code:

```python
class PDFFrame(wx.Frame):
    """
    The top level container for the panel and menu
    """

    def __init__(self):
        wx.Frame.__init__(self, None, title='PDF Creator')
        panel = PDFPanel(self)
        self.Show()


if __name__ == '__main__':
    app = wx.App(False)
    frame = PDFFrame()
    app.MainLoop()
```

All this code does right now is create the frame and the panel inside the frame. You will note that the last line of code starts the application object's main loop. This is what starts wxPython's event loop, which is basically an infinite loop that waits for the user to generate an event. An event in wxPython is when the user presses a button, moves the mouse over a widget, or otherwise interacts with your application.

When you run this code, you should get a user interface that looks something like this:

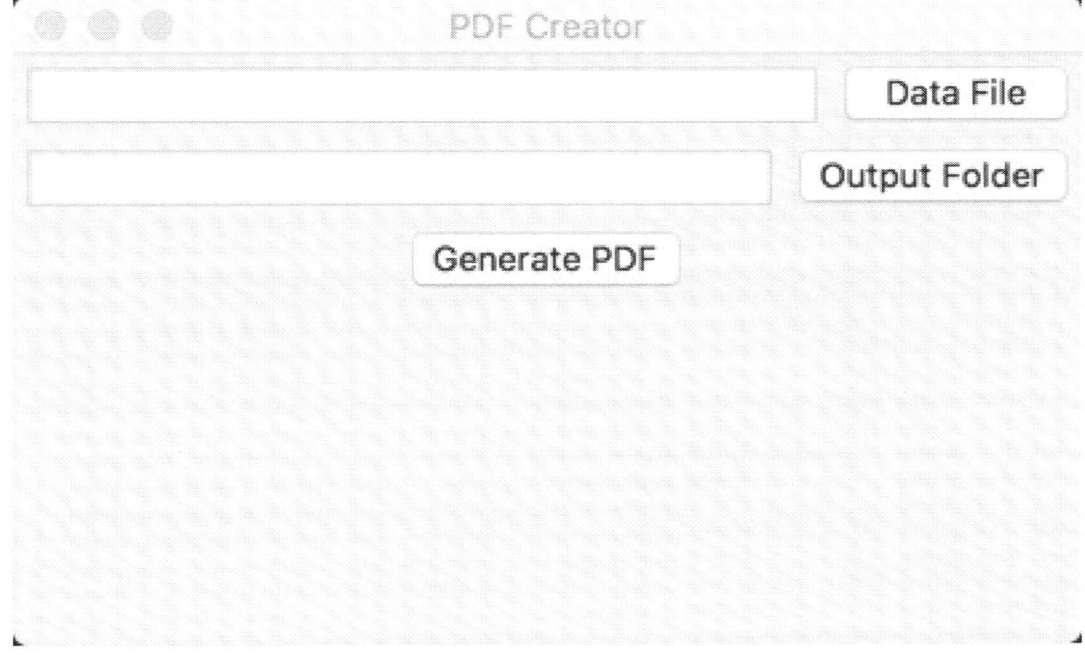

Fig. 13-2: First iteration of the wxPython user interface

That looks kind of like our mock-up, but we don't have the menu along the top of the frame yet. We will need that to make editing the config possible. Of course, if you want, you could add another button at the bottom to do that, but most applications put the edit preferences or edit config option in the menu.

Finishing the User Interface

Since this next step will require a decent sized chunk of code, we will create one more new version of our code base. Copy the contents of the **version_4** folder to a new folder called **version_5** so we can keep our new changes separate. Now open up your new copy of **gui.py** and update the **PDFFrame** class:

```
class PDFFrame(wx.Frame):
    """
    The top level container for the panel and menu
    """

    def __init__(self):
        wx.Frame.__init__(self, None, title='PDF Creator')
        panel = PDFPanel(self)
        self.create_menu()
        self.Show()
```

Here we add a new call to a method named **create_menu**. That was a simple change. Let's look at this new method though:

```
def create_menu(self):
    """
    Create the menu
    """
    menubar = wx.MenuBar()

    file_menu = wx.Menu()
    exit_menu_item = file_menu.Append(
        wx.NewId(), 'Exit', 'Exit the application')
    menubar.Append(file_menu, '&File')
    self.Bind(wx.EVT_MENU, self.on_exit, exit_menu_item)

    edit_menu = wx.Menu()
    config_menu_item = edit_menu.Append(
        wx.NewId(),'Config', 'Edit config')
```

Chapter 13 - Creating a PDF Library

```
    menubar.Append(edit_menu, '&Edit')
    self.Bind(wx.EVT_MENU, self.on_edit_config, config_menu_item)

    self.SetMenuBar(menubar)
```

Here we create a **wx.MenuBar** instance. This is a class that we use for creating the menu bar itself. Then we need to create **wx.Menu** objects to add then to our MenuBar. After creating a **wx.Menu** object, you can append menu items to them via the Menu's **Append** method. These require a unique identifier (**wx.NewId**), a label, and some help text that would appear in the Status Bar at the bottom of the frame, if we had one. Finally we bind the menu items to events using **self.Bind** and binding to **wx.EVT_MENU**, which is fired when someone clicks on a menu item in the menu.

Now let's write the last two methods that the menu items are bound to:

```
def on_edit_config(self, event):
    """
    Edit the configuration
    """
    dlg = config_editor.ConfigDialog()
    dlg.ShowModal()
    dlg.Destroy()

def on_exit(self, event):
    """
    Close the application
    """
    self.Close()
```

The **on_edit_config** event handler method will utilize a new module called **config_editor**. From there we call **ConfigDialog** to display a dialog that allows us to edit the configuration file. We also create an **on_exit** method that is used for closing our application. Make sure that you import the **config_editor** module at the top of the **gui.py** script.

Here is what the GUI should look like now:

Chapter 13 - Creating a PDF Library

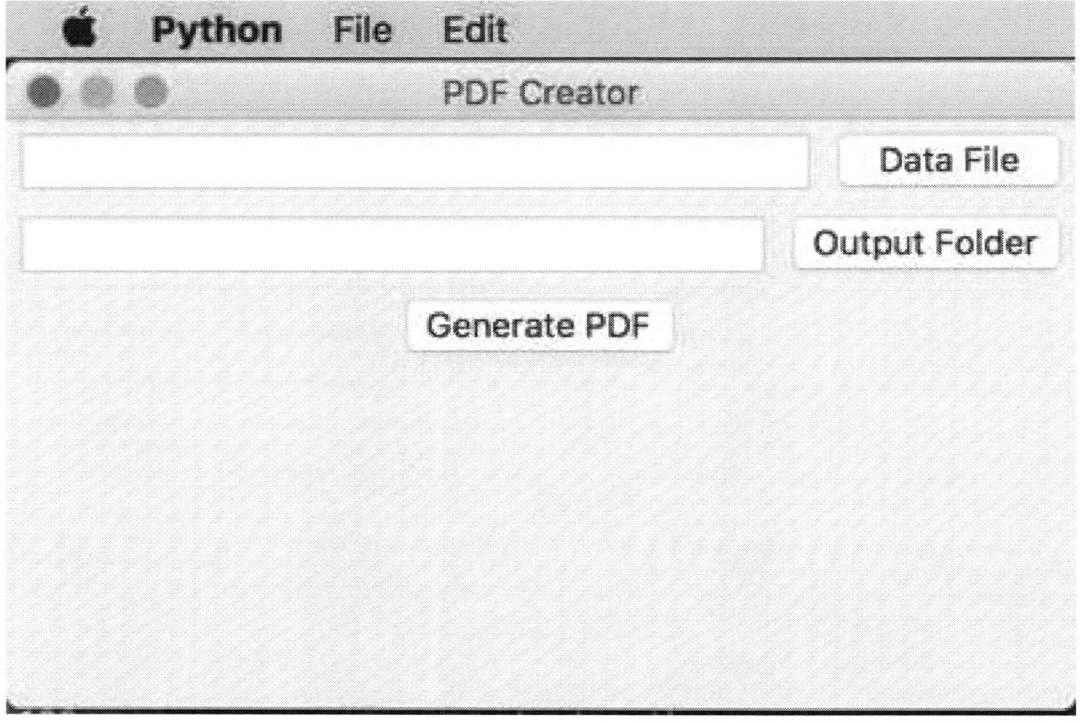

Fig. 13-3: Final iteration of main user interface

Now let's create a file called **config_editor.py** and save it to our **version_5** folder. Now we can start writing our module:

```
import configparser

import wx


class ConfigDialog(wx.Dialog):

    def __init__(self):
        wx.Dialog.__init__(self, None,
                           title='Edit Configuration',
                           size=(400, 400))
        self.main_sizer = wx.BoxSizer(wx.VERTICAL)

        config = configparser.ConfigParser()
        config.read('config.ini')
        config_dict = dict(config.items('General'))

        self.logo = wx.TextCtrl(
```

```python
        self, value=config_dict['logo_path'])
self.layout('Logo Path:', self.logo)

self.left_margin = wx.TextCtrl(
    self, value=config_dict['left_margin'])
self.layout('Left Margin:', self.left_margin)

self.right_margin = wx.TextCtrl(
    self, value=config_dict['right_margin'])
self.layout('Right Margin:', self.right_margin)

self.top_margin = wx.TextCtrl(
    self, value=config_dict['top_margin'])
self.layout('Top Margin:', self.top_margin)

self.bottom_margin = wx.TextCtrl(
    self, value=config_dict['bottom_margin'])
self.layout('Bottom Margin:', self.bottom_margin)

self.style = wx.TextCtrl(
    self, value=config_dict['style'])
self.layout('Style:', self.style)

btn_sizer = wx.BoxSizer()
save_btn = wx.Button(self, label='Save')
save_btn.Bind(wx.EVT_BUTTON, self.save)
btn_sizer.Add(save_btn, 0, wx.ALL|wx.CENTER, 5)

cancel_btn = wx.Button(self, label='Cancel')
cancel_btn.Bind(wx.EVT_BUTTON, self.cancel)
btn_sizer.Add(cancel_btn, 0, wx.ALL|wx.CENTER, 5)

self.main_sizer.Add(btn_sizer, 0, wx.ALL|wx.CENTER, 5)

self.SetSizer(self.main_sizer)
```

Here we subclass from **wx.Dialog**. The nice thing about dialogs in Python is that they basically have a **wx.Panel** built into them. However they do not allow the user to resize them, so that is kind of annoying. If you want a resizable dialog, then you would want to use a **wx.Frame** instead. Anyway, all this code is used to create the form that matches with the config file we created earlier in this chapter. We use a **layout** helper method here as well and we bind the Cancel and Save buttons to separate event handlers. Let's take a look at some of these other methods:

```python
def cancel(self, event):
    """
    Cancel / Close the dialog
    """
    self.Close()

def layout(self, lbl, txt):
    """
    Layout the label and text control widgets
    """
    size = (80, -1)
    hsizer = wx.BoxSizer()
    hsizer.Add(wx.StaticText(self, label=lbl, size=size),
               0, wx.ALL, 5)
    hsizer.Add(txt, 1, wx.ALL|wx.EXPAND, 5)
    self.main_sizer.Add(hsizer, 0, wx.EXPAND)
```

The **cancel** event handler method is just used to close our dialog. Note that we need to actually call a dialog's **Destroy** method to make it actually go away. Otherwise it will just kind of float around in memory. This is why we call the Destroy method on the dialog object in **gui.py**. Here we just want to close the dialog. This tells wxPython that it's no longer needed and will allow Python to continue to destroy it.

Next up is the **layout** method, which is just used for laying out the label and text controls on the dialog. The last method we will look at is our **save** method:

```python
def save(self, event):
    """
    Save the config to disk
    """
    config = configparser.ConfigParser()
    config.add_section('General')
    config.set('General', 'logo_path',
               self.logo.GetValue())
    config.set('General', 'left_margin',
               self.left_margin.GetValue())
    config.set('General', 'right_margin',
               self.right_margin.GetValue())
    config.set('General', 'top_margin',
               self.top_margin.GetValue())
    config.set('General', 'bottom_margin',
               self.bottom_margin.GetValue())
    config.set('General', 'style',
```

```
            self.style.GetValue())

with open('config.ini', 'w') as config_file:
    config.write(config_file)

dlg = wx.MessageDialog(
    parent=None,
    message='Config saved',
    caption='Config Saved',
    style=wx.OK|wx.ICON_INFORMATION
)
dlg.ShowModal()
dlg.Destroy()
self.Close()
```

Here we create a config object using Python's **configparser** library. Then we recreate the section and key / value pairs that we need using the text control's values. Finally we write the config back to disk by deleting the original and replacing it with whatever is in the text controls. Finally we pop up a dialog to tell the user that config was saved successfully. When the user closes this notification, we close the message dialog and the configuration edit dialog.

When the user goes to launch the configuration edit dialog, it should look something like this:

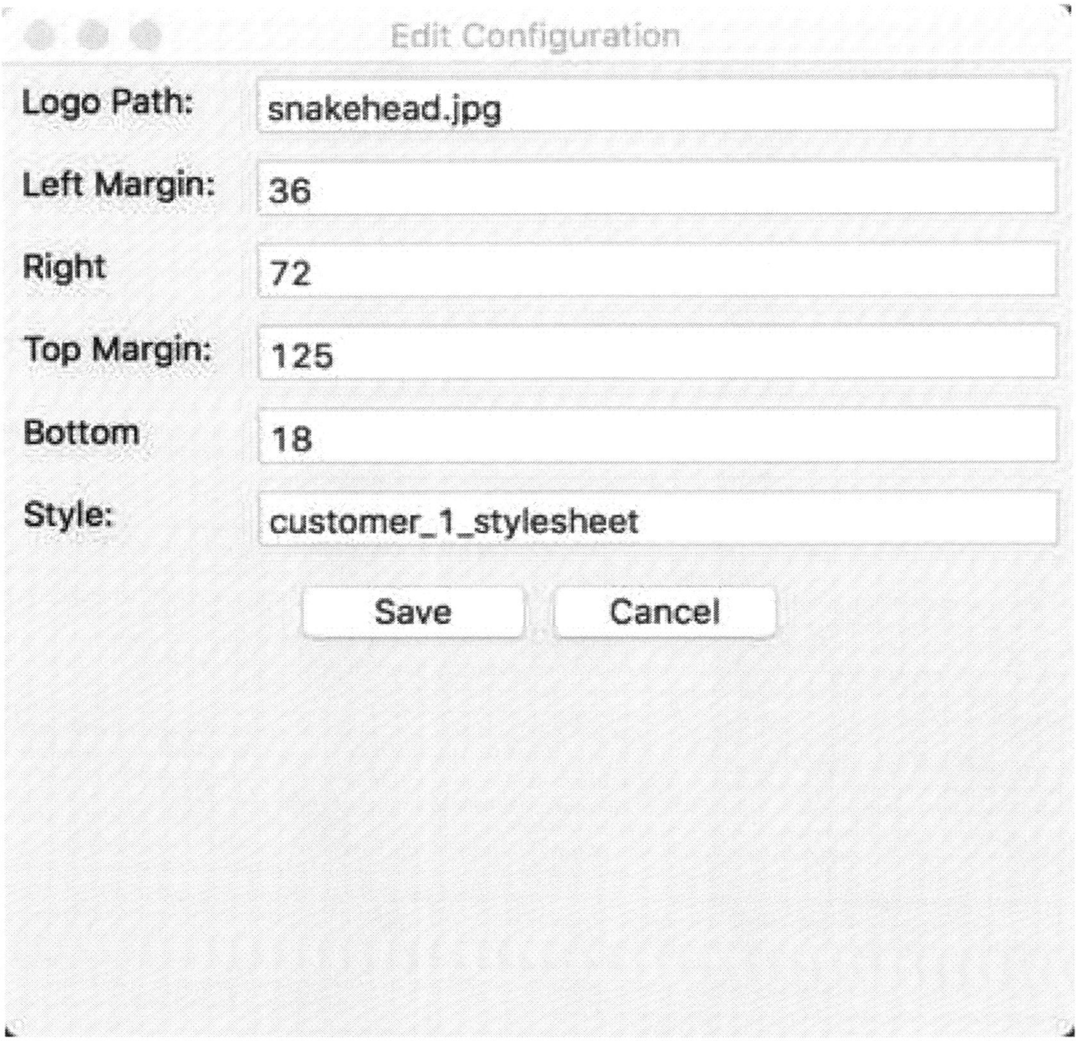

Fig. 13-4: Configuration editor user inteface

Try editing some of the values using your new user interface and then generate the PDF to see how the changes effect the result.

Wrapping Up

You should now have a decent idea of how to create some reusable modules of your own for generating PDFs. In this chapter we learned how to apply custom stylesheets. We also enhanced what we learned in previous chapters about using configuration files and data to generate PDFs. We learned how you can use a command line interface for these modules in addition to using the configuration file for controlling the look of the output. Finally we learned how to add a graphical user interface via the wxPython toolkit. Try playing around with the examples and changing them up a bit. You can also enhance the UI by adding a preview menu item or a help menu or add your own idea(s).

Chapter 14 - The PyPDF2 Package

The **PyPDF2** package is a pure-Python PDF library that you can use for splitting, merging, cropping and transforming pages in your PDFs. According to the PyPDF2 website, you can also use PyPDF2 to add data, viewing options and passwords to the PDFs too. Finally you can use PyPDF2 to extract text and metadata from your PDFs.

PyPDF2 is actually a fork of the original pyPdf which was written by Mathiew Fenniak and released in 2005. However, the original pyPdf's last release was in 2014. A company called Phaseit, Inc spoke with Mathieu and ended up sponsoring PyPDF2 as a fork of pyPdf

At the time of writing this book, the PyPDF2 package hasn't had a release since 2016. However it is still a solid and useful package that is worth your time to learn.

The following lists what we will be learning in this chapter:

- Extracting metadata
- Splitting documents
- Merging 2 PDF files into 1
- Rotating pages
- Overlaying / Watermarking Pages
- Encrypting / decrypting

Let's start by learning how to install PyPDF2!

Installation

PyPDF2 is a pure Python package, so you can install it using **pip** (assuming pip is in your system's path):

```
python -m pip install pypdf2
```

As usual, you should install 3rd party Python packages to a Python virtual environment to make sure that it works the way you want it to.

Chapter 14 - The PyPDF2 Package

Extracting Metadata from PDFs

You can use PyPDF2 to extract a fair amount of useful data from any PDF. For example, you can learn the author of the document, its title and subject and how many pages there are. Let's find out how by downloading the sample of this book from leanpub at https://leanpub.com/reportlab. The sample I downloaded was called "reportlab-sample.pdf". I will include this PDF for you to use in the Github source code as well.

Here's the code:

```
# get_doc_info.py

from PyPDF2 import PdfFileReader


def get_info(path):
    with open(path, 'rb') as f:
        pdf = PdfFileReader(f)
        info = pdf.getDocumentInfo()
        number_of_pages = pdf.getNumPages()

    print(info)

    author = info.author
    creator = info.creator
    producer = info.producer
    subject = info.subject
    title = info.title

if __name__ == '__main__':
    path = 'reportlab-sample.pdf'
    get_info(path)
```

Here we import the **PdfFileReader** class from **PyPDF2**. This class gives us the ability to read a PDF and extract data from it using various accessor methods. The first thing we do is create our own **get_info** function that accepts a PDF file path as its only argument. Then we open the file in read-only binary mode. Next we pass that file handler into PdfFileReader and create an instance of it.

Now we can extract some information from the PDF by using the **getDocumentInfo** method. This will return an instance of **PyPDF2.pdf.DocumentInformation**, which has the following useful attributes, among others:

- author
- creator
- producer
- subject
- title

If you print out the DocumentInformation object, this is what you will see:

```
{'/Author': 'Michael Driscoll',
 '/CreationDate': "D:20180331023901-00'00'",
 '/Creator': 'LaTeX with hyperref package',
 '/Producer': 'XeTeX 0.99998',
 '/Title': 'ReportLab - PDF Processing with Python'}
```

We can also get the number of pages in the PDF by calling the **getNumPages** method.

Extracting Text from PDFs

PyPDF2 has limited support for extracting text from PDFs. It doesn't have built-in support for extracting images, unfortunately. I have seen some recipes on StackOverflow that use PyPDF2 to extract images, but the code examples seem to be pretty hit or miss.

Let's try to extract the text from the first page of the PDF that we downloaded in the previous section:

```python
# extracting_text.py

from PyPDF2 import PdfFileReader


def text_extractor(path):
    with open(path, 'rb') as f:
        pdf = PdfFileReader(f)
        
        # get the first page
        page = pdf.getPage(1)
        print(page)
        print('Page type: {}'.format(str(type(page))))
        
        text = page.extractText()
        print(text)
```

```
if __name__ == '__main__':
    path = 'reportlab-sample.pdf'
    text_extractor(path)
```

You will note that this code starts out in much the same way as our previous example. We still need to create an instance of **PdfFileReader**. But this time, we grab a page using the **getPage** method. PyPDF2 is zero-based, much like most things in Python, so when you pass it a one, it actually grabs the second page. The first page in this case is just an image, so it wouldn't have any text.

Interestingly, if you run this example you will find that it doesn't return any text. Instead all I got was a series of line break characters. Unfortunately, PyPDF2 has pretty limited support for extracting text. Even if it is able to extract text, it may not be in the order you expect and the spacing may be different as well.

To get this example code to work, you will need to try running it against a different PDF. I found one on the United States Internal Revenue Service website here: https://www.irs.gov/pub/irs-pdf/fw9.pdf

This is a W9 form for people who are self-employed or contract employees. It can be used in other situations too. Anyway, I downloaded it as **w9.pdf** and added it to the Github repository as well. If you use that PDF instead of the sample one, it will happily extract some of the text from page 2. I won't reproduce the output here as it is kind of lengthy though.

Splitting PDFs

The PyPDF2 package gives you the ability to split up a single PDF into multiple ones. You just need to tell it how many pages you want. For this example, we will open up the W9 PDF from the previous example and loop over all six of its pages. We will split off each page and turn it into its own standalone PDF.

Let's find out how:

```
# pdf_splitter.py

import os
from PyPDF2 import PdfFileReader, PdfFileWriter


def pdf_splitter(path):
    fname = os.path.splitext(os.path.basename(path))[0]
```

```
    pdf = PdfFileReader(path)
    for page in range(pdf.getNumPages()):
        pdf_writer = PdfFileWriter()
        pdf_writer.addPage(pdf.getPage(page))

        output_filename = '{}_page_{}.pdf'.format(
            fname, page+1)

        with open(output_filename, 'wb') as out:
            pdf_writer.write(out)

        print('Created: {}'.format(output_filename))

if __name__ == '__main__':
    path = 'w9.pdf'
    pdf_splitter(path)
```

For this example, we need to import both the **PdfFileReader** and the **PdfFileWriter**. Then we create a fun little function called **pdf_splitter**. It accepts the path of the input PDF. The first line of this function will grab the name of the input file, minus the extension. Next we open the PDF up and create a reader object. Then we loop over all the pages using the reader object's **getNumPages** method.

Inside of the **for** loop, we create an instance of **PdfFileWriter**. We then add a page to our writer object using its **addPage** method. This method accepts a page object, so to get the page object, we call the reader object's **getPage** method. Now we had added one page to our writer object. The next step is to create a unique file name which we do by using the original file name plus the word "page" plus the page number + 1. We add the one because PyPDF2's page numbers are zero-based, so page 0 is actually page 1.

Finally we open the new file name in write-binary mode and use the PDF writer object's **write** method to write the object's contents to disk.

Merging Multiple PDFs Together

Now that we have a bunch of PDFs, let's learn how we might take them and merge them back together. One useful use case for doing this is for businesses to merge their dailies into a single PDF. I have needed to merge PDFs for work and for fun. One project that sticks out in my mind is scanning documents in. Depending on the scanner you have, you might end up scanning a document into multiple PDFs, so being able to join them together again can be wonderful.

When the original PyPdf came out, the only way to get it to merge multiple PDFs together was like this:

Chapter 14 - The PyPDF2 Package

```
# pdf_merger.py

import glob
from PyPDF2 import PdfFileWriter, PdfFileReader

def merger(output_path, input_paths):
    pdf_writer = PdfFileWriter()

    for path in input_paths:
        pdf_reader = PdfFileReader(path)
        for page in range(pdf_reader.getNumPages()):
            pdf_writer.addPage(pdf_reader.getPage(page))

    with open(output_path, 'wb') as fh:
        pdf_writer.write(fh)


if __name__ == '__main__':
    paths = glob.glob('w9_*.pdf')
    paths.sort()
    merger('pdf_merger.pdf', paths)
```

Here we create a **PdfFileWriter** object and several **PdfFileReader** objects. For each PDF path, we create a **PdfFileReader** object and then loop over its pages, adding each and every page to our writer object. Then we write out the writer object's contents to disk.

PyPDF2 made this a bit simpler by creating a **PdfFileMerger** class:

```
# pdf_merger2.py

import glob
from PyPDF2 import PdfFileMerger

def merger(output_path, input_paths):
    pdf_merger = PdfFileMerger()
    file_handles = []

    for path in input_paths:
        pdf_merger.append(path)

    with open(output_path, 'wb') as fileobj:
        pdf_merger.write(fileobj)
```

Chapter 14 - The PyPDF2 Package

```
if __name__ == '__main__':
    paths = glob.glob('fw9_*.pdf')
    paths.sort()
    merger('pdf_merger2.pdf', paths)
```

Here we just need to create the **PdfFileMerger** object and then loop through the PDF paths, appending them to our merging object. PyPDF2 will automatically append the entire document so you don't need to loop through all the pages of each document yourself. Then we just write it out to disk.

The **PdfFileMerger** class also has a **merge** method that you can use. Its code definition looks like this:

```
def merge(self, position, fileobj, bookmark=None, pages=None,
        import_bookmarks=True):
    """
    Merges the pages from the given file into the output file at the
    specified page number.

    :param int position: The *page number* to insert this file. File will
        be inserted after the given number.

    :param fileobj: A File Object or an object that supports the standard
        read and seek methods similar to a File Object. Could also be a
        string representing a path to a PDF file.

    :param str bookmark: Optionally, you may specify a bookmark to be
        applied at the beginning of the included file by supplying the
        text of the bookmark.

    :param pages: can be a :ref:`Page Range <page-range>` or a
    ``(start, stop[, step])`` tuple
        to merge only the specified range of pages from the source
        document into the output document.

    :param bool import_bookmarks: You may prevent the source
    document's bookmarks from being imported by specifying this as
    ``False``.
    """
```

Basically the merge method allows you to tell PyPDF where to merge a page by page number. So if you have created a merging object with 3 pages in it, you can tell the merging object to merge the next document in at a specific position. This allows the developer to do some pretty complex merging operations. Give it a try and see what you can do!

Chapter 14 - The PyPDF2 Package

Rotating Pages

PyPDF2 gives you the ability to rotate pages. However you must rotate in 90 degrees increments. You can rotate the PDF pages either clockwise or counter clockwise. Here's a simple example:

```
# pdf_rotator.py

from PyPDF2 import PdfFileWriter, PdfFileReader

def rotator(path):
    pdf_writer = PdfFileWriter()
    pdf_reader = PdfFileReader(path)

    page1 = pdf_reader.getPage(0).rotateClockwise(90)
    pdf_writer.addPage(page1)
    page2 = pdf_reader.getPage(1).rotateCounterClockwise(90)
    pdf_writer.addPage(page2)
    pdf_writer.addPage(pdf_reader.getPage(2))

    with open('pdf_rotator.pdf', 'wb') as fh:
        pdf_writer.write(fh)

if __name__ == '__main__':
    rotator('reportlab-sample.pdf')
```

Here we create our PDF reader and writer objects as before. Then we get the first and second pages of the PDF that we passed in. We then rotate the first page 90 degrees clockwise or to the right. Then we rotate the second page 90 degrees counter-clockwise. Finally we add the third page in its normal orientation to the writer object and write out our new 3-page PDF file.

If you open the PDF, you will find that the first two pages are now rotated in opposite directions of each other with the third page in its normal orientation.

Overlaying / Watermarking Pages

PyPDF2 also supports merging PDF pages together, or overlaying pages on top of each other. This can be useful if you want to watermark the pages in your PDF. For example, one of the eBook distributors I use will "watermark" the PDF versions of my book with the buyer's email address. Another use case that I have seen is to add printer control marks to the edge of the page to tell the printer when a certain document has reached its end.

For this example we will take one of the logos I use for my blog, "The Mouse vs. the Python", and overlay it on top of the W9 form from earlier:

Chapter 14 - The PyPDF2 Package

```python
# watermarker.py

from PyPDF2 import PdfFileWriter, PdfFileReader


def watermark(input_pdf, output_pdf, watermark_pdf):
    watermark = PdfFileReader(watermark_pdf)
    watermark_page = watermark.getPage(0)

    pdf = PdfFileReader(input_pdf)
    pdf_writer = PdfFileWriter()

    for page in range(pdf.getNumPages()):
        pdf_page = pdf.getPage(page)
        pdf_page.mergePage(watermark_page)
        pdf_writer.addPage(pdf_page)

    with open(output_pdf, 'wb') as fh:
        pdf_writer.write(fh)

if __name__ == '__main__':
    watermark(input_pdf='w9.pdf',
              output_pdf='watermarked_w9.pdf',
              watermark_pdf='watermark.pdf')
```

The first thing we do here is extract the watermark page from the PDF. Then we open the PDF that we want to apply the watermark to. We use a **for** loop to iterate over each of its pages and call the page object's **mergePage** method to apply the watermark. Next we add that watermarked page to our PDF writer object. Once the loop finishes, we write our new watermarked version out to disk.

Here's what the first page looked like:

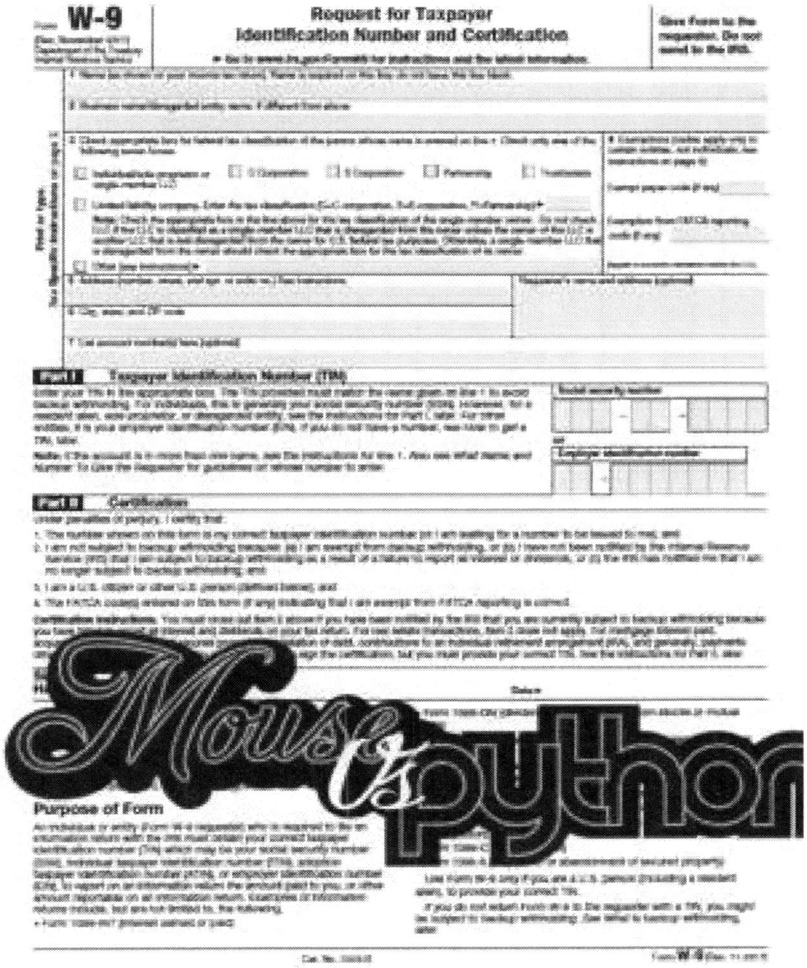

Chapter 14 - The PyPDF2 Package

Fig. 14-1: Watermark Example

That was pretty easy.

PDF Encryption

The PyPDF2 package also supports adding a password and encryption to your existing PDFs. As you may recall from Chapter 10, PDFs support a user password and an owner password. The user password only allows the user to open and read a PDF, but may have some restrictions applied to the PDF that could prevent the user from printing, for example. As far as I can tell, you can't actually apply any restrictions using PyPDF2 or it's just not documented well.

Here's how to add a password to a PDF with PyPDF2:

```
# pdf_encryption.py
```

```
from PyPDF2 import PdfFileWriter, PdfFileReader

def encrypt(input_pdf, output_pdf, password):
    pdf_writer = PdfFileWriter()
    pdf_reader = PdfFileReader(input_pdf)

    for page in range(pdf_reader.getNumPages()):
        pdf_writer.addPage(pdf_reader.getPage(page))

    pdf_writer.encrypt(user_pwd=password, owner_pwd=None,
        use_128bit=True)

    with open(output_pdf, 'wb') as fh:
        pdf_writer.write(fh)

if __name__ == '__main__':
    encrypt(input_pdf='reportlab-sample.pdf',
        output_pdf='encrypted.pdf', password='blowfish')
```

All we did here was create a set of PDF reader and write objects and read all the pages with the reader. Then we added those pages out to the specified writer object and added the specified password. If you only set the user password, then the owner password is set to the user password automatically. Whenever you add a password, 128-bit encryption is applied by default. If you set that argument to False, then the PDF will be encrypted at 40-bit encryption instead.

Wrapping Up

We covered a lot of useful information in this chapter. You learned how to extract metadata and text from your PDFs. We found out how to split and merge PDFs. You also learned how to rotate pages in a PDF and apply watermarks. Finally we discovered that PyPDF2 can add encryption and passwords to our PDFs.

Chapter 15 - The pdfrw Package

Patrick Maupin created a package he called **pdfrw** and released it back in 2012. The pdfrw package is a pure-Python library that you can use to read and write PDF files. At the time of writing, pdfrw was at version 0.4. With that version, it supports subsetting, merging, rotating and modifying data in PDFs. The pdfrw package has been used by the rst2pdf package (see chapter 18) since 2010 because pdfrw can "faithfully reproduce vector formats without rasterization". You can also use pdfrw in conjunction with ReportLab to re-use potions of existing PDFs in new PDFs that you create with ReportLab.

In this chapter, we will learn how to do the following:

- Extract certain types of information from a PDF
- Splitting PDFs
- Merging / Concatenating PDFs
- Rotating pages
- Creating overlays or watermarks
- Scaling pages
- Combining the use of pdfrw and ReportLab

Let's get started!

Installation

As you might expect, you can install pdfrw using pip. Let's get that done so we can start using pdfrw:

```
python -m pip install pdfrw
```

Now that we have pdfrw installed, let's learn how to extract some information from our PDFs.

Extracting Information from PDF

The pdfrw package does not extract data in quite the same way that PyPDF2 does. You may recall that PyPDF2 let's you extract an document information object that you can use to pull out information like author, title, etc. While pdfrw does let you get the Info object, it displays it in a less friendly way. Let's take a look:

Chapter 15 - The pdfrw Package

```
# reader.py

from pdfrw import PdfReader

def get_pdf_info(path):
    pdf = PdfReader(path)

    print(pdf.keys())
    print(pdf.Info)
    print(pdf.Root.keys())
    print('PDF has {} pages'.format(len(pdf.pages)))

if __name__ == '__main__':
    get_pdf_info('w9.pdf')
```

Here we import pdfrw's **PdfReader** class and instantiate it by passing in the path to the PDF file that we want to read. Then we extract the PDF object's keys, the information object and the Root. We also grab how many pages are in the document. The result of running this code is below:

```
['/ID', '/Root', '/Info', '/Size']
{'/Author': '(SE:W:CAR:MP)',
 '/CreationDate': "(D:20171109144422-05'00')",
 '/Creator': '(Adobe LiveCycle Designer ES 9.0)',
 '/Keywords': '(Fillable)',
 '/ModDate': "(D:20171109144521-05'00')",
 '/Producer': '(Adobe LiveCycle Designer ES 9.0)',
 '/SPDF': '(1112)',
 '/Subject': '(Request for Taxpayer Identification Number and Certification)',
 '/Title': '(Form W-9 \\(Rev. November 2017\\))'}
['/Pages', '/Perms', '/MarkInfo', '/Extensions', '/AcroForm', '/Metadata', '/Typ\
e', '/Names', '/StructTreeRoot']
PDF has 6 pages
```

If you run this against the **reportlaf-sample.pdf** file that I also included in the source code for this book, you will find that the author name that is returned ends up being:

- '<feff004d00690063006800610065006c00200044007200690073006300 6f006c006c>'

instead of "Michael Driscoll". I haven't figured out exactly why that is, but I am assuming that PyPDF2 does some extra data massaging on the PDF trailer information that pdfrw currently does not do.

Splitting

You can also use pdfrw to split a PDF up. For example, maybe you want to take the cover off of a book for some reason or you just want to extract the chapters of a book into multiple PDFs instead of storing them in one file. This is fairly trivial to do with pdfrw:

```python
# splitter.py

from pdfrw import PdfReader, PdfWriter

def split(path, number_of_pages, output):
    pdf_obj = PdfReader(path)
    total_pages = len(pdf_obj.pages)

    writer = PdfWriter()

    for page in range(number_of_pages):
        if page <= total_pages:
            writer.addpage(pdf_obj.pages[page])

    writer.write(output)

if __name__ == '__main__':
    split('reportlab-sample.pdf', 10, 'subset.pdf')
```

Here we create a function called **split** that takes an input PDF file path, the number of pages that you want to extract and the output path. Then we open up the file using pdfrw's **PdfReader** class and grab the total number of pages from the input PDF. Then we create a **PdfWriter** object and loop over the range of pages that we passed in. In each iteration, we attempt to extract a page from the input PDF and add that page to our writer object. Finally we write the extracted pages to disk.

Merging / Concatenating

The pdfrw package makes merging multiple PDFs together very easy. Let's write up a simple example that demonstrates how to do it:

```python
# concatenator.py

from pdfrw import PdfReader, PdfWriter, IndirectPdfDict

def concatenate(paths, output):
    writer = PdfWriter()

    for path in paths:
        reader = PdfReader(path)
        writer.addpages(reader.pages)

    writer.trailer.Info = IndirectPdfDict(
        Title='Combined PDF Title',
        Author='Michael Driscoll',
        Subject='PDF Combinations',
        Creator='The Concatenator'
    )

    writer.write(output)

if __name__ == '__main__':
    paths = ['reportlab-sample.pdf', 'w9.pdf']
    concatenate(paths, 'concatenate.pdf')
```

In this example, we create a function called **concatenate** that accepts a list of paths to PDFs that we want to concatenate together and the output path. Then iterate over those paths, open the file and add all the pages to the writer object via the writer's **addpages** method. Just for fun, we also import **IndirectPdfDict**, which allows us to add some trailer information to our PDF. In this case, we add the title, author, subject and creator script information to the PDF. Then we write out the concatenated PDF to disk.

Rotating

The pdfrw package also supports rotating the pages of a PDF. So if you happen to have a PDF that was saved in a weird way or an intern that scanned in some documents upside down, then you can use pdfrw (or PyPDF2) to fix the PDFs. Note that in pdfrw you must rotate clockwise in increments that are divisible by 90 degrees.

For this example, I created a function that will extract all the odd pages from the input PDF and rotate them 90 degrees:

Chapter 15 - The pdfrw Package

```
# rotator.py

from pdfrw import PdfReader, PdfWriter, IndirectPdfDict

def rotate_odd(path, output):
    reader = PdfReader(path)
    writer = PdfWriter()
    pages = reader.pages

    for page in range(len(pages)):
        if page % 2:
            pages[page].Rotate = 90
            writer.addpage(pages[page])

    writer.write(output)

if __name__ == '__main__':
    rotate_odd('reportlab-sample.pdf', 'rotate_odd.pdf')
```

Here we just open up the target PDF and create a writer object. Then we grab all the pages and iterate over them. If the page is an odd numbered page, we rotate it and then add that page to our writer object. This code ran pretty fast on my machine and the output is what you would expect.

Overlaying / Watermarking Pages

You can use pdfrw to watermark your PDF with some kind of information. For example, you might want to watermark a PDF with your buyer's email address or with your logo. You can also use the overlay one PDF on top of another PDF. We will actually use the overlay technique for filling in PDF forms in chapter 17.

Let's create a simple watermarker script to demonstrate how you might use pdfrw to overlay one PDF on top of another.

```
# watermarker.py

from pdfrw import PdfReader, PdfWriter, PageMerge

def watermarker(path, watermark, output):
    base_pdf = PdfReader(path)
    watermark_pdf = PdfReader(watermark)
    mark = watermark_pdf.pages[0]

    for page in range(len(base_pdf.pages)):
        merger = PageMerge(base_pdf.pages[page])
        merger.add(mark).render()

    writer = PdfWriter()
    writer.write(output, base_pdf)

if __name__ == '__main__':
    watermarker('reportlab-sample.pdf',
                'watermark.pdf',
                'watermarked-test.pdf')
```

Here we create a simple **watermarker** function that takes an input PDF path, the PDF that contains the watermark and the output path of the end result. Then we open up the base PDF and the watermark PDF. We extract the watermark page and then iterate over the pages in the base PDF. In each iteration, we create a **PageMerge** object using the current base PDF page that we are on. Then we overlay the watermark on top of that page and render it. After the loop finished, we create a PdfWriter object and write the merged PDF to disk.

Scaling

The pdfrw package can also manipulate PDFs in memory. In fact, it will allow you to create **Form XObjects**. These objects can represent any page or rectangle in a PDF. What this means is that you once you have one of these objects created, you can then scale, rotate and position pages or subpages. There is a fun example on the pdfrw Github page called **4up.py** that takes pages from a PDF and scales them down to a quarter of their size and positions four pages to a single page.

I decided to ask the creator of pdfrw, Patrick Maupin, if I could use a modified version of that example in this book to show some of the power of the pdfrw package. Here is my version:

Chapter 15 - The pdfrw Package

```python
# scaler.py

from pdfrw import PdfReader, PdfWriter, PageMerge


def get4(srcpages):
    scale = 0.5
    srcpages = PageMerge() + srcpages
    x_increment, y_increment = (scale * i for i in srcpages.xobj_box[2:])
    for i, page in enumerate(srcpages):
        page.scale(scale)
        page.x = x_increment if i & 1 else 0
        page.y = 0 if i & 2 else y_increment
    return srcpages.render()


def scale_pdf(path, output):
    pages = PdfReader(path).pages
    writer = PdfWriter(output)
    scaled_pages = 4

    for i in range(0, len(pages), scaled_pages):
        four_pages = get4(pages[i: i + 4])
        writer.addpage(four_pages)

    writer.write()

if __name__ == '__main__':
    scale_pdf('reportlab-sample.pdf', 'four-page.pdf')
```

The **get4** function comes from the **4up.py** script. This function takes a series of pages and uses pdfrw's **PageMerge** class to merge those pages together. We basically loop over the passed in pages and scale them down a bit, then we position them on the page and render the page series on one page.

The next function is **scale_pdf**, which takes the input PDF and the path for the output. Then we extract the pages from the input file and create a writer object. Next we loop over the pages of the input document 4 at a time and pass them to the **get4** function. Then we take the result of that function and add it to our writer object.

Finally we write the document out to disk. Here is a screenshot that kind of shows how it looks:

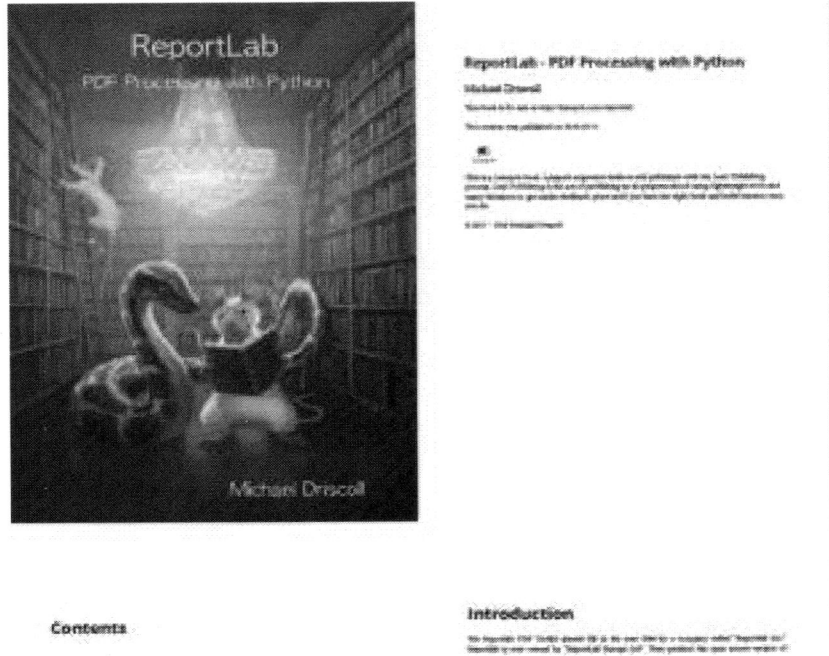

Fig. 15-1: Scaling 4 pages to 1

Now let's learn how we might combine pdfrw with ReportLab!

Combining pdfrw and ReportLab

One of the neat features of pdfrw is its ability to integrate with the ReportLab toolkit. There are several examples on the pdfrw Github page that show different ways to use the two packages together. The creator of pdfrw thinks that you may be able to simulate some of ReportLab's **pagecatcher** functionality which is a part of ReportLab's paid product. I don't know if it does or not, but you can definitely do some fun things with pdfrw and ReportLab.

For example, you can use pdfrw to read in pages from a pre-existing PDF and turn them into objects that you can write out in ReportLab. Let's write a script that will create a subset of a PDF using pdfrw and ReportLab. The following example is based on one from the pdfrw project:

```
# split_with_rl.py

from pdfrw import PdfReader
from pdfrw.buildxobj import pagexobj
from pdfrw.toreportlab import makerl

from reportlab.pdfgen.canvas import Canvas

def split(path, number_of_pages, output):
    pdf_obj = PdfReader(path)

    my_canvas = Canvas(output)

    # create page objects
    pages = pdf_obj.pages[0: number_of_pages]
    pages = [pagexobj(page) for page in pages]

    for page in pages:
        my_canvas.setPageSize((page.BBox[2], page.BBox[3]))
        my_canvas.doForm(makerl(my_canvas, page))
        my_canvas.showPage()

    # write the new PDF to disk
    my_canvas.save()


if __name__ == '__main__':
    split('reportlab-sample.pdf', 10, 'subset-rl.pdf')
```

Here we import some new functionality. First we import the **pagexobj** which will create a **Form XObject** from the view that you give it. The view defaults to an entire page, but you could tell pdfrw to just extract a portion of the page. Next we import the **makerl** function which will take a ReportLab canvas object and a pdfrw Form XObject and turn it into a form that ReportLab can add to its canvas object.

So let's examine this code a bit and see how it works. Here we create a reader object and a canvas object. Then we create a list of Form XForm objects starting with the first page to the last page that we specified. Note that we do not check if we asked for too many pages though, so that is something that we could do to enhance this script and make it less likely to fail.

Next we iterate over the pages that we just created and add them to our ReportLab canvas. You will note that we set the page size using the width and height that we extract using pdfrw's **BBox** attributes. Then we add the Form XObjects to the canvas. The call to **showPage** tells ReportLab that you finished creating a page and to start a new one. Finally we save the new PDF to disk.

There are some other examples on pdfrw's site that you should review. For example, there is a neat piece of code that shows how you could take a page from a pre-existing PDF and use it as the background for a new PDF that you create in ReportLab. There is also a really interesting scaling example where you can use pdfrw and ReportLab to scale pages down in much the same way that we did with pdfrw all by itself.

Wrapping Up

The pdfrw package is actually pretty powerful and has features that PyPDF2 does not. Its ability to integrate with ReportLab is one feature that I think is really interesting and could be used to create something original. You can also use pdfrw to do many of the same things that we can do with PyPDF2, such as splitting, merging, rotating and concatenating PDFs together. I actually thought pdfrw was a bit more robust in generating viable PDFs than PyPDF2 but I have not done extensive tests to actually confirm this.

Regardless, I believe that pdfrw is worth adding to your toolkit.

Chapter 16 - Extracting and Exporting Data from PDFs

There are many times where you will want to extract data from a PDF and export it in a different format using Python. Unfortunately, there aren't a lot of Python packages that do the extraction part very well. In this chapter, we will look at a variety of different packages that you can use to extract text. We will also learn how to extract some images from PDFs. While there is no complete solution for these tasks in Python, you should be able to use the information herein to get you started. Once we have extracted the data we want, we will also look at how we can take that data and export it in a different format.

Let's get started by learning how to extract text!

Extracting Text with PDFMiner

Probably the most well known is a package called **PDFMiner**. The PDFMiner package has been around since Python 2.4. It's primary purpose is to extract text from a PDF. In fact, PDFMiner can tell you the exact location of the text on the page as well as father information about fonts. For Python 2.4 - 2.7, you can refer to the following websites for additional information on PDFMiner:

- Github - https://github.com/euske/pdfminer
- PyPI - https://pypi.python.org/pypi/pdfminer/
- Webpage - https://euske.github.io/pdfminer/

PDFMiner is not compatible with Python 3. Fortunately, there is a fork of PDFMiner called **PDFMiner.six** that works exactly the same. You can find it here: https://github.com/pdfminer/pdfminer.six

The directions for installing PDFMiner are out-dated at best. You can actually use **pip** to install it:

```
python -m pip install pdfminer
```

If you want to install PDFMiner for Python 3 (which is what you should probably be doing), then you have to do the install like this:

```
python -m pip install pdfminer.six
```

The documentation on PDFMiner is rather poor at best. You will most likely need to use Google and StackOverflow to figure out how to use PDFMiner effectively outside of what is covered in this chapter.

Note: Even when using the **pdfminer.six** package, I have had reports that it doesn't fully work in Python 3. So if you want to use any of PDFMiner's advanced features, you may need to use Python 2.7 until they get that package completely converted over to Python 3.

Extracting all the text

Sometimes you will want to extract all the text in the PDF. The PDFMiner package offers a couple of different methods that you can do this. We will look at some of the programmatic methods first. Let's try reading all the text out of an Internal Revenue Service W9 form. You can get a copy here: https://www.irs.gov/pub/irs-pdf/fw9.pdf

Once you had the PDF properly saved off, we can look at the code:

```python
# miner_text_extraction.py

import io

from pdfminer.converter import TextConverter
from pdfminer.pdfinterp import PDFPageInterpreter
from pdfminer.pdfinterp import PDFResourceManager
from pdfminer.pdfpage import PDFPage


def extract_text_from_pdf(pdf_path):
    resource_manager = PDFResourceManager()
    fake_file_handle = io.StringIO()
    converter = TextConverter(resource_manager, fake_file_handle)
    page_interpreter = PDFPageInterpreter(resource_manager, converter)

    with open(pdf_path, 'rb') as fh:
        for page in PDFPage.get_pages(fh,
                                      caching=True,
                                      check_extractable=True):
            page_interpreter.process_page(page)

        text = fake_file_handle.getvalue()

    # close open handles
```

```
        converter.close()
        fake_file_handle.close()

        if text:
            return text

if __name__ == '__main__':
    print(extract_text_from_pdf('w9.pdf'))
```

The PDFMiner package tends to be a bit verbose when you use it directly. Here we import various bits and pieces from various parts of PDFMiner. Since there is no documentation of any of these classes and no docstrings either, I won't explain what they do in depth. Feel free to dig into the source code yourself if you're really curious. However, I think we can kind of follow along with the code.

The first thing we do is create a resource manager instance. Then we create a file-like object via Python's **io** module. If you are using Python 2, then you will want to use the **StringIO** module. Our next step is to create a converter. In this case, we choose the **TextConverter**, however you could also use an **HTMLConverter** or an **XMLConverter** if you wanted to. Finally we create a PDF interpreter object that will take our resource manager and converter objects and extract the text.

The last step is to open the PDF and loop through each page. At the end, we grab all the text, close the various handlers and print out the text to stdout.

Extracting text by page

Frankly grabbing all the text from a multi-page document isn't all that useful. Usually you will want to do work on smaller subsets of the document instead. So let's rewrite the code so it extracts text on a page-by-page basis. This will allow us to examine the text a page at a time:

```
# miner_text_generator.py

import io

from pdfminer.converter import TextConverter
from pdfminer.pdfinterp import PDFPageInterpreter
from pdfminer.pdfinterp import PDFResourceManager
from pdfminer.pdfpage import PDFPage

def extract_text_by_page(pdf_path):
    with open(pdf_path, 'rb') as fh:
        for page in PDFPage.get_pages(fh,
                                      caching=True,
```

```
                                check_extractable=True):
        resource_manager = PDFResourceManager()
        fake_file_handle = io.StringIO()
        converter = TextConverter(resource_manager, fake_file_handle)
        page_interpreter = PDFPageInterpreter(resource_manager, converter)
        page_interpreter.process_page(page)

        text = fake_file_handle.getvalue()
        yield text

        # close open handles
        converter.close()
        fake_file_handle.close()

def extract_text(pdf_path):
    for page in extract_text_by_page(pdf_path):
        print(page)
        print()

if __name__ == '__main__':
    print(extract_text('w9.pdf'))
```

In this example, we create a generator function that **yields** the text for each page. The **extract_text** function prints out the text of each page. This is where we could add some parsing logic to parse out what we want. Or we could just save the text (or HTML or XML) off as individual files for future parsing.

You will note that the text may not be in the order you expect. So you will definitely need to figure out the best way to parse out the text that you are interested in.

The nice thing about PDFMiner is that you can already "export" the PDF as text, HTML or XML.

You can also use PDFMiner's command line tools, **pdf2txt.py** and **dumppdf.py** to do the exporting for you if you don't want to try to figure out PDFMiner yourself. According to the source code of **pdf2txt.py**, it can be used to export a PDF as plain text, html, xml or "tags".

Exporting Text via pdf2txt.py

The **pdf2txt.py** command line tool that comes with PDFMiner will extract text from a PDF file and print it out to stdout by default. It will not recognize text that is images as PDFMiner does not support optical character recognition (OCR). Let's try the simplest method of using it which is just passing it the path to a PDF file. We will use the **w9.pdf**. Open up a terminal and navigate to the location that you have saved that PDF or modify the command below to point to that file:

Chapter 16 - Extracting and Exporting Data from PDFs

```
pdf2txt.py w9.pdf
```

If you run this, it will print out all the text to stdout. You can also make pdf2txt.py write the text to file as text, HTML, XML or "tagged PDF". The XML format will give to the most information about the PDF as it contains the location of each letter in the document as well as font information. HTML is not recommended as the markup pdf2txt generates tends to be ugly. Here's how you can get different formats output:

```
pdf2txt.py -o w9.html w9.pdf
pdf2txt.py -o w9.xml w9.pdf
```

The first command will create an HTML document while the second will create an XML document. Here is a sceenshot of how the HTML rendered from the PDFMiner conversion of the PDF:

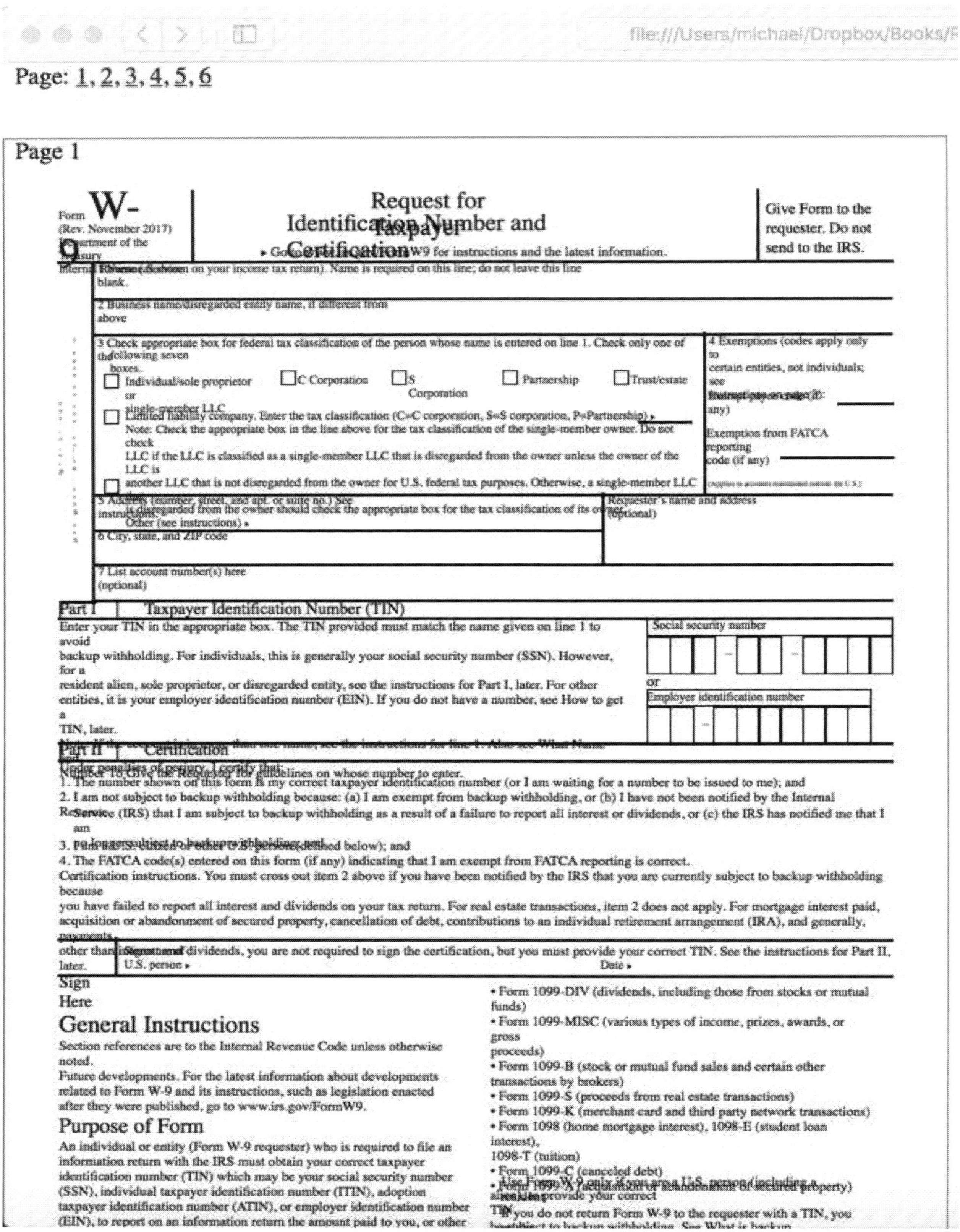

Fig. 16-1: HTML conversion of a PDF

As you can see, the end result looks a bit off, but it's not too bad. The XML it outputs is extremely verbose, so I can't reproduce it all here. However here is a snippet to give you an idea of what it looks like:

```
<pages>
    <page id="1" bbox="0.000,0.000,611.976,791.968" rotate="0">
        <textbox id="0" bbox="36.000,732.312,100.106,761.160">
            <textline bbox="36.000,732.312,100.106,761.160">
                <text font="JYMPLA+HelveticaNeueLTStd-Roman" bbox="36.000,736.33\
4,40.018,744.496" size="8.162">F</text>
                <text font="JYMPLA+HelveticaNeueLTStd-Roman" bbox="40.018,736.33\
4,44.036,744.496" size="8.162">o</text>
                <text font="JYMPLA+HelveticaNeueLTStd-Roman" bbox="44.036,736.33\
4,46.367,744.496" size="8.162">r</text>
                <text font="JYMPLA+HelveticaNeueLTStd-Roman" bbox="46.367,736.33\
4,52.338,744.496" size="8.162">m</text>
                <text font="JYMPLA+HelveticaNeueLTStd-Roman" bbox="52.338,736.33\
4,54.284,744.496" size="8.162"> </text>
                <text font="JYMPLA+HelveticaNeueLTStd-Roman" bbox="54.284,736.33\
4,56.230,744.496" size="8.162"> </text>
                <text font="JYMPLA+HelveticaNeueLTStd-Roman" bbox="56.230,736.33\
4,58.176,744.496" size="8.162"> </text
                ><text font="JYMPLA+HelveticaNeueLTStd-Roman" bbox="58.176,736.3\
34,60.122,744.496" size="8.162"> </text>
                <text font="ZWOHBU+HelveticaNeueLTStd-BlkCn" bbox="60.122,732.31\
2,78.794,761.160" size="28.848">W</text>
                <text font="ZWOHBU+HelveticaNeueLTStd-BlkCn" bbox="78.794,732.31\
2,87.626,761.160" size="28.848">-</text>
                <text font="ZWOHBU+HelveticaNeueLTStd-BlkCn" bbox="87.626,732.31\
2,100.106,761.160" size="28.848">9</text>
                <text></text>
            </textline>
```

Extracting Text with Slate

Tim McNamara didn't like how obtuse and difficult PDFMiner is to use, so he wrote a wrapper around it called **slate** that makes it much easier to extract text from PDFs. Unfortunately, it does not appear to be Python 3 compatible. If you want to give it a try, you may need to have **easy_install** available to install the **distribute** package, like this:

Chapter 16 - Extracting and Exporting Data from PDFs

```
easy_install distribute
```

I wasn't able to get pip to install that package correctly. Once it's installed though, you will be able to use pip to install slate:

```
python -m pip install slate
```

Note that the latest version is 0.5.2 and pip may or may not grab that version. If it does not, then you can install slate directly from Github:

```
python -m pip install git+https://github.com/timClicks/slate
```

Now we're ready to write some code to extract the text from a PDF:

```python
# slate_text_extraction.py

import slate

def extract_text_from_pdf(pdf_path):
    with open(pdf_path) as fh:
        document = slate.PDF(fh, password='', just_text=1)

    for page in document:
        print(page)

if __name__ == '__main__':
    extract_text_from_pdf('w9.pdf')
```

As you can see, to make slate parse a PDF, you just need to import slate and then create an instance of its **PDF** class. The PDF class is actually a subclass of Python's **list** builtin, so it just returns a list / iterable of pages of text. You will also note that we can pass in a password argument if the PDF has a password set. Anyway, once the document is parsed, we just print out the text on each page.

I really like how much easier it is to use slate. Unfortunately there is almost no documentation associated with this package either. After looking through the source code, it appears that all this package supports is text extraction.

Exporting Your Data

Now that we have some text to work with, we will spend some time learning how to export that data in a variety of different formats. Specifically, we will learn how to export our text in the following ways:

- XML
- JSON
- CSV

Let's get started!

Exporting to XML

The eXtensible Markup Language (XML) format is one of the most well known output and input formats. It is used widely on the internet for many different things. As we have already seen in this chapter, PDFMiner also supports XML as one of its outputs.

Let's create our own XML creation tool though. Here's a simple example:

```
# xml_exporter.py

import os
import xml.etree.ElementTree as xml

from miner_text_generator import extract_text_by_page
from xml.dom import minidom


def export_as_xml(pdf_path, xml_path):
    filename = os.path.splitext(os.path.basename(pdf_path))[0]
    root = xml.Element('{filename}'.format(filename=filename))
    pages = xml.Element('Pages')
    root.append(pages)

    counter = 1
    for page in extract_text_by_page(pdf_path):
        text = xml.SubElement(pages, 'Page_{}'.format(counter))
        text.text = page[0:100]
        counter += 1

    tree = xml.ElementTree(root)
```

```python
    xml_string = xml.tostring(root, 'utf-8')
    parsed_string = minidom.parseString(xml_string)
    pretty_string = parsed_string.toprettyxml(indent='   ')

    with open(xml_path, 'w') as fh:
        fh.write(pretty_string)
    #tree.write(xml_path)

if __name__ == '__main__':
    pdf_path = 'w9.pdf'
    xml_path = 'w9.xml'
    export_as_xml(pdf_path, xml_path)
```

This script will use Python's built-in XML libraries, **minidom** and **ElementTree**. We also import our PDFMiner generator script that we use to grab a page of text at a time. In this example, we create our top level element which is the file name of the PDF. Then we add a **Pages** element underneath it. The next step is our **for** loop where we extract each page from the PDF and save off the information we want. Here is where you could add a special parser where you might split up the page into sentences or words and parse out more interesting information. For example, you might want only sentences with a particular name or date / timestamp. You can use Python's Regular Expressions to find those sorts of things or just check for the existence of sub-strings in the sentence.

For this example, we just extract the first 100 characters from each page and save them off into an XML **SubElement**. Technically the next bit of code could be simplified to just write out the XML. However, ElementTree doesn't do anything to the XML to make it easy to read. It kind of ends up looking like minified javascript in that its just one giant block of text. So instead of writing that block of text to disk, we use **minidom** to "prettify" the XML with whitespace before writing it out. The result ends up looking like this:

```
<?xml version="1.0" ?>
<w9>
   <Pages>
      <Page_1>Form     W-9(Rev. November 2017)Department of the Treasury  Internal \
Revenue Service Request for Taxp</Page_1>
      <Page_2>Form W-9 (Rev. 11-2017)Page 2 By signing the filled-out form, you: 1\
. Certify that the TIN you are g</Page_2>
      <Page_3>Form W-9 (Rev. 11-2017)Page 3 Criminal penalty for falsifying inform\
ation. Willfully falsifying cert</Page_3>
      <Page_4>Form W-9 (Rev. 11-2017)Page 4 The following chart shows types of pay\
ments that may be exempt from ba</Page_4>
      <Page_5>Form W-9 (Rev. 11-2017)Page 5 1. Interest, dividend, and barter exch\
ange accounts opened before 1984</Page_5>
      <Page_6>Form W-9 (Rev. 11-2017)Page 6 The IRS does not initiate contacts wit\
```

```
h taxpayers via emails. Also, th</Page_6>
  </Pages>
</w9>
```

That's pretty clean XML and it's also easy to read. For bonus points, you could take what you learned in the PyPDF2 chapter and use it to extract the metadata from the PDF and add it to your XML as well.

Exporting to JSON

JavaScript Object Notation or JSON is a lightweight data-interchange format that is easy to read and write. Python includes a **json** module in its standard library that allows you to read and write JSON programmatically. Let's take what we learned from the previous section and use that to create an exporter script that outputs JSON instead of XML:

```python
# json_exporter.py

import json
import os

from miner_text_generator import extract_text_by_page


def export_as_json(pdf_path, json_path):
    filename = os.path.splitext(os.path.basename(pdf_path))[0]
    data = {'Filename': filename}
    data['Pages'] = []

    counter = 1
    for page in extract_text_by_page(pdf_path):
        text = page[0:100]
        page = {'Page_{}'.format(counter): text}
        data['Pages'].append(page)
        counter += 1

    with open(json_path, 'w') as fh:
        json.dump(data, fh)

if __name__ == '__main__':
    pdf_path = 'w9.pdf'
    json_path = 'w9.json'
    export_as_json(pdf_path, json_path)
```

Here we import the various libraries that we need including our PDFMiner module. Then we create a function that accepts the PDF input path and the JSON output path. JSON is basically a dictionary in Python, so we create a couple of simple top-level keys: **Filename** and **Pages**. The **Pages** key maps to an empty list. Next we loop over each page of the PDF and extract the first 100 characters of each page. Then we create a dictionary with the page number as the key and the 100 characters as the value and append it to the top-level Page's list. Finally we write the file using the **json** module's **dump** command.

The contents of the file ended up looking like this:

```
{'Filename': 'w9',
 'Pages': [{'Page_1': 'Form    W-9(Rev. November 2017)Department of the Treasury\
    Internal Revenue Service Request for Taxp'},
           {'Page_2': 'Form W-9 (Rev. 11-2017)Page 2 By signing the filled-out f\
orm, you: 1. Certify that the TIN you are g'},
           {'Page_3': 'Form W-9 (Rev. 11-2017)Page 3 Criminal penalty for falsif\
ying information. Willfully falsifying cert'},
           {'Page_4': 'Form W-9 (Rev. 11-2017)Page 4 The following chart shows t\
ypes of payments that may be exempt from ba'},
           {'Page_5': 'Form W-9 (Rev. 11-2017)Page 5 1. Interest, dividend, and \
barter exchange accounts opened before 1984'},
           {'Page_6': 'Form W-9 (Rev. 11-2017)Page 6 The IRS does not initiate c\
ontacts with taxpayers via emails. Also, th'}]}
```

Once again, we have some nice output that is easy to read. You could enhance this example with the PDF's metadata as well, if you would like to. Note that the output will change depending on what you want to parse out of each page or document.

Now let's take a quick look at how we could export to CSV.

Exporting to CSV

CSV stands for **comma separated values**. It is a pretty standard format that has been around a very long time. The nice thing about CSV is that Microsoft Excel and LibreOffice will open them up in a nice spreadsheet automatically. You can also open up CSV files in a text editor if you'd like to see the raw value.

Python has a built-in **csv** module that you can use to read and write CSV files. We will use it here to create a CSV from the text that we extract from the PDF. Let's take a look at some code:

Chapter 16 - Extracting and Exporting Data from PDFs

```
# csv_exporter.py

import csv
import os

from miner_text_generator import extract_text_by_page


def export_as_csv(pdf_path, csv_path):
    filename = os.path.splitext(os.path.basename(pdf_path))[0]

    counter = 1
    with open(csv_path, 'w') as csv_file:
        writer = csv.writer(csv_file)
        for page in extract_text_by_page(pdf_path):
            text = page[0:100]
            words = text.split()
            writer.writerow(words)


if __name__ == '__main__':
    pdf_path = 'w9.pdf'
    csv_path = 'w9.csv'
    export_as_csv(pdf_path, csv_path)
```

For this example, we import Python's **csv** library. Otherwise the imports are the same as the previous example. In our function, we create a CSV file handler using the CSV file path. Then we initialize a CSV writer object with that file handler as its sole argument. Next we loop over the pages of the PDF as before. The only difference here is that we split the first 100 characters into individual words. This allows us to have some actual data to add to the CSV. If we did not do this, then each row would only have one element in it, which isn't really a CSV file at that point. Finally we write out our list of words to the CSV file.

This is the result I got:

```
Form,W-9(Rev.,November,2017)Department,of,the,Treasury,Internal,Revenue,Service,\
Request,for,Taxp
Form,W-9,(Rev.,11-2017)Page,2,By,signing,the,filled-out,"form,",you:,1.,Certify,\
that,the,TIN,you,are,g
Form,W-9,(Rev.,11-2017)Page,3,Criminal,penalty,for,falsifying,information.,Willf\
ully,falsifying,cert
Form,W-9,(Rev.,11-2017)Page,4,The,following,chart,shows,types,of,payments,that,m\
ay,be,exempt,from,ba
Form,W-9,(Rev.,11-2017)Page,5,1.,"Interest,","dividend,",and,barter,exchange,acc\
ounts,opened,before,1984
Form,W-9,(Rev.,11-2017)Page,6,The,IRS,does,not,initiate,contacts,with,taxpayers,\
via,emails.,"Also,",th
```

I think this one is a bit harder to read than the JSON or XML examples, but it's not too bad. Now let's move on and look at how we might extract images from a PDF.

Extracting Images

Unfortunately, there are no Python packages that actually do image extraction from PDFs. The closest thing I found was a project called **minecart** that claims to be able to do it, but only works on Python 2.7. I was not able to get it to work with the sample PDFs I had. There is an article on Ned Batchelder's blog (https://nedbatchelder.com/blog/200712/extracting_jpgs_from_pdfs.html) that talks a bit about how he was able to extract JPGs from PDFs. His code is as follows:

```python
# Extract jpg's from pdf's. Quick and dirty.
import sys

pdf = file(sys.argv[1], "rb").read()

startmark = "\xff\xd8"
startfix = 0
endmark = "\xff\xd9"
endfix = 2
i = 0

njpg = 0
while True:
    istream = pdf.find("stream", i)
    if istream < 0:
        break
    istart = pdf.find(startmark, istream, istream+20)
```

Chapter 16 - Extracting and Exporting Data from PDFs

```
        if istart < 0:
            i = istream+20
            continue
        iend = pdf.find("endstream", istart)
        if iend < 0:
            raise Exception("Didn't find end of stream!")
        iend = pdf.find(endmark, iend-20)
        if iend < 0:
            raise Exception("Didn't find end of JPG!")

        istart += startfix
        iend += endfix
        print("JPG %d from %d to %d" % (njpg, istart, iend))
        jpg = pdf[istart:iend]
        jpgfile = file("jpg%d.jpg" % njpg, "wb")
        jpgfile.write(jpg)
        jpgfile.close()

        njpg += 1
        i = iend
```

This also did not work for the PDFs I was using. There are some people in the comments that do claim it works for some of their PDFs and there are some examples of updated code in the comments too. StackOverflow has variations of this code on it, some of which use PyPDF2 in some way or another. None of these worked for me either.

My recommendation is to use a tool like **Poppler** to extract the images. Poppler has a tool called **pdfimages** that you can use with Python's **subprocess** module. Here's how you could use it without Python:

```
pdfimages -all reportlab-sample.pdf images/prefix-jpg
```

Make sure that the **images** folder (or whatever output folder you want to create) is already created as pdfimages doesn't create it for you.

Let's write up a Python script that also executes this command and will make sure the output folder exists for you too:

```
# image_exporter.py

import os
import subprocess

def image_exporter(pdf_path, output_dir):
    if not os.path.exists(output_dir):
        os.makedirs(output_dir)

    cmd = ['pdfimages', '-all', pdf_path,
           '{}/prefix'.format(output_dir)]
    subprocess.call(cmd)
    print('Images extracted:')
    print(os.listdir(output_dir))


if __name__ == '__main__':
    pdf_path = 'reportlab-sample.pdf'
    image_exporter(pdf_path, output_dir='images')
```

In thie example, we import the **subprocess** and **os** modules. If the output directory does not exist, we attempt to create it. Them we use subprocess's **call** method to execute pdfimages. We use **call** because it will wait for pdfimages to finish running. You could use **Popen** instead, but that will basically run the process in the background. Finaly we print out a listing of the output directory to confirm that images were extracted to it.

There are some other articles on the internet that reference a library called **Wand** that you might also want to try. It is an ImageMagick wrapper. Also of note is that there is a Python binding to Poppler called **pypoppler**, although I wasn't able to find any examples of that package that did image extraction.

Wrapping Up

We covered a lot of different information in this chapter. You learned about several different packages that we can use to extract text from PDFs such as PDFMiner or Slate. We also learned how to use Python's built-in libraries to export the text to XML, JSON and CSV. Finally we looked at the difficult problem of exporting images from PDFs. While Python does not currently have any good libraries for this task, you can workaround that by using other tools, such as Poppler's pdfimage utility.

Chapter 17 - Filling in PDF Forms

Fillable forms have been a part of Adobe's PDF format for years. One of the most famous examples of fillable forms in the United States are documents from the Internal Revenue Service. There are lots of government forms that use fillable forms. There are many different approaches for filling in these forms programmatically. The most time consuming method I have heard about is to just recreate the form in ReportLab by hand and then fill it in. Frankly I think this is probably the worst idea, except when your company is in charge of creating the PDFs itself. Then that might be a viable option because you then have complete control over the PDF creation and the inputs that need to go into it.

Creating a Simple Form

We need a simple form to use for our first example. Fortunately, we created a simple form back in chapter 10 when we learned about ReportLab's built-in support for interactive forms. Here is the code we used in that chapter for generating a simple form:

```
# simple_form.py

from reportlab.pdfgen import canvas
from reportlab.pdfbase import pdfform
from reportlab.lib.colors import magenta, pink, blue, green

def create_simple_form():
    c = canvas.Canvas('simple_form.pdf')

    c.setFont("Courier", 20)
    c.drawCentredString(300, 700, 'Employment Form')
    c.setFont("Courier", 14)
    form = c.acroForm

    c.drawString(10, 650, 'First Name:')
    form.textfield(name='fname', tooltip='First Name',
                   x=110, y=635, borderStyle='inset',
                   borderColor=magenta, fillColor=pink,
                   width=300,
                   textColor=blue, forceBorder=True)
```

```
        c.drawString(10, 600, 'Last Name:')
        form.textfield(name='lname', tooltip='Last Name',
                       x=110, y=585, borderStyle='inset',
                       borderColor=green, fillColor=magenta,
                       width=300,
                       textColor=blue, forceBorder=True)

        c.drawString(10, 550, 'Address:')
        form.textfield(name='address', tooltip='Address',
                       x=110, y=535, borderStyle='inset',
                       width=400, forceBorder=True)

        c.drawString(10, 500, 'City:')
        form.textfield(name='city', tooltip='City',
                       x=110, y=485, borderStyle='inset',
                       forceBorder=True)

        c.drawString(250, 500, 'State:')
        form.textfield(name='state', tooltip='State',
                       x=350, y=485, borderStyle='inset',
                       forceBorder=True)

        c.drawString(10, 450, 'Zip Code:')
        form.textfield(name='zip_code', tooltip='Zip Code',
                       x=110, y=435, borderStyle='inset',
                       forceBorder=True)

        c.save()

if __name__ == '__main__':
    create_simple_form()
```

When you run this example, the interactive PDF form looks like this:

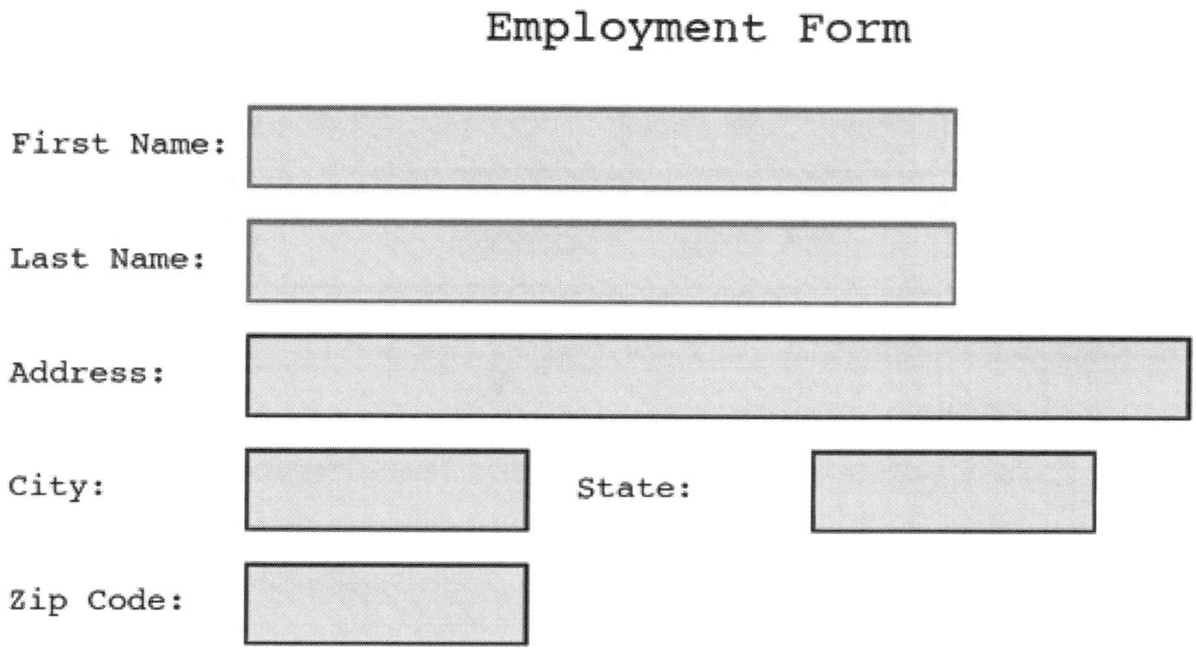

Chapter 17 - Filling in PDF Forms

Fig. 17-1: A simple fillable form created with ReportLab

Now we are ready to learn one of the ways that we can fill in this form!

Merging Overlays

Jan ChÄ™Ä‡ wrote an article on Medium (https://medium.com/@zwinny/filling-pdf-forms-in-python-the-right-way-eb9592e03dba) that contained several different approaches to this problem of filling in forms in PDFs. The first solution proposed was to take an unfilled form in a PDF and create a separate PDF using ReportLab that has the data we want to us to "fill" this form. The author then used **pdfrw** to merge the two PDFs together. You could theoretically use **PyPDF2** for the merging process too. Let's go ahead and take a look at how this approach might work using the **pdfrw** package.

If you haven't already installed pdfrw when you read chapter 15, then you will want to get started by installing it now:

```
python -m pip install pdfrw
```

Now that we have pdfrw installed, let's create a file called **fill_by_overlay.py**. We will add two functions to this file. The first function will create our overlay. Let's check that out:

Chapter 17 - Filling in PDF Forms

```python
# fill_by_overlay.py

import pdfrw
from reportlab.pdfgen import canvas


def create_overlay():
    """
    Create the data that will be overlayed on top
    of the form that we want to fill
    """
    c = canvas.Canvas('simple_form_overlay.pdf')

    c.drawString(115, 650, 'Mike')
    c.drawString(115, 600, 'Driscoll')
    c.drawString(115, 550, '123 Greenway Road')
    c.drawString(115, 500, 'Everytown')
    c.drawString(355, 500, 'IA')
    c.drawString(115, 450, '55555')

    c.save()
```

Here we import the **pdfrw** package and we also import the **canvas** sub-module from ReportLab. Then we create a function called **create_overlay** that creates a simple PDF using ReportLab's **Canvas** class. We just use the **drawString** canvas method. This will take some trial-and-error. Fortunately on Linux and Mac, there are decent PDF Previewer applications that you can use to just keep the PDF open and they will automatically refresh with each change. This is very helpful in figuring out the exact coordinates you need to draw your strings to. Since we created the original form, figuring out the offset for the overlay is actually pretty easy. We already knew where on the page the form elements were, so we can make a good educated guess of where to draw the strings to.

The next piece of the puzzle is actually merging the overlay we created above with the form we created in the previous section. Let's write that function next:

```
def merge_pdfs(form_pdf, overlay_pdf, output):
    """
    Merge the specified fillable form PDF with the
    overlay PDF and save the output
    """
    form = pdfrw.PdfReader(form_pdf)
    olay = pdfrw.PdfReader(overlay_pdf)

    for form_page, overlay_page in zip(form.pages, olay.pages):
        merge_obj = pdfrw.PageMerge()
        overlay = merge_obj.add(overlay_page)[0]
        pdfrw.PageMerge(form_page).add(overlay).render()

    writer = pdfrw.PdfWriter()
    writer.write(output, form)


if __name__ == '__main__':
    create_overlay()
    merge_pdfs('simple_form.pdf',
               'simple_form_overlay.pdf',
               'merged_form.pdf')
```

Here we open up both the form and the overlay PDFs using pdfrw's **PdfReader** classes. Then we loop over the pages of both PDFs and merge them together using **PageMerge**. At the end of the code, we create an instance of **PdfWriter** that we use to write the newly merged PDF out. The end result should look like this:

Fig. 17-2: A merged fillable form

Note: When I ran this code, I did receive some errors on stdout. Here's an example:

```
[ERROR] tokens.py:226 stream /Length attribute (171) appears to be too small (si\
ze 470) -- adjusting (line=192, col=1)
```

As I mentioned, this doesn't actually prevent the merged PDF from being created. But you might want to keep an eye on these as they might hint at a problem should you have any issues.

Other Ways to Fill Forms

I have read about several other ways to "fill" the fields in these kinds of PDFs. One of them was to take a PDF and save the pages as a series of images. Then draw rectangles at the locations you want to add text and then use your new image as a config file for filling out the PDF. Seems kind of wacky and frankly I don't want to go to all that work.

A better method would be to open a PDF in a PDF editor where you can add invisible read-only fields. You can label the fields with unique names and then access them via the PDF's metadata. Loop over the metadata and use ReportLab's canvas methods to create an overlay again and then merge it in much the same way as before.

I have also seen a lot of people talking about using Forms Data Format or FDF. This is the format that PDFs are supposed to use to hold that data that is to be filled in a PDF. You can use **PyPDFtk** and **PdfJinja** to do the form filling. Interestingly, **PyPDFtk** doesn't work with image fields, such as

Chapter 17 - Filling in PDF Forms

where you might want to paste a signature image. You can use **PdfJinja** for this purpose. However **PdfJinja** seems to have some limitations when working with checkboxes and radioboxes.

You can read more about these topics at the following links:

- https://yoongkang.com/blog/pdf-forms-with-python/
- https://medium.com/@zwinny/filling-pdf-forms-in-python-the-right-way-eb9592e03dba

Using the pdfforms Package

The package that I think holds the most promise in regards to simplicity to use is the new **pdfforms** package. It requires that you install a cross-platform application called **pdftk** though. Fortunately pdftk is free so that's not really a problem.

You can install pdfforms using pip like this:

```
python -m pip install pdfforms
```

To use pdfforms, you must first have it **inspect** the PDF that contains a form so it knows how to fill it out. You can do the inspection like this:

```
pdfforms inspect simple_form.pdf
```

If pdfforms works correctly, it will create a "filled" PDF in its "test" sub-folder. This sub-folder appears next to where pdfforms itself is, not where you run it from. It will fill the form with numbers in a sequential order. These are the **field numbers**.

The next thing you do is create a CSV file where the first column and row contains the name of the PDF. The other rows in the first column correspond to the field numbers. You enter the numbers of the fields that you want to fill here. Then you enter the data you want to fill use in the form in the third column of your CSV file. The second column is ignored, so you can put a description here. All columns after the third column are also ignored, so these can be used for whatever you want.

For this example, your CSV file might look something like this:

```
simple_form.pdf,,,
1,first name,Mike
2,last name,Driscoll
```

Once you have the CSV filled out, you can run the following command to actually fill your form out with your custom data:

```
pdfforms fill data.csv
```

The filled PDF will appear in a sub-folder called **filled** by default.

Now on to the bad news. I wasn't able to get this to work correctly on Windows or Mac. I got the **inspect** step to work on Windows, but on Mac it just hangs. On Windows, when I run the **fill** command it just fails with an error about not finding the PDF to fill.

I think when this package becomes less error-prone, it will be really amazing. The only major downside other than it having issues running is that you need to install a 3rd party tool that isn't written in Python at all.

Wrapping Up

After looking at the many different options available to the Python developer for filling PDF forms, I think the most straight-forward method is creating the overlay and then merging it to the fillable form PDF using a tool like pdfrw. While this feels a bit like a hack, the other methods that I have seen seem just as hacky and just as time consuming. Once you have the position of one of the cells in the form, you can reasonably calculate the majority of the others on the page.

Chapter 18 - Converting Markup to PDF

While ReportLab is great for laying out your PDFs programmatically in Python, sometimes you might want to write your documents using a type of markup. For example, you might have non-developers that need to be able to get their work turned into PDFs too. Now they could just use a print-to-PDF option. That actually works great in most applications. But what I am referring to are the people who know markup, like HTML, Markdown or restructuredText. There are a lot of tools out there to help you write well using a text editor and still get a nice PDF output.

We will look at just a handful of the ones that are currently available in this chapter.

rst2pdf

I personally really like restructuredText. This markup format used to be the format of choice for writing documentation in Python. I believe the current Python documentation is still written in restructuredText. This is also the format that the **Sphinx** documentation framework was originally based on. Sphinx is the documentation tool used for creating Python's documentation and the documentation used on the ReadTheDocs website. Of course, today Sphinx also supports Markdown and several other formats.

When I was first learning about how to write a book, I recalled that I had heard of a project called **rst2pdf** that a fellow named Roberto Alsina had created. It basically takes restructuredText as its input and then outputs a PDF using ReportLab underneath. It is an alternative to using LaTeX, which I won't be covering in detail in this chapter. You can read all about rst2pdf on its website here: http://rst2pdf.ralsina.me/stories/index.html or download the manual here: http://ralsina.me/static/manual.pdf

You can use **pip** to install rst2pdf:

```
python -m pip install rst2pdf
```

You will notice that when the install process is running, pip will also install and dependencies that rst2pdf requires. Now you need to write some markup. Here's a simple example:

```
Title
=====

Subtitle
--------
```

I am a paragraph. This word is **bold** and this one is *italicized*.

Let's save the markup in the example above to a file called **test.rst**. Now let's try converting this restructuredText file into a PDF. Open up a terminal and navigate to the location that you saved the file to. Then run the following command:

```
rst2pdf test.rst test.pdf
```

The first argument to rst2pdf is the path to the input file and the second argument is the path to the output file. The command should just return without any errors. Now if you open your **test.pdf** file, it should look something like this:

Title

Subtitle

I am a paragraph. This word is **bold** and this one is *italicized*.

Fig. 18-1: PDF Created from restructuredText

restructuredText supports pretty much any type of markup you can imagine. You can add a code block like this:

```
.. code-block:: python

    def doubler(x):
        return x * 2
```

This is an example of a **directive**. There are many other directives and you can even create custom ones. There are directives for inserting images, figures, tables, footnotes, sidebars and much much more! There are already several documents detailing what you can do with restructuredText and that is really outside the scope of this book. However, I highly recommend reading the documentation for restructuredText and then trying it out with rst2pdf.

If you look in the book's source code on Github, you will find that I have included a chapter (**intro.rst**) of this book in restructuredText format. You can use **rst2pdf** on this file too to see what kind of output it can generate with a more full-fledged example.

One final note on this topic is that when you installed rst2pdf it installed **docutils** as a dependency. Docutils includes tools for converting restructuredText to HTML, XML, LaTeX and more. So if you are looking for a versatile markup language, you might want to check restructuredText out.

WeasyPrint

WeasyPrint is a specialized beast. It is a "visual rendering engine for HTML and CSS that can export to PDF". It does not allow you to specify absolute positioning of elements on the page, but it does make pagination easy. You can read more about WeasyPrint on the ReadTheDocs website here: http://weasyprint.readthedocs.io

You can use **pip** to install WeasyPrint:

```
python -m pip install WeasyPrint
```

WeasyPrint had a minimum of 10 dependencies at the time of writing this book, so I definitely recommend installing this package into a virtual environment to test it out. You may also need to install non-Python dependencies, so be sure to read the installation instructions on the WeasyPrint website carefully. Once you have all of them installed, you can use WeasyPrint as an executable on the command line or by importing it into your Python code. We will look at both options. If you want to use the executable, you can do the following:

```
weasyprint http://weasyprint.readthedocs.io/en/stable/tutorial.html tutorial.pdf
```

This does a pretty good job of downloading the web page and turning it into a PDF. Here is a screenshot of how part of the first page turned out:

WeasyPrint
stable

- Installing
- Tutorial
  - As a standalone program
  - As a Python library
    - Quickstart
    - Instantiating HTML and CSS objects
    - Rendering to a single file
    - Individual pages, meta-data, other output formats, …
    - URL fetchers
    - Logging
  - WeasyPrint Navigator

Fig. 18-2: WeasyPrint PDF Example

Interestingly, when I tried to have WeasyPrint turn one of Python's documentation pages into a PDF, it didn't turn out quite right:

```
weasyprint https://docs.python.org/3/library/collections.html collections.pdf
```

In this case, it looks like we ended up with a PDF that has a bunch of the website's contents truncated off the bottom. Somehow WeasyPrint managed to create bookmarks for parts of the web page that it didn't actually render in the PDF. Regardless, it still made the pages look nice, even if it wasn't able to get all of the information.

Now let's take a moment and find out how you might use WeasyPrint in Python itself:

```
from weasyprint import HTML

html = HTML('https://www.blog.pythonlibrary.org/')
html.write_pdf('/tmp/test.pdf')
```

This code is the equivalent of calling the weasyprint executable we were using in the previous examples. Here we just use the **weasyprint** module's **HTML** class to basically turn a web page into an object that can then be turned into a PDF or PNG. In this case, we call the **write_pdf** method to create a PDF. One thing I noticed while using WeasyPrint is that it doesn't work very well with web pages that have a lot of dynamically loaded content.

Anyway, one cool extra that WeasyPrint provides is the ability to use custom CSS to style the HTML your download or create before turning it into a PDF. You just have to import the **CSS** class from the **weasyprint** module. You can give this class an inline stylesheet by passing it a string or you can pass it a file path. WeasyPrint also supports **font-face** rules in your CSS, although you will have to use its **FontConfiguration** class to make that work.

I personally think this is a pretty slick package for web developers or people who are just familiar with HTML / CSS.

Pandoc

Pandoc is well known as a "universal document converter". You can use it to convert documents created in many types of markup to HTML, Microsoft Word, epub, TeX formats, PDF and much more. I actually use Pandoc when I am writing my books to convert from restructuredText to Markdown. I have also used Pandoc for converting restructuredText to PDF and other formats. It is free software that is licensed under GPL. You can read all about it on Pandoc's website here: https://pandoc.org/

Pandoc defaults to converting Markdown to HTML, but it's trivial to make it do whatever conversion you want it to do.

Installing Pandoc is pretty easy as it is well supported on Windows, Mac and Linux. You can download the Windows installer from Pandoc's Github page, which also has a *.deb file, a Mac installer file and source tarballs. You can also install Pandoc using Mac'sbrew** package manager or the package manager of your choice on your Linux box.

Let's see how we might convert restructuredText to Markdown with Pandoc:

```
pandoc intro.rst -f rst -t markdown -o test.md
```

Here we pass pandoc a file path to a document that is in restructuredText format. The **-f** argument stands for "from" and is for telling Pandoc explicitly what the format of the input document is. The **-t** argument stands for "to" and tells Pandoc what to convert the document into. In this case, we specify that we want to convert to Markdown. The **-o** argument stands for "output" and tells Pandoc where to save the output. If you would like a more complex example of restructuredText, try downloading some of Python's documentation pages from Github. They are very interesting and will be good candidates for conversion to Markdown as well.

If you want to convert straight to PDF, then you need to tell Pandoc to use its LaTeX converter:

```
pandoc test.rst -f rst -t latex -o test-pandoc.pdf
```

When you run that, you should get a nicely formatted PDF. You will note that LaTeX converted the restructuredText a bit differently than rst2pdf did.

LaTeX

LaTeX (usually pronounced la-tec) is a typesetting system. A lot of scientific and technical writers use LaTeX to produce documentation. It is used especially by scientists for scientific documents. It is also free under the LPPL license. I personally know some authors who use LaTeX for writing their books. Some use it for every part of their book and others use it just for specific parts of their books. LaTeX has it's own special kind of markup that you will have to learn. Its markup is nothing like restructuredText, HTML or Markdown, so knowing those will not be of much help. I personally have never used LaTeX and do not plan to.

I only mention LaTeX because you will see it mentioned in a lot of other programs as an intermediary program. For example, in the previous section, Pandoc uses LaTeX to generate PDFs. You will find that a lot of conversion utility use LaTeX or a variant of it under the hood to do certain types of conversions.

Learning how to use LaTeX is way outside the scope of this book. There is a lot of documentation for this program on their website and a lot of good books on the subject that you can get too.

Wrapping Up

While this chapter was shorter than some of the previous ones, its intent was to help you learn about the many different tools you can use to convert markup to PDFs and other formats. My favorite is probably **rst2pdf** because I really enjoy using restructuredText. There are lots of other products for converting other types of markup to PDFs too. We looked at **WeasyPrint** for converting HTML / CSS documentation into PDFs. You could also use **docutils html2pdf** utility for the same purpose. If you like the Markdown format, then you can use **Pandoc** and many other utilities to convert that format to PDF. Finally we mentioned LaTeX in passing. This is a really powerful program for typesetting that you hopefully will never need to learn. But if you do, you can rest assured that it can make beautiful looking documentation and PDFs should you ever need to use it.

Chapter 19 - The PyFPDF Package

ReportLab is the primary toolkit that you can use for generating PDFs from scratch. However I have found that there is another one called **PyFPDF** or **FPDF for Python**. The **PyFPDF** package is actually a port of the "Free"-PDF package that was written in PHP. There hasn't been a release of this project in a few years, but there have been commits to its Github repository so there is still some work being done on the project. The PyFPDF package supports Python 2.7 and Python 3.4+.

This chapter will not be exhaustive in its coverage of the PyFPDF package. However it will cover more than enough for you to get started using it effectively. Note that there is a short book on PyFPDF called "Python does PDF: pyFPDF" by Edwood Ocasio on Leanpub if you would like to learn more about the library than what is covered in this chapter or the package's documentation.

Installation

Installing PyFPDF is easy since it was designed to work with pip. You can install this package just like you have all the others in this book:

```
python -m pip install fpdf
```

At the time of writing, this command installed version 1.7.2 on Python 3.6 with no problems whatsoever. You will notice when you are installing this package that it has no dependencies, which is nice.

Basic Usage

Now that you have PyFPDF installed, let's try using it to create a simple PDF. Open up your Python editor and create a new file called **simple_demo.py**. Then enter the following code into it:

Chapter 19 - The PyFPDF Package

```
# simple_demo.py

from fpdf import FPDF

pdf = FPDF()
pdf.add_page()
pdf.set_font("Arial", size=12)
pdf.cell(200, 10, txt="Welcome to Python!", ln=1, align="C")
pdf.output("simple_demo.pdf")
```

The first item that we need to talk about is the import. Here we import the **FPDF** class from the **fpdf** package. The defaults for this class are to create the PDF in Portrait mode, use millimeters for its measurement unit and to use the A4 page size. If you wanted to be explicit, you could write the instantiation line like this:

```
pdf = FPDF(orientation='P', unit='mm', format='A4')
```

I am not a fan of using the letter 'P' to tell the class what its orientation is. You may also use 'L' if you prefer landscape over portrait.

The PyFPDF package supports 'pt', 'cm' and 'in' as alternative measurement units.

If you go diving into the source, you will find that the PyFPDF package only supports the following page sizes:

- A3
- A4
- A5
- letter
- legal

This is a bit limiting compared to ReportLab where you have several additional sizes supported out of the box and you can set the page size to something custom as well.

Anyway, the next step is to create a page using the **add_page** method. Then we set the page's font via the **set_font** method. You will note that we pass in the font's family name and the size that we want. You can also set the font's style with the **style** argument. If you want to do this, note that it takes a string such as 'B' for bold or 'BI' for **Bold-Italicized**.

Next we create a **cell** that is 200 millimeters wide and 10 millimeters high. A cell is basically a flowable that holds text and can have a border enabled. It will split automatically if automatic page break is enabled and the cell goes beyond the page's size limit. The **txt** parameter is the text that you want to print in the PDF. The **ln** parameter tells PyFPDF to add a line break if set to one, which is what we do here. Finally we can set the alignment of the text to either be aligned (the default) or centered ('C'). We chose the latter here.

Finally we save the document to disk by calling the **output** method with the path to the file that we want to save.

When I ran this code, I ended up with a PDF that looked like this:

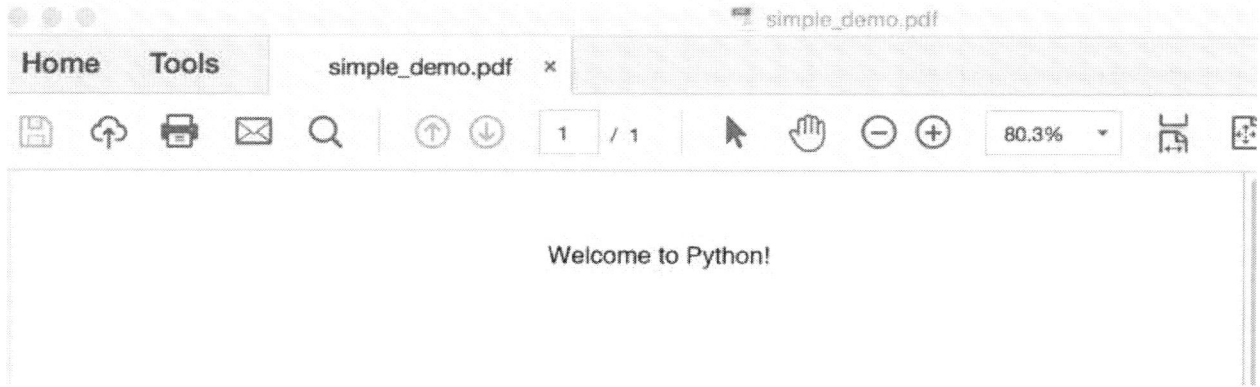

Fig. 19-1: PyFPDF Demo Example

Now let's learn a little bit about how PyFPDF works with fonts.

Working with Fonts

The PyFPDF has a set of core fonts hard-coded into its FPDF class:

```
self.core_fonts={'courier': 'Courier',
    'courierB': 'Courier-Bold',
    'courierBI': 'Courier-BoldOblique',
    'courierI': 'Courier-Oblique',
    'helvetica': 'Helvetica',
    'helveticaB': 'Helvetica-Bold',
    'helveticaBI': 'Helvetica-BoldOblique',
    'helveticaI': 'Helvetica-Oblique',
    'symbol': 'Symbol',
    'times': 'Times-Roman',
    'timesB': 'Times-Bold',
    'timesBI': 'Times-BoldItalic',
    'timesI': 'Times-Italic',
    'zapfdingbats': 'ZapfDingbats'}
```

You will note that Arial is not listed here even though we used it in the previous example. Arial is getting remapped to Helvetica in the actual source code, so you are not really using Arial at all. Anyway, let's learn how you can change fonts using PyFPDF:

```python
# change_fonts.py

from fpdf import FPDF

def change_fonts():
    pdf = FPDF()
    pdf.add_page()
    font_size = 8
    for font in pdf.core_fonts:
        if any([letter for letter in font if letter.isupper()]):
            # skip this font
            continue
        pdf.set_font(font, size=font_size)
        txt = "Font name: {} - {} pts".format(font, font_size)
        pdf.cell(0, 10, txt=txt, ln=1, align="C")
        font_size += 2

    pdf.output("change_fonts.pdf")

if __name__ == '__main__':
    change_fonts()
```

Here we create a simple function called **change_fonts** and then we create an instance of the FPDF class. The next step is to create a page and then loop over the core fonts. When I tried that, I discovered that PyFPDF doesn't consider the variant names of its core fonts as valid fonts (i.e. helveticaB, helveticaBI, etc). So to skip those variants, we create a list comprehension and check for any capital characters in the font's name. If there is one, we skip that font. Otherwise we set the font and the font size and write it out. We also increase the font size by two points each time through the loop. If you want to change the font's color, then you can call **set_text_color** and pass in the RGB value that you require.

The result of running this code looks like this:

Chapter 19 - The PyFPDF Package

Fig. 19-2: **PyFPDF Changing Fonts**

I like how easy it is to change fonts in PyFPDF. However the number of core fonts is pretty small. You can add TrueType, OpenType or Type1 fonts using PyFPDF though via the **add_font** method. This method takes the following arguments:

- family (font family)
- style (font style)
- fname (font file name or full path to font file)
- uni (TTF Unicode flag)

The example that PyFPDF's documentation uses is as follows:

```
pdf.add_font('DejaVu', '', 'DejaVuSansCondensed.ttf', uni=True)
```

You would call **add_font** before attempting to use it via the **set_font** method. I tried this on Windows and got an error as Windows couldn't find this font, which is what I expected. This is a really simply way to add fonts though and will probably work. Note that it uses the following search paths:

- FPDF_FONTPATH
- SYSTEM_TTFONTS

These appear to be constants that are defined either in your environment or in the PyFPDF package itself. The documentation does not explain how these are set or modified however, if you look closely at the API and the source code, it would appear that you would have to do the following at the beginning of your code:

```
import fpdf

fpdf.SYSTEM_TTFONTS = '/path/to/system/fonts'
```

The **SYSTEM_TTFONTS** is set to **None** by default otherwise.

Drawing

The PyFPDF package has limited drawing support. You can draw lines, ellipses and rectangles. Let's take a look at how to draw lines first:

```
# draw_lines.py

from fpdf import FPDF

def draw_lines():
    pdf = FPDF()
    pdf.add_page()
    pdf.line(10, 10, 10, 100)
    pdf.set_line_width(1)
    pdf.set_draw_color(255, 0, 0)
    pdf.line(20, 20, 100, 20)
    pdf.output('draw_lines.pdf')

if __name__ == '__main__':
    draw_lines()
```

Here we call the **line** method and pass it two pairs of x/y coordinates. The line width defaults to 0.2 mm so we increase it to 1 mm for the second line by calling the **set_line_width** method. We also set the color of the second line by calling **set_draw_color** to an RGB value equivalent to red. The output looks like this:

Chapter 19 - The PyFPDF Package

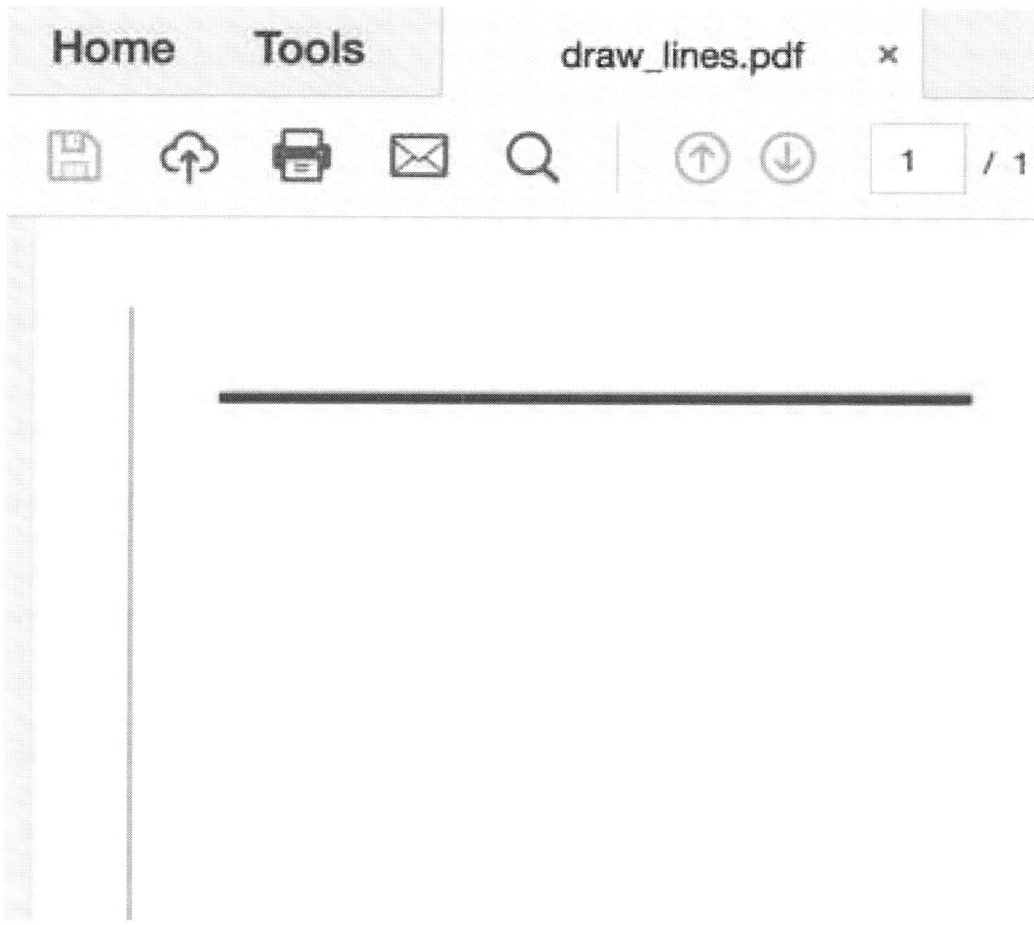

Fig. 19-3: PyFPDF - Drawing Lines

Now we can move on and draw a couple of shapes:

```python
# draw_shapes.py

from fpdf import FPDF

def draw_shapes():
    pdf = FPDF()
    pdf.add_page()
    pdf.set_fill_color(255, 0, 0)
    pdf.ellipse(10, 10, 10, 100, 'F')

    pdf.set_line_width(1)
    pdf.set_fill_color(0, 255, 0)
    pdf.rect(20, 20, 100, 50)
    pdf.output('draw_shapes.pdf')
```

```
if __name__ == '__main__':
    draw_shapes()
```

When you draw a shape like an **ellipse** or a **rect**, you will need to pass in the x and y coordinates that represent the upper left corner of the drawing. Then you will want to pass in the width and height of the shape. The last argument you can pass in is for **style** which can be "D" or an empty string (default), "F" for fill or "DF" for draw and fill. In this example, we fill the ellipse and use the default for the rectangle. The result ends up looking like this:

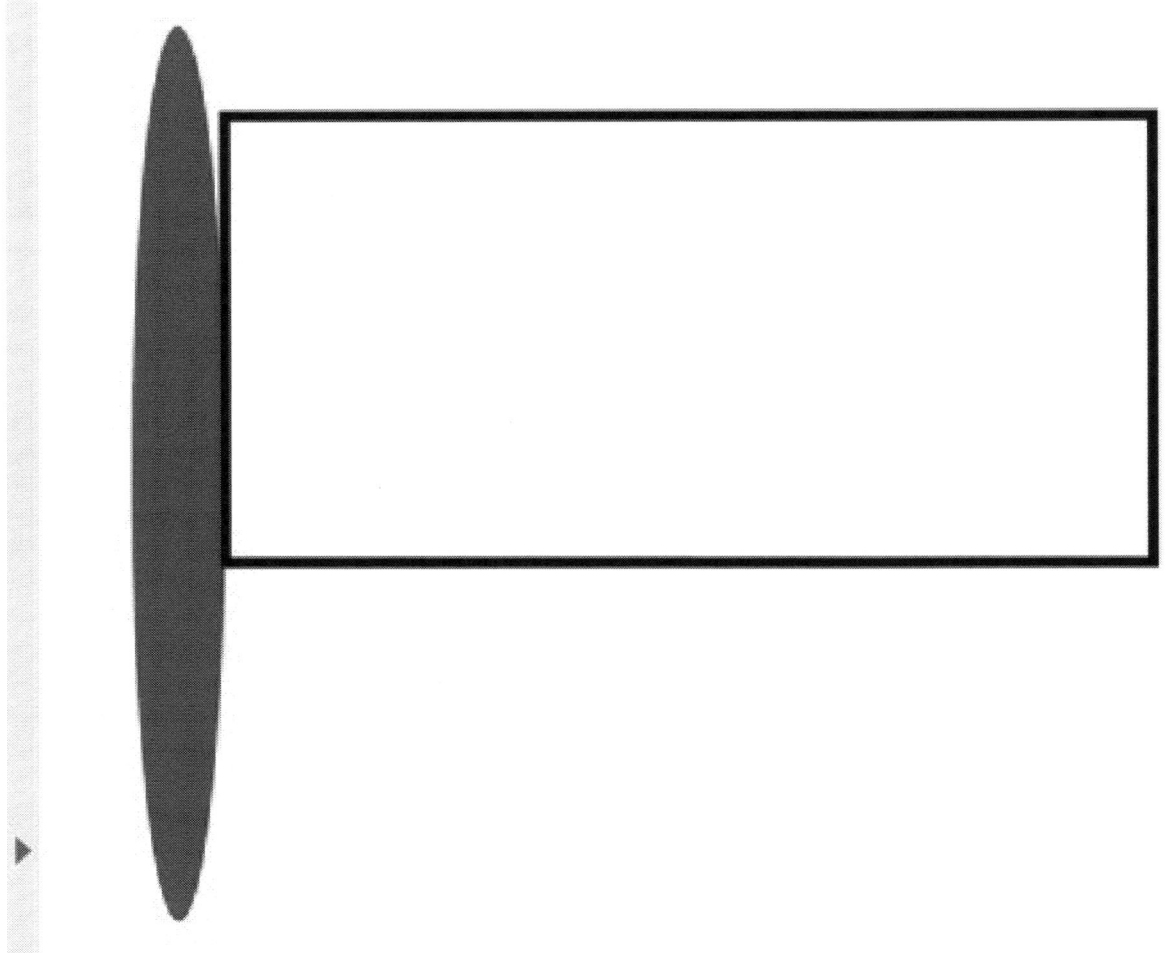

Fig. 19-4: PyFPDF - Drawing Shapes

Now let's learn about image support.

Adding Images

The PyFPDF package supports adding JPEG, PNG and GIF formats to your PDF. If you happen to try to use an animated GIF, only the first frame is used. Also of note is that if you add the same image multiple times to the document, PyFPDF is smart enough to only embed one actual copy of the image. Here is a very simple example of adding an image to a PDF using PyFPDF:

```
# add_image.py

from fpdf import FPDF

def add_image(image_path):
    pdf = FPDF()
    pdf.add_page()
    pdf.image(image_path, x=10, y=8, w=100)
    pdf.set_font("Arial", size=12)
    pdf.ln(85)  # move 85 down
    pdf.cell(200, 10, txt="{}".format(image_path), ln=1)
    pdf.output("add_image.pdf")

if __name__ == '__main__':
    add_image('snakehead.jpg')
```

The new piece of code here is the call to the **image** method. Its signature looks like the this:

```
image(name, x = None, y = None, w = 0, h = 0, type = '', link = '')
```

You specify the image file path, the x and y coordinate and the width and height. If you only specify the width or the height, the other is calculated for you and attempts to maintain the original proportions of the image. You can also specify the file type explicitly, otherwise it is guessed from the file name. Finally you can add a link / URL when adding the image.

When you run this code, you should see something like the following:

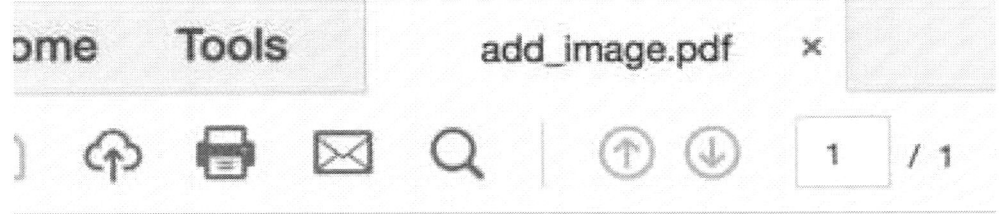

Fig. 19-5: PyFPDF - Adding an Image

Now let's learn how PyFPDF supports doing multipage documents.

Multipage Documents

PyFPDF had multipage support enabled by default. If you add enough cells to a page, it will automatically create a new page and continue to add your new text to the next page. Here is a simple example:

Chapter 19 - The PyFPDF Package

```python
# multipage_simple.py

from fpdf import FPDF

def multipage_simple():
    pdf = FPDF()
    pdf.set_font("Arial", size=12)
    pdf.add_page()
    line_no = 1
    for i in range(100):
        pdf.cell(0, 10, txt="Line #{}".format(line_no), ln=1)
        line_no += 1
    pdf.output("multipage_simple.pdf")

if __name__ == '__main__':
    multipage_simple()
```

All this does is create 100 lines of text. When I ran this code, I ended up with a PDF that contained 4 pages of text.

Headers and Footers

The PyFPDF package has built-in support for adding headers, footers and page numbers. The **FPDF** class just needs to be sub-classed and the the **header** and **footer** methods overridden to make them work. Let's take a look:

```python
# header_footer.py

from fpdf import FPDF

class CustomPDF(FPDF):

    def header(self):
        # Set up a logo
        self.image('snakehead.jpg', 10, 8, 33)
        self.set_font('Arial', 'B', 15)

        # Add an address
        self.cell(100)
        self.cell(0, 5, 'Mike Driscoll', ln=1)
        self.cell(100)
```

```python
            self.cell(0, 5, '123 American Way', ln=1)
            self.cell(100)
            self.cell(0, 5, 'Any Town, USA', ln=1)

            # Line break
            self.ln(20)

    def footer(self):
        self.set_y(-10)

        self.set_font('Arial', 'I', 8)

        # Add a page number
        page = 'Page ' + str(self.page_no()) + '/{nb}'
        self.cell(0, 10, page, 0, 0, 'C')

def create_pdf(pdf_path):
    pdf = CustomPDF()
    # Create the special value {nb}
    pdf.alias_nb_pages()
    pdf.add_page()
    pdf.set_font('Times', '', 12)
    line_no = 1
    for i in range(50):
        pdf.cell(0, 10, txt="Line #{}".format(line_no), ln=1)
        line_no += 1
    pdf.output(pdf_path)

if __name__ == '__main__':
    create_pdf('header_footer.pdf')
```

Since this is a fairly long piece of code, let's go over this piece-by-piece. The first section that we want to look at is the **header** method:

Chapter 19 - The PyFPDF Package

```
def header(self):
    # Set up a logo
    self.image('snakehead.jpg', 10, 8, 33)
    self.set_font('Arial', 'B', 15)

    # Add an address
    self.cell(100)
    self.cell(0, 5, 'Mike Driscoll', ln=1)
    self.cell(100)
    self.cell(0, 5, '123 American Way', ln=1)
    self.cell(100)
    self.cell(0, 5, 'Any Town, USA', ln=1)

    # Line break
    self.ln(20)
```

Here we just hard-code in the logo image that we want to use and then we set the font that we will be using in our header. Next we add an address and we position that address to the right of the image. You will notice that when you are using PyFPDF, the origin is the top left of the page. So if we want to move our text over to the right, then we need to create a cell with a number of units of measurement. In this case, we move the next three lines over to the right by adding a cell of 100 mm. Then we add a line break at the end, which should add 20 mm of vertical space.

Next up, we want to override the **footer** method:

```
def footer(self):
    self.set_y(-10)

    self.set_font('Arial', 'I', 8)

    # Add a page number
    page = 'Page ' + str(self.page_no()) + '/{nb}'
    self.cell(0, 10, page, 0, 0, 'C')
```

The first thing we do here is set the y-position of the origin on the page to -10 mm or -1 cm. This puts the footer's origin right above the bottom of the page. Then we set our font for the footer. Finally we create the page number text. You will note the reference to **{nb}**. This is a special value in PyFPDF that is inserted when you call **alias_nb_pages** and represents the total number of pages in the document. The last step in the footer is to write the page text on the page and center it.

The final piece of code to look at is in the **create_pdf** function:

```
def create_pdf(pdf_path):
    pdf = CustomPDF()
    # Create the special value {nb}
    pdf.alias_nb_pages()
    pdf.add_page()
    pdf.set_font('Times', '', 12)
    line_no = 1
    for i in range(50):
        pdf.cell(0, 10, txt="Line #{}".format(line_no), ln=1)
        line_no += 1
    pdf.output(pdf_path)
```

This is where we call the somewhat magical **alias_nb_pages** method that will help us get the total number of pages. We also set the font for the portion of the page that is not taken up by the header or footer. Then we write 50 lines of text to the document to make it create a multipage PDF.

When you run this code you should see a page that looks something like this:

Fig. 19-6: PyFPDF - Adding a Header / Footer

Now let's find out how you can create tables with PyFPDF.

Tables

The PyFPDF does not have a table control. Instead you have to build your tables using cells or HTML. Let's take a look at how you might create a table using cells first:

```python
# simple_table.py

from fpdf import FPDF

def simple_table(spacing=1):
    data = [['First Name', 'Last Name', 'email', 'zip'],
            ['Mike', 'Driscoll', 'mike@somewhere.com', '55555'],
            ['John', 'Doe', 'jdoe@doe.com', '12345'],
            ['Nina', 'Ma', 'inane@where.com', '54321']
            ]

    pdf = FPDF()
    pdf.set_font("Arial", size=12)
    pdf.add_page()

    col_width = pdf.w / 4.5
    row_height = pdf.font_size
    for row in data:
        for item in row:
            pdf.cell(col_width, row_height*spacing,
                    txt=item, border=1)
        pdf.ln(row_height*spacing)

    pdf.output('simple_table.pdf')

if __name__ == '__main__':
    simple_table()
```

Here we just create a simple list of lists and then loop over it. For each row in the list and each element in the nested row, we add a cell to our PDF object. Note that we turn the border on for these cells. When we finish iterating over a row, we add a linebreak. If you want the cells to have more space in the cells, then you can pass in a spacing value. When I ran this script, I ended up with a table that looked like this:

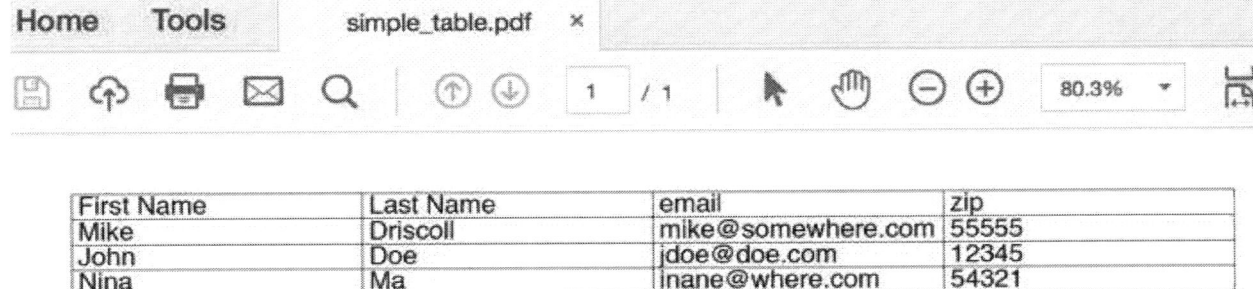

Fig. 19-7: PyFPDF - Adding a Simple Table

This is a pretty crude way to create tables though. I personally prefer ReportLab's methodology here. The alternative method is to use HTML to create your table:

```python
# simple_table_html.py

from fpdf import FPDF, HTMLMixin

class HTML2PDF(FPDF, HTMLMixin):
    pass

def simple_table_html():
    pdf = HTML2PDF()

    table = """<table border="0" align="center" width="50%">
    <thead><tr><th width="30%">Header 1</th><th width="70%">header 2</th></tr></\
thead>
    <tbody>
    <tr><td>cell 1</td><td>cell 2</td></tr>
    <tr><td>cell 2</td><td>cell 3</td></tr>
    </tbody>
    </table>"""

    pdf.add_page()
    pdf.write_html(table)
    pdf.output('simple_table_html.pdf')

if __name__ == '__main__':
    simple_table_html()
```

Here we use PyFPDF's **HTMLMixin** class to allow it to accept HTML as an input and transform that into a PDF. When you run this example, you will end up with the following:

Header 1	header 2
cell 1	cell 2
cell 2	cell 3

Fig. 19-8: PyFPDF - Adding a Simple Table using HTML

There are some examples on the website that use the Web2Py framework in conjunction with PyFPDF to create better looking tables, but the code was incomplete so I won't be demonstrating that here.

Transform HTML to PDF

The PyFDPF package has some limited support for HTML tags. You can create headings, paragraphs and basic text styling using HTML. You can also add hyperlinks, images, lists and tables. Check the documentation for the full list of tags and attributes that are supported. You can then take basic HTML and turn it into a PDF using the **HTMLMixin** that we saw in the previous section when we created our table.

```
# html2fpdf.py

from fpdf import FPDF, HTMLMixin

class HTML2PDF(FPDF, HTMLMixin):
    pass

def html2pdf():
    html = '''<h1 align="center">PyFPDF HTML Demo</h1>
    <p>This is regular text</p>
    <p>You can also <b>bold</b>, <i>italicize</i> or <u>underline</u>
    '''
    pdf = HTML2PDF()
    pdf.add_page()
    pdf.write_html(html)
    pdf.output('html2pdf.pdf')

if __name__ == '__main__':
    html2pdf()
```

Here we just use pretty standard HTML markup to design the PDF. It actually ends up looking pretty good when you run this code:

Fig. 19-9: PyFPDF - Creating a PDF with HTML

Web2Py

The Web2Py framework includes PyFPDF package to make creating reports in the framework easier. This allows you to create PDF templates in Web2Py. The documentation is a bit scarce on this subject, so I won't be covering this subject in this book. However it does appear that you can do halfway decent reports using Web2Py this way.

Templates

You can also create templates using PyFPDF. The package even includes a designer script that uses wxPython for its user interface. The templates that you can create would be where you want to specify where each element appears on the page, its style (font, size, etc) and the default text to use. The templating system supports using CSV files or databases. There is only one example in the documentation on this subject though, which is a bit disappointing. While I do think this part of the library holds promise, due to the lack of documentation, I don't feel comfortable writing about it extensively.

Wrapping Up

The PyFPDF package is a fairly nice project that let's you do basic PDF generation. They do point out in the FAQ that they do not support charts or widgets or a "flexible page layout system" like

ReportLab. They also do not support PDF text extraction or conversion like PDFMiner or PyPDF2. However if all you need are the bare bone basics to generate a PDF, then this library might work for you. I think its learning curve is simpler than ReportLab's is. However PyFPDF is nowhere near as feature-rich as ReportLab and I didn't feel like you had quite the same granularity of control when it came to placing elements on the page.

Appendix A - Adding SVG Files in ReportLab

ReportLab has native support for generating SVGs, but not for embedding SVGs in their PDFs. Fortunately, Dinu Gherman created the **svglib** package, a pure-Python package that can read SVG files and convert them to other formats that ReportLab can use. The svglib can be found on the Python Packaging Index here: https://pypi.python.org/pypi/svglib/ The official website for svglib is on Github here: https://github.com/deeplook/svglib

The svglib package will work on Linux, Mac OS and Windows. The website states that it works with Python 2.7 - 3.5, but it should work in newer versions of Python as well.

You can use svglib to read your existing SVG giles and convert them into ReportLab **Drawing** objects. The svglib package also has a command-line tool, **svg2pdf**, that can convert SVG files to PDFs.

Dependencies

The svglib package depends on **ReportLab** and **lxml**. You can install both of these packages using pip:

```
python -m pip install reportlab lxml
```

Installation

The svglib package can be installed using one of three methods.

Install the latest release

If you'd like to install the latest release from the Python Packaging Index, then you can just use pip the normal way:

```
python -m pip install svglib
```

Install from latest version from source control

On the off chance that you want to use the latest version of the code (i.e. the bleeding edge / alpha builds), then you can install directly from Github using pip like this:

```
python -m pip install git+https://github.com/deeplook/svglib
```

Manual installation

Most of the time, using pip is the way to go. But you can also download the tarball from the Python Packaging Index and do all the steps that pip does for you automatically if you want to. Just run the following three commands in your terminal in order:

```
tar xfz svglib-0.8.1.tar.gz
cd svglib-0.8.1
python setup.py install
```

Now that we have svglib installed, let's learn how to use it!

Usage

Using svglib with ReportLab is actually quite easy. All you need to do is import **svg2rlg** from **svglib.svglib** and give it the path to your SVG file. Let's take a look:

```python
# svg_demo.py

from reportlab.graphics import renderPDF, renderPM
from svglib.svglib import svg2rlg


def svg_demo(image_path, output_path):
    drawing = svg2rlg(image_path)
    renderPDF.drawToFile(drawing, output_path)
    renderPM.drawToFile(drawing, 'svg_demo.png', 'PNG')


if __name__ == '__main__':
    svg_demo('snakehead.svg', 'svg_demo.pdf')
```

After giving **svg2rlg** your path to the SVG file, it will return a drawing object. Then you can use this object to write it out as a PDF or a PNG. You could go on to use this script to create your own personal SVG to PNG converting utility!

Drawing on the Canvas

Personally, I don't like to create one-off PDFs with just an image in them like in the previous example. Instead, I want to be able to insert the image and write out text and other things. Fortunately, you can do this very easily by painting your canvas with the drawing object. Here's an example:

```
# svg_on_canvas.py

from reportlab.graphics import renderPDF
from reportlab.pdfgen import canvas
from svglib.svglib import svg2rlg

def add_image(image_path):
    my_canvas = canvas.Canvas('svg_on_canvas.pdf')
    drawing = svg2rlg(image_path)
    renderPDF.draw(drawing, my_canvas, 0, 40)
    my_canvas.drawString(50, 30, 'My SVG Image')
    my_canvas.save()

if __name__ == '__main__':
    image_path = 'snakehead.svg'
    add_image(image_path)
```

Here we create a **canvas.Canvas** object and then create our SVG drawing object. Now you can use **renderPDF.draw** to draw your drawing on your canvas at a specific x/y coordinate. We go ahead and draw out some small text underneath our image and then save it off. The result should look something like this:

Appendix A - Adding SVG Files in ReportLab

Fig. Appendix A-1: SVG on Canvas

Adding an SVG to a Flowable

Drawings in ReportLab can usually be added as a list of Flowables and built with a document template. The svglib's website says that its drawing objects are compatible with ReportLab's Flowable system. Let's use a different SVG for this example. We will be using the Flag of Cuba from Wikipedia. The svglib tests download a bunch of flag SVGs in their tests, so we will try one of the images that they use. You can get it here:

https://upload.wikimedia.org/wikipedia/commons/b/bd/Flag_of_Cuba.svg

I have also copied the image into the book's Github repository as well.

Once you have the image saved off, we can take a look at the code:

Appendix A - Adding SVG Files in ReportLab

```
# svg_demo2.py

from reportlab.platypus import SimpleDocTemplate
from svglib.svglib import svg2rlg


def svg_demo(image_path, output_path):
    drawing = svg2rlg(image_path)

    doc = SimpleDocTemplate(output_path)

    story = []
    story.append(drawing)

    doc.build(story)

if __name__ == '__main__':
    svg_demo('Flag_of_Cuba.svg', 'svg_demo2.pdf')
```

This worked pretty well, although the flag is cut off on the right side. Here's the output:

Fig. Appendix A-2: A Flag of Cuba SVG Example

I actually had some trouble with this example. ReportLab or svglib seems to be really picky about the way the SVG is formatted or its size. Depending on the SVG I used, I would end up with an **AttributeError** or a blank document or I would be successful. So your mileage will probably vary. I will say that I spoke with some of the core developers and they mentioned that **SimpleDocTemplate** doesn't give you enough control over the frame that the drawing goes into, so you may need to create your own **Frame** or **PageTemplate** to make the SVG show up correctly. A workaround to get the **snakehead.svg** to work was to set the left and right margins to zero:

```
# svg_demo3.py

from reportlab.platypus import SimpleDocTemplate
from svglib.svglib import svg2rlg


def svg_demo(image_path, output_path):
    drawing = svg2rlg(image_path)

    doc = SimpleDocTemplate(output_path,
                            rightMargin=0,
                            leftMargin=0)

    story = []
    story.append(drawing)

    doc.build(story)

if __name__ == '__main__':
    svg_demo('snakehead.svg', 'svg_demo3.pdf')
```

Scaling SVGs in ReportLab

The SVG drawings you create with svglib are not scaled by default. So you will need to write a function to do that for you. Let's take a look:

Appendix A - Adding SVG Files in ReportLab

```python
# svg_scaled_on_canvas.py

from reportlab.graphics import renderPDF
from reportlab.pdfgen import canvas
from svglib.svglib import svg2rlg


def scale(drawing, scaling_factor):
    """
    Scale a reportlab.graphics.shapes.Drawing()
    object while maintaining the aspect ratio
    """
    scaling_x = scaling_factor
    scaling_y = scaling_factor

    drawing.width = drawing.minWidth() * scaling_x
    drawing.height = drawing.height * scaling_y
    drawing.scale(scaling_x, scaling_y)
    return drawing


def add_image(image_path, scaling_factor):
    my_canvas = canvas.Canvas('svg_scaled_on_canvas.pdf')
    drawing = svg2rlg(image_path)
    scaled_drawing = scale(drawing, scaling_factor=scaling_factor)
    renderPDF.draw(scaled_drawing, my_canvas, 0, 40)
    my_canvas.drawString(50, 30, 'My SVG Image')
    my_canvas.save()

if __name__ == '__main__':
    image_path = 'snakehead.svg'
    add_image(image_path, scaling_factor=0.5)
```

Here we have two functions. The first function will scale our image using a scaling factor. In this case, we use 0.5 as our scaling factor. Then we do some math against our drawing object and tell it to scale itself. Finally we draw it back out in much the same way as we did in the previous example.

Here is the result:

Fig. Appendix A-3: SVG Scaled on Canvas

Using SVG Plots from matplotlib in ReportLab

Back in chapter 8, we learned how to create graphs using just the ReportLab toolkit. One of the most popular 2D graphing packages for Python is **matplotlib** though. You can read all about matplotlib here: https://matplotlib.org/. The reason I am mentioning matplotlib in this appendix is that it supports SVG as one of its output formats. So we will look at how to take a plot created with matplotlib and insert it into ReportLab.

To install matplotlib, the most popular method is to use pip:

```
pip install matplotlib
```

Now that we have matplotlib installed, we can create a simple plot and export it as SVG. Let's see how this works:

```python
import matplotlib.pyplot as pyplot

def create_matplotlib_svg(plot_path):
    pyplot.plot(list(range(5)))
    pyplot.title = 'matplotlib SVG + ReportLab'
    pyplot.ylabel = 'Increasing numbers'
    pyplot.savefig(plot_path, format='svg')

if __name__ == '__main__':
    from svg_demo import svg_demo
    svg_path = 'matplot.svg'
    create_matplotlib_svg(svg_path)
    svg_demo(svg_path, 'matplot.pdf')
```

In this code, we import the **pyplot** sub-library from matplotlib. Next we create a simple function that takes the path to where we want to save our plot. For this simple plot, we create a simple range of five numbers for one of the axes. hen we add a title and a y-label. Finally we save the plot to disk as an SVG.

The last step is in the **if** statement at the bottom of the code. Here we import our **svg_demo** code from earlier in this appendix. We create oru SVG image and then we run it through our demo code to turn it into a PDF.

The result looks like this:

Appendix A - Adding SVG Files in ReportLab

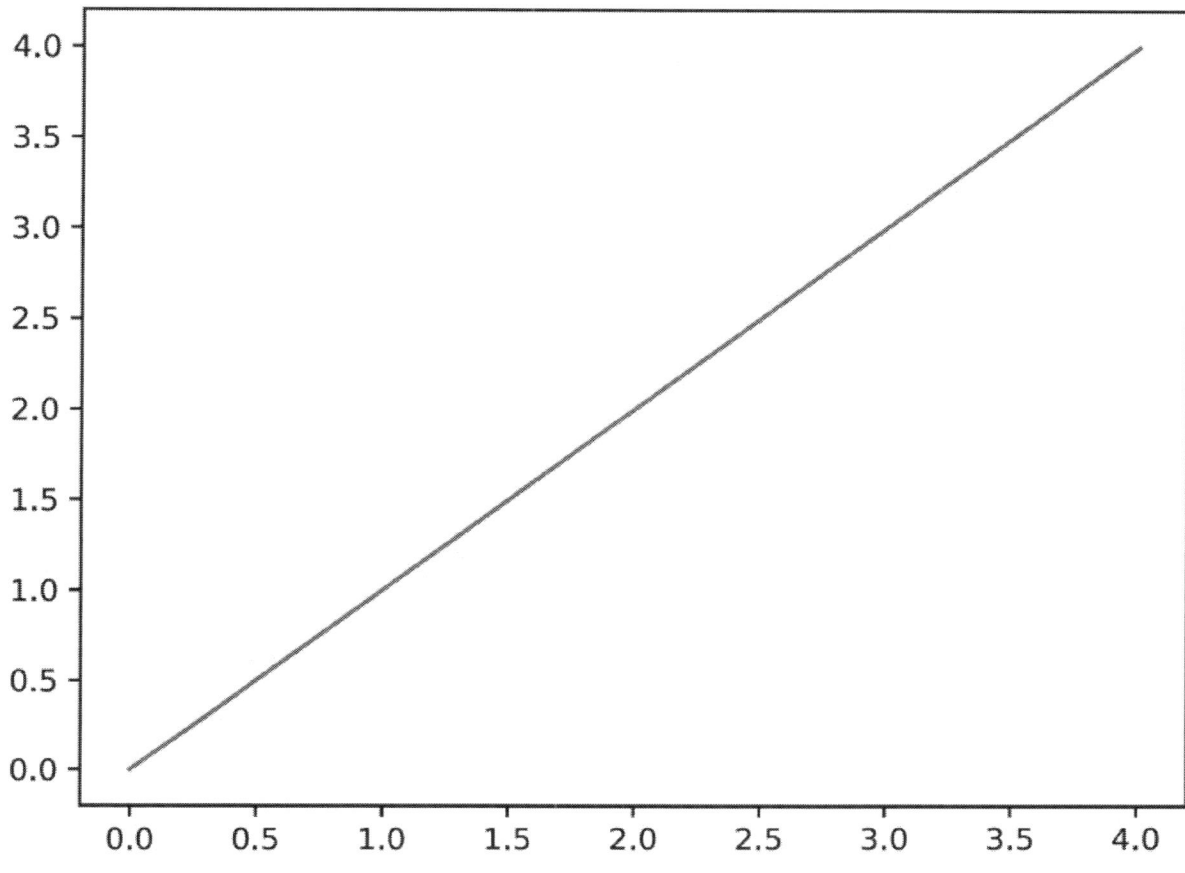

Fig. Appendix A-4: Matplotlib SVG in ReportLab

Using svg2pdf

When you install svglib, you also get a command-line tool called **svg2pdf**. As the name implies, you can use this tool to convert SVG files to PDF files. Let's look at a couple of examples:

```
svg2pdf /path/to/plot.svg
```

This command just takes the path to the SVG file that you want to turn into a PDF. It will automatically rename the output to the same name as the input file, but with the PDF extension. You can specify the output name though:

```
svg2pdf -o /path/to/output.pdf /path/to/plot.svg
```

The **-o** flag tells svg2pdf requires that you pass in the output PDF path followed by the input SVG path.

The documentation also mentions that you can convert all the SVG files to PDFs using a command like the following:

```
svg2pdf -o "%(base)s.pdf" path/to/file*.svg
```

This will rename the output PDF to the same name as the input SVG file for each SVG file in the specified folder.

Wrapping Up

The svglib is the primary method to add SVGs to ReportLab at the time of writing this book. While it isn't full featured, it works pretty well and the API is quite nice. We also learned how to insert a plot SVG created via the popular matplotlib package. Finally we looked at how to turn SVGs to PDFs using the svg2pdf command line tool.

Appendix B - Getting System Fonts

ReportLab does not have a way to get all the fonts that are installed on a system. In fact, Python itself has no good way to grab the fonts either. But I thought it would be fun to write a script that would grab all the TrueType fonts on your system and try to add them to your PDF. After much research, I thought I had found a handy answer with Python's built-in GUI toolkit, **Tkinter**:

```
>>> from tkinter import Tk, font
>>> root = Tk()
>>> font.families()
```

This code basically creates a **Tk** object which then allows us to query the operating system for installed font families and names. Alas, it does not provide us with the file paths to those families as far as I could find.

The fontTools Package

So I ended up using a package called **fontTools** from https://github.com/fonttools/fonttools. You can install it with **pip** like this:

```
python -m pip install fonttools
```

Once you have that installed, we can write some code to get the information that ReportLab requires!

Getting the System's Fonts

The first step is to figure out a way to find all the TTF files on your system. To do that, we can use ReportLab's **rl_settings**, which has some search paths built into it. Let's start by creating a file named **find_installed_fonts.py**. Here's how the code should start:

Appendix B - Getting System Fonts

```python
# find_installed_fonts.py

import os

from fontTools import ttLib
from reportlab import rl_settings

def find_installed_ttf_fonts():
    installed_fonts = []
    for folder in rl_settings.TTFSearchPath:
        if os.path.exists(folder):
            for entry in os.scandir(folder):
                if entry.name.endswith('.ttf'):
                    installed_fonts.append(entry.path)
    return installed_fonts
```

Here we import Python's **os** module as well as a couple of items from **fontTools** and ReportLab. Next we create a function where we loop over the paths in **TTFSearchPath**. For each folder we check if it exists on our system. The reason for this is that there are both Windows and Linux paths that are returned. Then we use **os.scandir** to walk the paths recursively for files that end with **.ttf**. When we find those paths, we add them to our **installed_fonts** list. You could improve this code by setting the entire file name to lowercase, but I will leave that step to the reader.

Now let's add another function to our script. This function will extract the font name from the TTF file using the **fontTools** package.

```python
def get_font_names(font_paths):
    fonts = {}
    for font in font_paths:
        tt = ttLib.TTFont(font)
        name = ''
        family = ''
        for record in tt['name'].names:
            if record.nameID == 4 and not name:
                if '\000' in str(record.string):
                    name = unicode(record.string, 'utf-16-be').encode('utf-8')
                else:
                    name = record.string
            elif record.nameID == 1 and not family:
                if '\000' in str(record.string):
                    family = unicode(record.string, 'utf-16-be').encode('utf-8')
                else:
                    family = record.string
```

```
            if name and family:
                break
        fonts[name] = font
    return fonts


if __name__ == '__main__':
    paths = find_installed_ttf_fonts()
    get_font_names(paths)
```

Here we create an empty dictionary that we will use to map our font names to their respective font files. This code is based on some used by the **TTFQuery** package (https://pypi.org/project/TTFQuery/), which is a useful wrapper around fontTools. Anyway, I was able to use this to extract font names pretty successfully.

Now we just need to write some ReportLab code to embed our newly found fonts into a PDF.

```
# system_font_demo.py

import find_installed_fonts

from reportlab.pdfbase import pdfmetrics
from reportlab.pdfbase.ttfonts import TTFont
from reportlab.pdfgen import canvas


def system_font_demo(my_canvas, fonts):
    pos_y = 750
    for font in fonts:
        try:
            ttf = TTFont(font, fonts[font])
        except:
            # Skip this font
            continue

        pdfmetrics.registerFont(ttf)

        my_canvas.setFont(font, 12)
        my_canvas.drawString(30, pos_y, font)
        pos_y -= 10
        if pos_y < 40:
            my_canvas.showPage()
            pos_y = 750
```

```python
if __name__ == '__main__':
    my_canvas = canvas.Canvas("system_font_demo.pdf")
    font_paths = find_installed_fonts.find_installed_ttf_fonts()
    fonts = find_installed_fonts.get_font_names(font_paths)
    system_font_demo(my_canvas, fonts)
    my_canvas.save()
```

For this example, we import our font finder script as well as a few items from ReportLab. For this example, we use ReportLab's **canvas.Canvas** class. For each font that we found on the system, we attempt to load it using ReportLab's **TTFont** class. I had some fonts that wouldn't load, so I wrapped this step in a **try/except**. Then we write out the font name and adjust the y coordinate so that each font is on a different line. When I ran this code, I ended up with several pages worth of fonts. Note that some fonts are rendered as boxes. I am guessing these fonts could not be embedded as-is so ReportLab did the best that it could.

Here is a screenshot of the first page:

Appendix B - Getting System Fonts

Fig. Appendix B-1: System Fonts

Wrapping Up

Now you have enough code that you will be able to access the pre-installed fonts on your system. You can updated this code as you see fit to add new font search paths or to look for other types of fonts besides TrueType.

Appendix C - Creating a Color Demo

ReportLab has many built-in colors included in **reportlab.lib.colors**. Unfortunately, there is no resource for seeing what these pre-made colors actually look like. So in this appendix, we will write some code that can generate a PDF that shows all the colors in the **reportlab.lib.colors** sub-module along with their ReportLab names.

Getting the Colors

If you open up ReportLab's **colors.py** file, you will find a long list of variables that represent the ReportLab color names. They are set using a function named **HexColor** that uses hexadecimal values for setting the color. The HexColor function returns a ReportLab **Color** object. So what we need to do is figure out how to access those color variables.

Let's take a look at some code that shows one way to do what we want:

```python
from reportlab.lib import colors
from reportlab.lib.pagesizes import letter
from reportlab.graphics.shapes import String, Rect, Drawing
from reportlab.platypus import Paragraph, SimpleDocTemplate

def color_demo():
    doc = SimpleDocTemplate("colors.pdf",
                            pagesize=letter)
    flowables = []
    for color in dir(colors):
        attr = getattr(colors, color)
        if isinstance(attr, colors.Color):
            drawing = Drawing(width=100, height=50)
            string = String(10, 10, color)
            rectangle = Rect(125, 10, 100, 35)
            rectangle.fillColor = attr

            drawing.add(string)
            drawing.add(rectangle)
            flowables.append(drawing)

    doc.build(flowables)
```

```
if __name__ == '__main__':
    color_demo()
```

Here we import a few items from ReportLab. We want to draw a rectangle and a label, so we import **Rect** and **String** from ReportLab's **shapes** sub-module. Then we use Python's **dir** command to get all the attributes and methods from the **colors** module. This will return a LOT of cruft that we just don't care about. So when we iterate over that list of items, we extract the object using Python's built-in **getattr** function and check if the "attribute" is an instance of the **Color** type. If it is, then we create a drawing and add a string with the color's name. We also add a rectangle that is filled with that color.

When you run this code you should get a multipage document that look something like this:

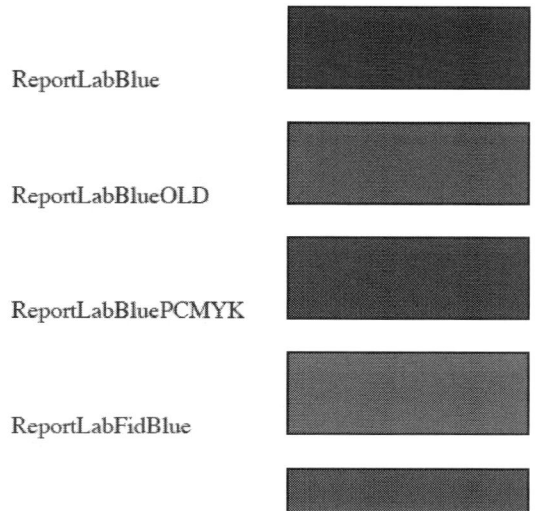

Fig. Appendix C-1: A Sample of the color chart

Wrapping Up

Being able to see what the color looks like before we attempt to use it is quite nice. You might want to use the code in this appendix to generate a listing of the colors and keep that file around to refer to or print it out and put them on the wall near your PC.

Afterword and Thanks

This book was a lot of fun to put together. I enjoyed learning how to do new things with ReportLab and Python. There are lots of really interesting Python packages that you can use to work with PDFs. In this book, we looked at the major ones:

- ReportLab
- PyPDF2
- pdfrw
- PyFPDF
- pdfminer
- rst2pdf
- WeasyPrint

I really hope you enjoyed learning how to create, edit and remix PDFs using Python. There are so many applications you can create using the information that you learned in this book. I hope you will let me know about some of the fun applications that you create.

I want to thank Axel Kielhorn, Keven Webb and Steve Barnes for all their suggestions and bug reports. I also want to thank the ReportLab developers for creating such a useful package and supporting it for so many years. Finally I want to thank the many other people who have written neat packages for manipulating PDFs with Python and a special thanks goes out to my readers for supporting me and this book!

Thanks, Mike

Made in the USA
Middletown, DE
04 August 2020